This volume brings together a wide-ranging collection of papers by Jeremy Waldron, one of the most internationally respected political theorists writing today.

The main focus of the collection is on the idea of rights, as it features in substantive debates in modern political philosophy. The first six chapters deal with freedom, toleration, and neutrality. Waldron defends the robust liberal principle that people have a right to act in ways that others disapprove of, even where their activities offend cherished beliefs or the norms of their community. The chapters that follow are concerned with socioeconomic rights. Waldron argues that poverty and homelessness, as much as intolerance or oppression, are affronts to individual liberty. The liberal ideal is that people are entitled to live life on their own terms. That ideal is undermined, not served, when the interest of some people in power, luxury, or comfort has the effect of excluding others forcibly from the resources they need to live.

The collection will be of particular interest to political philosophers, political scientists, and legal theorists.

Liberal rights

Cambridge Studies in Philosophy and Public Policy
GENERAL EDITOR: Douglas MacLean

The purpose of this series is to publish the most innovative and up-to-date research into the values and concepts that underlie major aspects of public policy. Hitherto most research in this field has been empirical. This series is primarily conceptual and normative; that is, it investigates the structure of arguments and the nature of values relevant to the formation, justification, and criticism of public policy. At the same time it is informed by empirical considerations, addressing specific issues, general policy concerns, and the methods of policy analysis and their applications.

The books in the series are inherently interdisciplinary and include anthologies as well as monographs. They are of particular interest to philosophers, political and social scientists, economists, policy analysts, and those involved in public administration and environmental policy.

Mark Sagoff: *The Economy of the Earth*
Henry Shue (ed.): *Nuclear Deterrence and Moral Restraint*
Judith Lichtenberg (ed.): *Democracy and the Mass Media*
William A. Galston: *Liberal Purposes*
R. G. Frey and Christopher W. Morris (eds.): *Violence, Terrorism, and Justice*
Elaine Draper: *Risky Business*
Ferdinand David Schoeman: *Privacy and Social Freedom*
Paul B. Thompson: *The Ethics of Trade and Aid*
Steven Lee: *Morality, Prudence, and Nuclear Weapons*
Dan Brock: *Life and Death*

Liberal rights

Collected papers 1981–1991

JEREMY WALDRON
PROFESSOR OF LAW AND PHILOSOPHY
UNIVERSITY OF CALIFORNIA AT BERKELEY

CAMBRIDGE
UNIVERSITY PRESS

PUBLISHED BY THE PRESS SYNDICATE OF THE UNIVERSITY OF CAMBRIDGE
The Pitt Building, Trumpington Street, Cambridge CB2 1RP, United Kingdom

CAMBRIDGE UNIVERSITY PRESS
The Edinburgh Building, Cambridge CB2 2RU, United Kingdom
40 West 20th Street, New York, NY 10011-4211, USA
10 Stamford Road, Oakleigh, Melbourne 3166, Australia

First published 1993
Reprinted 1997

Printed in the United States of America

Typeset in Palatino

A catalogue record for this book is available from the British Library

Library of Congress Cataloguing-in-Publication Data is available

ISBN 0-521-43024-0 hardback
ISBN 0-521-43617-6 paperback

For my mother
Joyce Annette Waldron
with love

Contents

vii

Acknowledgments

The essays collected in this volume were written over a ten-year period. The debts incurred in writing and thinking about them are too numerous to list here. I have been helped enormously by friends and colleagues in New Zealand, at Oxford, at the University of Edinburgh, at Cornell University, at the University of California at Berkeley, and throughout the scholarly community.

Academic writers too rarely acknowledge the institutions that provide an atmosphere of daily sustenance for their work, enabling them to grasp the hour here and the thirty minutes there that make all the difference to the pursuit of their projects. I have been fortunate in the encouragement I have received and particularly lucky in the deans and department chairs who have supported my writing in good times and bad. They are the people I particularly want to thank: Alan Musgrave and Bob Durrant at the University of Otago; David Goldey at Lincoln College, Oxford; Malcolm Anderson at Edinburgh; Henry Shue at Cornell; and, for the last five years, Jesse Choper, Shelly Messinger, Dan Rubinfeld, and Harry Scheiber at Boalt Hall and in the Jurisprudence and Social Policy Program at Berkeley. I am grateful also to Boalt Hall for summer stipends that supported work on some of these pieces in 1988, 1989, and 1990.

All these essays, bar the first, have been previously published, though each is presented here in a lightly revised form. I am most grateful to the editors and publishers who

ix

Acknowledgments

gave me permission to include the various pieces in the collection. The details are as follows:

"Theoretical foundations of liberalism" appeared originally in the *Philosophical Quarterly*, 37 (1987), pp. 127–50. It was the winner of that journal's annual essay prize in 1986.

"A right to do wrong" appeared originally in *Ethics*, 92 (1981), pp. 21–39. Published by the University of Chicago. © 1981 by the University of Chicago. All rights reserved.

"Locke, toleration and the rationality of persecution" appeared originally in Susan Mendus (ed.), *Justifying Toleration: Conceptual and Historical Perspectives* (Cambridge: Cambridge University Press, 1988), pp. 61–86. This article was also reprinted in *John Locke, a Letter Concerning Toleration: In Focus*, edited by John Horton and Susan Mendus (London: Routledge, 1991), pp. 98–124.

"Mill and the value of moral distress" appeared originally in *Political Studies*, 35 (1987), pp. 410–23.

"Rushdie and religion" appeared originally in the *Times Literary Supplement*, published by Times Newspapers in London, March 10–16, 1989, pp. 248 and 260. It appeared under the title "Too Important for Tact."

"Legislation and moral neutrality" appeared originally in Robert Goodin and Andrew Reeve (eds.), *Liberal Neutrality* (London: Routledge, 1989), pp. 61–83.

"Particular values and critical morality" appeared originally in the *California Law Review*, 77 (1989), pp. 561–89. It was a contribution to a symposium on "Law, community and moral reasoning," organized by Sanford Kadish, Robert Post, and Philip Selznick at Berkeley, September 30–October 1, 1988.

"Rights in conflict" appeared originally in *Ethics*, 99 (1989), pp. 503–19. Published by the University of Chicago. © 1989 by the University of Chicago. All rights reserved.

"Welfare and the images of charity" appeared originally in the *Philosophical Quarterly*, 36 (1986), pp. 463–82.

"John Rawls and the social minimum" appeared originally in the *Journal of Applied Philosophy*, 3 (1986), pp. 21–33.

Acknowledgments

"Social citizenship and the defense of welfare provision" appeared originally in the *British Journal of Political Science*, 18 (1988), pp. 415–43, under the title "Citizenship, social citizenship and the defense of welfare provision." It was coauthored with Desmond King.

"Homelessness and the issue of freedom" appeared originally in the *UCLA Law Review*, 39 (1991), pp. 295–324.

"Can communal goods be human rights?" appeared originally in *Archives européenes de sociologie*, 27 (1987), pp. 296–321. Reproduced with permission of *Archives européenes de sociologie*.

"When justice replaces affection: The need for rights" appeared originally in the *Harvard Journal of Law and Public Policy*, 11 (1988), pp. 625–47. It won the Institute for Humane Studies' Lon Fuller Prize in Jurisprudence in 1987.

"Rights and majorities: Rousseau revisited" appeared originally in John Chapman and Alan Wertheimer (eds.), *NOMOS XXXII: Majorities and Minorities*, Yearbook of the American Society for Political and Legal Philosophy (New York: New York University Press, 1990), pp. 44–75.

Desmond King was coauthor of the original version of Chapter 12, the piece on social citizenship. He not only gave permission for me to include the essay here, but generously allowed me to edit it, to fit in with the rest of the collection. I am particularly grateful to him for this, and for interesting me in the idea of social citizenship in the first place.

Finally, I would like to thank Terence Moore and his staff at Cambridge University Press for their support; Henry Shue, Jules Coleman, and Stephen Munzer for their encouragement on the project; and Rod Watanabe, Leslie Farrer, and Kiara Jordan for their help in getting things done at this end.

University of California, Berkeley　　　　　JEREMY WALDRON

Chapter 1

Liberal rights:
Two sides of the coin

I

The essays collected in this volume address a range of issues raised by the term "rights" in moral and political philosophy. They ask whether a person can have a right to do what is morally wrong. They consider whether rights embody values that may conflict with one another, and if so, whether they can be traded off in a sort of consequentialist balancing act. They explore the changes we would need to make in our familiar ways of thinking if we were to regard charity as a matter of entitlement. They ask about the relation between rights and citizenship. They attempt an answer to the question of whether rights can be held by groups. And they discuss the embodiment of moral entitlements in legal and constitutional arrangements.

I have called the collection "*Liberal* Rights" in order to emphasize, in the first instance, that these essays are grounded in the classic tradition of liberal political theory (a body of thought whose distinctive features I have tried to capture in Chapter 2). It is the tradition of thinkers like John Locke and John Stuart Mill. It is a heritage which prizes individuality, which requires social and political power to justify itself at the tribunal of people's interests as they themselves conceive them, and which – though it concedes the importance of culture and custom – insists, in Mill's words, that "[h]uman nature is not a machine to be built after a model" and that it is "the privilege and proper condition of

1

a human being . . . to use and interpret the experience [of his community] in his own way."[1]

Against this background, the essays explore traditional liberal themes such as religious toleration, the neutrality of the state, the distinction between ethics and politics, and the dangers of moral complacency and communitarian conformism. The picture they paint – and the aspiration that I hope the reader is left with – is of a society comprising men and women of high spirit and high ideals, each living life on his or her own terms, none of them worrying too much about each others' embarrassment or disapproval as they exercise their powers of practical reason autonomously, creatively, even provocatively. The society envisaged in this brand of liberalism has its radicals, its heretics, its blasphemers, and its deracinated apostates.[2] It does not ask dissenters to closet themselves smoldering in some cautiously constructed private realm; on the contrary, it expects dissent to blaze out in public to challenge and disconcert those who are taking things on faith or fashion.[3] It tolerates all this, not just because it expects society to progress thereby, but because it takes seriously the truism that the world we all share is the world in which each of us must make his or her life. We are social beings, we individuals, and the lives we have to lead must be lived in the light of day, not hidden away to cosset each others' sensibilities.

The essays are also *liberal* in a second sense. In the language of politics, particularly in the United States, "liberal" (the "L" word) means public policies designed to reduce inequality, to raise or at least maintain the level of welfare provision, and to regulate business and industry in the interests of health and safety at work, sexual and racial equality, environmental integrity, and the promotion of public goods. The themes of equality and social justice that underlie such politics are a major concern of mine in the second half of the collection.

The essays are not themselves exercises in public policy analysis, although one of them, Chapter 11 – the piece on homelessness – does address a particular crisis in modern

American life. For the most part, what I am doing in these pieces is examining some of the theoretical apparatus that is presupposed when we talk about rights to economic welfare as well as rights to civil and political liberty. Thus, for example, I discuss the concept of social citizenship,[4] the idea of a social minimum, the relation between property and charity, the practicability of socioeconomic rights, and the contractarian arguments of John Rawls. Though the essays that pursue these themes vary slightly in their direction and level of abstraction, the overall aim is to establish that no society can pride itself on respect for the individual if its social and economic structures have the effect of excluding large numbers of people from access to even the most elementary necessities of material life.

The liberal society I described a moment ago comprises, as I said, men and women of high spirit and high ideals, each living life freely and creatively on his or her own terms. But a society in which some are excluded from the means of life, whether or not this is done in the name of "property," does not answer to that aspiration. If we are to enforce rules to govern the use and allocation of resources, they must be rules designed and administered to respect the fact that every person has a life to lead. It is a cardinal principle of liberal thought that no one's interest in power, prominence, or luxury by itself justifies the coercive imposition of a restriction on others. A rule of ownership, however, is precisely such a restriction. Liberalism, then, in the second sense we have identified,[5] is a determination to apply that cardinal principle as much to rules of property as to other bases of restriction in social and political life.

II

I shall not, in this Introduction, attempt to summarize the chapters that follow. Each is self-contained and, I hope, largely self-explanatory. The essays are organized roughly as I have just intimated: a first bunch pursuing traditional liberal themes of ethical and religious liberty, and a second bunch applying liberal principles to socioeconomic concerns. Thus Chapters 3 through 8 address issues of toleration. They ask what attitude should be taken to individuals who pursue ideals or life-styles that conflict with the dominant mores and sensitivities of their community. Chapters 9 through 14 address the relation between rights and social justice. And Chapters 15 and 16 – which stand a little apart from the others – consider the importance of legal and constitutional structures in embodying individual rights.

In the remainder of *this* chapter I want to expand the argument sketched above, the argument connecting a commitment to liberalism in the traditional sense with a commitment to welfare provision and the reduction of economic inequality. I would like to summarize and discuss the various ways in which the idea of socioeconomic rights can be defended, exploring the connections between welfare rights and property, and between rights generally and social justice. Above all, I want to rebut some familiar objections to the idea of extending rights into this area of political concern.

III

According to the Universal Declaration of Human Rights (UDHR), adopted by the United Nations in 1948,

> Everyone has the right to a standard of living adequate for the health and well-being of himself and his family, including food, clothing, housing, medical care and necessary social services, and the right to security in the event of unemployment, sickness, disability, widowhood, old age or other lack of livelihood beyond his control.[6]

Not only that, but everyone has, according to the Declaration, "the right to work," "the right to just and favorable remuneration, ensuring for himself and his family an existence worthy of human dignity," "the right to education," and "the right to rest and leisure, including reasonable limitation of working hours and periodic holidays with pay."[7]

In international human rights circles, these socioeconomic claims are often referred to as "second-generation rights." First-generation rights are the traditional liberties and privileges of citizenship, covered by the first twenty articles of the UDHR: free speech, religious liberty, the right not to be tortured, the right to a fair trial, the right to vote, and so forth. Third-generation rights are the solidarity rights of communities and whole peoples rather than individuals. They include minority language rights, the right to national self-determination, and the rights that people may have to diffuse goods such as peace, environmental values, the integrity of their culture and ethnicity, and healthy economic development.[8] I shall not say much about third-generation rights in this chapter (they are discussed in detail in Chapter 14). But one way into the discussion of socioeconomic entitlement is to ask about the relation between first- and second-generation rights.

Much liberal thought in the twentieth century has focused on the question of whether it is possible really to enjoy civil liberties and political freedoms as they are traditionally understood, without also enjoying a fair degree of material security. For a while this debate was bogged down as an analytical dispute about the *meaning* of "liberty." Those who believed that traditional freedoms could not adequately be enjoyed by people who lacked the basic necessities of life were taken to be propounding a "positive" conception of liberty. It was assumed, accordingly, that they ran foul of Isaiah Berlin's strictures against confusing freedom with justice, or with equality, or with the sum of all good things. Defenders of "positive" freedom were accused of leading us down the road not only to socialism, but to a totalitarianism of "Newspeak," in which the coercion of the welfare state would be disguised and redescribed as the liberation of the true self from the shackles of its own empirical nature.[9]

That was always a confusion. For one thing, the conception of positive liberty that Berlin was discussing concerned the relation between liberty, on the one hand, and virtue and rationality, on the other, not the relation between liberty and

5

material well-being.[10] For another thing, Berlin made it perfectly clear that the traditional point about the *definition* of "freedom" could be argued without prejudice to the substantive issue of the *importance* for freedom of material well-being. In the text of his original article, Berlin was quite explicit:

> It is true that to offer political rights, or safeguards against intervention by the state, to men who are half-naked, illiterate, underfed, and diseased is to mock their condition; they need medical help or education before they can understand, or make use of, an increase in their freedom. What is freedom to those who cannot make use of it? Without adequate conditions for the use of freedom, what is the value of freedom?[11]

A few years later, in view of what he called "the astonishing opinions which some of my critics have imputed to me," Berlin underlined his attack on the pursuit of liberty without attention to social justice, on the evils of unrestricted *laissez-faire*, and on the social systems that permitted and encouraged it:

> I should perhaps have stressed (save that I thought this too obvious to need saying) the failure of such systems to provide the minimum conditions in which alone any degree of significant "negative" liberty can be exercised by individuals or groups, and without which it is of little or no value to those who may theoretically possess it. For what are rights without the power to implement them? I had supposed that enough had been said by almost every serious modern writer concerned with this subject about the fate of personal liberty during the reign of unfettered economic individualism – about the condition of the injured majority, principally in the towns, whose children were destroyed in mines or mills, while their parents lived in poverty, disease, and ignorance, a situation in which the enjoyment by the poor and the weak of legal rights to spend their money as they pleased or to choose the education they wanted (which Cobden and Herbert Spencer and their disciples offered them with every appearance of sincerity) became an odious mockery. All this is notoriously true.[12]

And *still*, he said, from the analytical point of view, "liberty is one thing, and the conditions for it are another."[13]

That last conviction was echoed a few years later in John Rawls's insistence in *A Theory of Justice* that "the inability to take advantage of one's rights and opportunities as a result of poverty and ignorance" is not to be counted "among the constraints definitive of liberty." A lack of means, he said, is to be counted as affecting the worth of one's liberty, not the extent of liberty itself.[14] Even so, Rawls did not believe, any more than did Berlin, that a society could pride itself on offering its poorer citizens liberty, in this narrow sense, without paying attention to their material condition. "The worth of liberty" means just what it says, despite the fact that it is regulated by a principle standing second in Rawls's lexical priorities. It binds the two principles of justice together, and indicates the importance of economic well-being in determining whether the liberties governed by the first principle are actually worth having.

In any case, the argument from first-generation to second-generation rights was never supposed to be a matter of conceptual analysis. It was rather this: if one is really concerned to secure civil or political liberty for a person, that commitment should be accompanied by a further concern about the conditions of the person's life that make it possible for him to enjoy and exercise that liberty. Why on earth would it be worth fighting for this person's liberty (say, his liberty to choose between A and B) if he were left in a situation in which the choice between A and B meant nothing to him, or in which his choosing one rather than the other would have no impact on his life?

The general argument to this effect has been developed by Henry Shue.[15] No one, Shue argues, can fully enjoy *any* right that he is supposed to have if he lacks the essentials for a reasonably healthy and active life. The rights that are most familiar to us, rights to civil and political liberty, evoke images of autonomy, rational agency, and independence. It is our interest in those underlying ideas that explains our allegiance to first-generation rights, but we know that things like mal-

7

nutrition, epidemic disease, and exposure can debilitate and finally destroy all the human faculties that such rights presuppose. There is no prospect of an individual living the sort of autonomous life we have in mind when we talk about liberty if he is in a state of abject and desperate need. His condition would be one of lethargy rather than agency, or, at best, action under the impulse of necessity rather than action governed by autonomous deliberation.

As it affects one's agency, desperate need also affects one's relation with others, leaving one open to exploitation, dependence, and coercion.[16] Indeed, famine and disease leave their victims more vulnerable to the forms of attack that rights theorists have traditionally been concerned about, such as state terrorism and other forms of physical violence. Those who are politically oppressed can sometimes flee, but those who lack essentials such as food can often do nothing and are, on their own, utterly helpless.[17]

This is a very general line of argument, relating the ideas of agency, autonomy, and independence to the need that people sometimes have for economic support and assistance. It asks rhetorically how anyone can call himself a partisan of liberty, and yet remain indifferent to the plight of those whose very agency is in danger of being overwhelmed by material need. The human autonomy that is at stake when we stop people from attacking or threatening one another is no less at stake when individuals are reduced by hunger or fear of destitution to desperate pleading for subsistence. If we truly respect human agency as an end in itself, we must follow that end where it leads and, in the circumstances of human life, that may well require us to attend to the needs of persons whose ability to function as agents is imperiled by poverty or disease or by the fear of those predicaments.

Particular versions of this argument can also be developed for specific rights. Many feminists argue, for example, that it is not enough for abortion to be a legally secured right, if all that means is that procuring an abortion is not a criminal offense. If a poor woman facing the immediate problem of an unwanted pregnancy is unable to take advantage of this liberty because she has no access to clinical services or cannot pay for the procedure, she is about as badly off as she would be if there were no legal liberty at all.[18]

Shue's claim was phrased in terms of what is necessary if a person is to *enjoy* some right that he has: "No one can fully, if at all, enjoy any right that is supposedly protected by society if he or she lacks the essentials for a reasonably healthy and active life."[19] This way of putting it may lead to some misunderstanding. "Enjoyment" need not mean taking pleasure in or deriving maximum advantage from the right. What enjoyment means is actually *having* the right, in the substantive sense in which the right is thought to be worth having. A person does not have the right to vote unless there is some reasonable prospect that he can cast his vote on election day and have it counted. He cannot be said to have or enjoy the right in this sense if, for example, there are no polling places nearby or if there is no transportation available to get him to the polls. By contrast, we may not infer from the right to emigrate a requirement that society subsidize trips abroad for anyone who wants them. The point in this case is that emigration be among the legal options a person can work toward (which it is not if there is a ban on leaving the country). But if the point of a given right is to ensure that a certain choice can actually be exercised at a certain time (and this is surely true of both the abortion case and the voting rights case), then it seems clear that facilitating the exercise may sometimes be as important as not obstructing it.

However, although these particular arguments about specific rights are important, we must not allow them to swamp the general issue. Even in the case of those rights – like the right to emigrate – which do not generate an immediate call on social assistance, there is still a background concern about destitution. If some people are kept in absolute penury with no hope at all of savings or of anything other than the most precarious subsistence, it *is* a mockery to say that they have the right to emigrate, for their position even so far as long-range planning is concerned is little different than it would

9

be if emigration were banned. One is reminded of the question David Hume posed embarrassingly for the Lockean theory of political obligation: "Can we seriously say, that a poor peasant or artisan has a free choice to leave his country, when he knows no foreign language or manners, and lives from day to day, by the small wages which he acquires?"[20] We must think not only about the relation between poverty and the actual enjoyment of the right, but also about the relation between poverty and the reasons for according people rights in the first place. First-generation rights, such as the right to emigrate, are predicated on some notion of respect and human dignity. People are to be treated not as captives in the land where they live, but as free and equal members of a community. Is neglect of their social or economic predicament consonant with that respect? At the moment, whole sections of society live as members of an underclass, left to their own devices in the poverty, hopelessness, and degradation of inner cities; and just as the boroughs in which they live have become "no-go" areas so far as the rest of us are concerned, so their predicament has become a taboo topic in the politics of a country determined to confine economic debate to "middle-class" issues.[21] I guess that in principle *some* social and economic neglect is consistent with the proclamation that we still take very seriously the autonomy, freedom, and dignity of those who are in such a predicament, the proclamation necessary to make sense of their still being accorded first-generation rights. But the tension can only be taken so far. After a while, the combination becomes unbelievable, and it is increasingly difficult for those who actually *urge* such neglect to maintain with a straight face that respect for the rights of those whose needs they are planning to ignore is still in fact their highest priority.

IV

A second argument for welfare rights is more direct than the one I have just outlined. Instead of saying that economic security is necessary if *other* (first-generation) rights are to be taken seriously, we might insist bluntly that socioeconomic needs are as important as any other interests, and that a moral theory of individual dignity is plainly inadequate if it does not take them into account. The advantage of this more direct approach is that it concedes nothing in the way of priority to first-generation rights. Morally, it maintains that death, disease, malnutrition, and economic despair are as much matters of concern as any denials of political or civil liberty. Where these predicaments are plainly avoidable, a refusal to do anything to address them is evidently an insult to human dignity and a failure to take seriously the unconditional worth of each individual. Liberals sometimes express concern about the proliferation of rights claims: too many rights, they say, debase the currency of entitlement.[22] But even if we are worried about this proliferation, it is by no means clear that rights based on economic need should be the ones to give way. The prevention or the remedying of economic deprivation is not a luxury: on the contrary, it attends to the primal necessities and vulnerabilities of human life.

Giving socioeconomic claims this sort of priority may be part of what some socialist and feminist critics intend when they urge liberals to abandon their concern for rights and replace it with a concern for *needs*. On the face of it, this suggestion is based on a misunderstanding. It confuses the content of a claim with the normative form in which that claim is couched. (It is like saying we should concentrate less on duties and more on truth telling!) The language of rights as it is nowadays understood is accommodating to a variety of human concerns. To invoke a right is to predicate a duty on some concern for a certain individual interest, and although the interest in question is often an interest in liberty, it might equally be an interest in the satisfaction of some material need. There used to be controversy in the analysis of rights about whether the concept presupposed an exclusive concern with liberty. The claim that it did has now largely been abandoned, and the language of rights is used to refer to any demand that an individual interest should be protected or promoted, made from the individual's own point of view, and accorded decisive moral importance. The issue of material needs and the socioeconomic rights that may be necessary to serve them thus becomes a substantial matter, not an analytic one.

How important are second-generation rights? Certainly, some of the ones set out in the UDHR do not appear to have the same air of urgency as first-generation rights like the right not to be tortured or the right to freedom of worship. Critics are fond of citing Article 24 in this connection:[23]

> Everyone has the right to rest and leisure, including reasonable limitation of working hours and periodic holidays with pay.

The provision is apt to summon up images of lazy union members sleeping on the job, while their officials enjoy Caribbean cruises at public expense. A guarantee of holidays with pay for everyone might seem a splendid utopian aspiration. But, for one thing, it sounds like a peculiarly Western ideal (and even in the West limited to those who are salaried or wage employees) and so hardly something we can call a universal *human* entitlement. For another thing, it simply seems to lack the moral urgency, the priority, the sense of being an indispensable part of the moral minimum, that we usually associate with rights.

I figure it is worth responding to these familiar points, because if we see what can be said for Article 24, it may be easier to understand what is at stake in some of the other more evidently compelling second-generation provisions.

Let's start with the hard bit: "periodic holidays with pay." The phrase is certainly infelicitous as an expression of a universal human need, but that does not mean there is no such need in back of this expression. There have been times (not too distant) and there are places (not too far away) where people have lived and worked in the following manner. Since age twelve, say, a man may have worked fourteen or fifteen hours a day at hard manual labor in a mine, a farm, or a mill, every day of every week, until he collapsed in his forties, worn out and perhaps ridden with some disease brought on by his working conditions. He may have done this to earn a bare subsistence for himself and his family, knowing that if he were ever to take a few days or a week off for some festival or to visit distant family members, the result might be that he was unable to buy food for that week or pay his rent. To demand "reasonable limitation of working hours" is to try and claw back some free time on a daily basis. In the history of labor's struggle with capital, this has been a constant and desperate theme, and anyone who denigrates its urgency simply doesn't know what he is talking about.[24] To demand in addition "periodic holidays with pay" is to try and claw back as well some larger blocks of leisure time, time measured in whole days rather than hours, so the rest of life can be led. There *is* a universal human interest – recognized (though not necessarily respected) in all cultures – in having longish periods (days rather than hours) of sustained respite from the business of securing subsistence, whatever that involves: fiestas (as opposed to siestas), holy days, vacations, communal celebrations, and so forth. "Periodic holidays with pay" expresses a particular culture-bound conception of that interest, but the wider interest is there and its importance in the constitution of a bearable human life is undeniable.[25]

The urgency of the other socioeconomic demands is more evident: health care, social security, a minimum standard of living. Humans live as embodied and needy beings in a material world populated also by others. We have seen that the liberal idea of rights proclaims the value of high-spirited individuals leading their lives proudly and independently, on their own terms. But this idea denies neither the neediness of human beings, nor the vicissitudes of human life, nor the importance of our relation to others. Because it is put forward as a moral claim, it amounts to the demand that we should organize our lives together, our use of material resources, and our forms of cooperation and exchange, so that such proud and independent lives are possible for all. The liberal demand is not predicated on any assumption that this independence is given naturally or magically. Like all moral ideals, it is something we have to work together to achieve for each other as individuals. In some circumstances that will involve checking the impulse to interfere with someone's life or activity; in other circumstances, particularly some of the extremities of human vicissitudes, it will involve an active commitment to intervene with support and assistance; in still other circumstances, what may be needed is the assurance or guarantee of support, not necessarily the support and assistance themselves. Above all, a commitment to the liberal ideal involves a sensitivity to the variety of ways in which it can be frustrated in a person's life. Leading a life on one's own terms can be undermined as much by the degradation and abject dependence of poverty, disease, or neglected old age as by any of the more traditionally recognized forms of violent political repression. When it is undermined through social and economic vicissitude, it is destroyed as decisively, and what is lost is just as valuable, from the liberal point of view, as when someone is tortured, imprisoned, or persecuted for the life he wants to lead.

It is sometimes said, nevertheless, that the moral requirement to respond to social and economic vicissitude is less stringent, or less of an obligation, than the requirement to refrain from, say, torture or persecution. The former is a matter of "imperfect" rather than "perfect" duty.[26] I have a perfect duty not to torture others, a duty that binds me stringently at all times in my behavior toward each other person. By contrast, it is said, I have only an imperfect duty to give alms to beggars: I am duty bound to give alms to some beggars some of the time, but I am not bound to give to every beggar who crosses my path, let alone every beggar who needs assistance. Now an imperfect duty can always be restated as a stringent duty: an imperfect duty to give alms amounts in effect to perfect duty not to be a person who never gives alms to anyone.[27] For our purposes, however, the point is supposed to be that imperfect duties (whether they are reformulated in this way or not) do not correlate with rights. If my duty is only not to refrain altogether from

14

almsgiving, it cannot be said of any particular beggar that he has a right to my charity.

I think the situation is a little more complicated than this. Compare two cases. (1) Smith, a testator who is disposed to leave most of his wealth to a dogs' home, may think that he has some obligation to leave something to some member of his family, as an indication that he has not repudiated family ties altogether. But his relatives may all be perfectly well-off. Because no one stands in need of his assistance, or in any special relation of desert, it may be quite acceptable for him to bestow a legacy on some arbitrarily selected niece, son, or cousin. He has, we may think, a familial obligation to benefit at least one of his relatives, but none of them has a right to receive such a benefit. (2) Jones, a wealthy philanthropist concerned about poverty, may recognize that there is a much wider array of indigents than he can possibly help. So he makes a selection, choosing to give his charity either to the neediest or to a random number of cases that are close to him or that he knows about. He does not reproach himself for violating the rights of those he does not help, but he recognizes their need and may recommend them to the charity of other philanthropic friends.

In both cases, we can see that there is an imperfect obligation in the Kantian sense, and we can see also that none of the possible beneficiaries has a right specifically against the person whose obligations we are considering (specifically against Smith, or specifically against Jones). There is an important difference, however. In case (1), each of the relatives has moral standing simply as a possible beneficiary of Smith's imperfect duty; there is nothing more to be said from a moral point of view about any given relative's situation than that. In case (2), by contrast, though each of the indigents is a possible beneficiary of Jones's imperfect duty, there *is* more to be said about their situation than that. Jones and his philanthropic friends may think that something has gone wrong if all of them end up (accidentally) lavishing their charity on the same few persons or if, after all of them have fulfilled their imperfect duties, some indigents have still not received any benefit at all. We may want to express this difference as follows. In case (2), though not in case (1), each of the potential beneficiaries has a *right* to assistance even though that right does not correlate with a perfect duty incumbent on any one in particular. We may want to say that a given indigent in (2) has a right to relief against all the world. It is not a right to receive charity from each person in turn, but it is a right against all the possible sources of charity taken together, and what this right requires for each individual benefactor depends in part on what other potential benefactors are doing or may reasonably be expected to do.

Someone might object that there can be no determinate right for the indigent unless it is correlated with a determinate duty incumbent on some person or persons in particular. But this view about the tightness of the relation between rights and duties is no longer reputable. Neil MacCormick has shown that even in technical legal relations, the determination of who has a right often precedes the determination of who has the corresponding duty and in some cases may even form part of the reason for assigning duties in one way rather than another.[28] Both Joseph Raz and Ronald Dworkin have argued that in political morality rights function as a ground for generating duties rather than merely as their correlate.[29] In any case, we must take care not to put the analytical cart before the substantive horse. Our concept of a right is loose enough to be defined in a way that accommodates what we want to use it to say. It would be crazy if a philosophically controversial view about the tightness of the relation between rights and duties were to preclude us from using the language of rights to mark the difference between what we think about case (1) and what we think about case (2), above.

A similar response can be made to the objection that imperfect duties simply do not correlate with rights at all, in any fashion. The response is that there is *something* importantly different between case (1) and case (2). Though both share some features of the traditional notion of imperfect duty, case (2) connotes the additional idea of a duty being generated by a concern for the morally compelling interests of a beneficiary. That is the idea that may plausibly be marked using the notion of a right. Once again, the difference is not going to go away whatever terminology we use. If someone desires, for purely verbal reasons, to confine the term "imperfect duty" to cases like (1) where there is no right-based element at all, that is fine. We shall just choose some other words to express what we want to say about (2).

The analysis that we have been developing indicates an interesting role for the state in relation to duties of the sort we have discerned in case (2).[30]

Part of the difficulty faced by private philanthropists like Jones is that they cannot always coordinate their charity so that all the needy cases are covered. The rights of the needy, as I have outlined them in this example, give Jones and the others a reason – I think a compelling reason – to pay attention to the problem of coordination. If some system is in place which ensures that the limited charity of each philanthropist is brought into rational relation with that of each of the others, it is morally incumbent on each of them to participate in that scheme. Often (though not always – international aid provides a partial counterexample), the welfare state functions in effect as a clearinghouse for these imperfect obligations. It takes from each person an amount that is not enough to cover all the needy but is sufficient to discharge his imperfect obligation, and it distributes that carefully to those who need it, ensuring that people's imperfect obligations are discharged in a way that ultimately respects the fact that they arise out of the needs of others.

Someone might complain finally that it is wrong to *enforce* an imperfect duty. But if that is an objection, it must be made out substantively. There is nothing in the *concept* of imperfect duty to justify the complaint, for the difference between perfect and imperfect duty has to do with the occasions for performance, not issues of moral importance and not issues of enforceability.

17

V

There is a famous passage in *Anarchy, State and Utopia* where Robert Nozick voices a complaint about arguments similar to those I have been developing. He says that although it seems a nice idea to base human rights on material needs, in the real world the resources required to satisfy these needs may already be owned by private individuals. He argues that if private property entitlements in fact cover all the relevant resources, there is nothing to be done: the property rights that particular individuals have over particular things simply "fill the space of rights, leaving no room for general rights to be in a certain material condition."[31]

This complaint assumes that claims based on need occupy a relatively superficial role in a general theory of economic entitlement. It is as though we first determine who owns what, and then determine whose needs are left unsatisfied and what is to be done about them. Some of Nozick's claims suggest this is unavoidable: "Things come into the world already attached to people having entitlements over them."[32] He thinks this is clearest in the case of body parts: you may need *these* kidneys or *this* retina, but my entitlement to them is necessarily prior to yours for we cannot even grasp my status as a person without comprising in that status a rightful claim to the limbs, cells, and organs that make me who I am.[33] But it is important also for the external objects that people make: "Isn't it implausible that how holdings are produced and come to exist has no effect at all on who should hold what?"[34] The trouble with welfare rights, on this account, is that they "treat objects as if they appeared from nowhere, out of nothing,"[35] like manna from heaven. "[I]s *this* the appropriate model," he asks, "for thinking about how the things people produce are to be distributed?"[36]

I have colleagues who say they find it difficult to explain why Nozick's book, universally excoriated as it is, has been so influential.[37] But the virtue and the challenge of his analysis are that they force us to confront these issues of moral priority. In our discussion in Section IV, we assumed a wealthy philanthropist who had certain imperfect obligations so far as the distribution of *his* wealth to the poor was concerned. Like much analysis of charity and poverty in the literature, that discussion assumed that we already knew who owned what (the wealth was *his*) and that the issue of welfare rights concerned the circumstances under which people had an obligation to contribute, or could be forced to contribute, out of their own largesse to relieve the needs of others. Nozick observes correctly that this way of understanding things is superficial. The idea of welfare rights, he argues, the idea that a person's right to use or receive resources might be based generally on need rather than on some particular relation between *this* person and *this* thing, poses an immense challenge to our understanding of property entitlement. The notion of entitlement will never be secure if it is always subject to subsequent challenge on this basis. Therefore, he thinks, we have to choose: either particular people have acquired property entitlements in particular things, or people in general have a right to material and economic security, even when they cannot provide it for themselves. One or other can be true, but not both. We do not have to accept Nozick's own resolution of this dilemma to agree with him about the importance of confronting it honestly and explicitly.

Nozick's position, you will recall, is that "particular rights over things fill the space of rights, leaving no room for general rights to be in a certain material condition." He maintains that the alternative is to stipulate the general rights first, and then try to fit particular property entitlements around them. "[T]o my knowledge," he says, "no serious attempt has been made to state this 'reverse' theory."[38] I doubt that he is correct in that last point,[39] but certainly he is right to insist that a serious defense of welfare rights must involve the statement of this alternative approach to justice and property.

I suggest, then, that we should regard rights based on material need as *fundamental* in our theory of human access to and use of resources. Instead of making these rights the basis of a duty of charity incumbent on existing property holders, we are to take them as a basis for calling property arrangements themselves into question; the existence of unsatisfied material need thus becomes an objection not just to the way property rights are being exercised (selfishly, thoughtlessly, and so forth) but to the very shape and distribution of property entitlements themselves. In proclaiming welfare rights, we are not begging property holders to be a little more generous. We are asking the deeper question: by what right do they claim to hold something as exclusively their own in face of others' abject need? We insist that property must answer at the tribunal of need, not the other way round.

This reversal of priorities is a bit like the way we ought to think about political or democratic rights. On a superficial view, we start from the position of subjection to authority, and then we plead for a participatory role in that authority. We try to give reasons why government should be democratic rather than nondemocratic in character. But on a deeper liberal view, the starting point is each person's right to govern himself:

> [F]or really I think that the poorest he that is in England has a life to live as the greatest he; and therefore truly, sir, I think it's clear, that every man that is to live under a government ought first by his own consent to put himself under that government; and I do think that the poorest man in England is not at all bound in a strict sense to the government that he has not had a voice to put himself under;[40]

The tone of rights in this passage is not *"Please* let me have a say," but rather "How *dare* you try to govern me without my being a participant in that governance?" The liberal position is that the basis of all sovereignty and all political power is the people's right, individually and together, to govern themselves. Similarly, the logic of welfare rights is not "Please let me sleep on your land," but rather "How *dare* you erect fences around land that people may need to sleep on?" A commitment to welfare rights reflects a view that the basis of all property is the general human right to live (and, indeed, to lead a decent life) by using the land and the resources that exist in the world and that seem, in Locke's words, to be "serviceable for [our] Subsistence."[41] On the liberal view, the fundamental point about justice and rights in the economic sphere is the inestimable worth of each individual leading a life on his own terms, and the apparent existence of sufficient resources to enable everyone to do so. From this starting point, the appropriation of large masses of those resources by some, to the complete exclusion of large numbers of others, is an insult to human dignity rather than something to which a dignitarian theory of rights should defer.

Nozick, as we have seen, meets all this with a "How dare you?" of his own: "How dare you try to satisfy your needs out of something someone else has *made?*" But he is too honest a philosopher to stick with this for long. Nozick recognizes that any theory of producers' entitlement must be predicated on some prior theory of the *initial* acquisition of resources – of raw materials, land, and other factors of production. We cannot talk of producers' rights until we have a theory that deals with "the issues of how unheld things may come to be held, the things that may come to be held by these processes, the extent of what comes to be held by a particular process, and so on."[42] Elsewhere I have argued that the issue of acquisition that Nozick makes fundamental is precisely the issue of how we are to deal with manna from heaven.[43] There are all these resources just lying around, and all these needy people. The resources might (if we let people use them) give rise to producers' entitlements. But before we do that, we must develop principles for their use that respect each person's fundamental right to derive sustenance from this world that is our common heritage.[44]

Almost all serious theories of property recognize that constraint, in one way or another.[45] John Locke recognizes it, in part by allowing a right of recourse to all property in the last resort for the needy,[46] and in part by his well known concern to link the justification of private property with the proposition that legitimate appropriation leaves "enough and as good . . . in common for others."[47] Nozick, despite his exclusionist bluster, recognizes it too: "A process normally giving rise to a permanent bequeathable property right in a particular thing will not do so if the position of others no longer at liberty to use the thing is thereby worsened."[48] Few are willing to say that property rights are justified utterly without reference to the interests or needs of those whom they exclude from access to resources. The reason is obvious: to justify a property right in X is not only to feel justified *oneself* in coercively excluding others from X, but to justify *their* recognition of a *duty* to refrain from using X even when one is not around to physically defend it. I argue in Chapter 2 of this collection that the whole liberal enterprise of justification is essentially justification-*to* those who are to be constrained by the duties and burdens of social life. Not only must we have something to say in defense of our property rights; we must have something to say *to* those for whom our property rights are property duties, something that addresses their interests and concerns.

All this is by way of showing that the liberal defense of welfare rights should root itself in the foundations of our theory of property, economy, and justice. It is not a luxurious accretion to liberal philosophy, in the way that talk of "*second-generation*" rights might suggest. Rights to decent subsistence, of the sort we find in Articles 22–28 of the Universal Declaration, are fundamental to our conception of the dignity and the inherent claims of men and women, endowed with needs as well as with autonomy, in a world that contains the resources that might (if others let them) enable them to live. What *is* new or additional is the legal guarantee of welfare provision, the welfare state. The advantage of the account I have been outlining is that we can view that provision as the political tip of a very large theoretical iceberg. It is a reflection in our political practice of claims that go very deep, and it may well be best for us to think of it as little more than a hesitant first step toward a complete overhaul of the system of ownership – a system whose failure to respect fundamental human rights is indicated by the fact that people continue to be without access to the resources they need in order to live.

VI

The line of argument developed in the previous section may also be used to respond to a common criticism of second-generation rights: that they are impracticable or too expensive or too demanding. Some critics argue that socioeconomic rights violate the logical principle *"Ought* implies *can."* Many states, they say, do not have the resources to provide even minimal economic security for masses of their citizens, and since states differ considerably in this regard, it hardly makes sense to regard economic provision as a matter of universal human entitlement.[49]

However, the alleged impossibility in many of these cases often stems from an assumption that the existing distribution of property remain largely undisturbed. When a conservative government in the West says, in response to some plea for welfare provision, "The money simply isn't there," what is usually meant is that it would be impolitic to try and raise it from existing property holders and income earners by taxation. The more radical challenge posed by these rights to the underlying distribution of wealth and income is simply ignored.

The same is true in the international context. To refute the claim that economic security is a human right, it is not enough to show that states like Somalia and Bangladesh cannot make this provision for their citizens. Though a person's own state is the primary bearer of the duties correlative to his rights, the mark of a human right is that it is held by each individual against the whole world. If the Somali government cannot feed its citizens, then the governments (and thus the citizens) of other countries must consider their responsibility in the matter. Just as civil and political rights call in question imperial and geopolitical structures that sustain tyranny and oppression, so economic rights call in question the present

23

global distribution of resources. Once matters are put this way, it becomes pretty clear that the *"ought"* of human rights is being frustrated, not by the *"can't"* of impracticability, but usually by the *"shan't"* of selfishness and greed.

Still, someone may press the question: aren't these socio-economic rights awfully demanding? First-generation rights require only that we and our governments refrain from various acts of tyranny and oppression. They are "negative" rights correlative to duties of omission, whereas socioeconomic rights are correlative to positive duties of assistance. An advantage of negative rights is that they never conflict with one another, for one can perform an infinite number of omissions at any given moment. With positive rights, we have to consider the inherent scarcity of the resources and services that are called for.[50]

However, the correlation of first- and second-generation rights with the distinction between negative and positive rights simply will not stand up. Many first-generation rights (for example, the right to vote) require the positive establishment and maintenance of certain frameworks, and all of them make costly claims on scarce police and forensic resources. The right to vote is not a matter of the negative freedom to mark a cross against the name of one's favorite politician, and it is not secured by the individual simply being left alone to do this as and when he pleases. The vote must be counted and given effect in a political system that determines leadership and authority. To vote is to exercise a Hohfeldian *power*, and to demand the right to vote is to demand that there be a political system in which the exercise of that power is rendered effective along with its similar exercise by millions of other individuals.

Those first-generation rights – such as free speech and freedom of worship – which *can* be conceived in the first instance as matter of negative freedom, still require more from the government than that it simply stay its hand. We set up governments to *protect* our rights, not simply to respect them (what would be the point of that?). All serious political theorists recognize that protection is costly,[51] and that therefore first-generation rights – as much as socioeconomic entitlements – impose costs and raise questions about priorities for us all.

In Chapter 9 I argue that each right is best thought of not as correlative to one particular duty (which might then be classified as a duty of omission or as a positive duty of action or assistance), but as generating successive waves of duty, some of them duties of omission, some of them duties of commission, some of them too complicated to fit easily under either heading. The right not to be tortured generates a duty not to torture people, but it also generates a duty to investigate complaints of torture, a duty to pay one's share for the political and administrative setups that might be necessary to prevent torture, and so on. As far as second-generation rights are concerned, they too may be correlated with duties that are positive or negative, depending on the context. If people are actually starving, their rights make a call on our active assistance, but if they are living satisfactorily in a traditional subsistence economy, the right may require we simply refrain from any action that could disturb that state of affairs. We talk sometimes as though it only happens by misfortune that people are starving and that the only issue rights raise in the matter is whether we should put ourselves out and come to their aid. But people often starve as a result of what we do as well as what we don't do. The right to a decent subsistence constrains (and provides a moral framework for evaluating) all the actions we are tempted to perform that might affect the livelihood of others.[52]

For another thing, it needs to be understood that where resources are scarce relative to human wants, *any* system of rights or entitlements will seem demanding to those constrained by it. If an economic system includes provision for welfare assistance, it may seem overly demanding to taxpayers. But if it does not include such provision, the system of *property rights* will seem overly demanding to the poor, requiring as it does that they refrain from making use of resources (owned by others) that they need in order to survive. As usual, the question is not whether we are to have a system of demanding rights, but how the costs of the demands are to be distributed.

VII

Thinking about scarcity and practicability does have one important advantage: it forces proponents of second-generation rights to take seriously issues of distributive justice. An unhappy feature of the language of rights is that it expresses demanding moral claims in a sort of "line item" way, presenting each individual's case peremptorily, as though it brooked no denial, no balancing, no compromise. That feature of rights has always troubled those who are sensitive to the fact that individuals live in a social environment where the things that they may reasonably expect must be adjusted constantly to reflect similar expectations on the part of others. The language of absolute and uncompromisable demands is inapt to capture anything important about our moral situation in such an environment.

Qualifying the air of absolutism is not the same, however, as derogating from the individualism of rights discourse. It remains important that the moral claims we are weighing against one another are the claims of individuals. They are claims made by each man and woman in regard to leading a life on his or her own terms. We must not push the idea of balance and compromise in a direction that makes us lose sight of that. Claims of right are not like individual satisfactions in the utilitarian calculus: mere *ingredients* in something else – a social sum or a social average – taken to be of overriding importance.[53] Nor is this readiness to balance claims of right against one another the same as a willingness to submerge them in the overarching value of community. In modern political philosophy, the idea of community represents values quite distinct from, and controversial in relation to, the rights of individuals.[54] The idea of community is certainly not the natural or obvious matrix (anymore than the calculus of utility is the natural or obvious matrix) on which

26

claims of right are to be brought into relation with one another.

If we want a matrix of compromise that more adequately reflects the individualistic character of rights claims, we must turn instead to the modern discussion of justice. John Rawls's work is a paragon of such discussion. What he calls "the circumstances of justice" indicate the conditions under which compromise and cooperation are both possible and necessary. Natural resources and human energies, though not desperately scarce, are not so abundant that there are no hard choices to be made; individuals and groups have different ends and purposes which lead them to make conflicting demands on those resources.[55] The problem of justice for Rawls is the problem of defining a viable institutional structure of cooperation adequately reflecting the worth and intrinsic importance of the claims each individual can make. He argues that this problem is best approached by asking what principles for institutional design would be chosen by the individuals in question if they were bargaining on a basis of freedom and equality to settle the terms of their association with one another.[56] I do not want to go into the details of that construction here, nor do I want to suggest that the modern discussion of justice is necessarily or exclusively Rawlsian.[57] I mention Rawls's theory to indicate the existence of ways of thinking about the balancing of individual claims that avoid both the brutal aggregative trade-offs and the immersion of the particular in the communal that characterize, respectively, utilitarian and communitarian accounts of sharing the world with others.

Modern theorists have not written nearly enough about the relation between liberal theories of rights and liberal theories of justice. Let me conclude this section with a gesture toward such an account.

Familiar claims of right will figure as both inputs and outputs, so far as theorizing about justice is concerned. They function as *inputs* inasmuch as they help constitute our sense of what it is to take each individual seriously. The content of familiar rights helps indicate the sorts of beings we are dealing with, what are likely to count for them as goods and harms, and broadly what it is to respect such beings in the quest for fair terms of human association. That people are normally taken to have the right of freedom of worship, the right to participate in politics, and the right to work, helps us *frame* the problems of justice that a society of such persons gives rise to. It indicates, for example, that an approach to the problem of justice like that of Thomas Hobbes in *Leviathan* may not be altogether adequate since it neglects important aspects of the respect we are used to demanding from one another.

We expect or we hope that many familiar claims of right will also figure among the *outputs* of an adequate theory of justice. We hope that an institutional structure set up in this way can offer certain guarantees to individuals, though they may not be so strong or so unqualified as those we had in mind before we remembered the need to balance our own claims against those made by others. For example, we may go in with a sense that respecting a human being means respecting his freedom of worship, but come out (of the balancing process) with a religious guarantee that is perhaps modified by a recognition that children, for example, must be given an adequate education and not left at the mercy of their parents' convictions, and that certain aspects of religious practice must on occasion give way to independently grounded exigencies of public administration.

In Rawls's theory, the basic liberties secured by the First Principle operate in roughly this way: the rights that emerge are not *exactly* the strident claims for absolute freedom people might start off with, but they embody a familiar sense of what it is reasonable to claim in behalf of each individual in a world where similar claims by others impose competing demands on scarce space and resources.[58]

With regard to socioeconomic claims the picture is slightly more complicated. We go into the discussion of justice with the sense that people are not just the disembodied wraiths of libertarian ideology, but needy individuals subject to vicissitudes of embodiment and materiality: we must have food and shelter, we must work, we get sick, we grow old, we are often dependent, and so on. A preliminary sense of the importance of all this – I mean its importance to each of us as individuals, not just its importance to society – is conveyed by provisions like the second-generation rights we have been discussing. That sense is then reflected in the account given of primary goods, and in the recognition to which we have already alluded (in Section III, above) that a principle for the distribution of liberty needs to be complemented by a principle addressing the distribution of the means of material well-being.

Things are a little less clear at the output end, however. Rawls is anxious that the task of a theory of justice not be understood simply as an allocation of distributive shares: who gets what when and how? "We must not assume," he says, "that there is much similarity from the standpoint of justice between an administrative allotment of goods to specific persons and the appropriate design of society."[59] Thus, for example, Rawls's "Difference Principle" is not to be interpreted as dictating that the worst-off group be *given* a certain share of resources. The effect of the principle is that when we are designing or (more likely) evaluating and reforming the network of rules and procedures that constitute the institutional structure of society, we should do so in a way that is oriented toward the advantage of the worst-off group. The institutions should be designed to operate on the assumption that when the system is working, outcomes are evaluated purely procedurally. We are not to meddle with the outcomes of a just institutional structure even if we think that by doing so we could make the array of outcomes even *more* just from a distributive point of view.

In his book on social justice, the anti-egalitarian writer F. A. Hayek has taken these comments to indicate that the difference between Rawls's approach and his own is "more verbal than substantial."[60] Rawls's work, he says, has been "wrongly . . . interpreted as lending support to socialist demands."[61] He takes Rawls to agree with his own central claim that "[j]ustice is not concerned with those unintended consequences of a spontaneous order [such as a market] which have not been deliberately brought about by anybody."[62]

I think Hayek is mistaken about this, and that he exaggerates the implications of Rawls's refusal to consider the justice of particular allocations of goods. Rawls's position may be illuminated as follows. Suppose that, on one occasion, the institutions of our economy happen to yield a distribution of wealth, D_1, that is judged inferior in terms of the Difference Principle to another distribution D_2. Should we immediately interfere and reallocate wealth so that we change D_1 into D_2? Rawls's answer, like Hayek's, is "No." For Hayek the matter ends there, but for Rawls there is a further question to be addressed: can we change the institutional structure to render it more likely in the future that the normal operation of our economy will yield distributions like D_2 rather than D_1? The answer to this may also be "No," because the proposed change might be incompatible with institutional virtues like publicity, stability, and the rule of law.[63] The new institutions being suggested may not, as it were, hold up as institutions. Still – and this is what Hayek overlooks – the answer is not *necessarily* "No." If change is possible and if the resulting institutional structure would be viable, stable, and so forth, then we are *required* as a matter of justice to implement it, for the Difference Principle just *is* the requirement that we arrange (and, if necessary, rearrange) our institutions so that social and economic inequalities are to the greatest benefit of the least advantaged. Thus, for example, if we find ourselves in a market society that lacks basic welfare provision, we have to consider whether the institutional structure of a market economy would be wrecked qua institutional structure by the addition of what Rawls calls a "transfer branch," charged with administering a social minimum. Would that make it impossible for the economic structure as a whole to operate predictably, publicly, impersonally, and in accordance with other institutional virtues? Hayek has devoted a large part of his life to arguing that it would, that the modern regulated welfare state is incompatible with the rule of law.[64] It is pretty clear that Rawls disagrees with him about that,[65] but the deeper disagreement is that Rawls thinks it is the job of a theory of justice to select principles for evaluating economic institutions along exactly these lines, whereas Hayek denies that that is a legitimate concern about justice.[66]

I have taken this digression into the Hayek–Rawls misunderstanding because I want to stress that in a theory of justice like Rawls's we cannot guarantee that socioeconomic rights will emerge in a familiar or predictable form. As an abstract matter we can say, with the drafters of Article 25 of the UDHR, that everyone has "the right to a standard of living adequate for the health and well-being of himself and his family." But that may not necessarily emerge as a specific legal or constitutional guarantee: a just society may not have a *rule* to that effect, or even any particular agency charged with administering this standard. There may be a variety of provisions and arrangements, ranging from tax breaks to educational opportunities to rent control (or its abolition) to unemployment insurance schemes, all of which taken together may represent the best (and *genuinely* the best) that can be done in an institutional framework to honor the underlying claim for the individuals in whose behalf it can be made.

That may upset people who think it more important that a right be *proclaimed* than that it be secured.[67] It may upset those who are uninterested in the viability of social institutions and in rule of law values. But people who strike these attitudes should reflect a little on the role rights are supposed to play in our social and political evaluations. It has been a common and I think correct assumption that the language of rights takes its place not just in moral philosophy, but also in *political* philosophy. At a minimum, this means that we reserve the language of rights for moral considerations we think it appropriate to enforce.[68] Enforcement, however, is just one dimension of the general issue that distinguishes political from moral philosophy: the willingness to consider the embodiment of various moral concerns in the *institutional* arrangements of human society. Once we see that as the distinctive perspective of political philosophy, we begin to see the inadequacy of the approach that leaves rights as simply programmatic claims, without considering how they fit together as a system and how the rights of one person might be made compatible, concretely not just in theory, with the rights of another.

VIII

The approach I took in the last section may also upset those who want to maintain at all costs that each individual right is absolute, and who in consequence refuse to face issues of scarcity, conflict, and moral priority. I discuss in Chapter 9 one of the sources of this insistence. The modern preoccupation with rights is partly a response to the trade-offs that characterize utilitarian calculations. Rights were supposed to express limits on what could be done to individuals for the sake of the greater benefit of others. But if rights themselves involve conflicts and balancing, it looks as though there is no getting away from the casuistry and complex moral calculations thought to be the hallmark of more blatantly consequentialist theories.

I have some sympathy with this, but, as I also argue in Chapter 9, the insistence on absolutism does not make the conflicts go away; it doesn't make the situations that appear to call for trade-offs disappear. Those situations are not something that consequentialists and their fellow travelers have perversely *invented* in order to embarrass moral absolutists. It is not the theorist's fault that there are sometimes several drowning people and only one lifeguard. As I said earlier, the world turns out not to be the sort of place to which absolute moral requirements are an apt response. If we insist on the absoluteness of rights, there is a danger that we may end up with no rights at all, or, at least, no rights embodying the idea of real concern for the individuals whose rights they are. At best, we will end up with a set of moral constraints whose absoluteness is secured only by the contortions of agent-relativity, that is, by their being understood not as concerns focused on those who may be affected by our ac-

32

tions but as concerns focused on ourselves and our own integrity.[69]

The proper response to situations posing conflicts and dilemmas is not to deny that they exist or protect the term "rights" from being contaminated by them. It is to face up to the challenges they pose with the clearest sense we can get of the intrinsic worth of each individual's well-being and independence in a world also inhabited by others. Unless that sense becomes hopelessly attenuated, it is exactly what we should identify as our theory of rights. Rights are not to be thought of as moral absolutes, waiting, tragically unemployed, on the sidelines of a world riven by distasteful conflict and hard choices. On the contrary, they are supposed to be our best and most honest individualist response to such a world. Whatever can be said to address those conflicts and those choices, in the name of the liberal ideal of high-spirited men and women each leading a life on his or her own terms – *that* is what our theory of rights should be.

To summarize: my discussion in this chapter has shown three things. First of all, it has shown that individuality, individual well-being, and individual independence really *are* at stake in the sorts of situations second-generation rights address. We cannot plausibly claim to respect the idea of persons leading lives on their own terms while neglecting the vicissitudes of poverty, material insecurity, famine, disease, and the exclusion of some from the resources of the earth by the property claims of others. Rights – or the idea of rights – simply *have* to have a presence in these areas.

Second, I hope I have shown that proponents of socioeconomic rights must really face up to the conflicts posed in these areas. Such rights are not to be left at the level of particular Articles in a Declaration. Instead they are to be integrated into a general theory of justice, which will address in a principled way whatever trade-offs and balancing are necessary for their institutionalization in a world characterized by scarcity and conflict.

Third – and here I leave my own arguments and gesture toward those of others – I hope it is clear that there are ways

33

of addressing such questions of justice which manage to preserve a sense of fundamental respect for individual persons, while simultaneously accepting the need for compromise on particular formulaic claims. We first learn about rights from slogans, but we quickly find, as we turn to political philosophy, that the truth about respecting each person in a world populated by billions is more complicated than any slogan can possibly capture. If we can preserve our determination to face up to that complexity without losing our sense of individual worth, then and, I think, only then, will we prove ourselves true partisans of liberal rights.

Chapter 2

Theoretical foundations
of liberalism

I

The terms "socialism," "conservatism," and "liberalism" are like surnames and the theories, principles, and parties that share one of these names often do not have much more in common with one another than the members of a widely extended family. If we examine the range of views that are classified under any one of these labels, we may find what Wittgenstein referred to in another context as "a complicated network of similarities overlapping and criss-crossing... sometimes overall similarities, sometimes similarities of detail";[1] but we are unlikely to find any set of doctrines or principles that are held in common by all of them, any single cluster of theoretical and practical propositions that might be regarded as the *core* or the *essence* of the ideology in question.

Partly this is because those who call themselves "liberal" or "socialist" or "conservative" have never had anything like complete control over the use of that terminology: an opponent is often happy to call a view "liberal" which many self-styled liberals would repudiate. But mostly it is because of the way political theories have developed. With the exception, and it is quite a recent exception, of socialist thought developed explicitly in the wake of Karl Marx and under the auspices of the First and Second Internationals, political theories in the West have not been constructed self-consciously under any ideological rubric or classification. Locke did not write the *Two Treatises* in order to be a liberal, any more than

Burke wrote *Reflections on the Revolution in France* in order to be a conservative. Rather, each was developed as *a* theory of government, *a* theory of society, or *a* theory of political economy, and was intended to be judged as a contribution to a debate that knew no ideological frontiers and in which almost all thinking people of the time were interested. By the same token, these bodies of theory were not developed in isolation from one another. From the point of view of the modern classifications, they seem hopelessly eclectic and impure pieces of work. Those we call "liberals" would think nothing of responding to, drawing on, or admitting to having been influenced by the works of those we call "conservatives" or "socialists." And so it is fruitless, not only to look for a core of *common* characteristics, but also to think that we can find *distinguishing* or *peculiar* characteristics which differentiate views in one tradition from views in another. Liberal moderatism fades into conservatism; the conservative's concern for community matches the socialist's; the socialist claims to take the liberal concern for freedom more seriously than the liberals themselves; and so on. To push the metaphor a little further, we are dealing not only with cases of "family resemblance," but with resemblance and difference in the context of three (or more) great families which, though rivals, have engaged over the centuries in extensive intermarriage and alliance. Indeed it is plausible to argue that in the case of socialism, we are talking of a new family that has broken away from an older liberal stock,[2] so that often we must expect to find characteristics in a "socialist" theory which quite closely resemble those of their repudiated liberal cousins.

In this chapter, I want to argue that liberalism rests on a certain view about the justification of social arrangements, and that this view helps us to understand some of the differences and some of the similarities between liberalism and other ideologies. Briefly, I shall argue that liberals are committed to a conception of freedom and of respect for the capacities and the agency of individual men and women, and that these commitments generate a requirement that all aspects of the social world should either be made acceptable or be capable of being made acceptable to every last individual. I believe that this view or something like it underpins many of the most characteristic and distinctive liberal positions. But, as I have formulated it, the view is one that many liberals may not recognize, and there may be other aspects of their beliefs that can be supported independently of these ideas. I do not want to deny that. What follows is "one view of the cathedral," so to speak:[3] a *reconstruction* of the foundations of liberalism that may be fertile in the generation of new ideas in this tradition of political theory.

But though there is this aspect of rational reconstruction, I am not going to attribute to liberals premises that are self-evident or arguments that are uncontroversial. There are some very deep tensions in the liberal view of human nature, freedom, and society, and it would be a poor account that sought to cover them up. So far from wanting to conceal or underestimate the tensions and difficulties in the liberal tradition, I hope the account that I am going to give will help to cast some light on them as well.[4]

II

Etymology suggests an association between "liberalism" and "liberty"; and while the word "liberal" has other connotations – of generosity, broadmindedness, and tolerance – it is clear enough that a conviction about the importance of individual freedom lies close to the heart of most liberal political positions.

Of course, even a generalization this vague may be difficult to sustain. Ronald Dworkin insists that liberals are more deeply committed to an ideal of equality than to any ideal of liberty, and he even rejects the commonplace view that liberal politics consists in striking a distinctive balance between these competing ideals.[5] Certainly a strong commitment to liberty in the economic sphere is more likely to be associated with political conservatism than with liberalism, particularly as those terms are understood in North America.

Those who plead for freedom of contract, for the freedom of property owners to do as they please with their land, and for the liberation of business from bureaucratic regulation, may think of themselves as "libertarians"; but they will be as anxious as their opponents that the term "liberal" should not be used to characterize these positions. However, it does not follow that those who *do* call themselves liberals are unconcerned about liberty, even in economic life. For one thing, many liberals will argue that right-wing economists have abused and wrongfully appropriated the language of freedom: they affect to be concerned with freedom generally, but it turns out to be the freedom of only a few businessmen that they are worried about and not the freedom of those they exploit or those constrained by the enforcement of their property rights. Freedom for the few, these liberals will say, is an unattractive political ideal since, under plausible assumptions, it means oppression and constraint for the many. A more attractive ideal would be equal freedom for everyone.[6] But it is unlikely that that is going to justify anything like the characteristic positions of New Right politics and economics. In other words, there are resources in a *liberal* commitment to freedom with which the "libertarianism" of economic conservatives can be opposed.[7]

Second, we should recall that even if liberty in economic life is an uncharacteristic concern of modern liberalism, a commitment to individual freedom in other areas is absolutely central. In politics, liberals are committed to intellectual freedom, freedom of speech, association, and civil liberties generally. In the realm of personal life, they raise their banners for freedom of religious belief and practice, freedom of life-style, and freedom (provided again that it *is* genuine freedom for everyone involved) in regard to sexual practices, marital affairs, pornography, the use of drugs, and all those familiar liberal concerns. Dworkin maintains that these positions are all derivative from a fundamental commitment to equality of concern and respect;[8] but it seems to me that equality of respect, at least, cannot be understood in this context except by reference to a conviction about the importance of liberty (for everyone).

A third point is much more important. Freedom or liberty is a concept of which there are many conceptions.[9] Since some of these conceptions are not associated with the liberal tradition, it is unsatisfactory to say simply that liberals are committed to (equal) liberty and leave the matter there.

The debate over the proper conception of liberty has been bitter and sometimes deadly. Many who call themselves liberals (but who might be labeled "conservatives" or "libertarians" by their opponents) take their stand on what is termed a *"negative"* conception of liberty: a person's liberty is simply the extent to which he can act unconstrained by literal obstruction or interference from others. This view is referred to by its opponents as an "impoverished," "infantile," or "philistine" theory of freedom, while libertarians themselves describe less negative conceptions as "fraudulent" and potentially "despotic."[10] The intensity and single-mindedness with which positions are taken and defended in this debate are surprising. Liberty is a concept which captures what is distinctive and important in human agency as such and in the untrammeled exercise of powers of individual deliberation, choice, and the intentional initiation of action. Surely no one can really believe that what this *is* is something simple or self-evident, or that there can never be honest disagreements in this area. Human agency, will, and the initiation of action is a profoundly complicated business: it is the locus of one of the most intractable problems in metaphysics, and it is also the source of some of the deepest exultation and despair in human experience. Our sense of what it is to have and exercise freedom is bound up with our conception of ourselves as persons and of our relation to value, other people, society, and the casual order of the world. From the point of view of moral and political philosophy, then, human agency is a rich seam of value which competing conceptions of freedom mine in differing ways. I do not want to suggest that rival conceptions should be immune from criticism. But just because of the richness and complexity of this seam of value, it seems odd for a philosopher to say: "Here is my conception of freedom; this is all there is to freedom; all other conceptions are utterly unintelligible and unappealing to me."

To say then that a commitment to *freedom* is the foundation of liberalism is to say something too vague and abstract to be helpful, while to say that liberals are committed fundamentally to a particular *conception* of liberty is to sound too assured, too dogmatic about a matter on which, with the best will in the world, even ideological bedfellows are likely to disagree. All the same, there are positions in the debate about freedom which it is characteristically liberal to repudiate, and it may be worth giving them some brief attention.

Much of that debate has been concerned with a proper understanding of the relation between freedom and social order. Some philosophers say there is a definitional connection between freedom and social order: *real* freedom (sometimes, freedom for the *true* self) just *is* submission to and participation in the order of a good society. Others maintain that freedom is lost or the principle of liberty is violated whenever *any* rule of social order is enforced, no matter how well grounded it is in the requirements of social life. Liberalism, it seems to me, repudiates both of these extreme positions.

In "Two Concepts of Liberty," Isaiah Berlin described as "positive freedom" a package of views which included the identification of the "true self" with the order of one's community, state, or class and the identification of freedom for that self with the willing discharge of social or communal responsibilities.[11] An example of this may be found in Hegel's view that "the state in and by itself is the ethical whole, the actualization of freedom," and that "in duty [by which Hegel means laws and institutions perceived from a subjective point of view] the individual finds his liberation."[12] The trouble with this, from a liberal perspective, is that it seems to rule out the possibility of an individual standing back from that form of social order and subjecting it to critical evaluation.

If a person's true self is thought to be partly or wholly constituted by the social order, then that self cannot ask the critical question "Is this the sort of order *I* accept? Is it one that *I* would have chosen?" Or, if this question *is* asked, it is to be regarded as the alienated bewilderment of one who is divorced from his true self, rather than as a genuine exercise of freedom. This view of freedom, then, is at odds with the liberal insistence that all social arrangements are subject to critical scrutiny by individuals, and that men and women reveal and exercise their highest powers as free agents when they engage in this sort of scrutiny of the arrangements under which they are to live.

Connected with this is a long-standing uneasiness in the liberal tradition about the establishment of any disjunction between the "true" subject of freedom and the self as it appears in the subjective consciousness of the individual concerned. To use a phrase from the philosophy of mind, there is *something it is like* to be me[13] – the occurrent subjective experience of my thoughts, fears, preferences, desires, and intentions. To talk about my freedom, on the liberal view, is to talk about the role *I* play in the determination of my actions, where "I" is understood in the sense of what it is now like to be me; it is not to talk about the thought or decision-making of an entity cleansed of the "false consciousness" that characterizes my present experiences and desires. Sometimes liberals are accused of taking the beliefs and preferences of individuals as given and hence of ignoring the fact that forms of society may determine forms of consciousness and the structure and content of preferences.[14] But liberals need not be blind to the possibility of preferences changing, either autonomously or along with changes in social structure and social expectations. Provided this possibility of change is in principle something that people as they are can recognize in themselves and take into account in their reflective deliberations, then it can be accommodated perfectly well in a liberal account of freedom.

I do not want to pretend that this is an easy position to adopt. As we shall see later, liberalism is also bound up in large part with respect for rationality, with the discipline of self-knowledge and clear-sightedness, and with the celebration of the human capacity to grasp and understand the world. But those capacities are not always in play when people make decisions about how to act. So that sense of the importance of *reason* in human decision-making is bound to introduce some tension into a theory organized around respect for decisions made by individual men and women as they are in ordinary life.

So far we have said that the liberal rejects the view that social order is constitutive of individual freedom. But is he committed to the opposite extreme – that the impositions and restraints of social life are necessarily *violations* of individual freedom? Partisans of negative liberty in the Berlin tradition are apt to answer quickly "Yes" and qualify that by adding that such violations are often justified by respect for other values or for the freedom of other individuals.[15] But I think the matter is more complicated than that. The question has to be whether liberty – *in any sense in which liberty is thought to be important* – is attacked or undermined whenever a rule of social conduct is enforced. Consider the position of a person bound by a contract he has freely entered into: if that contract is enforced against him, is anything important lost so far as his liberty is concerned? Surely a negative answer is plausible in this case. Though he may be forced or coerced by the threat of court action, it is pursuant to an arrangement that he has chosen, and it would be a poor conception of freedom which did not leave room for the possibility of individuals binding themselves in this way.[16] Something similar may be said about social rules. If the rule is one that the citizen has agreed to, surely little that is important in relation to liberty is lost if it is subsequently enforced against him. If we take his agreement seriously, we may see that as something more like the consummation of his freedom than a violation of it. But if the rule is simply *imposed*, without reference to the consent of those who are to be bound by it, then something important in this connection *is* lost – namely, the capacity of human agents to determine for themselves

42

how they will restrain their conduct in order to live in community with others. That capacity will have been pushed aside in the name of social order, as though it were something of no consequence; and that *is* an attack on what we should conceive as the importance of freedom. Now, in each case, the mechanics of enforcement may be exactly the same: coercion is applied to an agent who experiences it as a constraint on decision-making, and certain actions are impelled or obstructed as a result. But though action has been determined and agency interfered with in both cases, the value of freedom has been more seriously attacked in the second case than in the first.

So liberals need not take an anarchist approach to the problem of social order. They can concede that the enforcement of social rules involves actions which characteristically and in familiar circumstances threaten freedom and threaten it seriously. But since it is possible for an individual to *choose* to live under a social order, to *agree* to abide by its restraints, and therefore to use his powers as a free agent to commit himself for the future, the enforcement of such an order does not *necessarily* mean that freedom as a value is being violated.

III

The relationship between liberal thought and the legacy of the Enlightenment cannot be stressed too strongly. The Enlightenment was characterized by a burgeoning confidence in the human ability to make sense of the world, to grasp its regularities and fundamental principles, to predict its future, and to manipulate its powers for the benefit of mankind. After millennia of ignorance, terror, and superstition, cowering before forces it could neither understand nor control, mankind faced the prospect of being able at last to build a *human* world, a world in which it might feel safely and securely at home. Empiricism made this an optimism on behalf of the individual mind: there was a sense abroad that it was possible, in principle, for *each individual* to understand the world in this way, and indeed it was maintained that there was no *other* way in which the world could be understood except by an individual mind.[17]

The drive for individual understanding of the world is matched in Enlightenment thought by an optimism at least as strong about the possibility of understanding society. In one aspect, this optimism is the basis of modern sociology, history, and economics. But it is also the source of certain normative attitudes – I want to say distinctively *liberal* attitudes – toward political and social justification. It is the source of an impatience with tradition, mystery, awe, and superstition as the basis of order, and of a determination to make authority answer at the tribunal of reason and convince us that it is entitled to respect. If life in society is practicable and desirable, then its principles must be amenable to explanation and understanding, and the rules and restraints that are necessary must be capable of being justified to the people who are to live under them. The social world, even more than the natural world, must be thought of as a world *for us* – a world whose workings the individual mind can grasp and perhaps manipulate deliberately for the benefit of human purposes.

The view that I want to identify as a foundation of liberal thought is based on this demand for a justification of the social world.[18] Like his empiricist counterparts in science, the liberal insists that intelligible justifications in social and political life must be available in principle for everyone, for society is to be understood by the individual mind, not by the tradition or sense of a community. Its legitimacy and the basis of social obligation must be made out to each individual, for once the mantle of mystery has been lifted, *everybody* is going to want an answer. If there is some individual to whom a justification cannot be given, then so far as *he* is concerned the social order had better be replaced by other arrangements, for the status quo has made out no claim to *his* allegiance.

Stated in this way, the demand for justification has obvious affinities with the somewhat older idea, present in the natural law tradition of medieval and early modern thought, of the social contract and government by consent.

> Men being, as has been said, by Nature, all free, equal and independent, no one can be put out of this Estate, and subjected to the Political Power of another, without his own *Consent*. The only way whereby any one devests himself of his Natural Liberty, and *puts on the bonds of Civil Society* is by agreeing with other Men to joyn and unite into a Community, for their comfortable, safe and peaceable living one amongst another, in a secure Enjoyment of their Properties, and a greater Security against any that are not of it.[19]

The ideas expressed here have a positive and a negative side. Negatively, they involve the denial that being governed is natural to human persons: being governed, on the contrary, is something people invent and take upon themselves, for reasons, in an act of free choice. We may find it hard to imagine anyone choosing to live outside *all* political frameworks. But, on this view, there is nothing perverse or unnatural about standing back from the social order and putting it to the test of individual critical evaluation. Positively, these ideas suggest that the constitution of a good society is best represented as something which will have been chosen by the people living under it, something whose main features are as intelligible to them as the charter of a club of which they are founding members, designed by them in order to serve the purposes that brought them together in the first place.

The idea of individual choice here performs two related functions: it may serve as a basis for political legitimacy or it may serve as a basis for political obligation (or it may do both). Sometimes, when I give my consent to an arrangement, I make it permissible for *other* people to do what it would otherwise be impermissible for them to do; and sometimes my agreement also makes it impermissible for *me* to do what it would otherwise be permissible for me to do. (For example, the first but not the second idea is involved when I consent to a surgical operation.)

In traditional theories of the social contract, both aspects are involved. By agreeing to be governed (under certain arrangements) an individual makes it permissible for others, usually the instituted agencies of government, to exercise power over him in ways that might otherwise not be permissible; for example, they may now physically prevent him from taking the law into his own hands when he thinks he has been wronged, whereas previously it may have been wrong for them to do this. At the same time, he also takes an obligation on himself: to use the same example, whereas before he was morally at liberty to punish someone who had wronged him, now he has an obligation to refrain from doing so and to submit the matter to the community or the courts instead.

When people have discussed the liberal idea of the social contract, attention has often focused exclusively on the issue of obligation. I think this is a pity. There are all sorts of difficulties with contract accounts of political obligation which do not affect contract accounts of legitimacy to anything like the same extent.

Some of these difficulties relate to the application of the underlying idea of consent as an action with moral effect. In the case of political obligation, contract theory rests on the view that we ought to obey the law, accept unpalatable political decisions without resistance, and suffer the sacrifices that our society may demand of us simply because we have made a *promise*. I find that an improbable view. We all think promise-breaking is wrong, no doubt; but is it so conclusively and momentously wrong that people should be prepared to put up with hardship, oppression, mortal danger, and even death (in the story of Socrates) just because they promised to obey? Very few of us think this even about the explicit promises that are given in personal life, and so it is no wonder we balk when such requirements are said to be based on some of the things political philosophers have taken to be sufficient indications of consent.

None of this is helped by the lack of philosophical agreement on exactly *why* we ought to keep our promises. The
least substantial account is this: that saying the words themselves – "I promise to obey" or whatever – just *is* the assumption of an obligation, and that is all there is to it.
Hobbes, for example, seems on very weak ground when he
says of a political agent "that he ought to perform for his
promise sake" or because going back on his word and dis-
obeying would involve him in some kind of verbal contradiction.[20] But his account becomes more convincing when he
tells us that the strongest reasons for keeping a contract are
the reasons one had for making it in the first place. Certainly
this is what he says about political obligation *in extremis:*

> The Obligation a man may sometimes have, upon the Com-
> mand of the Soveraign to execute any dangerous, or dis-
> honourable Office, dependeth not on the Words of our
> Submission; but on the Intention; which is to be understood
> by the End thereof.[21]

But then in this sort of account the act of consent itself is
almost redundant. At most it serves as an indication that the
reasons now being given for obedience are reasons that the
agent has at least once found compelling.[22] Maybe, however,
our consent binds us in a political context because of the
reliance that others place on us. Morally this is the most attractive theory. But then as Michael Walzer has pointed out,
the resulting obligation may be just one among a number of
competing obligations based on reliance that we have to other
people.[23]

These difficulties do not arise so acutely in relation to the
legitimating function of consent. Why does my consent make
it permissible for someone to do something to me which
would otherwise be impermissible? The reason lies first, in
our need for control over what happens to us, as part of our
general interest in controlling the course of our lives, and
second, in the fact that as social beings we can help, assist,
and enjoy one another in various ways. Giving individuals

the power of consensual legitimation helps to reconcile these two important elements – our individual need for control and the desirability of our interaction with others. In a political context, these reflect our liberty or autonomy, on the one hand, and the potential gains from social cooperation, on the other. Making consent the source of political legitimacy provides a basis on which these gains can be realized without any serious threat to freedom.

Consider now the traditional objection that as a matter of fact most societies have *not* been set up on a contractual basis. Most were established as a result of external force or internal dissension.[24] Even in the few cases where states have been consensually instituted, the practice has never been established of giving each new arrival, as it were, an opportunity of expressing or withholding consent to the society into which he has been born. The laws treat us as bound willy-nilly to obey them and leave us little realistic alternative if we find them for some reason repugnant.

Once again, these objections pose difficulties for the theory of political obligation. Some liberals have resorted to the idea of *tacit* consent. According to Locke, everyday actions like enjoying property in a jurisdiction or even traveling on the highway can count as consent for the purposes of political subjection.[25] But the crucial question to ask of such accounts is always: "What would count as the withholding of consent?" If there is no plausible answer, then it is clear that the concept is not really pulling its weight in the argument for obligation. "Emigration" is the traditional reply; but in the modern world that is simply not a real possibility for most people. For most of us, citizenship and obligation are determined by birth not choice, and very few modern liberals are prepared to say that things would be much different in this regard even in a perfectly just society.

The other familiar tactic is to move from a requirement of actual to one of *hypothetical* consent. Later I shall argue that hypothetical consent is an important idea in the liberal tradition. But to see that it is of no help at all in the theory of obligation, we need only consider the inference "You *would have* consented, therefore you *are* obliged." We may, as Robert Nozick suggests, "learn much from seeing how the state could have arisen, even if it didn't arise that way," but we shall not learn anything about *our* obligations.[26]

The idea that consent might be the basis of political legitimacy is, however, much easier to rescue from the traditional objections to social contract theory. An example will illustrate. Normally it is wrong for a surgeon to operate on a person's body without his consent. But sometimes after accidents people are left unconscious and incapable of consenting to procedures that may be necessary to save their lives. In these circumstances, we believe the surgeon should ask: "*Would* the patient give his consent *if* he were in a position to do so?" If the answer is affirmative, the operation may be morally legitimate, even though as it happens the patient never recovers and is unable to ratify the agreement given on his behalf. Now perhaps there are instances where this sort of hypothetical consent is not sufficient. For example, we may not use the face of an unconscious person in an advertisement for sleeping pills even if there is reason to believe that he would have agreed to act as a model if he were conscious. So there are limits to how far hypothetical consent can confer legitimacy on what would otherwise be wrongful interferences. Still, even in these cases we may think that this sort of wrongness is a matter of degree, and that interfering with someone without his consent, but in a way in which he would have agreed to be treated had he been asked, is *less wrong* than interfering with him in a way in which, even hypothetically, he would never have agreed to be treated. If so, hypothetical consent at least *makes a difference* to the wrongness of interference, even though it may not always in itself be enough to make that interference legitimate. (It is worth noting that *nothing similar* happens in the case of obligation. A hypothetical promise by itself does not add a scintilla of obligation to a person's moral position.)

Though legitimacy and obligation are sometimes treated as two sides of the same coin, these considerations suggest that they may come apart in social contract theory. The classic case is posed by Hobbes: a group of people who have wrongfully resisted their sovereign may rightfully be put to death by the sovereign but they have no obligation to submit to execution or to refrain from conspiracy to escape.[27] Another instance is found in a certain view of civil disobedience. It is often said that those who break the law in order to conscientiously protest some injustice have no right to complain if the law is enforced against them. Though this may mean that they have a duty to surrender themselves to the authorities, it may also mean that the rightness of their disobedience does not in itself entail the wrongness of punishing them.[28] Unless we want to insist that it is never right for the state to force people to do anything unless they are violating an obligation that they have to do it (and a moment's reflection reveals the inadequacy of *that* position), then we must accept that a regime may be morally legitimate even though disobedience to its laws is not always morally wrong.

Anyway, political legitimacy will be the focus of the rest of this chapter. I want to present liberalism as, at bottom, a theory about what makes political action – and in particular the enforcement and maintenance of a social and political order – morally legitimate. The thesis that I want to say is *fundamentally* liberal is this: a social and political order is illegitimate unless it is rooted in the consent of all those who have to live under it; the consent or agreement of these people is a condition of its being morally permissible to enforce that order against them. (I state that here as a *necessary* condition, leaving open the possibility that liberals may want to allow other things to vitiate political legitimacy besides lack of consent.) Understood in this way, the liberal position provides a basis for arguing against some arrangement or institution inasmuch as one can show that it has not secured, or perhaps could not secure, the consent of the people. And it provides a basis for arguing in favor of an arrangement or institution if one can show that no social order which lacked this feature could possibly secure popular consent.

IV

The thesis I have outlined can be understood in slightly different ways, for liberalism is not a monolithic tradition. One of the most important differences – between voluntaristic and rationalistic accounts of political legitimacy – corresponds to the distinction between actual and hypothetical consent.

If emphasis is placed on the role of *will* in the individual choice of government, then hypothetical consent will not be viewed as an adequate substitute for the actual consent of the citizen. A given social order will be regarded as unfree – as a violation of the free capacities of its citizens – unless and until they agree to its laws in some explicit act of choice and adoption. On this sort of voluntarist account, the requirement that the laws be actually agreed to is indispensable for freedom. Rousseau's theory in *The Social Contract* – his insistence that the general will must be *expressed* by the people on a regular basis and his violent rejection of representation in the making of the laws – is about as close as we get to this voluntarism in the liberal tradition.[29]

But even this sort of approach may concede that there is more than one way a social order may be oriented to the norm of actual consent. Though a social order not legitimated by actual consent may be unfree, that unfreedom can be mitigated by our recognition that it is at least *possible* to imagine people giving it their consent. Such an order can be described in terms of hypothetical consent, and though it is unfree from a voluntarist point of view, is surely not so bad in terms of unfreedom as one to which consent cannot even be imagined. So though the liberal requirement may be interpreted strictly and radically – undermining the legitimacy of many if not all existing societies – it need not be left with nothing to say or no discriminations to make between societies that fall into this category. If the lack of actual consent is to be remedied, the first step must be reform of the society so that consent becomes an imaginable option. Hypothetical contractarianism provides the basis for that step to be taken.

By contrast, there are a number of liberal views which come

close to repudiating the actual *will* aspect of consent altogether. The clearest case of a nonvoluntarist theory of the social contract is that of Kant. In his work on political philosophy, Kant insists that since "the will of another person cannot decide anything for someone without injustice," the law must be based on "the will of the entire people."[30] But though he calls that will the basis of "the original contract," he goes on to say:

> But we need by no means assume that this contract . . . based on a coalition of the wills of all private individuals in a nation to form a common, public will for the purposes of rightful legislation, actually exists as a *fact*, for it cannot possibly be so. . . . It is in fact merely an *idea* of reason, which nonetheless has undoubted practical reality; for it can oblige every legislator to frame his laws in such a way that they could have been produced by the united will of a whole nation. . . . This is the test of the rightfulness of every public law. For if the law is such that a whole people could not *possibly* agree to it (for example, if it stated that a certain class of *subjects* must be privileged as a hereditary *ruling class*), it is unjust; but if it is at least *possible* that a people could agree to it, it is our duty to consider the law as just, even if the people is at present in such a position or attitude of mind that it would probably refuse its consent if it were consulted.[31]

So the standard Kant proposes is a relaxed one. Not only can a social order be made legitimate without actual consent, but even the barest possibility of consent is enough to justify the law.

In modern political philosophy, the Kantian approach has been taken up by John Rawls. According to Rawls, the basic structure of society is to be evaluated according to principles presented as those that would be chosen by free and rational individuals coming together in a position of initial equality to settle the terms of their association.[32] But again, the idea is not a voluntaristic one:

> No society can, of course, be a scheme of cooperation which men enter voluntarily in a literal sense. . . . Yet a society sat-

isfying the principles of justice as fairness comes as close as a society can to being a voluntary scheme, for it meets the principles which free and equal persons would assent to under circumstances that are fair. In this sense its members are autonomous and the obligations they recognize self-imposed.[33]

The test of a just society, then, is not whether the individuals who live in it have agreed to its terms, but whether its terms *can be represented* as the object of an agreement between them.

In all of this, it is important to remember that theories of actual and hypothetical consent are not independent of one another. A theory of hypothetical consent obviously defines limits for a theory of actual consent: showing that something *could not be* consented to is a way of showing that it *has not been* consented to. If reasons can be given in hypothetical contract theory why certain sorts of arrangements would not be the subject of an agreement they may be sufficient to cast doubt, for moral purposes, on the reality of any putative *actual* consent to such arrangements. Not every utterance of the phonemes "I consent" counts for the purposes of legitimacy (let alone obligation). The act of agreement must be minimally intelligible to count as the sort of thing that can have the moral effects consent is supposed to have; and that intelligibility cannot wholly be divorced from some consideration of the substance of what is alleged to have been agreed to.[34] In early modern contract theory, this approach led to what Richard Tuck has described as a radical strategy of interpretative charity. For example:

> [N]o man can be supposed so void of common sense (unless an absolute Fool, and then he is not capable of making any Bargain) to yield himself so absolutely up to anothers disposal. ... So that I conceive that even a Slave ... in the state of Nature, where he hath no civil power to whom to appeal for Justice, hath as much right as a Son or Child of the Family, to defend his life, or what belongs to him, against the unjust violence or Rage of his Master.[35]

That strategy was used to undermine the suggestion that slavery and absolutism might be based on the free alienation of liberty.

Whereas this use of hypothetical contract draws on the idea that something *could* not be agreed to, the idea that something *should* not be agreed to has also been deployed. Much of Locke's theory has this character. Some of our natural rights are held by us on trust from our creator and we *may* not (that is, we are not in a moral position to) bargain them away. An actual case of someone "giving" his sovereign the right to kill him at will, therefore, has no greater moral effect than someone purporting to sell the property of another.[36] More recently, Rawls has deployed a procedural idea to similar effect. In his argument against utilitarianism, he says:

> I shall rely upon the fact that for an agreement to be valid, the parties must be able to honor it under all foreseeable circumstances. There must be a rational assurance that one can carry through. . . . [W]hen we enter an agreement, we must be able to honor it even should the worst possibilities prove to be the case. Otherwise we have not acted in good faith.[37]

Thus, for example, people who believe there is a chance of utilitarianism justifying slavery and who believe that as slaves in a utilitarian regime they would be inclined to resistance and disobedience must not sign up for utilitarian principles of justice. They are morally precluded from entering into an agreement that may turn out to have consequences they cannot accept. If this argument goes through, there is no way that utilitarian principles can be represented as an object of agreement in Rawls's "original position."

But it is worth noting that this sort of criticism leaves utilitarianism standing in an ambiguous relation to the liberal tradition.[38] There is obviously a sense in which it *is* a liberal theory: it is individualist in its hedonism, liberal in its acceptance of men and women as they actually are, egalitarian in its claim that the pleasure and suffering of the beggar count for as much as those of a king, and modern in its imposition of a rational and intelligible standard as a criterion of political evaluation. In the eighteenth and early nineteenth centuries, Bentham and the utilitarians were at the forefront of the attempt to demystify society, to throw its workings open to the light of individual reason, and to set out in an explicit and formulaic way intelligible principles of political morality. But utilitarians were always wary of the idea of social contract, and modern criticisms have highlighted at least one reason for that. Because of the way in which utilitarians aggregate individual harms and benefits, it is plausible to argue that the outcomes of their reasoning can be made acceptable in the end only to those who gain from the operation of the felicific calculus; if there are any net losers and if their loss is drastic then neither the utilitarian computations nor the principles that generate them can be made universally acceptable. Sensitivity to this prospect of being relegated to the margins of the liberal tradition has made many utilitarians scurry for answers to objections like these: perhaps drastic losses would never occur, or perhaps the risk of incurring them would nevertheless be a good bet considering what each person stands to gain, or perhaps some form of "two-level" or "indirect" utilitarianism can be established which does justice to our liberal intuitions on these matters.[39] These are arguments we cannot go into here.

When we move from asking what people actually accept to asking what they *would* accept under certain conditions, we shift our emphasis away from the will and focus on the *reasons* that people might have for exercising their will in one way rather than another. Doing so involves certain dangers for the liberal. Real people do not always act on the reasons we think they might have for acting: the reasonableness of the actors in our hypothesis may not match the reality of men and women in actual life.

This bears acutely on the issue of the liberal response to the ethical and religious pluralism of the modern world. Some liberals celebrate the diversity of beliefs, commitments, ideals, and life-styles held and practiced in our community.

Others accept simply as a matter of fact that that diversity is irreducible to a single orthodoxy, no matter how rationally compelling that orthodoxy may be.[40] Still, others are convinced by Mill's arguments that any attempt to homogenize the ethical or religious life of our society would be ethically and socially disastrous.[41] Whichever of these views is taken, a liberal society is envisaged as one in which people will practice and pursue a variety of opposing and incommensurable life-styles. But how then is it possible for these same people to live peaceably together and accept the same forms of social justification? The liberal strategy has been to search for underlying interests and beliefs shared in common which may be appealed to in the justification of our institutional arrangements: the basic needs of nature, certain desired objects that are means to the pursuit of any ideal, common general beliefs about how the world works, similar modes of argument and reason, and so on. But in addition to that liberals must also assume that all ethical commitment has a common form: that there is something like *pursuing a conception of the good life* that all people, even those with the most diverse commitments, can be said to be engaged in.[42] The recognition of such an underlying form was crucial in the emergence of religious toleration: those of different faiths had to be able to recognize one another as *worshipping a god*, each in his own way, and to identify with one another in that regard. Modern liberalism attempts to express a similar idea for all aspects of life-style. The hunch is that, although people do not share one another's ideals, they can at least abstract from their experience a sense of *what it is like to be committed to an ideal of the good life;* they can recognize this in others and they can focus on it as something to which political justification ought to be addressed.[43]

These seem to be the minimal assumptions of "reasonableness" which the liberal has to make if the project of social justification is to get off the ground at all.[44] But many will challenge the universality of this conception of "reason." They will say that people in fact exhibit different basic wants and needs, different fundamental beliefs about the world, and utterly disparate modes of reasoning. More seriously, it is arguable that many individual and communal commitments do not have the shape that the liberal envisages. Some people's commitments are so overwhelming that they appear to swamp the basic human concerns, giving us reason to doubt the universal validity of the framework sketched above. Other people's commitments are so inextricably bound up with their sense of themselves that they find it impossible to abstract from them: they will be repelled by the thought that their ideals share a common form with those of people they despise, and they will be outraged that political justification should require them to think in that way. Even more worrying, some may find themselves with commitments so fervent that they cannot be pursued except through the endeavor to impose them on others. Faced with these possibilities, the liberal has a hard choice. Either he concedes that his conception of political judgment will be appealing only to those who hold their commitments in a certain "liberal" spirit, or he must look for a form of social order in which not only those with different ideals, but those with different views about the legitimacy of imposing their ideals, can be accommodated. Since the prospects for a social order of this kind are not very promising, the former more robust response seems the only one available.[45] But if this line is taken, we must abandon any claim about the "neutrality" of liberal theory.[46] The liberal will have to concede that he has a great many more enemies (real enemies – people who will suffer under a liberal dispensation) than he has usually pretended to have. This, then, is the cost of the move from actual consent theory with its emphasis on will to hypothetical consent theory with its emphasis on liberal reason.

V

I have concentrated my discussion on the idea of social contract, not because all liberals take that idea seriously, but because it expresses in a clear and provocative form a view I believe most liberals do share: that the social order must be one that can be justified to the people who have to live under it. We have seen that the Enlightenment impulse on which this is based is the demand of the individual mind for the intelligibility of the social world. Society should be a *transparent* order, in the sense that its workings and principles should be well-known and available for public apprehension and scrutiny. People should know and understand the reasons for the basic distribution of wealth, power, authority, and freedom. Society should not be shrouded in mystery, and its workings should not have to depend on mythology, mystification, or a "noble lie."[47] As Rawls puts it, the basic structure of society should be "a public system of rules":

> Thus the general awareness of their universal acceptance should have desirable effects and support the stability of social cooperation. . . . Conceptions that might work out well enough if understood and followed by a few or even by all, so long as this fact were not widely known, are excluded by the publicity condition.[48]

Is there any tension between this requirement of transparency and the equally characteristic liberal commitment to privacy in certain areas of social life? Many liberals believe that it is important to establish a distinction between the public and the private aspects of a person's life – between those activities for which he is accountable to society (those which are to be open to evaluation and criticism by others) and those that are not. The problem is that privacy here is not usually the privacy of solitude, but rather the privacy of the family and (in classical but not in modern liberalism) the privacy of the workplace. But these are areas in which, on any realistic social understanding, important issues of power and hence legitimacy arise. That leads to a genuine dilemma. Some liberals may be happy with the panopticism of a Bentham:

> A whole kingdom, the whole globe itself, will become a gymnasium, in which every man exercises himself before the eyes

of every other man. Every gesture, every turn of limb or feature, in those whose motions have a visible impact on the general happiness, will be noticed and marked down.[49]

But others will view this with alarm. Freedom from the public gaze, they will argue, is an indispensable condition for the nurture of moral agency: people need space and intimacy in order to develop their liberty.[50] Others may raise again the fears about social homogeneity that we have already mentioned. It is easy to imagine Bentham's gymnasium becoming a place in which everyone casts sidelong glances at his neighbor to ensure that all are going through exactly similar motions.[51] But to the extent that these lines of thought are taken seriously, liberals leave themselves open to the charge of being less than wholehearted about the legitimation of *all* structures of power in modern society.

Connected with this is an issue about the transparency of economic processes. The demand for a society whose workings are demystified and open to the rational scrutiny of the individual mind is one that characterizes certain forms of socialism as well as the liberal tradition. Marx, for example, looked forward to a society in which all aspects of economic life would be subject to explicit human control, as opposed to a situation in which people see themselves at the mercy of market forces which they cannot understand or manipulate.[52] As Steven Lukes puts it:

> [T]he ideal society to which Marx expectantly looked forward would be one in which, under conditions of abundance, human beings can achieve self-realization in a new, transparent form of social unity, in which nature, both physical and social, comes under their control.[53]

What then distinguishes the Marxist from the liberal in this respect? Marxists believe that transparency is simply unavailable in relation to present forms of "liberal" society. For one thing, people as they are are so burdened by the mystifications of capitalist ideology as to be incapable of apprehending the true basis of social order. But more important, they insist that as long as liberal society remains committed to some form of market order, the demand for transparency can never be satisfied.

The point is an interesting and intriguing one. Liberals are attracted to markets for all sorts of reasons. Some of them are pragmatic: we fear the political consequences of vesting too much power in the hands of social planners.[54] Others are based on considerations of right: only in a market can people exercise their property entitlements to the full.[55] But the most persuasive argument remains that of economic efficiency: Adam Smith's claim that in pursuing his own self-interest in a market context, each individual is "led by an invisible hand to promote an end that was no part of his intention." The "invisibility" of the promotion of social benefit is something that does not trouble liberal economists: as Smith puts it, it is none the worse for society that the resultant social good was no part of anyone's intention.[56] But that is an idea that Marxists find deeply repellent. What they see as the *reality* of social and economic life – people producing cooperatively for one another's benefit – is made invisible by a mask or appearance of self-interest and competition. The workings of society, as they actually are, are hidden behind the curtain of capitalist economics, and we are asked to accept an imaginary view of those workings because any attempt to bring them consciously under our control would lead to worse consequences than if we remained in our state of mystification. Of course, many Marxists challenge the view that markets *are* efficient, and some also challenge the equity of the distributions that result. But their deepest worry concerns the opacity of this form of social order. One liberal response here might be to say there are different conceptions of intelligibility involved. When we talk of an invisible hand, it is not that we do not *understand* how markets generate efficient outcomes. We do: it is just that our understanding of them precludes their replacement by more direct forms of social control. The Marxist, I believe, is working with a more manipulative or technocratic conception of understanding: a process has not been made humanly intelligible unless there is a sense in which humanity can, as it were, take it over, not only representing it in thought but reproducing its workings in the concrete form of deliberate agency.[57] But both conceptions are rooted in what I called earlier the Enlightenment impulse. And I think the fact that a common value of social transparency is being deployed here helps to explain why many liberals also believe that the "anarchy" of the market is an insult to human intelligence and why they feel the attractions of some form of planned economy even though they stop short of anything like a commitment to communism.

VII

I said at the beginning that we must not expect to find a clear set of propositions sufficient to distinguish all forms of liberalism from all forms of socialism and conservatism. But I hope the broad outline of a distinction is clear. Liberals demand that the social order should in principle be capable of explaining itself at the tribunal of each person's understanding. Conservatives are likely to repudiate that as the arrogance of individualism:

> We are afraid to put men to live and trade each on his own private stock of reason; because we suspect that the stock in each man is small, and that individuals would do better to avail themselves of the general bank and capital of nations and of ages.[58]

They will celebrate the fact that the social order depends for its efficacy on a degree of mystery, illusion, and sentiment – all "the decent drapery of life" which the liberal pulls aside in the name of rational justification. By contrast, as we have seen, socialists are more sympathetic to the rationalist and humanist impulses on which liberalism is based. Of course, they will say, a good society is one that is penetrable and manipulable by the reason of free individuals acting in concert. But they share none of the liberals' optimism about the possibility of legitimating existing societies in this way. The opacity of capitalist economy and the alienating and corrupting effects of exploitation mean that all hope of a genuinely free and open society must be postponed indefinitely until class conflict has had its day. Liberals alone remain committed – ambiguously, uncertainly, and precariously – to the prospect and possibility of freedom in the present, that is, individual freedom for people like us in the social world with which we are familiar. Neither burdened by a mystifying heritage of tradition nor bought off by the promise that freedom will come for all at its historically appointed time, the liberal individual confronts his social order *now*, demanding respect for the existing capacities of his autonomy, his reason, and his agency.

Chapter 3

A right to do wrong

I

It seems unavoidable that, if we take the idea of moral rights seriously, we have to countenance the possibility that an individual may have a moral right to do something that is, from the moral point of view, wrong. Consider the following actions.

> Someone uses all the money that he has won fairly in a lottery to buy racehorses and champagne, refusing to donate any of it to a desperately deserving charity.
>
> An individual joins an organization he knows has racist leanings, such as the National Front in the United Kingdom; he canvasses support for it among a credulous electorate, and exercises his own vote in its favor.
>
> Somebody offers deliberately confusing, though not untrue, information about the policies of a political party to a confused and simpleminded voter in an attempt to influence his vote.
>
> An athlete takes part in sports competition with the representatives of a racist state, despite the fact that this profoundly demoralizes those who are struggling for the liberalization of that state.
>
> Antiwar activists organize a rowdy demonstration near a cenotaph service on Remembrance Day.
>
> A man refuses to give a stranger in the street the time

of day when he asks for it or coldly and rudely rebuffs attempts at conversation in a railway compartment.

Our opinions as to the morality of these actions may differ, and, in real life, our judgments would turn on details and background elements that have to be left out when one is sketching examples such as these. But in each case we can easily imagine circumstances and backgrounds in which the following is a possible, even perhaps the most plausible, moral response: the action in question is morally wrong, but nevertheless it is an action that the agent has a moral right to do. Thus someone might say, "It is surely wrong to canvass support for an organization with racist leanings, but equally surely it is something people have a moral right to do." Or he might say, "Certainly, athletes have a moral right to compete in sports with racially selected teams if they want to, but nevertheless it is something that they should not do." This sort of double-barreled response is not unfamiliar in political discourse. But it *sounds* paradoxical, or it sounds as if the person who is making it is equivocating. So the question that I want to examine in this chapter is whether there is any *real* inconsistency underlying the appearance of paradox or equivocation in this sort of response. When somebody says of an action, "Action A is wrong" and adds "... but you have a right to do it," is he expressing his own uncertainty or indecision as between two contrary positions? Or does the conjunction of these two judgments actually represent a single coherent position that is open to a logically scrupulous person making judgments from the moral point of view?

Obviously, at least some of our uneasiness about the idea of a right to do wrong can be explained away on purely terminological grounds. The *noun* "right" (as in "You have a *right* to join the National Front") is apt to be confused with the *adjective* "right" (as in "You are *right* to join the National Front"), and the latter term is, of course, an antonym of "wrong." So it is perhaps inevitable that the noun "right" tends to acquire by association some color of this antonymy. In a more lucid language, such a connotation might be avoided by having a word for *rights* (say, "claims" or "entitlements") which is different in sound and appearance from the adjective we use for the property *rightness*.

But this glib move does not do away with very many of our misgivings. The connection between the noun "right" and the adjective "right" is not a matter of accidental homonymy, like "pitch" (as in "cricket pitch") and "pitch" (as in "pitch black"), nor is it even merely a matter of common etymology, like "bank" (as in "bank overdraft") and "bank" (as in "river bank"). The connection between "right" and "right" is generally supposed to be more subtle and substantial than that. It is widely believed that statements about rights can be analyzed ultimately into statements about rightness and wrongness or into "ought" statements, or that both sets of statements are commonly reducible to statements about the realization of goodness or consequential value. The paradox of a right to do wrong is serious because it threatens to introduce incoherence into all these reductive enterprises. Such a threat cannot be removed simply by substituting a fresh string of letters for one of the delinquent terms.

II

The language of rights is now a familiar part of moral discourse. It should not be necessary to emphasize that the topic here is *moral* rights, not legal rights – no matter how the former are supposed to be related to the latter. There is no paradox in the suggestion that someone may have a *legal* right to do an act that is morally wrong. Just as individuals may have legal duties that require them to perform wrong acts (for example, serve in unjust wars), so they may have legal rights that entitle them to perform actions that are wrong from the moral point of view. This seems possible, whether "legal right" is construed as standing for a Hohfeldian privilege (indicating merely the absence of a legal duty constraining the right-bearer with respect to the action specified) or whether it stands for the stronger claim-right (indicating that others have certain duties to the right-bearer in respect of the action specified).[1] I may be legally at liberty to perform a certain act even though that act is not permissible from the moral point of view; or, others may have a legal duty to me to refrain from interfering with my performance of a certain act, even though the act is morally wrong and their interference morally permissible. All this seems quite straightforward. But legal rights are not our topic here.

When we come to examine the less straightforward topic of moral rights, we find that some moral philosophers have rejected out of hand the possibility that individuals have rights to do what is morally wrong. In 1798, William Godwin wrote, "There cannot be a more absurd proposition than that which affirms the right of doing wrong."[2] More recently, some philosophers seem to have adopted conceptions of moral rights such that the proposition

1. P has a moral right to do A

simply *entails* the negation of

2. P's doing A is morally wrong.

That is, they have adopted conceptions which make the moral permissibility of an action part of what is asserted when it is claimed that the action is the subject of a moral right. For instance, John Mackie says that a moral right is the conjunction of two elements – a moral freedom and a claim-right. The contribution made by the former element to the proposition that an individual has a right to do some act is this; that the act in question is one that the individual is not morally required not to do. Since a wrong act is an act we *are* morally required not to do, it follows, on Mackie's account, that one cannot have a moral right to do an action that is morally wrong.[3]

Philosophers are by no means unanimous on this. In recent jurisprudence, both Ronald Dworkin[4] and Joseph Raz[5] have insisted that there is no contradiction in the claim that a morally wrong act may be the exercise of a moral right. But neither Raz nor Dworkin has provided any detailed argument for this position. In what follows, I shall show that the conjunction of propositions 1 and 2 above is not, as Mackie suggests, a logical falsehood, and that the fact that it is not tells us a great deal about the nature of moral rights and their function in moral theory.

It may be thought that the issue between Mackie and myself is simply this: is it the case that the formal analysis of a rights statement always reveals, among other things, a Hohfeldian privilege? Or, more bluntly: do moral rights contain moral privileges? If they do, then the acts which are the subject matter of moral rights cannot be acts prohibited by the moral duties of the right-bearer, and, in this sense, one cannot have a moral right to do what is morally wrong. Unfortunately matters are not so simple. Hohfeld's account of privileges was designed to cope with the analysis of normative systems in which duties were perfectly correlative with claim-rights, as they are, for the most part, in contract, tort, and property law. In such systems, a privilege (being the absence of a duty with respect to some action) is just someone else's lack of a right with respect to that action. The duties whose absence is indicated by a privilege are always and only duties imposed by the rights of others. There is no conception of normative constraints on action other than duties in this strictly correlative sense and, thus, no conception of normative permissibility apart from the lack of constraints defined in this very narrow way.

The trouble with applying this neat analysis to the language of morals is that, in the moral sphere, notions like *duty, wrongness,* and *permissibility* are – though relevant to rights – not confined to the area of rights. Some actions are impermissible, actions that we have a duty not to do, because they are infringements of the rights of others. But actions may also be morally impermissible or more generally subject to moral criticism for other and more subtle reasons. They may be seen as wrong because they are vicious, or because they fall short of the standard required by some ideal or principle which is conceived as a constraint independent of moral rights. So, since wrongness does not necessarily involve the violation of rights, there is more to the question of whether one can have a moral right to do what is morally wrong than the simple question of whether moral rights are capable of coming into conflict.

I suppose we could *define* a sense of "morally wrong" so that it applied only to infringements of moral rights. If we were to adopt this artificial way of talking, *then* the issue would just be the Hohfeldian one outlined above. But resolution of that issue would beg the much more interesting question of the relation between the language of moral rights and the rest of moral language in all its exuberance, including those uses of "wrong" and "impermissible" that are not already tied into an artificial reconstruction of rights talk.

III

In analyzing a problem of this sort, the professional philosopher will be tempted to apply W. D. Ross's distinction between prima facie and actual duties.[6] The distinction is supposed to operate as follows.

When they are stated in general terms, the intuitively apprehended demands of morality often appear to contradict one another. My duty to tell the truth may conflict in a particular case with my duty not to cause distress. My duty to keep a promise to meet someone at a certain time may conflict with my duty to give aid to someone else along the way. If one and the same act is the subject of conflicting moral requirements, we have to insist that the general principles of duty which generate the conflict cannot *both* be regarded as stating the individual's *actual* duty with regard to that act in those circumstances. They cannot both be regarded as indicating what, all things considered, he ought to do. An individual's actual duty cannot be determined until the requirements of all the general principles applicable to the situation in which he finds himself have been weighed and considered. The application of a *single* general principle to a particular case, in advance of this process of weighing and considering, yields only the conclusion that the act in question is what we call a prima facie duty – something which we might conclude would be our duty *tout court* were it not for the fact that other moral considerations are relevant as well.

Obviously, if there is anything in this distinction between prima facie duty and actual duty, it can be applied equally to rightness and wrongness. Since the idea of duty leads to the idea of the wrongness of the failure to do one's duty, we can talk about prima facie wrongness and actual wrongness in a similar sort of way. It has been argued that the distinction can also be extended to moral rights; indeed, some theorists have claimed that, without such a distinction between prima facie and actual rights, theories of human rights become manifestly implausible.[7] Since a general right like the right to liberty may have to be set aside in some cases in favor, say, of the right to life or the right to a decent standard of living, particular cases where these rights conflict cannot be analyzed without recourse to the distinction between prima facie and actual moral constraints.

Is this distinction of any use in analyzing our paradox of a right to do wrong? At first sight, maybe. Perhaps what are involved when somebody conjoins

1. P has a moral right to do A

and

2. P's doing A is morally wrong

are not final all-things-considered judgments but tentative prima facie judgments about P's doing A, each capable of entering into the balance of considerations to establish what, in the final analysis, ought to be done. We may rewrite 1, then, as

1A. P has a prima facie moral right to do A,

meaning that, under one description at least, P's doing A is the exercise of a moral right, but withholding our final assessment until the significance of all the possible descriptions of P's doing A is considered. And similarly, 2 is now

2A. P's doing A is prima facie morally wrong.

69

Understood in this way, the conjunction of 1A and 2A is, of course, not incoherent: neither of the judgments purports to state a final position, and their juxtaposition indicates only that they are both to be weighed in the balance, along with any other judgments relevant to the moral character of P's doing A, to determine what we are finally to say about the matter.

But there is a bit of an ambiguity here. Consider 2. When we shift from 2 to 2A, we indicate that we are to be understood as expressing only a prima facie rather than a final moral judgment. But in saying this we may mean either of two things. (i) We may mean that it is not to be understood as a final judgment *even so far as the wrongness of P's doing A is concerned*. That is, there may be other considerations to be weighed before we finally conclude that P's doing A is morally wrong, quite apart from whether P has a right to do it. (ii) Or we may mean that it *is* to be understood as *a final judgment so far as the wrongness of P's doing A is concerned*, but that the judgment remains prima facie inasmuch as the issue between it and 1 or 1A is still outstanding. Of these two interpretations of the claim that we are making a prima facie rather than a final moral judgment, the rendering of 2 as 2A seems better suited to (i). Similarly, there are two possible interpretations of 1A: (i) that it is not a final judgment even about moral rights, and (ii) that it is final about rights but not final vis-à-vis 2 or 2A. Again, the rendering of 1 as 1A seems better suited to the former interpretation.

But from our point of view, it is the latter interpretation, (ii), of the prima facie claims that is the more interesting. We are more interested in the case where a judgment which is final so far as the rightness or wrongness of P's doing A is concerned confronts a judgment that is final so far as the issue of whether P has a moral right to do A is concerned. Take one of the examples from the list at the start of the chapter: we may have balanced up all the conflicting principles and considerations that bear on the issue of whether voting for the National Front is *wrong* (for example, on the one hand, British society as we know it is in danger of cultural collapse, and, on the other hand, the National Front is a dangerous racist organization); we may have weighed up all the conflicting principles and considerations that bear on the issue of whether one has a moral *right* to vote for the National Front (for example, on the one hand, being free to vote for the party of one's choice is a necessary right in a true democracy, and, on the other hand, there is a chance that one's vote is being given to a party that would itself reject the democratic process); and we may have reached verdicts that are final in each of these two areas of morality. The question, then, is this: can the distinction between prima facie and actual moral requirements be of any further use in analyzing the confrontation between these two verdicts?

It is difficult to see how it could be. The distinction between prima facie and actual moral requirements is designed for the analysis of cases in which the agent is pulled in opposite directions by a number of general moral requirements whose applicability to this situation he acknowledges. But, whereas it is clear that the judgment expressed in 2, conceived of as a final judgment about the wrongness of the action, pulls the agent in a certain direction – in the direction of refraining from A – it is not at all clear that the judgment expressed in 1, even conceived as a final judgment about P's rights, pulls him in the opposite direction, or indeed in any direction at all.

This point can be understood more clearly in terms of the idea of reasons for action. Obviously, anyone who acknowledges the truth of 2 or 2A recognizes a reason for not doing A in the sorts of circumstances in which P is placed. That, at least in part, is what acknowledging the truth of 2 amounts to. But although 2 provides a reason for *not* doing A, there is no corresponding reason *in favor of* doing A provided by an acknowledgment of 1. To assent to the proposition that I have a right to perform some action is not thereby to acknowledge any reason for performing that action.[8] For instance, I have a moral right to marry the partner of my choice (if she will have me), but that does not provide me with any reason whatever for getting married, let alone for marrying anyone in particular. If I say, "I have a right to marry anyone I choose but I am determined to remain celibate," there is nothing logically odd, not even slightly logically odd, about that conjunction. Perhaps it will be argued that in remaining a bachelor I am in fact exercising the right in question, since the right to marry may be thought to include the right to refuse to get married. (Similarly, choosing to remain silent may be thought of as an exercise of the right of free speech, and so on.) But this point – important as it is – only reinforces my argument. The moral right in itself gives me no reason for undertaking any one course of action rather than another. Thus the fact that P has a right to do A does not of itself give rise to any reason in favor of A which is capable of competing with and being balanced against the reason for not doing A provided by the acknowledged wrongness of the act. So the distinction between prima facie and actual moral requirements, tailored as it is to the analysis of cases in which moral reasons for acting conflict, is inappropriate for the analysis of the tensions that arise in the case of our paradox of a right to do wrong.

IV

Rights, I have said, do not provide reasons for acting, at least not for the people who have them. The same point can be presented another way. If, in some situation, I ask a friend, "What shall I do?" he has not given me any advice at all, he has not prescribed any action, if he answers, "You have a right to do A." By the same token, if somebody asks me, "Why did you vote for the National Front candidate?" or "Why did you spend all that money on racehorses and champagne?" or "Why did you marry someone you loathed?" the answer, "I was exercising my moral rights," is not an appropriate reply. At best it amounts to a refusal to reply, like the retort, "Because I wanted to." Certainly, the reply, "I had a right to do A," goes no way toward *justifying* the doing of A. To justify an action is to show the standard to which in the circumstances it conformed or the worthiness of the goal that it was intended to advance. To adduce a right is not to do either of these things.

This point has often been overlooked. For instance, A. I. Melden opens his book *Rights and Persons* with the claim: "Actions which would otherwise be arbitrary and capricious may be quite reasonable when they are in fact cases in which rights are being exercised."[9] But that is precisely what is *not* the case. If an action appears arbitrary or capricious, if, for example, I stand on my head for a week facing west in a public place, or marry somebody I loathe, or burn my stock certificates in a fit of pique, or vote randomly in a general election, my action when questioned is not made to appear one iota more reasonable or defensible, nor is a spectator the slightest bit more likely to understand why I did it, when I reply, "I had a right to do it; I was exercising my right." The spectator may concede that the reply is *true*, but that concession need not in any way diminish his puzzlement or indignation at my behavior.

In what contexts, then, *is* this reply helpful or appropriate? The cutting edge of the claim that P has a right to do A is the correlative claim that other people are morally required to refrain from interfering with P's performance of A. If P has a right to do A, then it follows that it is wrong for anyone to try to stop P from doing A. Thus the assertion, "I have a moral right to do A," is entirely appropriate when my act is challenged in the sense that somebody threatens to interfere coercively. For example, I may be halfway through my speech in favor of the National Front when a radical member of the audience interrupts me, saying, "Give me one good reason why I shouldn't stop you making such an evil racist speech." In these circumstances, the reply, "I have a moral right to make the speech," is, if true, a sufficient answer. Although it does not provide *me* with any reason or justification for acting, my right provides the radical with a reason for not interfering.

Our paradox of a right to do wrong arose out of the conjunction of two propositions:

73

1. P has a moral right to do A

and

2. P's doing A is morally wrong.

We have seen that 1 entails

3. It is morally wrong for anyone to interfere
with P's doing A.

The first step toward an understanding of why our paradox does not involve a contradiction is to realize that 2 and 3 are perfectly compatible. 2 does not entail

4. It is morally permissible for someone to interfere with
P's doing A,

which would obviously contradict 3 and therefore 1.

That the wrongness of an act does not by itself entail the moral permissibility of interfering with it is obvious on a number of grounds. First, in almost every case, the act of interfering with wrongdoing will have a significance over and above the mere stopping of the wrongdoing and the suppression of its consequences. It may put the interferer at risk; it may involve the expenditure of public money or the use of other scarce resources such as police manpower; it may enhance or tarnish the reputation of the police; and so on. It may even, as the Christian ethic argues, distract the interferer from the task of his own self-improvement or be the occasion for a sinful act of moral self-indulgence. Clearly, none of these factors is relevant to the issue of whether P's doing A is right or wrong. But they *are* directly relevant to the permissibility of someone's proposed interference with P's doing A. For these reasons, then, it is necessary to drive a wedge between 2 and 4.

It may be thought that driving a wedge between 2 and 4 diminishes the prescriptivity of 2. After all, I can hardly assert 2 sincerely, with its full prescriptive force, and yet remain completely indifferent to the conduct in question. But there is an important distinction to be drawn between self and

other here. If I utter 2 sincerely, I commit myself to avoiding
A in the sorts of circumstances in which P is placed. But I
do not commit myself to interfering with P's action. Tolerating wrongdoing does not make me hypocritical or weak
willed; I am weak willed only to the extent that I perform
actions myself that I believe to be wrong, and I am hypocritical only if I purport to believe that certain actions are
wrong that I myself perform. The difference between self
and other is this. To stop *myself* from performing wrong
actions, no special act of prevention is required; I need only
steel myself to my duty (assuming of course that I am not
in the grip of any sort of duress or compulsion). But to stop
others from performing wrong acts (even when their behavior
is as voluntary as my own), other positive acts must be performed by me beyond the mere giving of my sincere assent
to the moral judgment in question. And, of course, these
other acts will have moral ramifications of their own.

In practice, these distinctions get a bit blurred. Depending
on the circumstances, on the personal relationships involved,
and so on, merely *telling* someone that he should not do A
may be a highly effective way of *getting* him to stop A-ing.
The line at which mere prescription and admonition stop and
coercion begins is a fine one. Even the mere expression of
disapproval – the raised eyebrow or the icy stare – may be
felt as a positive show of force. Also, inasmuch as a morality
forms part of a way of life, and inasmuch as a person's way
of life is defined in part by the persons with whom he chooses
to associate, the prescriptivity of a *personal* moral judgment
may lead an agent to impose social sanctions of the most far-
reaching kind on those around him. There are, then, considerable difficulties in distinguishing interference from mere
condemnation, and it should not be thought that driving a
wedge between 2 and 4 in our formal reconstruction of the
positions involved does anything to remove them. But it
would be a mistake to abandon the point in the face of these
difficulties. What we can say is this: to the extent that expressing an opinion on a moral matter has any effect on the
world (over and above its inherent prescriptive effect on the

actions of the person expressing it), the issue of whether one ought to express the opinion is a separate issue – a separate *moral* issue – from the issue of the correctness of the opinion itself. The expression of a moral judgment may have any number of effects in the world: it may disturb the peace in a library; it may reveal one's position to enemy soldiers; it may upset one's mother; or it may coercively interfere with another's freedom. It is not necessary to be a consequentialist to see that in all such cases there is a clear distinction to be drawn between the issue of the *truth* of a moral judgment and the issue of the rightness or wrongness of expressing it. So long as these distinctions are kept in mind, it will be clear that, since 4 does not follow from 2, then 2 and 3 are logically compatible.

We have seen that 1 and 2, the two sides of our paradox, are compatible at least to the extent that 2 does not contradict one of the most important consequences of 1, namely, 3. But while obviously 1 entails 3, it is not obvious that their relation is one of equivalence. Mackie's position, for example, was based on the inference of a further consequence from 1 – an assertion of moral permissibility.[10] So a more general argument is needed to show, against Mackie and others, that there is nothing *else* in 1 that 2 could contradict.

The same point can be put another way. The considerations I have given in favor of driving a wedge between 2 and 4 apply to *all* cases of wrongdoing, not just those cases of wrongdoing protected by a moral right. In *every* situation where someone does something that is wrong, it is a further question whether it would be right or permissible to interfere with the wrongdoing. But when we move to the cases where there are moral *rights* involved, there is a feeling that the fact that the agent had a right to do what he did provides a *special* reason for not interfering that is not present in the ordinary cases of wrongdoing. So what we have to do now is to make sure that there is nothing in this special reason for noninterference, provided by rights, which is inconsistent with the claim that the action in question is wrong.

In the following section I shall show that we can capture

the special reasons against interference provided by rights in a way that does not commit us to rejecting the possibility of a right to do wrong. To this end, I shall provide an argument showing that the *function* of rights in moral theory precludes the imposition of any general requirement on rights to the effect that actions that one has a right to perform must be actions that it is morally permissible for one to perform.

V

The argument I am going to introduce relies on something I want to call the *generality* of moral rights. The statement that an individual P has a moral right to perform a particular action A never stands on its own. It is usually supported by indicating that A is a member of a certain set of actions any of which P has a right to perform in the circumstances. Characteristically, the claim about P's doing A is seen as a particular instance of a more general claim, that P has the right to perform actions of a certain type. For example, when we say that an individual has a right to join the National Front, this claim is defended and debated, not on its own merits, but on the basis of its connection with the wider claim that the individual has the right to join any political group he likes, or, if he chooses, to refrain from political activity altogether. It is put forward as an instance of the right of free political association. Similarly, when I say that a certain person has the right to publish a particular book, that claim is not contested or defended on its own merits alone but in terms of the wider claim that he has a right to free expression of his views – that is, a right to perform any of a number of activities, ranging from addressing a meeting at his workplace to writing a letter to the local newspaper. The general claim is not inferred, as it were, inductively from the more specific claims ("He has the right to publish the book, and he has the right to address his workmates, and he has the right to send a letter to the newspaper – so therefore he must have the right to free expression in public"). The order of argument is the other way round. We establish the general claim and then derive the more specific propositions from it.

Of course, not all argument about rights takes place at the general level. There may be argument as to whether a particular case really is an instance of the wider claim; for example, does the right of free expression include a right constraining the editor of the local newspaper to actually publish my letter? But even here, argument at the level of particular cases looks up and refers back all the time to the nature of the argument for the more general right.

Notice that generality, in this sense, is not the same as what R. M. Hare has called the "universalisability" of evaluative language.[11] A judgment is universalizable if it either is, or is supported by, a judgment in which there are no terms referring to particulars. But a judgment may eschew all reference to particulars and so be universal in Hare's sense and still fail to be general in the sense that I have outlined. For example (moving for a moment from the language of rights to that of deontological prescriptions), the prescription, "One should never tell lies to one's wife on the morning of her birthday" is *less* general than "Don't ever deceive me," even though the former is universal and the latter is not. The greater generality of "Don't ever deceive me" consists just in its application to a wider range of actions than the former prescription. Generality and universality, then, are two different dimensions in terms of which prescriptions may be described, though it is worth reminding ourselves that generality is a matter of degree, whereas a statement is either universal or it is not.[12]

Hare has insisted throughout his work that universalizability is a *logical* feature of evaluative language. I wish to make no such claim on behalf of generality, even in the limited fragment of evaluative language that comprises the language of rights. Nevertheless, it is, I think, significant that many rights-claims have this feature: particular claims, as well as being universalizable, are also liable to be argued for in terms of a wider, more general right. In particular, this seems to be true of the very rights that are most likely to feature in the paradox of a right to do wrong; it seems to be true, for instance, of all the rights-claims that could be applied to the situations described at the start of this chapter. This, as I shall show, is no coincidence.

Before we go on, it is necessary to add an important qualification. The language of rights is far from being a homogeneous fragment of the language of morals and political theory. It includes not only the traditional liberal claims of the right to free speech, to freedom of worship, and so on, in terms of which my argument has been couched so far, but also the more radical "positive" rights to free medical care, decent housing, and other basic assistance from the state and from one's fellow citizens. It also includes claims of *special* rights – the rights both positive and negative that arise out of interpersonal transactions such as promises and contracts.

In the case of these last two categories, the thesis that rights statements are not just universalizable but also general seems less appropriate. There is no question of defending, say, P's right to emergency first aid in an accident on the basis of some more general right of P's to choose among any of a number of alternative goods and services. The link with individual choice which seems so important in the case of the liberal rights, and which is probably the basis of the universality feature, seems a little out of place here. If human choice is important in cases like this, it is so only as a general justifying value lurking in the background; we might say, for instance, that the reason people have a right to free medical care is that, without such a right, any freedom of choice in other areas of life would be so insecure as to be empty. But the immediate subject matter of the right (the receipt of medical care) itself involves no choice.

This is even more apparent in the case of special rights. If I have a right arising out of a promise to use your cottage for the weekend, then that is all I have a right to. There is no more general right that I have in terms of which my right to use your cottage could be defended and which also indicates other particular rights that are open to me.

I suppose that if one were, in Aristotle's words, out to

defend a thesis at all costs, one might insist that the rights described in both these cases each covers at least two choices open to the right-bearer. In the case of the promissory right, I may choose either to use the cottage in accordance with the permission granted to me by its owner or not to use it. So my promissory right covers a plurality of actions. And even in the case of a straightforward right of receipt, such as the right to first aid in an accident, one might want to draw a distinction between *being given a good*, which is a purely passive condition, and *receiving or accepting a good*, which seems to have a slightly more active flavor to it. So if the right to first aid is redescribed as the right to *accept* first aid, and not just the right to *be given* first aid, then it too may be seen to cover a plurality of actions open to the right-bearer.[13]

I shall not pursue this line of thought here. Anyone who wants to apply my case for the coherence of the paradox of a right to do wrong to cases of special or positive rights of receipt is welcome to set up some such line of argument. But I prefer to concentrate on cases where the generality and choice elements are clearly prominent, for these are the cases where the paradox arises most acutely.

Particular rights statements can be thought of as clustered into groups represented by general rights statements. As indicated earlier, the main characteristic of this general clustering is its relation to justification: debate and justification normally take place at the level of the general rights statements, not at the level of the particular ones. What we contest or defend is not just the right to do A, but a general right which is the right to choose A or B or C or D.

It is important for understanding the notion of a right to do wrong to see in general terms how justification here usually proceeds. As we have seen, the cutting edge of a rights-claim is the claim it entails about the wrongness of interfering with the action that the right-bearer has chosen. So what is defended or contested when a general right is in dispute is the claim that choice within a certain range is not to be interfered with. This claim in turn is usually defended on the basis of the *importance* of the choices in the range in question for the lives of the individuals who are making them. In the ranges of action to which a theory of rights draws attention, individual choices are seen as crucial to personal integrity. To make a decision in these areas is, in some sense, to decide what person one is to be. Some theorists attribute this importance indiscriminately to *all* the choices that an individual makes in his life, and so his rights to perform particular actions are organized into just one cluster under the auspices of a general right to liberty. But most rights theorists recognize that some of the choices that individuals make are more important than others.[14] There are certain types of choices, certain key areas of decision-making, which have a special importance for individual integrity and self-constitution. Particular theorists may differ as to what these key areas are, but, over the centuries, a certain liberal consensus has evolved: individuals' political activities, their intimate relations with others, their public expressions of opinion, their choice of associates, their participation in self-governing groups and organizations, particularly political organizations and labor unions, their choice of an occupation – all these have been regarded as particularly important in people's definitions of themselves.

In each of these areas, from time to time, a number of alternative actions are possible. That is why the claim that someone has the right to perform one particular action does not stand alone: the claim is understood in the light of the more general proposition that the range of options in which that action is located represents an important area of choice for that person. Moreover, that is why the fact that an individual has the right to perform some particular action does not in itself provide a *reason* for his performing that action. For the claim that he has the right to perform it refers us to the wider area of decision, in which the action is located and in which alternatives are available, and asserts only that his decision-making in this area is to be protected. To protect decision-making is not to provide a reason for the making of any particular decision.

In the light of all this, it is easy to see why we cannot

exclude the possibility that a person has a right to perform some action that is wrong. Presumably, the actions in each of the clusters covered by a general right will each be either morally required, morally prohibited, or morally indifferent. Or, to phrase it a little less rigidly, each action protected by a right will, in its particular circumstances, be an action that is *called for* from the moral point of view, or an action that is *subject to moral criticism* or an action on which *morality has nothing of importance to say*. (For simplicity, I am ignoring supererogatory acts; their inclusion would not affect the argument except to make it a bit more complicated.)

Now suppose we were to agree with Mackie, for instance, that only morally permissible actions can be the subject of moral rights. Then the protected choices would be limited to actions that are called for from the moral point of view and actions that are morally indifferent; wrong actions or actions subject to moral criticism would be excluded. But once this restriction had been imposed it would be bound to escalate further. For, if an action is *called for* from the moral point of view, then any alternative to it that is not called for (that is, any merely indifferent alternative) immediately becomes impermissible and so would be excluded. Thus, if we applied Mackie's condition and allowed only right and indifferent acts to figure as the subject of rights, then the right actions would soon start to dominate. And to the extent that right actions became the dominant subject matter of rights, rights would lose what we have regarded up to now as their crucial link with the notions of choice and alternatives. One might have the right to do *the right thing* in given circumstances, but only at the cost of not having the right to do anything else in those circumstances. Rights would become what they are at times for Locke – merely the duties of the right-bearer perceived from a subjective point of view.[15]

It may be argued that this domination of rights by right action need not be total even on Mackie's proposal for, except under very rigorous moralities (such as Godwin's utilitarianism),[16] there are many choice situations in which a number of permissible alternatives are open to the agent, none of which is actually called for from the moral point of view.

However, this possibility reveals even greater danger for the idea of moral rights. Suppose that, in view of the argument just developed, we were to modify Mackie's proposal slightly, so that right actions as well as wrong actions were excluded, leaving only morally indifferent actions as the subject matter for rights. Then we seem to be faced with two possibilities, equally objectionable.

The first is that, by limiting rights to actions that are morally permissible, we would impoverish the content of our theory of rights. To implement the proposal under consideration, we would have to countenance some sort of lexical ordering whereby the morality of rightness and wrongness, duty and obligation, requirement and prohibition, even virtue and vice was allowed first into the field of action to pick out as its domain those actions that were of particular moral concern. The morality of rights would be allowed to enter the field only when that process had been completed, to clean up the leftovers, as it were. But *what* would be left over when the morality of rightness and wrongness had had its say? The answer seems to be: the banalities and trivia of human life. The decision to begin shaving on chin rather than cheek, the choice between strawberry and banana ice cream, the actions of dressing for dinner and avoiding the cracks on the sidewalk – these would be the sorts of actions left over for the morality of rights to concern itself with. But these are actions which – apart from the argument here under consideration – would be *least likely to be regarded as an appropriate subject matter for rights*. The areas of decision that we *normally* associate with rights would, on this account, be miles out of range. Because of the very importance that leads us to regard them as subject matter for rights, those areas of decision are bound to be of concern to the other aspects of morality and thus are bound to be excluded from the area of moral indifference where rights are permitted their limited sway. In other words, if rights were confined to actions that were morally indifferent, actions on which the rest of morality had nothing to say, then rights would lose the link with the *importance* of certain individual decisions which, as we have seen, is crucial in their defense.

The other possibility is to let the morality of rights into the field first and to exclude from the domain of rightness and wrongness, duty and obligation, requirement and criticism any action preempted by the morality of rights. But this is equally unacceptable. The decisions that one makes in exercising one's rights are supposed to be decisions that shape the character and direction of one's life and, in some sense, define the person one is to be. It is quite implausible to suppose that the rest of morality could be silent here, that the ethics of rightness and wrongness, goodness and evil, duty and obligation, and virtue and vice could have nothing to say on matters of this importance. When we say, for example, that individuals have the right to marry whom they will or to speak their minds on matters of public moment, we cannot mean to claim that particular actions of these kinds are sealed off from moral criticism and evaluation. Apart from anything else, the decisions in question cannot be made in an existentialist vacuum. Those who are making them will ask others for advice and for their opinions and evaluations of the various alternatives under consideration. And replies will come not just from those who have some personal interest at stake in the decision but also from those – like parents, priests, politicians, and philosophers – who are capable of seeing and evaluating the chosen actions as emergent fragments of an overall pattern of life. Since exercising a right involves making an important choice, it is incredible to suppose that the practice of assessing, evaluating, guiding, and criticizing important choices – the practice we call "morality" – should be inapplicable to the exercise. To exclude the rest of morality from the evaluation of these choices, and yet to insist that the choices in question are still somehow important (indeed, to justify the exclusion on the basis of this importance), is to come perilously close to self-contradiction.

Let me begin to sum up. I have spoken as if the morality

of rights and the morality of rightness and wrongness – the morality that gives rise to statements like 1 and the morality that gives rise to statements like 2 – were distinct. And so they are, for they have distinct functions: the former has the function of protecting choices and the latter the function of guiding them. But they cannot be distinct in their range of application: it cannot be the case that a choice is so important that it needs to be protected but yet so unimportant that guidance is out of the question. If we attempt to allot a distinct sphere of action to each of these fragments of morality, we will end up by impoverishing at least one of them.

If we take the idea of moral rights seriously, then, and if we draw the connections with the ideas of choice and of the importance of certain areas of decision that I have outlined, it is necessary to insist that wrong actions as well as right actions and indifferent actions can be the subject of moral rights. The clusters of actions subsumed under our general rights are likely to include, in the circumstances that face us, actions that would be stupid, cowardly, tasteless, inconsiderate, destructive, wasteful, deceitful, and just plain wrong, as well as actions that are wise, courageous, cultured, compassionate, creative, honest, and good. This may seem messy to a certain austere type of analytic mind, but it involves no contradiction, as far as I can see, and it is the only way to reconcile the importance of moral rights, as a distinctive ingredient in ethical theory, with the diversity and the wide range of standards of ethical evaluation.

VI

We have seen that the possibility of a right to do wrong, far from being a contradiction in terms, is actually required by the way in which rights function in moral theory and the basis on which we argue for them. Even after these arguments have been given, however, the sense of paradox is likely to linger. I will conclude by offering some explanations of this.

The residual sense of paradox in the idea of a right to do

wrong has four main sources. The first is the terminological consideration I mentioned at the very start of the chapter:[17] the associative link between the noun "right" and the adjective "right" is so strong that some feeling of the latter's antonymy with "wrong" is bound to rub off on the former.

The second source is connected with this. The language of rights is put to many uses, and sometimes a sentence like 1 is used just to say that P's doing A was right or at least morally permissible – and no more.[18] This usage is perhaps more noticeable in the second-person negative: "You had no right to do that" is often used as though it were interchangeable with, "You shouldn't have done that." We are all guilty of this usage at times, and it is an obvious source of misgiving about the conjunction of 1 and 2. (It should perhaps be noted also that this is not the only alternative use to which the language of rights is put. Often rights statements are used as though "right" were loosely synonymous with authority in such a way that "You had no right to do that" is equivalent to "It was not for you to do that" said, for example, to someone who had purported to act in loco parentis. In this sense of "right," there do not seem to be any problems with the idea of a right to do something that is wrong.)[19]

The third source was also alluded to earlier. It may be thought that it is, in the last resort, impossible both to guide choices and to protect them. If we take a sufficiently brutal (perhaps emotivist) view of moral interaction, we may believe that, when somebody tells me that A is wrong, he cannot claim to be respecting my right to do A. To say that an act is wrong, to condemn its performance, and to urge others not to do it – surely all that comes down, in the end, it may be said to the very sort of coercion which is ruled out when we say that the action is one which there is a moral right to perform. But it should be obvious that the whole drift of this chapter depends on a rejection of that way of looking at things. As Austin and Hare have stressed, there *is* a distinction to be drawn between telling a person to do something and making him do it;[20] so that even if saying that A is wrong involves telling P not to do A, still we can distinguish between moral guidance and coercive interference. But it has to be admitted that, in real life, this distinction is a perilously fine one, and that its fineness is one of the contributing sources of our residual misgivings about the idea of a right to do wrong.

The fourth and final source is based on the pragmatics of rights talk. There is, as we have seen, no prescriptive incompatibility between 1 and 2: there is nothing in the assertibility conditions of 1 to rule out its conjunction with 2. But now consider the *pragmatics* of the first-person assertion, "I have a right to do A." In real life, such an assertion is not often offered as a contribution to ethical theory – it is most often uttered by someone who intends to do A and is responding to moves by other people to prevent his carrying out that intention. There is something odd about having the intention to do A and sincerely believing that A is wrong. There is an important logical link, alluded to already in this chapter, whose precise nature has not and will not be explained until we have satisfactory theories both of weakness of will and of the relation between prima facie wrongness and actual wrongness, between intending to do A and *dissenting* from the judgment, "My doing A is wrong." And so the pragmatic link that holds between the assertion, "I have a right to do A," and the intention to do A, coupled with the semantic link between the assertion, "My doing A is wrong," and *not* intending to do A, is likely to remain as another source of residual misgiving about the idea of a right to do wrong.

Chapter 4

Locke, toleration, and the rationality of persecution

I

In this chapter I am going to discuss John Locke's argument for toleration, or, more accurately, the main line of argument which appears in Locke's work *A Letter on Toleration*.[1] I shall not say very much about the development of Locke's views on the subject, or about the debate on religious toleration in which Locke, first as an academic then as a political agitator, was involved, or about the historical circumstances of the *Letter's* composition.[2] No doubt these are worthy subjects for a paper, but not, I think, for a set of essays devoted mainly to toleration as an issue in modern political philosophy. I want to consider the Lockian case as a political argument – that is, as a practical intellectual resource that can be abstracted from the antiquity of its context and deployed in the modern debate about liberal theories of justice and political morality.[3] To put it bluntly, I want to consider whether Locke's case is worth anything as an argument which might dissuade someone here and now from acts of intolerance and persecution.[4]

There is a further somewhat more abstract reason for examining the Lockian argument. In its content and structure the Lockian case for toleration is quite different from the more familiar and more commonly cited arguments of John Stuart Mill.[5] Even if, as I shall claim, it turns out to be an inadequate and unconvincing argument, one that in the last resort underestimates the complexity of the problem it addresses, still its distinctive structure and content tell us a lot about the possibilities and limits of liberal argumentation in this area. Those insights and the contrast with the more familiar arguments of Mill may contribute considerably to our understanding of modern liberal theories of toleration and the "neutral" state.[6]

II

I have said that I shall concentrate on the main line of argument in the *Letter on Toleration*. But perhaps it is worth saying a word or two about one subordinate line of argument that I will largely overlook in the rest of my discussion.

At the beginning of the *Letter*, Locke takes some pains to emphasize the peculiarly Christian character of toleration. "The toleration of those that differ from others in matters of religion," he maintains, is not only consistent with and "agreeable to" the Gospel of Jesus Christ (p. 16), but actually required by Christian teaching. Persecution, he points out, with the denial of love and charity which it involves, is repugnant to the Christian faith (pp. 14–16).

Historically, there is no doubting the importance of this aspect of Locke's case. As an ad hominem argument addressed to the Christian authorities, it exposes an evident and embarrassing inconsistency between the content of their theory and their practice in propagating it. It is significant that much of the immediate reaction to the publication of the *Letter* concerned this part of the Lockian case; many of the issues taken up in Locke's boring and inordinately repetitive *Second*, *Third*, and (mercifully) uncompleted *Fourth Letters on Toleration* had to do with the argument from Christian premises.[7]

But, however effective this argument might have been, it is uninteresting from a philosophical point of view. We are interested in the question of whether the state *as such* is under a duty of toleration and we want an argument addressed to state officials in their capacity as wielders of the means of coercion, repression, and persecution. An argument which addresses them instead in their capacity as members of a Christian congregation is insufficiently general to be philosophically interesting because it leaves us wondering what if anything we would have to say to someone who proposed persecution in the name of a more militant and less squeamish faith. Certainly, it would be an untidy and unsatisfactory state of affairs if we had to construct a fresh line of argument for toleration to match each different orthodoxy that was under consideration.

Locke, I think, recognizes this, and the bulk of the *Letter* is devoted to considerations which proceed on a more general front and purport to show the *irrationality* of intolerance and not just its uncongeniality to a particular religious point of view. That is the argument – Locke's attempt to show that religious persecution is irrational – that I want to examine in this chapter.

III

An argument for toleration gives a reason for not interfering with a person's beliefs or practices even when we have reason to hold that those beliefs or practices are mistaken, heretical, or depraved. (Questions of toleration do not arise in relation to beliefs or practices which are regarded as good or true.[8])

I take it this is *not* achieved simply by announcing that the enforcement of correct religious belief or practice is not the *function* of the state, or by saying, in the famous terms of the Wolfenden Report, that matters of religion, like personal morality and immorality, are "not the law's business."[9] That sort of talk just begs the question. At most it gives us the *conclusion* we want, but it does not help us to argue for that conclusion. Locke, I am afraid, is often interpreted as having said little more than this. For example, in the entry under "Toleration" in his *Dictionary of Political Thought*, Roger Scruton gives the following account of Locke's argument:

[I]t is not within the competence of the state to discern the truth of religious doctrines, nor is it the function of the state to save men's souls; rather the state exists to protect men's rights and may use force to that end alone. *Hence*, there ought to be toleration in matters of religion.[10]

Hearing this sort of functionalist talk, we do well to remember Max Weber's observation that it is impossible to define the state in terms of its functions and that historically "there is scarcely any task that some political association has not taken in hand."[11] Among all the tasks that states have undertaken, the question of which fall into the class of the *proper* functions of government is an important one; but it has to be a matter of argument, not of essentialist definition.

Since the state cannot be defined in terms of its functions, the best way of defining it, Weber suggested, was in terms of its characteristic *means:* the means, such as the organized monopoly of legitimate force in a given territory, which are deployed to carry out whatever ends a state may happen to undertake.[12] Now if we can give such a *modal* definition of the state – if we can define it in terms of its distinctive and characteristic means – then we may have the basis for an argument about its proper ends or functions along the following lines:

A state by definition is an organization which uses means of type M. Means of type M are ill fitted for producing ends of type E. They never produce E-type effects (but perhaps at best mockeries or travesties of them). Therefore it is irrational to use M-type means in order to produce (genuine) E-type effects – and irrational in one of the most straightforward and least contestable instrumental senses. Thus, given the types of means that it uses, it is irrational for the state to pursue E-type ends. Therefore – and in this sense – the pursuit of E-type ends cannot be one of the proper functions of government.

That, it seems to me, is the form of an interesting and evidently acceptable line of argument. It is an argument from available means to possible ends – from a modal definition to a (negative) functionalist conclusion. In a very compressed form, it captures the structure of the main line of argument in the *Letter on Toleration*.

Like Weber, Locke defines the state in terms of the characteristic means at its disposal. In the *Second Treatise*, he tells us: "Political power...I take to be a right of making laws with penalties of death."[13] Similarly, in the *Letter on Toleration* he distinguishes the means available to the magistrate from those available to the ordinary man of good will in civil society. "Every man is entitled to admonish, exhort, and convince another of error, and lead him by reasoning to accept his own opinions. But it is the magistrate's province to give orders by decree and compel with the sword" (p. 19). Looking at the matter in more detail, Locke characterizes the power of the magistrate at three levels. Sometimes it is described symbolically in terms of the paraphernalia of force and terror, "fire and the sword" (p. 15), "rods and axes" (p. 28), and "force and blood" (p. 37). Sometimes it is described (along Weberian lines) in terms of the way force is organized in a political community: "the magistrate is armed with force, namely with all the strength of his subjects" (p. 17).[14] And sometimes it is characterized in legalistic terms – "impartially enacted laws" (p. 17), "laying down laws" (p. 28), and "legal censure" (p. 39) – and in terms of punishments such as the deprivation of property (p. 15), imprisonment (p. 18), mutilation and torture (pp. 15 and 18), and execution (p. 15). The emphasis is everywhere on *force*: that is, on the coercive nature of penalties – "if no penalties are attached to them, the force of laws vanishes" (p. 19) – and, somewhat less important, on the possibility of direct physical compulsion. The fact that governments and their officials work by coercive force while other organizations do not is the fundamental premise of Locke's argument and the basis of his distinction between church and state.[15]

It is true that Locke says a number of things which might lead a careless reader to believe that he wants to define government in functional terms. Early in the *Letter*, he says in an apparently definitional tone: "The commonwealth seems to me to be a society of men constituted only for preserving and advancing their civil goods" (p. 17), where civil goods are defined as "life, liberty, bodily health, . . . and the possession of outward things" etc. (p. 17). But he makes it absolutely clear in the *Letter* that he regards this as something to be established, as a task to be fulfilled (p. 17). He takes it as the conclusion, not a premise, of his argument;

> that the whole jurisdiction of the magistrate is concerned only with those civil goods, and that all the right and dominion of the civil power is bounded and confined solely to the care and advancement of these goods; and that it neither can nor ought in any way to be extended to the salvation of souls, the following considerations seem to me to prove. (pp. 17–18)

And then he gives the arguments that I shall examine in a moment. Elsewhere in the *Letter* the functional theory of government is described explicitly as a *conclusion* (p. 19) and as something which in the course of his argument he has *proved* (p. 28). Those like Scruton and also J. D. Mabbott (in his summary of Locke's arguments) who represent it as a premise are therefore doing Locke a grave disservice.[16]

Having defined government in terms of its means, Locke argues that those means – laws, threats, the sword – are not capable of producing genuine religious belief in the minds of citizens who are subjected to them. Sincere and genuine (as opposed to feigned or counterfeited) belief cannot be produced by these means; so it is irrational for the authorities to use them for that purpose. Thus, from a rational point of view, the state, defined in the way Locke wants to define it, cannot have among its functions that of promoting genuine religion. Since, on Locke's definition, toleration is nothing but the absence of force deployed for religious ends,[17] it follows that the state is rationally required to be tolerant.

That is a preliminary summary of a sophisticated argument. It gives us an idea of the lay of the land; and it has the merit of indicating by inequitable exaggeration the extent of the argument's defects and limitations. Let me now discuss it in a little more detail.

IV

The crux of the argument – the step which dominates it and on which everything else depends – is the claim that religious belief cannot be secured by the coercive means characteristic of the state. This is the essence of Locke's challenge to the rationality of religious persecution: what the persecutors purport to be up to is something that, in the nature of the case, they cannot hope to achieve.

To make this case, he needs to show that this is true *in principle*. It is not enough to show that coercion is *inefficient* as a means of religious discipline or that it is less efficient than the citizens' means of argument and persuasion. That would leave open the possibility of using coercion as a last resort, and it would also make the case for toleration vulnerable to a reassessment of the relative values of the various effects of coercive action. Locke needs to show impossibility. He must show that there is a gap between political means and religious ends which cannot in principle be bridged.

On Locke's account, that causal gap between political coercion and religious belief is framed by two important propositions: (1) that coercion works by operating on a person's will, that is by pressurizing his decision-making with the threat of penalties; and (2) that belief and understanding are not subject to the human will, and that one cannot acquire a belief simply by intending or deciding to believe. If I do not believe in the truth of the Resurrection, for example, there is nothing I can do, no act of will that I can perform, to *make* myself believe it. (There is no way of holding my mouth or concentrating which is going to get me into the state of having this belief.) Of course, I may change my mind about the Resurrection, and people often do. But there is a sense in which even if that happens it is not my doing: it happens rather as a result of the work of what Locke calls "light and evidence" on the understanding and not as the upshot of *my* conscious decision-making.

The effect of these two claims – that coercion works through the will and that belief is not subject to the will – if

94

they are true, is to render religious belief or unbelief effectively immune from coercive manipulation. Laws, Locke says, are of no force without penalties (p. 18), and the whole point of penalties is to bring pressure to bear on people's decision-making by altering the payoffs for various courses of action, so that willing one particular course of action (the act required or prohibited by law) becomes more or less attractive to the agent than it would otherwise be. But this sort of pressurizing is crazy in cases of actions which men are incapable of performing no matter how attractive the payoff or unattractive the consequences. Sincerely believing a proposition that one takes to be false is an action in this category. As Locke puts it: "What is gained in enjoining by law what a man cannot do, however much he may wish to do it? To believe this or that to be true is not within the scope of our will" (p. 41). The imposition of belief, then, by civil law has been exposed as an absurdity. Intolerance and persecution, at least for religious reasons, have been shown to be irrational.

This is the sort of conclusion every moral philosopher dreams of when he starts out making an argument. To justify his belief that a certain practice is wrong, he does not want to have to appeal in a Humean fashion to contingent desires and attitudes: he can never be certain that his audience shares them, and even if they do this sort of argument often appears to establish nothing more than the undesirability of the practice. He wants to be able to show (if he can) that the wrong practice is also an irrational practice – that it involves in itself the sort of inconsistency or rational absurdity which every philosopher wants to avoid in his life as well as in his arguments.[18] Everyone in his audience – or at least everyone in his philosophical audience – accepts standards of rationality; they are the tools of the trade, even for one who is, in other respects, the most rabid of moral skeptics. The possibility of appealing to those standards to establish substantive moral conclusions has been one of the recurring dreams of Western moral philosophers, at least since Kant. (It finds its latest manifestation in the work of Alan Gewirth.[19]). And here, in the *Letter on Toleration*, we find John Locke engaged in an attempt to do the same sort of thing.

v

That is the crux of Locke's argument for toleration. Before going on to indicate some of the difficulties in the argument, I want to make two or three general observations.

The first is that this argument for toleration does not rest on any religious doubt, religious skepticism, or epistemic misgivings in relation either to the orthodox position Locke is considering or to the beliefs and practices that are being tolerated. It is sometimes said that toleration is the child of doubt, and that there are philosophical as well as historical connections between the rise of secular liberalism and the decline of religious certainty. It is also said that there are philosophical as well as historical connections between liberal doctrine and doubts about the objectivity of ethics.[20] I have to confess that these conceptual connections escape me; and that the view that moral noncognitivism generates a principle of ethical laissez-faire seems simply incoherent.[21] Locke (like most of the great thinkers in the early liberal tradition) has little truck with arguments of this sort. He is adamant that there is a God, that his existence can be established very readily,[22] that this God requires certain things of us in the way of ethical practice, belief, and worship, and "that man is obliged above all else to observe these things, and he must exercise his utmost care, application and diligence in seeking out and performing them" (pp. 42–3). We should, however, note that although Locke believed that there is "only one way to heaven," he did suggest that the case for toleration might be even stronger if there were more than one right answer to questions about religious practice: "If there were several ways, not even a single pretext for compulsion could be found" (p. 29). But this is a mistake. The truth of something like religious pluralism (analogous to the moral pluralism that Joseph Raz discusses[23]) would still leave open the question of what to do about those heretics who, faced with a whole array of different routes to salvation, *still* persisted in choosing a deviant path. Just as, faced with a variety of goods, men may still choose evil, so, faced with a variety of true religions, men may still choose error and blasphemy.

Certainly, Locke confidently believed that most of the groups and sects he proposed to tolerate (such as Jews who disbelieved the New Testament and heathens who denied most of the Old) had got these matters objectively wrong. He was prepared to "readily grant that these opinions are false and absurd" (p. 41). His argument did not depend on any misgivings about contemporary orthodoxy (though in fact he did not support contemporary Anglicanism in all the details of its faith and liturgy); nor was it based on any suspicion, however slight, that at the last trump the sects that he proposed to tolerate might turn out to have been right all along. His position was rather that a false belief, even if it is objectively and demonstrably false, cannot be changed by a mere act of will on the part of its believer, and that it is therefore irrational to threaten penalties against the believer no matter how convinced we are of the falsity of his beliefs. Locke's view is not like the main theme in J. S. Mill's essay *On Liberty* that persecution is irrational because it tends to suppress doctrines which may turn out to have been worth preserving (for one reason or another).[24] It is more like Mill's subordinate argument that the state of mind produced by coercive indoctrination is so far from genuine belief as to call in question the rationality of one who is trying to inculcate it.[25]

There is one line of argument present in the *Letter* which may make us think that Locke was taking a skeptical position on religious matters. Locke was concerned that if a magistrate were to require certain religious beliefs or practices of us, there would be no guarantee that the religion he favored would be correct.

Princes are born superior in power, but in nature equal to other mortals. Neither the right nor the art of ruling carries with it the certain knowledge of other things, and least of all

true religion. For if it were so, how does it come about that
the lords of the earth differ so vastly in religious matters?
(p. 30)

But at most this is skepticism about the religious discernment
of princes, not skepticism about religion as such. Locke maintains that "a private man's study" is as capable of revealing
religious truth to him as the edicts of a magistrate (p. 29).
He insists that each man is *individually* responsible for finding
"the narrow way and the strait gate that leads to heaven"
(p. 19) and that God will excuse no man for a failure to
discharge this responsibility on grounds of duress or obedience to orders. If the magistrate makes a mistake and I
obey him, then *I* bear the responsibility and the cost I face
may be everlasting perdition: "What security can be given
for the kingdom of heaven?" (p. 30). Locke adds one further
point which, in his view, "absolutely determines this controversy" (p. 32) by distinguishing religious from other forms
of paternalism:

> even if the magistrate's opinion in religion is sound, . . . yet, if
> I am not thoroughly convinced of it in my own mind, it will
> not bring me salvation . . . I may grow rich by an art that I
> dislike, I may be cured of a disease by remedies I distrust; but
> I cannot be saved by a religion I distrust, or by a worship I
> dislike. It is useless for an unbeliever to assume the outward
> appearance of morality; to please God he needs faith and in-
> ward sincerity. However likely and generally approved a med-
> icine may be, it is administered in vain if the stomach rejects
> it as soon as it is taken, and it is wrong to force a remedy on
> an unwilling patient when his particular constitution will turn
> it to poison. (p. 32)

One may be forced to be free, to be healthy or to be rich,
but "a man cannot be forced to be saved" (p. 32). Religious
truth must be left to individual conscience and individual
discernment. So there are certainly individualistic doubts
about the abilities of princes; but none of these points is

consistent with any more far-reaching doubts about truth or knowledge in matters of religion.

There is one further line of argument connected with this which has a slightly stronger skeptical content. This is the worry at the back of Locke's mind that an argument for the imposition of Christian beliefs and practices by a Christian magistrate would seem to yield, by universalization, an argument for the imposition of pagan beliefs and practices by a pagan magistrate:

> For you must remember that the civil power is the same everywhere, and the religion of every prince is orthodox to himself. If, therefore, such a power be granted to the civil magistrate in religious matters, as that at Geneva he may extirpate by force and blood the religion which there is regarded as false or idolatrous, by the same right another magistrate, in some neighbouring country may oppress the orthodox religion, and in the Indies the Christian. (p. 37)[26]

Notice that this is a good argument only against the following rather silly principle: (P1) that the magistrate may enforce *his own* religion or whatever religion *he thinks* is correct. It is not a good argument against the somewhat more sensible position (P2) that a magistrate may enforce the religion, whatever it may be, which is *in fact* objectively correct. It may, of course, be difficult to tell, and perhaps impossible to secure social agreement about, whether the view that the magistrate believes is correct is in fact the correct view. (P2 is what Gerald Dworkin has called a "non-neutral" principle, and the social implementation of nonneutral principles is always problematic.[27]) But opposition to intolerance based on awareness of these difficulties is not opposition to intolerance as such, but only opposition to particular cases of it. Suppose, however, that the notion of objective truth in religious matters were a chimera. Would we then be able to make any distinction between P1 and P2? It may be thought that the answer is "No" and therefore (working backward) that Locke, who saw no difference between them, must have been skeptical about the objectivity of religious belief. And one does get a sense, especially in the *Third Letter concerning Toleration*, that Locke may be inclined to move in this direction.[28] Even so, a rigorous skeptic could still draw a distinction between P1 and P2. If there were no objective truth, P1 could be implemented as before (perhaps on Hobbesian grounds of public order[29]); but P2 would not now license the enforcement of any religious belief at all.

VI

The second general point I want to make concerns the way in which the case for toleration fits into the general structure of Locke's political philosophy.

I am not sure whether we ought to attach any significance to the fact that the subject of religious toleration is not mentioned at all in the *Two Treatises of Government*. There may be a historical explanation: if we take the *Letter on Toleration* to have been drafted after 1685[30] and we accept something like Peter Laslett's dating of the composition of the *Two Treatises*,[31] then we can say that Locke may well not have formulated his final tolerationist position sufficiently clearly at the time the *Treaties* were drafted to include reference to it there. Even so, it is surprising. Religious toleration was one of Locke's abiding preoccupations and one of the most contested political issues of the age. It is odd that he should make no reference to it in a treatise concerned with the functions and limits of government.

Indeed, the occasional references to religion in the *Second Treatise* indicate, if anything, that the legitimate Lockian state need not be a secular one at all. In the chapters on resistance and revolution, Locke suggests that a people may be entitled to rise up against their Prince if he has by his actions or negligence endangered "their estates, liberties, lives . . . and perhaps their religion too."[32] He implies throughout that the failure of the later Stuarts to prosecute and enforce the laws against Catholicism amounted to subversion of the constitution.[33] (This, however, is complicated by the fact that even in the *Letter on Toleration* Locke indicated that he was disposed to exclude Catholics, as he excluded atheists, from the scope of the toleration that he was arguing for [pp. 45–7]. We cannot go into the grounds for this here; but it had to do mainly with his suspicion that members of both classes would make bad citizens.) The indications in the *Second Treatise* seem to be that a legitimate state may have an established and constitutionally sanctioned religion and an established pattern of religious discrimination; and that it would be permissible for Lockian individuals to agree on such arrangements when they moved out of the state of nature.

However, I am inclined to regard these indications as superficial: arguably they have more to do with the political events of the 1670s than with Locke's deepest convictions in political philosophy. I want to see now whether it is possible to accommodate the argument for toleration within the framework of the political theory of the *Second Treatise*.

The view in the *Second Treatise* is that a state has no greater power than that delegated to it by its citizens. Specifically, what the magistrate has at his disposal is the executive power which everyone previously had in the state of nature to prosecute and punish transgressions of natural law.[34] This power is resigned into the hands of the community and entrusted to the magistrate on entry to civil society. No doubt the magistrate will organize that power efficiently, making it much more effective than the sum of the dispersed powers of the same individuals in the state of nature.[35] (That, after all, is the point of the shift to civil society.) But the substance of the power is exactly the same as the individuals' natural right to punish.

The question about toleration, then, is a question not just about the limits of *state* force but about the limits of the use of force by any agency or any individual at all. (It is significant that in Locke's discussion of excommunication [p. 23], he insists that, while it is permissible for a church, like any private club, to expel a recalcitrant member, nevertheless "care must be taken that the sentence of excommunication carry with it no insulting words or rough treatment, whereby the ejected person may be injured in any way, in body and estate.") So since the doctrine applies to individual force, let us consider its application to individuals in the state of nature who have retained their natural right to punish: do they have a right to punish heretics and persecute religious deviance? If they do, there seems no reason why that power should not be vested in the community as a whole when civil society is set up. Let us assume for the sake of argument (what Locke certainly believed, as we saw in Section V above) that the heresy whose toleration is in question really *is* heresy and that the members of the deviant religious sect really *are* acting in defiance of God's commands so far as their beliefs and practices are concerned. If a heretic is defying God's law (and remember that the law of nature, for Locke, derives all its normative force from the fact that it is God's law), do the rest of us have a natural right to punish him? On Locke's view the natural right to punish has two purposes – *reparation* for wrongful injury done, and *restraint* in the sense of coercive deterrence.[36] Clearly, reparation is out of the question in the religious case. Locke takes the Protestant view that a heretic does no injury to anyone but himself and God (pp. 42–3) – and, of course, it is not for us to collect compensation on behalf of the Almighty. That leaves the function of restraint. But if the argument of the *Letter* goes through, then restraint is also out of the question, since coercive deterrence can have no effect on the formation or maintenance of heretical beliefs. The right to punish may not be exercised in these cases, then, because it would serve no useful purpose, and punishment when it serves no useful purpose is wrong on the Lockian account.[37] So, since individuals have no right to punish heretics, governments cannot acquire any such right either, for "[n]obody can transfer to another more power than he has himself."[38] It follows that it is wrong to set up any sort of confessional state or established church when we move out of the state of nature, if this is going to involve the use of political power for religious purposes.

This argument would not work were Locke to countenance any sort of retributive justification for punishment. For we might then be justified in using force and inflicting pain and loss on heretics simply to punish them for their (undoubted) sins without any further purpose of deterrence, reform, or reparation in mind. Force used in this way could not be conceived as a means to any end apart from the immediate infliction of suffering; its employment, therefore, could not be criticized as irrational in the sense of being incapable of attaining the ends at which it was aimed. In a recent book, W. von Leyden has argued that Locke's theory of punishment *is* (partly) retributive.[39] If he is correct, then there is a gap in the argument for toleration. But the passages cited by von Leyden do not support his view. It is true that Locke says that punishment should be such as to make the criminal "repent" of his crime.[40] But since repentance involves, among other things, forming the belief that one's criminal conduct was wrong, the same argument can be used to establish that force is inapposite to this end as Locke used to establish that it was inapposite to more direct coercion and deterrence. Von Leyden notes that Locke makes occasional use of the language of retribution and desert: but when "retribute" is used early in the *Second Treatise* Locke immediately links it in a definitional way to reparation and restraint;[41] moreover he uses "desert" only in the sense of proportionality[42] and he is adamant elsewhere in the *Treatise* that proportionality of punishment is strictly determined by the damage that has been suffered and thus by the reparation that is to be recouped.[43]

VII

The third general point I want to make about Locke's argument concerns its structure and the sort of toleration it entails.

Locke's position is a *negative* one: toleration, as he says in his *Second Letter* on the subject, is nothing but the absence or "removing" of force in matters of religion.[44] The argument is about the irrationality of coercive persecution and it entails nothing more than that that sort of activity ought not to be undertaken. There is nothing about the positive value of religious or moral diversity. Unlike Mill, Locke does not see anything to be gained from the existence of a plurality of views, or anything that might be lost in monolithic unanimity. His argument does not justify a policy of fostering religious pluralism or of providing people with a meaningful array of choices.

More important, Locke's negative argument is directed not against coercion *as such*, but only against *coercion undertaken for certain reasons* and with certain ends in mind. The argument concerns the rationality of the would-be persecutor and his purposes; it is concerned about what happens to his rationality when he selects means evidently unfitted to his ends. Coercion, as we know, is on Locke's view unfitted to religious ends. But if it is being used for other ends to which it is not so unfitted (such as Hobbesian ends of public order), there can be no objection on the basis of this argument, even if *incidentally* some church or religious sect is harmed. The religious liberty for which Locke argues is defined *not* by the actions permitted on the part of the person whose liberty is in question, but by the motivations it prohibits on the part of the person who is in a position to threaten the liberty. It is what Joseph Raz has called "a principle of restraint."[45] Thus it is not a right to freedom of worship as such, but rather, and at most, a right not to have one's worship interfered with for religious ends.

This point is emphasized quite nicely by an example that Locke uses toward the end of the *Letter on Toleration*. In the course of considering various practices that heathen sects may engage in, Locke takes up the case of animal sacrifice. He begins by saying that if people want to get together and sacrifice a calf, "I deny that that should be forbidden by law" (p. 36). The owner of the calf is perfectly entitled to slaughter the animal at home and burn any bit of it he pleases. The magistrate cannot object when the slaughter takes on a religious character – for the element that makes it a religious *sacrifice* (and therefore an affront to God in the eyes of decent Anglicans) is precisely the internal aspect of belief which political power can never reach. *However,* Locke goes on, suppose the magistrate wants to prohibit the killing and burning of animals for nonreligious reasons:

> if the state of affairs were such that the interest of the commonwealth required all slaughter of beasts to be forborne for a while, in order to increase the stock of cattle destroyed by some murrain; who does not see that in such a case the magistrate may forbid all his subjects to kill any calves for any use whatever? But in this case the law is made not about a religious but a political matter, and it is not the sacrifice but the slaughter of a calf that is prohibited. (p. 37)

Of course, the *effect* of the economic ban on animal slaughter may be exactly the same as a ban that is religiously inspired. Perhaps in both cases the religious sect in question will die out as its congregation, deprived of their favorite ceremony, drift off to other faiths. What matters for Locke's purposes is not coercion as such or its effects, but the reasons that motivate it. If the reasons are religious, the coercion is irrational. But if the reasons are economic or political, then the argument for toleration gets no grip despite the fact that the coercion may discriminate unequally in its consequences against a particular group. There may, of course, be other arguments against this sort of inequity, but they are not based on a Lockian principle of toleration.

I emphasize this point because it seems relevant to some modern formulations of the liberal position on religion, personal morality, and conceptions of the good life. Ronald Dworkin and Bruce Ackerman have formulated that position in terms of a requirement of *neutrality*: the state and its officials are required to be *neutral* as between the various moral conceptions of the good life that various citizens may hold.[46] But what does neutrality involve? Is it just a requirement of impartiality or is it some stronger constraint of equal treatment? Does it involve, as Alan Montefiore has claimed, an effort to help and hinder the contending parties in equal degree?[47] And if it does require such evenhandedness, is it in practical terms *possible* for a government to be neutral in that sense?

In Locke's account of toleration, we have the basis for a conception of neutrality which is very narrow indeed and quite light in the burden that it places on the liberal state. The government and its officials are required to be neutral only in the *reasons* for which they take political actions. They must not act *in order to* promote particular religious objectives. Beyond that no wider neutrality is required. They need pay no attention to the evenness of the impact of their actions on those with whom they are dealing.

Compare now the conceptions of neutrality generated by other familiar lines of liberal argument. If we wanted to use John Stuart Mill's argument about the dialectical value of religious, philosophical, and ethical diversity, our conception of neutrality would be somewhat more strenuous. For if a sect, such as the animal sacrifice cult, dies out as a result of government action, that is a loss to religious and cultural diversity, and therefore a loss to the enterprise of seeking the truth, no matter what the reason for the action was. *Mill's* liberal government, unlike Locke's, must take care to see that diversity is not threatened even incidentally by its actions; and if it is threatened, it must weigh carefully the value of the loss against the other ends it hopes to achieve by the coercion.[48] If our argument for neutrality has to do with the respect a government owes to the autonomous moral and religious development of its citizens, again a more strenuous requirement than Locke's will be generated. The government will be obliged not merely to refrain from religiously or morally inspired persecution, but to avoid any action which, in its effects, may frustrate or undermine individuals' choices and their self-constitution in these areas.

An important point emerges from all this. The idea of liberal neutrality, like that of toleration, is an abstract concept in political theory of which various conceptions are possible.[49] These conceptions differ considerably in the practical requirements they generate and the burdens they impose on governments. Which conception we opt for is not a matter of preference – it is not a matter of which we find more congenial to our political "intuitions." It is a matter of the *line of argument* that we want to put forward. Locke's argument yields one conception of neutrality, Mill's another, and so on. It follows that an enterprise like that of Bruce Ackerman, in his book *Social Justice in the Liberal State*, is completely misguided. Ackerman puts forward a principle of liberal neutrality which he claims can be defended by any one of at least four distinct lines of argument. (Both Mill's argument and something like Locke's feature on his menu.[50]) He professes indifference as to which line of justification is adopted, claiming that the liberal ought to be as tolerant about that issue as he is about conceptions of the good life.[51] If I am right, this promiscuity about justification may have disastrous consequences. The different lines of argument do not converge on a single destination: each argument yields a distinct conception which in turn generates distinct and practically quite different principles of political morality and social justice. The liberal cannot afford to be indifferent or offhand about the justificatory task. The line of justification that is taken *matters* for the articulation of the position he wants to adopt.

VIII

Let us return, finally, to the details of the Lockian argument. The nub of the case, you will recall, was his claim that there is an unbridgeable causal gap between coercive means and religious ends – the gap which, as I put it, is framed by these two propositions – "Coercion works on the will" and "Belief cannot be affected by the will." So long as these two frames remain in place, the irrationality of using coercive means for religious ends is evident.

We have seen one reason for questioning the first of these propositions. Coercion may be applied to a person not to put pressure on his will but simply to punish him, retributively, for the wrong he has done. But it is with the second of the two propositions that I am now chiefly concerned.

The second proposition is not argued for by Locke at any length in the *Letter on Toleration*. All Locke says is that "[l]ight is needed to change men's opinions, and light can by no means accrue from corporeal suffering" (p. 19). One looks naturally to the *Essay concerning Human Understanding* for further elaboration, for the claim is primarily epistemological in character. We find there very little in the way of argument either. Locke does touch on the point in Book IV of the *Essay*,[52] but what he says is not entirely congenial to the argument put forward in the *Letter*.

The basic position that Locke defends in the *Essay* is that "[o]ur knowledge is *neither wholly necessary, nor wholly voluntary*." He explains two senses in which knowledge is not voluntary. First, "[m]en that have senses cannot choose but have some *ideas* by them," and what a man sees (for example) he cannot see otherwise than he does: "It depends not on his will to see that *black* which appears *yellow*, nor to persuade himself that what actually *scalds* him feels *cold*; the earth will not appear painted with flowers, nor the fields covered in verdure, whenever he has a mind to it: in the cold winter, he cannot help seeing it cold and hoary."

Second, once ideas have been received, the processes of the understanding go to work on them more or less automatically. Once men have received ideas from their senses, "if they have memory, they cannot but retain some of them; and if they have any distinguishing faculty, cannot but perceive the agreement or disagreement of some of them with one another. And if men have in their minds names for these ideas, then propositions expressing the agreement or disagreement which their understanding has discerned will necessarily be accepted as true."[53]

None of this is subject to the will so none of it can be coerced. Thus far the toleration argument is supported. What, then, according to the *Essay* is voluntary in the formation of beliefs? Locke answers: "all that is *voluntary* in our knowledge is the *employing* or withholding any of our faculties from this or that sort of object, and a more or less accurate survey of them."[54] Though a man with his eyes open cannot help but see, he can decide which objects to look at, which books to read, and more generally which arguments to listen to, which people to take notice of, and so on. In this sense, if not his beliefs then at least the sources of his beliefs are partly under his control.

All this is evidently true. But it opens up a first and fatal crack in the framework of Locke's argument for toleration. Suppose there are books and catechisms, gospels and treatises, capable of instructing men in the path of the true religion, if only they will read them. Then although the law cannot compel men coercively to believe this or that, it can at least lead them to water and compel them to turn their attention in the direction of this material. A man may be compelled to learn a catechism on pain of death or to read the gospels every day to avoid discrimination. The effect of such threats and such discrimination may be to increase the number of people who eventually end up believing the orthodox faith. Since coercion may be applied to religious ends by this indirect means, it can no longer be condemned as in all circumstances irrational.

The case is even stronger when we put it the other way round. Suppose the religious authorities know that there are certain books that would be sufficient, if read, to shake the faith of an otherwise orthodox population. Then, although again people's beliefs cannot be controlled directly by coercive means, those who wield political power can put it to work indirectly to reinforce belief by banning everyone on pain of death from reading or obtaining copies of these heretical tomes. Such means may well be efficacious even though they are intolerant and oppressive; and Locke, who is concerned only with the rationality of persecution, provides no argument against them.

Once we catch the drift of this criticism, we begin to see how the rest of Locke's case falls apart. His case depended on the Protestant importance he attached to sincere belief: "all the life and power of true religion consists in the inward and full persuasion of the mind; and faith is not faith without believing." So long as our attention is focused on the state of belief itself and *its* immunity from interference, Locke's argument is safe. But now we are starting to look at the epistemic apparatus that surrounds and supports belief – the apparatus of selection, attention, concentration, and so on – which, although it does not generate belief directly, nevertheless plays a sufficient role in its genesis to provide a point of leverage. Even if belief is not under the control of one's will, the surrounding apparatus may be; and that will be the obvious point for a rational persecutor to apply his pressure.

Perhaps the following response may be made on Locke's behalf.[55] What matters for the purposes of true religion is genuine belief. To be genuine, belief must be based on the free and autonomous activity of the mind, choosing and selecting its own materials and its own evidence, uncoerced and undetermined by outside factors. Belief-like states generated in the mind of an individual on the basis of a coerced input of ideas are not genuine in this sense; they are more like the states of mind of an individual who has been brainwashed or subjected incessantly to propaganda. Such an individual may look like a believer from the outside – and he may even feel like a believer from the inside (he is not merely mouthing formulas to evade punishment) – but nevertheless, in virtue of the history of their causation, his beliefs do not count as genuine.[56] Since it is genuine belief that the religious authorities are interested in securing, it will therefore be irrational for them to resort even to the sort of indirect coercion I have been describing.

I have two worries about this response. First, it is difficult to see why the "free" input of ideas should *matter* so much in determining what counts as genuine belief. We have said already that it is not a phenomenological matter of whether beliefs generated in this way *feel* more genuine than beliefs generated on the basis of coercively determined input. So is the point rather that belief-like states which are not "genuine" in this sense cannot perform some or all of the *functions* we expect beliefs to perform? Are they functionally deficient in some way? Are they, for example, like brainwashed "beliefs," peculiarly resistant to logical pressure and to requirements of consistency? That, I suppose, is a possibility. But I find it hard to imagine what sort of epistemology or philosophy of mind could possibly connect the *external* conditions under which sensory input was acquired with the functional efficacy of the beliefs generated on the basis of that input. If I am forced at the point of a bayonet to look at the color of snow, is my consequent belief that snow is white likely to function differently from the corresponding belief of someone who did not need to be forced to take notice of this fact?

Second, this approach appears to place such great demands on the notion of *genuine belief* as to lead us to doubt the genuineness of everything we normally count as a belief in ordinary life. In *most* cases (not just a few), the selection of sensory input for our understanding is a matter of upbringing, influence, accident, or constraint; freedom (in any sense that might plausibly be important) and autonomy seem to play only minor roles. If this yields the conclusion that most religious belief is not "genuine" anyway, then we have offered the persecutors an easily defensible position: they can now say that their intention is not to inculcate "genuine" belief (since that is impossible for most people anyway), but simply to generate in would-be heretics beliefs which are the same in content and status as those of the ordinary members of orthodox congregations. Against this proposal, it would seem, Locke has nothing to say.

We may attack the relation between belief and *practice* in the constitution of religious faith in a similar sort of way. Locke is relying on the view that practice – outward conformity to certain forms of worship – by itself without genuine belief is nothing but empty hypocrisy which is likely to imperil further rather than promote the salvation of the souls of those forced into it. But this is to ignore the possibility that practice may stand in some sort of generative and supportive relation to belief – that it too may be part of the apparatus which surrounds, nurtures, and sustains the sort of intellectual conviction of which true religion, in Locke's opinion, is composed. So here we have another point of leverage for the theocrat. A law requiring attendance at Matins every morning may, despite its inefficacy in the immediate coercion of belief, nevertheless be the best and most rational indirect way of avoiding a decline in genuine religious faith.

Some of these points were raised by Jonas Proast in a critique of Locke's *Letter,* to which the latter responded in his *Second* and subsequent *Letters concerning Toleration.*[57] Proast had conceded Locke's point that beliefs could not be imposed or modified directly by coercive means, but he insisted that force applied "indirectly and at a distance" might be of some service in concentrating the minds of recalcitrants and getting religious deviants to reflect on the content of the orthodox faith.[58] Force may be unable to inculate truth directly, but it may remove the main obstacles to the reception of the truth, namely "negligence" and "prejudice."[59]

Despite the enormous amount of ink that he devoted to his response, Locke failed to provide any adequate answer to this point. He said that it would be difficult to distinguish sincere and reflective dissenters from those whose religious dissent was negligent, slothful, or based on removable prejudice; and he insisted that it would certainly be wrong to use force indiscriminately on all dissenters when its proper object could only be a certain subset of them. That is undoubtedly correct. But now the case in principle against the use of force in religious matters has collapsed into a purely pragmatic argument: force *may* be serviceable, only it is likely to be difficult to tell *in which cases* it will be serviceable. In place of the knock-down argument against the use of political means for religious ends, we have an argument to the effect that political means must not be used indiscriminately for religious ends. Because the in-principle argument has collapsed, the sharp functional distinction between church and state that Locke was arguing for goes with it. We can no longer say that the magistrate's power is *rationally inappropriate* in the service of true religion. Everything now depends on how sure the magistrate is that the deviants he is dealing with have prejudiced and negligent minds. It is impossible, therefore, to agree with J. D. Mabbott that Locke provides a "complete and effective" response to Proast's critique.[60] On the contrary, the response he provides completely demolishes the substance of his position.

IX

I do not see any other way of reconstructing Locke's argument to meet the criticisms that I have outlined. Religious faith, and more generally moral commitment, are complex phenomena. Yet Locke has relied, for his indictment of the rationality of persecution, on a radical simplification of that complexity. A charge of irrationality based on that sort of simplification is likely to be returned with interest!

It is possible that the gist of Locke's position is correct. Perhaps at a very deep level, there *is* something irrational about intolerance and persecution; perhaps ultimately reason and liberal commitment do converge in this respect. But, on the face of it, it seems unlikely that this convergence is going to take place at the level of *instrumental* rationality. Censors, inquisitors, and persecutors have usually known exactly what they were doing, and have had a fair and calculating idea of what they could hope to achieve. If our only charge against them is that their enterprise was hopeless and instrumentally irrational from the start, then we perhaps betray only our ignorance of their methods and objectives, and the irrelevance of our liberalism to their concerns. If by their persistence they indicate that they *do* have a viable enterprise in mind, there comes a point when the charge of instrumental irrationality must be dropped (on pain of misunderstanding) and a more direct challenge to their actions taken up.

At this point, what one misses above all in Locke's argument is a sense that there is anything *morally* wrong with intolerance, or a sense of any deep concern for the *victims* of persecution or the moral insult that is involved in the attempt to manipulate their faith. What gives Locke's argument its peculiar narrowness is that it is, in the end, an argument about agency rather than an argument about consequences. It appeals to and is concerned with the interests of the persecutors and with the danger that, in undertaking intolerant action, they may exhibit a less than perfect rationality. Addressed as it is to the persecutors in *their* interests, the argument has nothing to do with the interests of the victims of persecution as such; the latter interests are addressed and protected only incidentally as a result of what is, in the last resort, prudential advice offered to those who are disposed to oppress them.

We have already seen that an argument based on a concern for the moral interests of the potential victims of intolerance would differ considerably from Locke's argument. Not being an argument about rational agency, it would not merely be a principle of restraint on reasons, but would generate more strenuous and more consequentially sensitive requirements for political morality. Perhaps this is why Locke avoided that line. But one cannot help feeling, too, that part of the explanation lies in the fatal attraction of ethical rationalism: that if only we can show that intolerance is irrational we may be excused from the messy business of indicating reasons why it is *wrong*.

Chapter 5

Mill and the value of moral distress

I

In the modern discussion of pornography and obscenity – and in the perennial liberal debates about freedom, toleration, and neutrality – it remains unclear what or how much should be made of the fact that people in one group find the views, the tastes, or the life-style of others in their community *disturbing*. Even if an action (or a book or a film) is not directly harmful, in the sense that it does not actually contribute to the causation of injury, loss, or damage, still it may be perceived as indecent, insulting, degrading, threatening, or distressing in less tangible ways. In the pornography debate, in particular, there is much to be said for the view that politicians and philosophers have concentrated too long on what pornography *does* (what it causes) and too little on what it *is* or what it represents, especially as far as women are concerned. That balance is now gradually being redressed, but further consideration of the issues involved in this shift of concerns is certainly necessary.[1] Undoubtedly one of the main characteristics of pornography (though one which it shares with the best art and literature) is that it *disturbs* us and makes us uneasy. That, I suppose, can be regarded as one of its *effects*, and, to the extent that people do not like being disturbed, to the extent that being disturbed in this way *hurts*, such an effect may be regarded as one of the *harmful* consequences of pornography and therefore as a basis for part of the case in favor of its prohibition. Alternatively, it may be argued that these negative effects accrue only because of moral views and prejudices that are held already by those who suffer from them, and therefore that they provide no distinct basis for prohibition apart from whatever arguments can be constructed out of the moral views and prejudices themselves.[2]

A full consideration of the issues here would involve untangling the various ideas that come together when we talk about a person being *disturbed* by another's behavior: the perception of threat, the perception of insult, the perception of symbol or representation, the vehemence of moral condemnation, the feeling of outrage, the elements of pity, contempt, sublimated guilt, shame, and so on. These need to be distinguished and their connections with one another carefully investigated in order to be able to deal sensitively with the variety of cases that can be accumulated under this general heading.[3] A full consideration would also mean exploring the way in which each of these strands is perceived in the various traditions of liberal and nonliberal argument: we must not assume, for example, that the Kantian argument for toleration and the Millian argument for toleration treat *moral outrage* or *threat* or *perceived insult* in the same way. On the contrary, these elements will be assigned different roles in different arguments, even when those arguments are driving toward substantially the same conclusion. There is, then, a lot to be done before we have anything like a satisfactory account of the relation between the fact that something is disturbing and a proposal that it ought to be prohibited.

My aims in the present chapter are very modest. I want to concentrate on what I shall call the element of moral distress – the fact that someone is distressed because of what he takes to be the immorality or the depravity of another's behavior. (Think, for example, of the distress many citizens experience when they see two men kissing passionately or when they consider what those two get up to in their bedroom at night.) I want to consider the place of this sort of distress, this element of disturbance, in what is perhaps the

most influential of the modern liberal arguments for toleration – the argument in John Stuart Mill's essay, *On Liberty*.

If we approach the issue of the social enforcement of ethical
and religious standards in terms of Mill's famous Harm Principle – the principle which holds that "the only purpose for
which power can be rightfully exercised over any member
of a civilized community, against his will, is to prevent harm
to others"[4] – we face the following question. Does moral
distress of the kind I have mentioned count as *harm* for the
purposes of Mill's principle?

Theoretically, at least, the question is an important one. It
is true that moral conservatives and perfectionists have not
usually relied on the existence of these harms to justify the
enforcement of their moral views. From their perspective,
that would be a rather sordid and self-interested approach;
they prefer to attack the Harm Principle directly rather than
squeeze out an interpretation of it congenial to their commitments.[5] Instead, Mill's critics make use of the problem to
discredit the Harm Principle, and to show the folly of imagining that there can be a sphere of individual morality and
immorality which in principle does not affect the interests of
other people.[6] The liberal, then, for his part, is interested in
the problem not because he imagines that conservatives will
try to justify the moralistic use of power on this basis, but
because of the implicit challenge posed to the meaning and
point of the principle he has invoked to protect individual
liberty.

One possible approach that the liberal might take is to
concede that moral distress falls within the scope of the Harm
Principle, but to insist that it is, on the whole, outweighed
by the pain that would be involved in the prohibition of the
conduct that occasions it.[7] After all, the fact that one's conduct harms another is, on Mill's account, only a necessary
not a sufficient justification for intervention; once harm is
established, everything depends on a calculation of the costs
and the benefits of preventing it.[8] The point of the Harm
Principle is to establish a threshold which must be crossed

before utilitarian calculations of that sort are even in order, not to elevate every little incident of harm into a pretext for prohibition. But this approach seems unsatisfactory, from a liberal point of view, for two reasons. First, it makes the case against the enforcement of ethical and religious standards rather more precarious than liberals have usually been willing to concede. On this approach the liberty, for example, of a religious minority will depend on how large the opposing majority is and on the intensity of the popular feeling directed against them. If the majority is very large and the feeling very intense, then the "harm" (to the "interests" of the majority) that could be prevented by persecution might greatly outweigh the harm that persecution would cause. But one's liberal instincts suggest that the case for toleration becomes *more* not less compelling the smaller and less popular the group whose liberty is in question. Second, if we agree that ethical and religious conviction is in part a matter of feeling and that everyone who takes his convictions seriously is to some degree upset when he discovers that others do not share them, it seems odd that the mere existence of moral distress should be sufficient to cross the threshold test established by the Harm Principle. For then what work is the principle doing? What cases of the enforcement of morals could it possibly exclude? The answer is: only those cases which are not really taken seriously by the moralists anyway. That is why I suggest that the problem of morality-dependent harm poses a threat not just to the operation, but to the very coherence, of the Harm Principle. If a moralist's *natural* and *predictable* response to deviance is sufficient to count as his being harmed, then the idea of deploying a *Harm* Principle to limit the enforcement of conventional morals seems hopelessly ill-conceived.

The question of moral distress has been considered many times in the vast literature that has accumulated around Mill's essay.[9] I want to argue that if we approach it in terms of Mill's *arguments* for the Harm Principle, we get an answer which is clear, unequivocal, and surprising: far from providing the basis of an argument for prohibition, moral distress on Mill's account is actually a *positive* feature of deviant actions and life-styles; the outrage and disturbance that deviance evokes is something to be welcomed, nurtured, and encouraged in the free society that Mill is arguing for.

II

Let me begin with one or two comments about methodology and interpretation. The problem of whether moral distress should be regarded as *harm* for the purposes of Mill's principle is not one that can be resolved by a logical analysis of the concept of harm or by looking up "harm" in a dictionary. There is at least one sense of the term in which anyone who is discomforted and distressed by an activity is *eo ipso* harmed by it (he experiences what feels from the inside remarkably like pain), even if there are other narrower senses, which an analytically minded liberal might want to invoke, which do not cover this type of experience. When we are faced, in this way, with rival conceptions of harm, the question is then not what "harm" *really* means, but what reasons of principle there are for preferring one conception to another in the present context. A similar point can be made about the maneuver, common among Mill scholars, which insists that his principle was concerned only with harm to individual *interests*.[10] The concept of interest is also a contested one. There are conceptions in terms of which moral distress has an indubitably adverse effect on one's interests:

> Suppose that Jones is a devout Calvinist or a principled vegetarian. The very presence in his community of a Catholic or a meat-eater may cause him fully as much pain as a blow in the face or theft of his purse. . . . If the existence of ungodly persons in my community tortures my soul and destroys my sleep, who is to say that my interests are not affected?[11]

And there are, as I shall argue, conceptions in terms of which one's interests should be said to be promoted rather than disserved by the experience of moral distress.[12] Once again, the question is not what "interests" *really* means, but rather what reasons of principle there are for preferring one conception of interests to another in this context.

When we are considering a text like *On Liberty*, we need to remember that a doctrine such as the Harm Principle is not a piece of legislation, and questions posed in jurisprudence and political philosophy about how it is to be understood are not questions of statutory construction. As a pronouncement it has no authority in itself. The principle is presented in Chapter 1 of *On Liberty* as the upshot of an argument which Mill is about to present, and the only meaning or interest it can possibly have for us lies in its relation to that justificatory argument.[13] If we accept, as I think we must, that terms such as "harm" and "interests" (like "power," "liberty," and "law") have no clear or indisputable meaning awaiting our analysis, and that they rather pick out concepts whose nature it is to be contested from different evaluative standpoints, then the question is not simply which is the better conception of harm, but which conception answers more adequately to the purposes for which the concept is deployed. In the context of *On Liberty*, those purposes are established by Mill's *arguments* for freedom of opinion and life-style, that is, by his account of what we have to lose if liberty in those areas is withheld.

III

On Liberty contains several arguments in favor of individual freedom of thought, discussion, and life-style. The most important of these are based on the desirability of what I am going to refer to as *ethical confrontation* – the open clash between earnestly held ideals and opinions about the nature and basis of the good life. Ethical confrontation should be understood to include conflicts on all sorts of issues – moral, philosophical, political, and religious – and to range from verbal debate on the one hand to the demonstration and flaunting of rival life-styles on the other. On Mill's view, the main argument against interference with individual liberty was that it diminished the occasion and opportunity for ethical confrontation in this sense.

Mill's attitude to confrontation was far from nihilistic; he did not take any satanic delight in the prospect of a *bellum omnium contra omnes* in the ethical realm. Although he denied the existence of any *one* solution to the problem of the good life, he certainly believed that there were objectively better and worse solutions.[14] As much as any of his perfectionist critics, he believed that genuine moral progress was possible. But progress, Mill insisted, was certainly not *guaranteed* under modern conditions; he rejected as a "pleasant falsehood" the dictum that truth always triumphs and that the good will come out on top in the end.[15] He saw a real danger that contemporary society might become stuck in a mire of prejudice and mediocrity, a danger of its becoming "another China"[16] – a more worrying analogue to the "stationary society" that he foresaw in the realm of economics.[17] If we want our society to remain progressive, Mill said, we must work at it, and the disappearance of ethical confrontation would be alarming evidence that we were failing in that task.

What contribution does ethical confrontation make to progress? The contribution, on Mill's account, is of two sorts. First, it contributes to the emergence of new and better ideas. Second, it makes an important contribution to the way ideas are held in society.

The first argument depends on a roughly dialectical account of ethical progress. It is a safe assumption that neither the prevailing doctrines in a society (if there are any) nor their main rivals express the whole truth about the human condition and the good life; most current doctrines contain elements of the truth and moral progress is a matter of the development of new doctrines that take up half-truths from here and there, and generate syntheses which have somewhat greater verisimilitude than the views out of which they grew. Mill does not believe that this process of synthesis can be contrived deliberately by any individual moralist acting on his own.

Truth in the great practical concerns of life is so much a question of the reconciling and combining of opposites that very few have minds sufficiently capacious to make the adjustment with an approach to correctness, and it has to be made by the rough process of a struggle between combatants fighting under hostile banners.[18]

Similarly, brand new ideas do not spring up ready formed in the minds of their proponents; they emerge phoenix-like from "the collision of adverse opinions"[19] in the antagonism of open debate and confrontation.

The second argument concerns not the ideas themselves, but the way they are held. According to Mill, progress is empty and the truth about the good life not worth pursuing, if the views that result are not held in a lively and committed spirit with a full awareness of their meaning and significance for human life and action. When ideas and life-styles clash in open debate, each is put on its mettle, and its adherents are required continually to reassert and therefore to reexamine the content and grounds of their views. No view, however popular, can afford to take its preeminence for granted in an atmosphere of open controversy; each person will take his view seriously and will be made acutely aware in the course of the debate of all its implications for his life and practice. So, if a given creed has anything to offer, ethical confrontation will bring it out; and if it has darker, hidden implications, those will emerge too in the course of earnest and committed debate about its desirability.[20] Without that challenge, the prevailing view, even if it is the soundest view, is likely to take on the character of an empty prejudice or "a few phrases learned by rote."[21] In this condition, a truth is worthless because it does not inform one's action to any significant extent; the valuable kernel of a half-truth lies hidden behind the blandness of its verbal repetition; and a falsehood poses no real provocative challenge to those who might be capable of refuting it.

Further, Mill was convinced that humans themselves benefit, morally and intellectually, from involvement in ethical confrontation. Partly this is a matter of the development of a certain sort of open-mindedness – the open-mindedness that results when each is intellectually alert to the possibility of criticism and cares passionately about its adequate rebuttal. This is not the so-called open-mindedness of the dilettante – the man who is willing to debate and defend an idea whether he believes it or not. As we shall see, Mill is almost as frightened of that attitude as he is of the dead weight of prejudice.[22] He is looking instead for committed open-mindedness – the openness of a man who is anxious to listen and respond to criticism precisely because he takes his view seriously and is interested in it as a view about the good life or whatever and not just as a verbal habit from which he finds it psychologically difficult to dissociate himself. Partly too it is a matter of the way in which an idea is held and of the effect on a person of full commitment to one view rather than another. Mill seems to be suggesting that, in an environment of confrontation, commitment heightens and alerts the mental faculties, whereas in an atmosphere of conformity we get

> the cases, so frequent in this age of the world as almost to form the majority, in which the creed remains, as it were, outside the mind, incrusting and petrifying it against all other influences addressed to the higher parts of our nature; manifesting its power by not suffering any fresh and living conviction to get in, but itself doing nothing for the mind or heart except standing sentinel over them to keep them vacant.[23]

For these reasons, Mill thinks ethical confrontation is indispensable for genuine moral progress in society. The existence of a plurality of opinions clashing with one another is, he asserted, the only explanation of the progressive character of western civilization to date. But at a time when economic and social forces are making society increasingly homogeneous and the variety of circumstances is diminishing, it becomes even more important not to interfere with what remains of individuality and the clash of ideas that it generates.[24]

So much is this so, that Mill suggests it might be necessary to *manufacture* dissent if it does not offer itself spontaneously. Even in the utopian circumstance of genuine ethical consensus, the lack of intellectual contention and antagonism would be "no trifling drawback" from the universal recognition of the truth.[25] Fortunately, that is not a problem we have to face:

> If there are any persons who contest a received opinion, or who will do so if law or opinion will let them, let us thank them for it, open our minds to listen to them, and rejoice that there is someone to do for us what we otherwise ought, if we have any regard for either the certainty or vitality of our convictions, to do with much greater labour for ourselves.[26]

IV

I do not propose to examine the merits of these arguments. But if there is anything in them at all, then they suggest a striking revaluation of moral offence and distress. Ethical confrontation, we have seen, is a positive good for Mill: it improves people and it promotes progress. But ethical confrontation is not a painless business. It always hurts to be contradicted in debate, if one takes seriously the views one is propounding, and it is distressing to be faced with examples of life-styles which pose a genuine challenge to the validity and grounds of one's own. People are naturally disturbed when they are involved in the collision of opinions. If nobody is disturbed, distressed, or hurt in this way, that is a sign that ethical confrontation is not taking place, and that in turn, as we have seen, is a sign that the intellectual life and progress of our civilization may be grinding to a halt. In those circumstances, we saw that Mill would propose a desperate remedy: we would have to manufacture ethical conflict in order to shake the complacency of accepted views and generate the shock, distress, and disturbance that were missing.

If, on the other hand, widespread moral distress *is* detectable in the community, then far from being a legitimate ground for interference, it is a positive and healthy sign that the processes of ethical confrontation that Mill called for are actually taking place. That a man is morally distressed by another's homosexuality, for example, is for Mill a sign, first, that he takes his own views on sexual ethics seriously, second, that he recognizes now the need to reassert vigorously the grounds of his own convictions, being confronted so dramatically and disturbingly with a case of its denial, and third – if (as is probable) the moral truth about sexual relations is the monopoly neither of his opinion nor its rival – it is a sign that ideas are struggling and clashing with one another in the way that Mill thought most likely to lead to the final emergence of a more balanced and sober truth about human sexuality.

Think what would be entailed by an interpretation which regarded moral distress as sufficient to cross the threshold established by the Harm Principle. What ought to be taken as evidence that freedom of thought and life-style was promoting progress would be invoked instead as a prima facie reason for interfering with that freedom. A sign of vitality would be cited as a necessary condition for legitimately suppressing that vitality. A symptom of progress would be deployed as a justification for acting in a way that would bring progress to a halt. If we assume that Mill took his own arguments seriously, we must say that this cannot have been his view. Since he believed that ethical confrontation was indispensable for moral and social progress, and since he used this as his main argument for individual liberty, it seems odd to suggest that he could have regarded the pain of debate and the distress of moral challenge as reasons for waiving the general ban on interference with personal liberty. Progress through the collision of opinion is the premise of Mill's liberalism. The sensitivity of the opinions involved in these collisions cannot therefore be taken as a basis for arguments justifying the restriction of liberty.

In a recent note, David Gordon has argued that moral distress might count as harm for the purposes of Mill's principle, provided it did not "arise from the holding of false moral views, judged by a correct account of morality."[27] But this account cannot be squared with Mill's arguments either. I shall leave aside the point that this requires the assessor of harm to be already in possession of the moral truth before he can determine which views should be heard in public debate and which life-styles flaunted. For Mill the more important point is that moral distress arising from a correct moral view indicates that the truth is being challenged, the view scrutinized, and therefore the mind of the true believer kept open and alert to the importance of the creed to which he (correctly, on this hypothesis) clings. If moral challenges were to be suppressed because of the sensibilities of those in possession of the truth – indeed if those sensibilities were even to be regarded as a reason for suppression – then the dangers of moral prejudice, intellectual stagnation, and the "incrustation" of the mind, which Mill knew could affect the truth as much as falsehood, would rear their heads again.

For these reasons, the concept of harm in Mill's principle cannot intelligibly be construed in a way that includes moral distress of the kind I have been discussing.

V

If the problem of moral distress is simply the problem of offense and disturbance occasioned by the fact that others hold or practice conceptions of the good that one regards as immoral or depraved, then the points I have just made dispose of it. Sometimes, however, the problem is confused with another one – the problem of the distress occasioned by the *manner* in which a rival conception of the good is expressed. People often say that they are distressed, and some may claim to be harmed, by seeing a life-style they detest *flaunted* or exhibited *aggressively* in front of them. I think Mill's argument has the capacity to deal with this problem also.

The first thing to say is that the good effects of ethical confrontation, on Mill's account, will not accrue unless views are put forward passionately, forcefully, and directly, in a manner that opponents of those views cannot practicably ignore. At the end of Chapter 2 of *On Liberty*, Mill has to deal with the (typically English) suggestion "that the free expression of all opinions should be permitted on condition that the manner be temperate."[28] He is rightly suspicious of any temperateness proviso:

> If the test be offence to those whose opinions are attacked, I think experience testifies that this offence is given whenever the attack is telling and powerful, and that every opponent who pushes them hard, and whom they find it difficult to answer, appears to them, if he shows any strong feeling on the subject, an intemperate opponent.[29]

Intemperance in this sense is as indispensable for progress as the confrontation which it generates, on Mill's account. A "temperate" debate would be one in which views were compared and exchanged in dilettante fashion without any real moral or intellectual engagement on either side.

(In this connection, it is worth noting that when Mill described his father in his *Autobiography*, he cited as a virtue the fact "that he, in a degree once common, but now unusual, threw his feelings into his opinions," and went on:

> Those, who having opinions which they hold to be immensely important, and their contraries to be prodigiously hurtful, have any deep regard for the general good, will necessarily dislike, as a class and in the abstract, those who think wrong what they think right, and right what they think wrong.[30]

It is a very common error to confuse liberalism with the lack of this strong feeling, but Mill insists that vehemence and toleration are perfectly compatible, and that "none but those who do not care about opinions, will confound this with intolerance."[31])

Mill does concede that "the manner of asserting an opinion ... may be very objectionable and may justly incur severe censure."³² He has in mind the use of personal invective, sarcasm, vituperative language, and so on. Clearly, these tactics can be distressing, and the distress they occasion adds little to the forcefulness (for Mill's purposes) of the debate or confrontation into which they are introduced. For this reason they are to be condemned and restrained by popular opinion (though Mill is still adamant that "law and authority have no business" in restraining them³³). He also believes that they are more common tactics on the side of orthodoxy than of heterodoxy and that there is "more need to discourage offensive attacks on infidelity than on religion."³⁴ For our purposes, the important point is that the distress occasioned by sarcasm and vituperation is not to be regarded as a morality-dependent harm. I can be "harmed" in this sense as much by the sarcastic inculcation of a creed that I am disposed already to believe as by the vituperative objections of an ethical opponent. The harm (if that is what it is) is done by the calculated attack on personality and self-confidence involved in sarcasm and vituperation, not by the attack, however shocking, on the substance of one's views. So Mill's condemnation of this sort of thing, like his later (though, on his own admission, much less well thought out) condemnation of bad manners,³⁵ adds little to the case for bringing moral distress within the scope of his Harm Principle.

Another suggestion often made in relation to Mill's Harm Principle is that an action may be "harmful" if performed in public even though it would harm no one if it were performed in private. What society generally regards as immorality should be tolerated provided it is practiced in the privacy of one's own bedroom (or wherever) and not brought into the public view. On this account, the public/private distinction is primarily a matter of *geography* rather than a question of the different nature of the moral standards involved.

It is tempting to interpret Mill's distinction between self-regarding and other-regarding actions along similar lines, so that a self-regarding action is paradigmatically an action performed behind closed doors. I think this temptation should be resisted.[36] If moral progress depends, as Mill claims, on struggle and confrontation between opposing views of the good life, the last thing we want is that people should conceal or disguise from others the fact that their opinions or life-styles are different. The moral, philosophical, and religious confrontation that Mill is calling for must be *public* confrontation between the practicing adherents of rival and antagonistic ethics. Otherwise the benefits to society – not just to the antagonists but also to "the calmer and more dispassionate bystander"[37] – will not be realized. Indeed, one possibility that worries Mill is this – that eccentric, novel, and heretical life-styles might be coerced by public opinion and collective mediocrity back into the purely private lives of those who practice them. In those circumstances, the ideas themselves may survive, but their existence will make little contribution to the general good if, as Mill puts it, "the most active and inquiring intellects find it advisable to keep the general principles and grounds of their convictions within their own breasts."[38] The alternative views will

> never blaze out far and wide, but continue to smoulder in the narrow circles of thinking and studious persons among whom they originate, without ever lighting up the general affairs of mankind with either a true or a deceptive light.[39]

Mill's argument for liberty commits him to the view that such "reticence on the part of heretics" is a social evil, and I think he would regard the modern idea (made popular since the findings of the Wolfenden Report[40]) that we should confine our deviant practices to the privacy of our own bedrooms, and never show them off to our neighbors, with similar disquiet.

When Mill talks, at the beginning of the essay, about a "sphere" of self-regarding action, we must not think of the boundaries of the sphere in quasi-physical terms, as though they were barriers blocking off the awareness of one's action from people liable to be affected by that awareness. (They are not like "transmitter shields" in Bruce Ackerman's "liberal" utopia, allowing anyone to screen out stimuli that he finds distressing.[41] Mill, I think, would be horrified by the suggestion in Ackerman's work that liberalism might involve the physical realization of this intellectual atomism.) Paradoxically, perhaps, the argument for freedom in relation to "self-regarding" actions rests on the hope and the possibility that the progress of moral debate, the struggle between rival views, and therefore (at least indirectly) the course of others' lives, will in fact be affected by those actions.

There is an isolated paragraph in Chapter 5 of *On Liberty* where Mill appears to subscribe to the view that there are some actions, harmless in private, which if done publicly may constitute indecency and therefore be liable to legitimate prohibition.[42] This is a difficult passage to accommodate and one on which Mill, on his own account, found it unnecessary to dwell. He does however make it clear that it is not the deviance or the perceived or actual immorality of the actions in question which makes their public performance indecent; rather it is a matter of the *type* of action that it is. For example, on this view, *all* forms of public copulation might be regarded as indecent, *including* marital sex in the missionary position for the sole and only purpose of procreation, not just sodomy, fellatio, masturbation, etc.[43] So if the spectacle of indecency is to be regarded as harmful, the harm involved is not (straightforwardly) moral distress, in the sense with which we are concerned.

Even so, I find this passage the most difficult to reconcile with the overall tendency of Mill's argument. There is, surely, a debate to be had about the merits of public lovemaking;[44] and making love in public would be, on Mill's own account, an important contribution to the initiation or the course of such a debate. If copulation in public were banned on the grounds that it is "bad manners" or offends against public decency, it is difficult to see how people could ever get a real sense of the issues involved in this argument, or even of what their own views actually entailed. The danger here, as I see it, is that the very "despotism of custom" which, according to Mill, is the deadliest enemy of individuality and progress, might creep in under the cover of standards of decency to threaten those values all over again.[45]

For this reason, I think the passage we are considering should charitably be overlooked in our reconstruction of Mill's view. If it is not, even the whole basis of his argument for liberty is called into question.[46] At any rate, this isolated passage apart, it is clear that the argument of *On Liberty* does not license the conclusion that putative immorality should be kept from public view.

VI

I have said that Mill is precluded, by his arguments for liberty, from taking moral distress and offence seriously as a form of harm for the purposes of his Harm Principle. In a recent article, Ted Honderich has suggested that this is incompatible with Mill's underlying utilitarianism. "If Mill is Utilitarian with respect to the proper rules for society, how can he be taken to ignore distress when it happens to be the morality-dependent kind?"[47] After all, no one is denying the reality of this distress, nor does our argument depend at all on the view that those concerned are "putting it on" in order to gain some sort of unfair advantage in the utilitarian calculus.[48] The distress is there, on any account, and Honderich is worried by the suggestion that a self-confessed utilitarian might be disposed not to take it seriously. On Honderich's interpretation, Mill *does* include this distress as a form of harm, and dismisses it (to the extent that he does) only on the basis that it is quantitatively inconsiderable.[49]

This last move, however, will not do. Mill describes societies in which the overwhelming majority are revolted by, say, the sexual, religious, or dietary habits of a few.[50] If moral distress counts at all in utilitarian calculation, then there can be no evident or clear-cut case for tolerating this minority deviance. Since Mill believed that there *was* such a case for toleration, no matter how strong and widespread the revulsion, he cannot have held the view that Honderich attributes to him.[51]

Actually, Honderich is mistaken about the character of Mill's utilitarian theory. Mill's utilitarianism is not a Benthamite calculus of pleasures and pains, or of satisfactions and dissatisfactions, of all sorts. The value on which liberty is based is certainly utility, on Mill's account, but, as he insists in his introduction to the essay, "it must be utility in the largest sense, grounded on the permanent interests of man as a progressive being."[52] I take it that this passage refers, not merely to the nature of Mill's utilitarian *computations* (for example, taking a long-run rather than a short-run view, etc.), but to the character of his utilitarian *values* – the fundamental values which he thinks will be promoted by his libertarianism. A considerable part of *On Liberty* is devoted to showing what it is for man to be "a progressive being" and what his interests in such a condition are. These are the interests whose promotion Mill's utilitarianism seeks to maximize.

If we accept the arguments about progress in Chapter 2 of *On Liberty* and spontaneity in Chapter 3, it is not then open to us to say that distress or resentment when one's preconceptions are challenged goes against one's interests as a progressive being. A creature who defined his interests – even in part – in terms of being free from the shock and perturbation of ethical debate and being free from anxiety about the grounds or validity of his opinions would be like the satisfied (and no doubt morally complacent) "fool" mentioned in *Utilitarianism*.[53] Mill is adamant, in the latter work, that there is a distinction between *happiness*, understood as the leading value of his ethical system, and mere contentment or satisfaction.[54] By insisting that distress and uneasiness under the impact of ethical confrontation are negative values for Mill, Honderich is driving the theory back toward the very Benthamism that Mill wanted to repudiate.

It is certainly true that Mill wants to argue, in consequentialist fashion, that the benefits of free discussion and of the open struggle between competing conceptions of the good life outweigh the costs of such confrontation. The costs include the bad effects of people believing falsehoods (Mill concedes, with common sense, that "it is dangerous and noxious when opinions are erroneous"[55]) and the dangers of people practicing life-styles that are actually depraved. They include also the tendency for religious and philosophical sectarianism to be "heightened and exacerbated" by the freest discussion.[56] (In certain circumstances, where sectarianism may lead to violence, these costs are so great as to outweigh the benefits of liberty.[57]) But, in Mill's calculations at any rate, the costs of freedom do *not* include the distress occasioned by contradiction or the pain and shock of forceful debate. Those are not experiences which a progressive being has a genuine interest in avoiding and they are therefore not negative values or costs in relation to the permanent interests of man as a progressive being.

Chapter 6

Rushdie and religion

It seems a shallow understatement to say that the threat to Salman Rushdie's life is a threat to free speech. Threats to free speech are things like film censorship, the Official Secrets Act, and the withdrawal of programs from television. The penalties we think of are fines, High Court injunctions, perhaps suspended jail sentences. Not book burnings, the consignment of an author to hell, and the offer of eternal bliss and a million dollars to anyone who sends him there. Not rioting, with scores already dead, hostages threatened, bookstores bombed, and an author in hiding under armed guard for perhaps the rest of what's left of his life.

The Ayatollah Khomeini's murderous anathema raises issues that go deeper and wider than free speech, as it is usually understood. They go deeper because they probe beneath the ideal of toleration to ask about the conditions under which people of different religious outlooks can live together peacefully in society. That issue is not so easy as it looks. How can there be peace when people disagree about what is sacred and what is profane, and when what is known to be sacred evokes the most devout respect on the one hand and all the kaleidoscopic irony of modern literature on the other?

There are other aspects too that make it a wider matter than free speech usually is. When we talk about free speech, we are most often talking about a particular constitutional provision (for example, the American First Amendment) or a particular set of laws. But evidently *The Satanic Verses* is not an issue for just one society. Although Salman Rushdie is a British citizen, he lives (or lived until terror confined him to a guarded room) *in the world*, as so many moderns do. Born in Bombay, he makes his home in England and he travels regularly to America, Europe, India, and elsewhere. He lives and works in a circle of authors, publishers, critics, and commentators that effortlessly transcends national boundaries. The scope and reach of his novels are cosmopolitan. If he contributes to the marketplace of ideas, it is a world market. When he offends religious sensibilities, they are those of a world religion. This is not just a British subject being set upon by Iran. This is Salman Rushdie, citizen of the world, in confrontation with Islam.

Nor is it simply an enlightened West confronting an older, foreign preenlightenment tradition. Things are not so easily divided. Every society in which such an author might live is already a microcosm of the world, of East and Middle East and West: Rushdie's book was burned in Bradford and banned in Ottawa weeks before he was damned in Teheran.

Our understanding of free expression has got to be as wide and cosmopolitan as the context in which this problem has arisen. We know that Iran imprisons, tortures, and kills its own dissident writers, for example. Should we condemn that, or is that the imperious imposition of our values on a culture we do not understand? A vague respect for national sovereignty and some muddled thoughts about relativism incline us to tread carefully. We know also that countries like Iran try to remain impervious to outside influences. They ban the importation of corrupt and blasphemous material. And again, part of us wants to say that that's a matter for them.

But the relativist approach is of no use in the Rushdie affair. That "their" ways are not our ways is now the problem, not a solution. The question is whether we shall have free expression *in the world* or not – whether some of the inhabitants of the world are to be threatened with death by others for what they write. No doubt, different cultures, different faiths bring their disparate perspectives to that question. But it needs one answer. Liberals cannot say open-mindedly that the killing of Rushdie by a Shiite Muslim would be as valid for the Muslim as literary hubris is for Rushdie. We cannot agree or afford to differ on who has the right to live. This is the place where we have to abandon our relativism and stand and fight for what matters.

That it is an issue for the world does not mean it is for the United Nations or some yet-to-be-established New World Order. There was indeed something gratifying about the speed with which the European Community nations responded to the crisis, just as there was something shameful about the late and pusillanimous response of the American administration. But respect for rights is ultimately not a matter for government, and respect for freedom in the world does not presuppose an international state. It is a matter of what the people of the world are willing to live with. When John Stuart Mill wrote *On Liberty*, he addressed it to his fellow citizens, not their government, because he was sure the threat to individuality and freedom came from society "executing its own mandates" rather than from the agency of the State. He did not argue for an enforced constitution or a Bill of Rights, but for "a strong barrier of moral conviction" to protect the freedom of thought and debate. It may be a lost cause, but we must do everything we can to make the case for freedom of expression, freedom from this sort of terror, to those with whom we share the world. Without that, legal or international protection for literary freedom is as fragile and as fearful as the police line that is guarding Salman Rushdie at this moment.

The deeper issues are posed when we remind ourselves that Islam did not invent book burning – or author burning, for that matter. We have been this way before. Those who waded through blood to plead for toleration in the sixteenth and seventeenth centuries knew that it was religion that was special, and that there was nothing self-evident about the idea that people of different faiths might get along. Faith treats of eternal life and eternal suffering, prospects in comparison with which earthly laws and earthly sanctions pale into insignificance. A church invests the most mundane objects and actions with immense importance, at once furnishing our culture with the richest symbolism and laying it out as the most deadly minefield of offence and misunderstanding. Religion confers a meaning on the otherwise brutish facts of life and death, mind and body, sex and family – a meaning that people long for and embrace. Yet it is those meanings that divide us; if we do not understand life and death in the same way how can we possibly agree on how to share the world?

To appeal to another for toleration is to invoke some value we both share. It is to say that something like knowledge, or freedom, or security, or even the bare possibility of a decent life for all will be imperiled unless we find a modus vivendi. But we cannot make that plea if we have no interests in common, or if all our interests are colored differently by our rival faiths and outlooks. If someone is convinced that life is literally not worth living, truth not worth seeking, or freedom not worth exercising in the company of the infidel, there is no foothold for argument.

Even if we have that foothold of common interest, it gets us only half the way. There is no evading the fact that lives erected on this common basis may differ profoundly in faith, meaning, and aspiration. Some are devout Muslims, some are Jews, some are Hindus, some are Catholics, some are Christian fundamentalists, some are fervent atheists, some are just trying to make it through their lives. What respect is due to those differences? How gingerly must we treat one another's religious sensibilities? Rushdie's critics say that he should have dealt more delicately, more seriously with the themes that he raised, or else avoided them altogether. What are we to say about that?

Toleration, mutual respect, live-and-let-live, can be conceived in different ways. On what we might call a one-dimensional account, toleration involves leaving people entirely alone with their faith and sensibilities. We are all to take care not to say anything that criticizes or cuts across the religious convictions of anyone else. If you believe that Jesus is the Son of God, who am I to contradict you? If I am the fool who says that there is no God, you must be equally circumspect. And both of us must take care not to say anything that treads on the sensibilities of someone who believes that it is the Koran that is the Word Incarnate.

But faith cannot be sealed off in this way. The religions of the world make *rival* claims about the nature and being of God and the meaning of human life. It is not possible for me to avoid criticizing the tenets of your faith without stifling my own. So mutual respect cannot possibly require us to refrain from criticism, if only because criticism of other sects is implicit already in the affirmations of any creed.

A second kind of toleration concedes this, and adds a dimension of debate. Criticism and discussion between rival faiths is fine and unavoidable, but two-dimensional toleration insists that it must be serious, earnest and respectful in its character. If I disagree with you about the existence of God, I may put forward my arguments, but I must do so in a way that is circumspect and inoffensive, taking full account of the fact that your religious beliefs are not just your *views*, but convictions which go to the core or essence of your being. I must be sensitive to the role these beliefs play in your life, and not deal with them lightly, sarcastically, or insultingly.

According to this model, *The Satanic Verses* went wrong, not in saying things against Islam, but in the offensive tone that it took. Rushdie spun fantasies, told ribald jokes, rehearsed heresies, used obscene language to make the points he wanted to make. He mocked the sacred, instead of asking us soberly to reconsider some doctrine.

Two-dimensional toleration would seem to combine the values of truth seeking – which John Stuart Mill made so much of in his essay *On Liberty* – with a principle of respect. It leaves room for debate, but it eschews mockery, offence, and insult. Above all it enables us to understand notions like sacrilege and blasphemy not as ideals internal to any religion, but as principles embodying what we owe to one another as humans, in respect for deeply held convictions.

But as soon as we say that, we begin to see the fallacy of two-dimensional toleration. What is serious and what is offensive, what is sober and what is mockery – these are not neutral ideas. They come as part of the package, and different religions define them in different ways. In some rabbinical traditions, theological debate proceeds through the telling of jokes. Some Muslim sects regard it as an unspeakable affront if a woman participates in religious discussion, no matter how sober her tone. For a long time in the Christian west, it was regarded as a capital mockery of the Almighty if one not in holy orders dared to debate the ways of God with man. This is exactly what we should expect; the demeanor with which religious disputation is to be conducted is itself an issue on which religious views are taken. It is bound up with the fact that faith addresses the deepest issues of truth, value, and knowledge. There is nothing necessarily privileged about the norms of civility that we call moral seriousness, and indeed requiring religious controversy to observe the ponderous debating rules of a Midwestern Rotary Club may be the worst, not the best, of both worlds.

By the same token, it is fatuous to think that there is a way of running a multicultural society without disturbance or offence. When Mill made his argument for free discussion, the disturbance of complacency and the shaking of faith were positive values in the debate. It is hard to see how free expression could do its work if it remained psychologically innocuous. In any case, there are some who hold their beliefs so devoutly that even the most sober and respectful criticism would count as a mortal insult to their personality. Some are so devout that the mere presence of the ungodly is more than they can bear. If the questions are as important as they seem, then distress at others' answers is part of the price of addressing them. Sensitivity is not trumps in this game; the stakes are already too high for that.

It would be different if religious faith were like a certain sort of posture or state of being, so that the seriousness with which one held oneself were not to be mocked by anyone else. But religious commitments have content: they address issues that have significance not only for one believer, but at least potentially for everyone. Is there a God? What is God like? What are His (or Her) purposes with us? What are we like? Why is there evil? These questions matter; nothing is more important. It cannot be that one person's style of answering (or even the style of a billion believers) precludes others from addressing the questions in the style that seems appropriate to them.

We are pushed, then, toward three-dimensional toleration. Persons and peoples must leave one another free to address the deep questions of religion and philosophy the best way they can, with all the resources they have at their disposal. In the modern world, that may mean that the whole kaleidoscope of literary technique – fantasy, irony, poetry, wordplay, and the speculative juggling of ideas – is unleashed on what many regard as the holy, the good, the immaculate, and the indubitable.

How could it be otherwise? Either the issues are important or they are not. If they are, we know that they strain our resources of psyche and intellect. They drive us to the limits of linear disputation and beyond, for they address the edgy, the shy, the disturbing, the frightening, the knowable, and the unthinkable. The religions of the world make their claims, tell their stories, and consecrate their symbols, and all that goes out into the world too, as public property, as part of the cultural and psychological furniture which we cannot respectfully tiptoe around in our endeavor to make sense of our being. We have to do what we can with the questions, and make what we can of the answers that have been drummed into us.

It is sometimes said tritely that secular humanism is a religion like any other. The grain of truth in that view is that the issues the great religions address are implicitly issues for all of us. But if that's the case, the great religions cannot lay down the terms on which those issues are dealt with. For example, we all cast about for an understanding of ourselves, our bodies, and the intense experience of our sexuality. We find in our culture tales of pure and holy men, like Mohammed, and even the claim that God has taken human form, flesh and blood, in the person of Jesus Christ. Now incarnation itself is not a straightforward idea, and it beggars belief to say we are required to think about it without dealing edgily with the question of Christ's sexuality. In general, our view of the body is so bound up with what we are taught about holiness that we cannot prohibit the association of the sacred and the sexual in our attempt to come to terms with ourselves. Some may be able to hold the two apart, but their piety cannot clinch the issue of how others are to deal with this experience.

By the same token, we all cast about for an understanding of evil in the world. There is disease, there are great crimes, children are killed in their millions, the heavens are silent, and there seems no sense in it. We know the great religions address the issue shyly and indirectly, with a cornucopia of images and stories. Satan lays a wager with God that Job, a good and holy man, can be brought by misfortune to curse Him to His face – a story which, if it were not already in the Bible, might have earned its publisher a firebomb or two. The point is not a cute *tu quoque:* it is that no one even within the religious traditions thinks this can be addressed without the full range of fantastic and poetical technique. Once again, respect for the sensitivities of some cannot in conscience be used to limit the means available to others to come to terms with the problem of evil. It is already too important for that.

Three-dimensional toleration is not an easy ideal to live with. Things that seem sacred to some will in the hands of others be played with, joked about, taken seriously, taken lightly, sworn at, fantasized upon, juggled, dreamed about backward, sung about, and mixed up with all sorts of stuff. That is what happens in *The Satanic Verses*. It is not a solemn theological disquisition, and it is not to be defended as such. Nor is it to be defended as a work of art that just happens to include some regrettable passages. Like all modern literature, it is a way of trying to make sense of human experience. It touches on some problems that Islam addresses, and it invokes images and narratives with which Islam has colored Rushdie's world. It does so playfully and kaleidoscop-ically, but that doesn't mean that the themes matter less to the author than they do to the millions of the faithful.

It may be too late to make a case for Salman Rushdie's freedom from terror and the threat of assassination. But if we make a plea for others like him in the world, it must be on this high ground – that the great themes of religion matter too much to be closeted by the sensitivity of those who are counted as the pious. There is no other way we can live together and respect each other's grappling with life.

Chapter 7

Legislation and moral neutrality

I

In this chapter, I want to discuss some aspects of the modern liberal theory of legislation and state action. In particular, I want to consider what I shall call *"the doctrine of liberal neutrality,"* expounded by philosophers like Ronald Dworkin, Bruce Ackerman, and Robert Nozick.[1] But though I shall be concentrating on the suggestions that have been made in these recent writings (together with some rather less explicit arguments in John Rawls's *A Theory of Justice*[2]), the themes that I shall be discussing have a rich heritage. The idea of neutrality is only the most recent attempt to articulate a position that liberals have occupied for centuries: the ancestry of the idea may be traced back through John Stuart Mill's essay *On Liberty* and Immanuel Kant's *Metaphysical Elements of Justice* at least as far as John Locke's *Letter Concerning Toleration* and maybe even further.[3] It is the latest expression of a view that liberals have always held about the attitude the state should take to the personal faith and beliefs of its citizens.

We talk about *the* liberal view and *the* doctrine of liberal neutrality, but one of the points I hope to make in this chapter is that there are in fact *several* such views, each based on premises and yielding practical requirements that differ subtly from those involved in each of the others. It is not my intention to single out and defend any one of these views in particular as the one we ought to adopt. I am taking on the more modest task of sorting out the work that needs to be done before *any* view of this kind can be defended.

II

We have to start somewhere. Perhaps the clearest expression of the modern doctrine is found in Ronald Dworkin's paper "Liberalism." As Dworkin put it, the doctrine requires that legislators (and other state officials)

> must be neutral on what might be called the question of the good life, or of what gives value to life. Since the citizens of a society differ in their conceptions [of what makes life worth living], the government does not treat them as equals if it prefers one conception to another, either because the officials believe that one is intrinsically superior, or because one is held by the more numerous or powerful group.[4]

The idea that Dworkin is getting at here is quite familiar to anyone who has read his Locke or his John Stuart Mill. It is the idea of tolerance, of secularism, of the state standing back from religion and personal ethics. But it is worth remarking that Dworkin's *formulation* of the liberal position is quite new; I mean its formulation in terms of the image of *neutrality*. I am not aware of the use of this image by any liberal writer to express such a position prior to 1974. In a book published just before the Second World War, T. S. Eliot occasionally referred to the secular conception of the state which he opposed, and which he believed existed in Britain in 1939, as "the idea of a neutral society."[5] But I have managed to find no evidence that any liberal view that Eliot was opposing was ever actually formulated in these terms. The image of neutrality, then, is relatively new to the liberal tradition. I believe it is a promising and helpful image (helpful not only in expressing the liberal position but also in highlighting some of its difficulties). But it is easy to misunderstand – the more so because it may be discredited automatically by being associated with other contexts in which the term "neutrality" has been deployed, particularly the discredited chimera of "value-neutrality" in the social sciences which was widely canvassed in the 1950s and 1960s and which remains alive in some corners even today.[6] I hope that in this chapter I can dispel some of the more obvious and more probable misunderstandings that may arise from the use of this image to express the liberal attitude toward ethical diversity.

III

The first thing to note about the use of the image is that neutrality itself is far from a straightforward concept. Certainly the recent debate has shown that it is not particularly amenable to uncontroversial logical analysis.[7] We can say a bit about it by way of analysis, but not much.

The concept of neutrality presupposes a *contest* between two or more sides (two or more people, parties, teams, nations, religions, ideals, values) and it focuses attention on a third or additional party whose actions and status are in question and to whom either the term "neutral" or the term "nonneutral" is to be applied. It is not necessarily the judicial or quasi-judicial image of the "triad" – plaintiff, defendant, judge – though of course that is an area where the image is often invoked. The third party's status and actions which are in question may or may not include an attempt to mediate between the other two. (Sometimes the concern is merely whether the third party can go "neutrally" about his own business ignoring the conflict between the other two as far as possible.)

The neutrality of the third party is a matter of his relation to the contest between the other two. In attempting to pin this down, two points of reference can be identified. (1) If the third party takes part in the contest in the same way and on the same terms as the sides by whose actions and interactions it is constituted, he can never be described as neutral. (2) If the actions or existence of the third party can have no impact on the contest at all, either on its course or on its outcome, then the question of his neutrality does not arise.

Those are our fixed points. In between we have all the cases in which the third party has or might plausibly be thought to have an effect on the contest to the detriment or frustration of the interests of either side. That is the situation of most third parties in relation to most disputes, and that is, so to speak, the *domain* of the concept of neutrality. The concept of neutrality is the concept of a range of actions open to the third party which are not to count (for some purpose – in determining, for example, whether it is appropriate to retaliate, or whether the contest is fair) as involvement or participation in the contest. The immediate function of the concept is to mark a division in the domain somewhere between our two fixed points, between actions that count as noninvolvement and actions that count as involvement in the contest.

There is always some point to this division of the middle area into a realm of noninvolvement and a realm that counts as being involved. In the context of international law, one can think of various reasons we have (we, the international community) for wanting to draw such a line: the containment of conflict; preservation of the possibility of mediation and honest broking; the need to allow international trade and diplomacy to proceed even while a conflict between nations is going on; and so on. These reasons will be different in different contexts. A particular set of reasons, together with the sorts of demarcations they suggest, will define a particular *conception* of neutrality.[8] Thus in international law, the reasons which make it seem desirable to the international community that there be such a thing as a neutral status provide the basis of a particular conception of how and where the line between third parties' involvement and noninvolvement in a conflict is to be drawn. Inasmuch as people may give different accounts of those reasons, or map them out as a demarcation in different ways, there will be competing conceptions of neutrality at work in international law.

As well as the reasons that there are for having such a thing as neutral status, there will also be reasons which particular third parties – in international law, reasons which particular nations – have for wanting to be on one or other side of that line. Just as the idea of neutrality is not self-evident, so a policy of neutrality is not self-justifying. Some states are neutral out of distaste for war; others for reasons of survival; others for reasons of domestic politics. It is obviously crazy in international affairs to expect a neutral state to have neutral reasons for its neutrality. Neutrality is not vitiated by the fact that it is undertaken for partial or self-interested reasons. One does not, as it were, have to be neutral all the way down. This point, as we shall see, is very important for an understanding of the logic of the liberal doctrine.

As I have indicated, the idea of neutrality is probably most at home in the context of international law – in the doctrine that any sovereign state may opt to be neutral in relation to any war or conflict between other nations in which it is not *ab initio* involved, and that if it publicly exercises this option, it acquires certain duties, rights, and powers which are in theory enforceable in international tribunals. But even in international law, the meaning of "neutrality" is not fixed and uncontroversial (mostly because of changes and shifts in the two sets of reasons I mentioned in the preceding paragraphs). Two illustrations of the way the doctrine changes may be of some interest.

On the traditional doctrine, a neutral government has a duty to refrain from helping either of the belligerent powers; but it is not required to prohibit or prevent its private citizens from trading with one of the belligerent countries or offering loans or whatever. That doctrine works fine in a world in which most economies are organized on a laissez-faire basis and in which there is a clear distinction between government action and private trade. But what conception of neutrality are we to adopt for cases where the putatively neutral state itself controls the economic activity of its society – directly or indirectly through nationalized agencies? No easy answer is available; it is partly a matter of what it is reasonable to expect from a country if it is to secure the advantages of neutrality (should the price be economic self-immolation?), and, on the other hand, of what it is reasonable for the other belligerents to put up with before acting against the putatively neutral party. No amount of purely logical analysis can tell us how the concept is to be deployed to deal with problems like this.[9]

Second, it may be worth saying something about the precarious history of the doctrine of neutrality in international law. If one reads Hugo Grotius or any of the natural law writers of his generation, one will find that the modern doctrine of neutrality is rejected at least in relation to those conflicts that can be classified under the heading of "just wars." The traditional idea of the just war is profoundly hostile to the doctrine of neutrality, for it is the idea of a war which one of the belligerents is morally justified in waging and in respect of which it may reasonably expect the support and cooperation of other powers. In that circumstance, the idea that a nation was entitled to stand back impartially, helping and hindering one party no more than the other, was regarded as morally misguided.[10] The modern doctrine of neutrality emerged only as the idea of a just war – or rather the idea of a *demonstrably* just war – became discredited. (The work of the Swiss jurist Emeric de Vattel was seminal in this respect.[11]) If there was no clear way of picking and choosing between the justice of the belligerents' causes, then there was no way states could be thought to be under a *duty* to intervene, and so a liberty to sit on the sideline, and the attachment of rights and duties to the exercise of that liberty, was the logical conclusion. But, by the same token, whenever the doctrine of the just war is resurrected (even implicitly, as it was in the latter stages of the Second World War, or as in the claim that a war – like the Korean War or the conflict in the Gulf – might have the status of an international police action) then again the doctrine of neutrality goes into decline. For evidence of this, we need only look at the wholesale and flagrant violation of what would normally be neutral duties by the United States in 1940–1, parading itself both as neutral in the conflict between Britain and Germany and, at the same time, as "the arsenal of democracy," supplying enormous amounts of military equipment and intelligence to the British. We may look also at the considerable international criticism that was directed at the decision of a state like the Irish Republic to remain aloof from the war against the Nazis *pour épater les anglais.*

It would be fascinating to draw a parallel between the disrepute of neutrality in relation to just wars, and the criticisms that are directed at the doctrine with which we are concerned – the liberal doctrine of moral neutrality – in relation to what certain moralists would see as the "just war" being waged (say) by Christian values against the values of secular humanism. But I will not pursue the analogy.

What I did mean to stress was that even on its home turf, neutrality is far from a straightforward or uncontested concept. And that is to say nothing of its use in other contexts: the concept of neutralism (as distinct from neutrality) in international diplomacy; the idea of neutrality as a judicial ideal; ideas of neutral colors, neutral tastes, neutral chemicals; the alleged neutrality of meta-ethical analysis; the idea of value-neutrality in the social sciences (with which, as I said, liberal neutrality is often confused); neutrality in education; and so on. All this means that we are dealing with a host of images of neutrality, not a single image. If they are united by anything at all, it is by their all being conceptions of the abstract concept I outlined earlier (and it has to be pretty abstract to fit some of them in!). Thus, when liberals talk about the desirability of morally neutral legislation, it is simply not clear so far which of these conceptions they want us to bring to mind.

One issue of definition, in particular, is very important. When a liberal like Dworkin says that a legislator must be neutral as between competing conceptions of the good life, is he talking about neutrality so far as the legislator's *intention* is concerned, or is he talking about the neutrality of the *effects* of the legislator's actions?

A number of writers – Alan Montefiore, for example, and I think, Joseph Raz – have interpreted liberal neutrality as concerning primarily the *consequences* of legislative action: the legislator must take care that his laws are even-handed in their effects on competing conceptions of the good life.[12] On this account a neutral law must not increase the chances of, say, a hedonistic life-style flourishing at the expense of adherence to traditional Christian values. It must enhance or retard the prospects of these life-styles to the same degree. This conception gives rise to enormous problems. The main theoretical difficulty is the postulation of some baseline relative to which differential effects of state action may be measured. In practical terms it is a difficult requirement to live up to, because it is so hard to predict what the effect of a law is going to be on life-styles and mores. If that is how neutrality were to be understood, we should have grave doubts about whether it was ever reasonable to require legislators to be neutral.

However, instead of that, the liberal may be talking instead about neutrality of intention – that is, neutrality in relation to the motives and reasons that the legislator uses to justify his laws. He may say – and I think this was John Stuart Mill's view (at least in Chapter 1 of *On Liberty* – the argument in Chapter 2 points in the other direction) that power must not be exercised over people for nonneutral reasons.[13] Thus, for example, the fact that a law against Sunday trading would accord with the requirements of a sabbatarian faith is not a good reason for having such a law; but the fact that it is necessary to prevent shop employees from being overworked may be. And the latter reason can be a good reason, and the legislation neutral on that account, even though the law undoubtedly benefits sabbatarian over nonsabbatarian sects. John Locke gives another example in his *Letter on Toleration*: a prohibition on the slaughter of cattle may particularly disadvantage a religious sect that focuses on animal sacrifice; but it will be justified nevertheless if an economic or public health reason can be given for the ban.[14] One and the same law, then, would be permitted or not permitted by the neutrality constraint depending on what the reasons for it were.

This looks as though it will also be a hard doctrine to apply in practice, because of the difficulty of telling what the reasons behind a particular piece of legislation were. But that may be an unnecessary worry. Perhaps the doctrine of liberal neutrality ought to be understood primarily as a basis for political morality in a narrow sense – that is, as a basis for each lawmaker to evaluate his own intentions – rather than as a doctrine for evaluating legislation as such. Or perhaps it can be seen as a constraint on the reasons *we* deploy in our reconstruction of the justification of some rule we support (whatever its original intention was). We should not think of political morality simply as a set of principles for judging outcomes. Its primary function is to guide action and to constrain practical thought.

Which of these conceptions should the modern liberal adopt? Nozick seems to favor the second;[15] so it seems does Dworkin, though he is not entirely consistent on this.[16] Bruce Ackerman oscillates freely between the two, depending on what he wants to use the neutrality constraint to rule out.[17] Certainly, Raz and other critics of liberalism are happier attacking the first (equality of consequences) conception than the second (motivational) one.

My hunch is that this is not a matter we can simply *decide*. It is not a matter of peering at the rival conceptions to see which is most congenial to our "intuitions" or which best approximates some dictionary definition. It is a question of the ultimate argument or justification that we want to bring forward in favor of liberal neutrality. Is our argument for neutrality based on moral skepticism? Is it based on a commitment to the positive value of ethical diversity? Is it based on a faith in moral progress like that of John Stuart Mill? Is it based on the importance of autonomy and the evil of coercion? Is it based on political worries about entrusting legislators with the moral authority perfectionism would involve? Or is it, as Dworkin suggests, derived from some deep ideal of equal respect? All these are arguments that can be, and have been, made in favor of the doctrine. The thing to remember is that a policy of liberal neutrality, in the sense of conception X, may not be susceptible to the same line of justification as a policy of liberal neutrality, in the sense of conception Y.

For example, the argument from moral skepticism may yield or justify one conception of neutrality (arguably the intentionalist one), while the pluralistic line of argument may be more congenial to consequentialist concern. If moral skepticism yields an argument for neutrality (which, by the way, I doubt),[18] it is (presumably) because there is something irrational about acting on moralistic reasons which in the nature of things cannot be known to be true; but then there is nothing irrational about action which differentially affects some moral creed if that is not the reason motivating one's action. If the value of moral pluralism yields an argument for neutrality, it proceeds presumably *via* the claim that we ought to be careful that our legislative action (whatever its intentions) does not accidentally diminish the diversity of moral life-styles.

Different lines of argument for the liberal position will generate different conceptions of neutrality, which in turn will generate different and perhaps mutually incompatible requirements at the level of legislative practice. Since we cherish our deep values and our justificatory arguments more dearly than we cherish any particular posited conception of neutrality, it will be the justification we favor which determines our interpretation of the concept, rather than the other way round.

This, by the way, is sufficient to wreck much of the basis of Bruce Ackerman's book, *Social Justice in the Liberal State*. Ackerman believes that it is possible, and indeed desirable, for us to be as liberally noncommittal about the justification of neutrality as we are about the issue of the good life itself. He thinks we should be neutral not only about ethical ideals, but about the justification of neutrality as well.[19] However, if there are two or more competing conceptions of neutrality, and one is the upshot of one line of argument, and another the upshot of another, then Ackerman's "liberal" strategy is simply a recipe for incoherence.

What emerges, then, is the centrality and inescapability of argument and justification so far as the liberal is concerned. The proponent of neutrality cannot afford to be negligent about the task of justifying the position he wants to embrace (as Dworkin is, for example[20]), because justifying it is part and parcel of the task of articulating it. By the same token he cannot afford, like Ackerman, to be indifferent about it or promiscuous across an array of different justifications. Neutrality is not a straightforward concept and we are in no position to say what conception of it we have adopted unless we have some idea already of why neutrality should be thought to matter. (This, I take it, is a general point about conceptual analysis. The study of concepts like *law*, and *freedom*, and *power*, and *democracy* cannot be undertaken in a normative vacuum. Unless, for example, we have some idea of why it might *matter*, why it might be thought a matter of *concern* whether something is a law or not, we cannot sensibly choose among rival conceptions of this concept. Unless we have an idea of the difference it makes whether a given relation counts as a power relation or not, we cannot specify a particular conception of power. Justificatory argument in political theory and jurisprudence must precede conceptual analysis, not the other way round.)[21]

IV

I have argued that in order to illuminate the concept of neutrality, an adequate liberal theory has to indicate why neutrality is required. Apart from this vital task, an adequate theory also has to explain two other things. (1) It has to explain exactly *who* is required to be neutral. If the answer focuses on legislators and those who have political power, then some explanation has to be given of why the duty of neutrality is particularly incumbent on them. (2) It has to explain who or what exactly the legislator (or whoever) is required to be neutral between. The latter task means saying something about what a conception of the good life is, and how conceptions of the good life may differ from those other values and principles (like justice, for example) that no legislator could possibly be expected to be neutral about. Let me say a little about each of these tasks.

The first point to note is that although the liberal insists that *legislators* should be neutral on the question of what constitutes the good life, he does not insist that people in general should be neutral on that question, or that neutrality is, in general terms, some sort of moral or intellectual virtue that we all should strive for.[22] Indeed, it would be absurd to suggest that neutrality on the question of what makes life worth living is in general a good thing or that it is a duty incumbent on everyone in all situations. Not everyone can be neutral on this question without the whole business of evaluating ways of life and making choices between them coming to an end. If the concept of a good life has a *use*, then neutrality cannot be required of everyone, since *good* itself is an evaluating, discriminating concept. Or, even if it is not formally incoherent, a general requirement of neutrality has no place in liberal theory. Of course individual citizens must have ideas of their own about the good life, and they should align and orient their lives to one conception rather than another. If I am deciding which profession to enter, where to live, whom to love and marry, whether to have children, what tastes to cultivate, and so on, my deliberations and decisions will be based on – or will, wholly or partially, reveal – what *I* think makes life worth living. If my account is not the same as that of my neighbor, I may be criticized by him for the content of the particular view I hold ("What a depraved or silly way to lead one's life!"), but it would be quite inappropriate for him to criticize me just for having and acting on a view.

The requirement of neutrality is generally taken to be specific to *political* morality. It is not wrong for someone to favor a particular conception of the good life, but it is wrong for him in his capacity as legislator (and presumably as voter) to favor such a view.[23] Unlike courage or honesty, neutrality is not a virtue whose estimation in the case of political actors is explained as a special case of its estimation in the world at large. It is a specifically political virtue. There is something special about political life that makes us require this of those involved in it.

This special feature need not be something that is confined to legislation. It may characterize certain other types of human actions as well, if they share with legislation whatever the characteristic is which, in this regard, distinguishes legislation from other ordinary forms of activity. In defining this characteristic, most liberal theories have concentrated on the relation between legislation and force, or between legislation and coercion. Laws, it is said, bear down on individuals by violence, restraint, and the threat of sanctions; and the suggestion is usually that these are not elements we want operating in the moral sphere or for the pursuit of moralistic purposes.

The underlying argument here may be the view held by John Locke (and perhaps also Immanuel Kant) that force and coercion are simply useless in the realm of morals anyway, because a person's allegiance to a conception of the good life is a matter of his inner commitment, which is not altogether under his control, rather than of his external conduct, which is. If it is not under his control, there is no hope of sanctions or other incentives working to change his mind. So the use of sanctions in the moral sphere is hopeless. On this account, nonneutral action by the legislator is simply irrational: the use of means which are singularly ill-adapted to the end he claims to be pursuing.[24]

Alternatively, the justification may be the more modern point that in our commitment to freedom we attach particular value to a person's autonomous organization of his own life – to his own reflection on desires, plans, and projects, and to his own deliberate effort to shape his life into a meaningful whole. On this account, what is wrong with the coercion associated with law is that it usurps and interferes with that process, leaving at best an individual life that has been shaped externally and heteronomously in accordance with someone else's conception of the good, but that has none of the particular value attaching to an autonomously organized life. And there are other ways in which the coercive character of legislation may be thought inappropriate in the moral sphere.

Here, once again, there is a point to be made about the primacy of justification. It is notoriously difficult to draw a sensible line between conduct that counts as coercive and conduct that merely counts as persuasive. Knowing how to draw this line is not a matter of being familiar with a dictionary. It is a matter of knowing how and why coercion is thought to be a worry, and of working out how far and to what extent the grounds of that worry apply in a particular case. Suppose a government makes no attempt to impose a Christian ethic with sanctions, but its most powerful orators constantly use broadcasting media to preach Christian values. Is this coercion or not? Is it a case that should fall within the ambit of the neutrality constraint? Or suppose the government offers tax incentives to those who organize their family life in what it takes to be a morally respectable way. Is this a mere offer of favor, or is it, too, coercive? We cannot tell, until we know *why* coercion matters and what deep values are reflected in our determination to focus on the coercive aspect in paradigm cases, rather than on some other aspect of the matter. Until we know that, we won't have the evaluative equipment to consider the puzzles at the margin. Similar considerations obviously apply to the way we approach the problem of how far allegedly coercive interactions in private life – in the family or in schools or in the workplace – should be brought within the ambit of the neutrality constraint.

V

The other point was that we will want to know who or what, exactly, legislators are required to be neutral between. This is the area in which the liberal doctrine is most commonly misunderstood.

Liberal neutrality is not and cannot be the doctrine that legislation should be neutral in relation to *all* moral values.

It is certainly not the doctrine that legislation should be "value-free," whatever that might mean. Those ideas are incoherent. Neutrality is itself a value: it is a normative position, a doctrine about what legislators and state officials ought to do. It is a doctrine that holds that it is wrong for certain considerations to enter the political arena; it is a doctrine which holds out neutrality in political activity as right and good. At the beginning of his essay "Against Moral Disestablishment," Neil McCormick suggests that the liberal may want to get around this point by distinguishing moral theories *about* legislation from the deployment or application of moral value *in* and *through* legislation. Perhaps the liberal holds the moral principle that legislation should never be used to enforce moral values.[25] That would perhaps not be incoherent, but still it would not capture the liberal view, as it has usually been understood. For liberals regard neutrality not only as a value that legislators ought to be constrained by, but also as a value that they ought to enforce (on other people attempting to exercise power in a nonneutral way). Another way of putting this is to say simply: in his own behavior but also in regard to the behavior of the people under him, the legislator is not to be neutral about neutrality.

If this is correct, an important consequence about justification follows immediately. The doctrine of liberal neutrality cannot coherently be justified by any general appeal to moral skepticism – that is, by any appeal to emotivism or relativism about values as such. As Ronald Dworkin puts the point, neutrality is required, "not because there is no right and wrong of the matter, but because that is what is right."[26] Moral skepticism and moral relativism are usually understood in terms that make them applicable across the board to all value statements. If they apply to any, they apply to all. Emotivist noncognitivism, for example, is a thesis about all evaluative language: it is the thesis that the characteristically evaluative or normative aspect of a moral judgment is always to be understood in terms of the expression and evocation of attitudes, not in terms of any cognitive aspect that would make it sensible to ask whether such a judgment were true. Now, liberal neutralism is undoubtedly an evaluative and normative position: it guides legislative conduct, and it evaluates legislative outcomes or purposes. So, if emotivism, or anything like it, is correct, then liberal neutralism – as much as any *particular* conception of the good life – is to be understood simply as the expression and attempted evocation of certain emotions and attitudes about certain forms of activity. If the noncognitivist or skeptical aspect of the emotivist theory gives us a reason not to enforce particular conceptions of the good life, then it also gives us a reason not to enforce the doctrine of liberal neutrality; that is, it gives us a reason not to enforce the view that conceptions of the good life ought not to be enforced. (Another way of putting this is to say that we cannot derive an *"ought"* – not even a liberal *"ought"* – from a meta-ethical *"is."*)

I am not saying, by the way, that liberalism depends on a rejection of emotivism, nor do I want to imply that one can be a liberal only if one believes in the objectivity of liberal values. As a matter of fact, most liberal thinkers (Locke, Kant, Mill, certainly) have believed that both the rectitude of liberal principles and the superiority of certain ways of life over others *could* be objectively established. Few have tried to argue for toleration from a premise of skepticism. (So there is no support for Roberto Unger's suggestion that liberalism, from its inception, "has been in revolt against objective value." The only philosopher Unger cites to support his assertion is Hobbes; and of course the significant thing about Hobbes is that his theory became most *il*liberal on those areas of ethics where he was most skeptical, notably in relation to the details of religious faith and worship.[27]) The point to be made is simply that liberal toleration and neutrality cannot be justified on the basis of skepticism. The meta-ethical issue is quite independent of the issue about liberalism.

There is also one other argument against using moral skepticism to justify liberal neutrality. If (which I deny) but *if* moral skepticism were to give the rational legislator no reason to prefer one conception of the good life over another in his legislation, it would presumably also give the rational citizen no reason to favor one conception over another either, even in his private life or his least obtrusive dealings with others. This violates the constraint we have already noted, that a justification for liberal neutrality should explain why neutrality is a *political* not a universal requirement.

What we seem to be driving toward is that the liberal legislator has to be sensitive to certain discriminations amongst values or principles, or types of values or principles. Some types of values (for example, liberal values) he *is* prepared to uphold and enforce. Other types he is not. Some values and principles, like the doctrine of neutrality and the liberal theory of justice are the proper concern of the law; other values and principles are, to use the "brief and crude terms" of the Wolfenden report, "not the law's business."[28] But meta-ethical theories do not make such discriminations among principles or among values; their conclusions, whether they are cognitivist or noncognitivist, apply across the board. Perhaps P. F. Strawson's discussion in "Social Morality and Individual Ideal," and R. M. Hare's distinction, in *Freedom and Reason*, between moral views and "fanatical" ideals, are attempts to challenge this, and to argue for a discriminating meta-ethic; but, even if they work, I am not sure that the discriminations they come up with are the ones the liberal wants.[29]

What sorts of principles and values will the liberal legislator *not* want to be neutral between? The principle of neutrality itself is the most obvious example, but it may be worth mentioning one or two others. There may be certain goods which can reliably be said to be regarded as values by everyone, no matter what their conception of the good life. This is the category of what Rawls calls "primary goods": the examples he gives include health, bodily integrity, wealth, self-respect, negative liberty, some degree of education, and so on.[30] If there are any identifiable goods in this category (and it is, of course, controversial whether there are), the legislator may regard it as his proper function to see that they are provided, on some basis or another, to citizens. Moreover, he will have to formulate a framework of principles and institutions to govern the supply and distribution of these goods. He will have to take care that his formulation of these principles and institutions does not wrongly discriminate between the adherents of various conceptions of the good life. But if a class of these goods can be specified, the attempt to provide principles for their distribution will not in itself be a violation of the doctrine of neutrality for all that those principles fall into the general category of morality. If the importance of having some structure of principles and institutions to perform this task can be established on neutral grounds, then other values may also come into play. That structure will be constituted in part by a legal system, and if anything like Lon Fuller's theory of the "internal morality of law" is correct, then legislators will be committed to certain values, and arguably to their enforcement, simply by the nature of their task.[31]

If these are the values and principles whose enforcement and articulation in the social and legal framework the liberal might be prepared to countenance, what are the sorts of values that are being ruled *out* of consideration by the neutrality doctrine?

In John Locke's theory of toleration, the concern was chiefly about various forms of religious faith. The state was required to be neutral on the question of what constituted the conditions for individual salvation and the question of what beliefs and practices were required of us as conditions for salvation by our almighty creator. In more recent formulations the scope is much wider. According to John Stuart Mill, society should stay neutral as far as possible on the whole question of life-style in its dealings with individual citizens. In the modern formulations with which we are concerned, the term that is used is "individual conceptions of the good life" (or sometimes just "individual conceptions of the good"). By this is meant something like individual beliefs about what gives meaning to life, or what it is for a person's life to be meaningful. According to Dworkin, almost everyone has such a conception, though many are far from explicit:

Each person follows a more or less articulate conception of what gives value to life. The scholar who values a life of contemplation has such a conception; so does the television-watching, beer-drinking citizen who is fond of saying. "This is the life," though of course he has thought less about the issue and is less able to describe or defend his conception.[32]

One's conception of the good includes one's aims in life, the goals and values that guide things like career choice, as well as one's tastes and other preferences. Rawls provides a longer account which focuses on the same raw material, but gives a clearer view of the structural elements which go to make an assemblage of tastes, aims, and ideals into a *conception*.[33]

The dominant theme in modern liberalism is that an individual conception of the good life is a plan of life or a strategy for living that an individual uses as a basis for making and reflecting on his more important decisions and for scheduling his enjoyments and setbacks (to the extent that he has any control over them). His conception, moreover, defines what is to count as a setback or an enjoyment for him; and it defines for him the things that are most, and least, important in his life. The idea of a conception of the good life need not be that of a fully worked out *plan*, in the sense of a detailed career trajectory ("I will be married by 25, vice-president of the company by 35, golf champion by 40" and so on).[34] But it does seem to involve the notion that an individual is in a position to view his life so far and his prospects for the future, at any point, as a whole, so that he can ask himself not just "What have I done?" and "What will I do?", but "What in general – am I doing?" One's conception of the good life may change from time to time, though it is probably part of the idea that it not change *too* often (for example, with every particular decision or choice that one makes), otherwise it would not perform its function. By seeing our lives in this way, we view ourselves as enduring beings, not just in the sense in which our bodies endure, but in the sense that there is a reflective unity of value. We do not see ourselves as successions of agent slices, each time making decisions on the desires and impulses of the moment without any sense of larger integration between past, present, and future.

It is also important to the modern notion that a conception of the good life not be seen in purely prudential terms: it is not just the exercise of scheduling our activities so as to maximize over the course of our lives the satisfaction of the preferences we happen to find ourselves afflicted with. The development of a conception of the good is seen as a more reflective business than that. It involves a process whereby the individual stands back and distances himself, from time to time, from his occurrent desires, and determines autonomously whether these are the sorts of desires he wants to be motivated by. In *choosing* his motivations, rather than regarding them as mere afflictions, the individual associates the business of binding his life into a unity with a process of evaluation: each tries to determine a basis for his action that will be *good* by his own lights.[35]

Now, it is precisely because forming a conception of the good life involves making an *evaluation* that legislators may be tempted to interfere. For who is to say that an individual, acting on his own resources, is going to make a good evaluation? Suppose millions of individuals choose to be motivated by desires for pornography or other morally corrupt tastes. Nothing in the liberal notion of a conception of the good life rules this out. Liberal neutrality is the doctrine that legislators should not interfere with the individual process of making these evaluations; they should not even use their power to try and make it more likely that good evaluations will be made rather than bad ones. This will seem a crazy and wrongheaded doctrine, unless the liberal can show that there is something important about each individual making evaluations of this kind for his *own* life which is both independent of, and of a greater order of moral importance than, the moral worth of the particular evaluations he in fact makes. At the very least, he must show that the attempt legislatively to modify these evaluations has itself a certain dis-value which is both independent of, and of a greater order of moral concern than, the dis-value in people's autonomous decision-making that the moralistic legislator may be trying to avoid. There is not space here to discuss the various liberal views that have been put forward in this regard. But the account of why individuals making their own evaluations is positively important, or of why legislators' interference is negatively important (quite apart from the moral worth of their particular legislative aim), will be the backbone of the liberal justification of neutrality; and by the arguments we have already developed, it will determine the details of what it is to be neutral.

VI

Though we have defined it in a secular way, the notion of a conception of the good life is a very wide one. We can include under it not only an individual's tastes and life-style but also his religious faith and ethical ideals. The notion purports to offer a more comprehensive account of the proper objects of liberal solicitude than, say, John Locke's account in *A Letter Concerning Toleration*. It is notorious that in this pamphlet, Locke asserted that toleration was to be confined to the adherents of religions only (and then only *some* religions – Roman Catholicism, for example, was implicitly excluded), and not extended to atheists.[36] Whatever the force of Locke's particular argument for that exclusion, the present account makes no such stipulation. Any attempt to say what is important and unimportant in a human life counts as a conception of the good life; it does not matter particularly what the source of that view may be.

A number of critics, however, have challenged the generality of the liberal theory. As it has been described here, the notion of a conception of the good life seems to involve a very *individualistic* account of the way in which meanings are created in people's lives. The stress has been on an individual planning his *own* life, shaping it into a meaningful whole *for himself*, choosing *for himself* what is to count as a motivating consideration, and so on. Of course, the liberal is not suggesting that this is something individuals do in utter isolation from one another. He recognizes that people acquire their tastes, values, and concerns and that they articulate, reflect on, and modify their tastes, values, and concerns largely through their interaction with others. One line of criticism to which he must respond challenges him to say why the heteronomy caused by the moralistic legislator differs from the moral heteronomy that flourishes at large in human life, in the various casual or deliberate ways human beings may affect and manipulate one another's values.

But there is a more serious line of objection that goes as follows. As a matter of fact, not all the ethical views (or even religious faiths) held by individuals are individualistic conceptions of the good life of the sort I have described. Not all of them are even life plans *for an individual*, or for giving meaning and coherence to the moments of an *individual* life. (After all, as Derek Parfit has argued, why think there is anything important about the intertemporal series of experiences that, for us, constitutes an individual life, as opposed to the simultaneous *and* intertemporal series of experiences that constitutes the life of a group, say, or society?[37]) Some people regard the business of forming a coherent individual life for themselves as secondary to involvement in activities whose meaning is oriented to the coherence of a community, a congregation, or a nation. What becomes of these people on the liberal account? It looks as though their ethical views are not treated equally with individualistic ones, for their conception of what makes human life worth living may involve activities of proselytism, regimentation, and perhaps even coercion – in order to get their community into a certain shape – which the liberal theory will condemn. The difficulty is that the reasons the liberal offers for condemning activities of these kinds by these people are reasons that they will see as already nonneutral, already biased toward an individualistic account of human fulfillment.

This objection was put forward forcefully in Thomas Nagel's review of Rawls's book. The liberal principles that Rawls embraces, Nagel argues, the social choice situation that he envisages, and the classes of primary goods that he defines, are all oriented toward the pursuit of individual life plans. Far from being neutral, the liberal idea (according to Nagel) presupposes a commitment to a particular individualistic (the term used is sometimes "Protestant") conception of goodness "according to which the best that can be wished for someone is the unimpeded pursuit of his own path, provided it does not interfere with . . . others." This presupposition, he says, has the nonneutral effect of "discounting the claims of those conceptions of the good that depend heavily on the relation between one's own position and that of others."[38]

On this objection, liberal neutrality is bogus neutrality, since the liberal aims to be neutral only between conceptions of the good that are already tailored to fit an individualistic framework. Many conceptions of the good are communitarian in character: they presuppose a structure of civic, social, economic, political, and perhaps religious relations and institutions of various sorts. Since the liberal is committed not to tolerate the determination of social structures by ethical or religious ideals, he necessarily rules these communalistic conceptions out of court. (Indeed, if one wanted to be charitable, one could put Locke's exclusion of Roman Catholicism in this category.) This shows, according to the objection, that the doctrine of liberal neutrality is inconsistent and perhaps self-defeating.

I hope I have stated this objection fairly, for it is a common worry, and it is important to understand why it is unjustified. To see why it fails, we need to bear in mind two crucial propositions about neutrality. First, neutrality as a policy is never, in any context, self-justifying: one is always neutral in a particular conflict for a reason, and it is obvious that one cannot then be neutral about the force of that reason. Second, a policy of neutrality in relation to one dispute does not commit a party to a policy of neutrality in all disputes; it does not even commit him to a policy of neutrality in other disputes in which one of the belligerents in the dispute in which he is neutral is involved. (*A* may be neutral in the conflict

between B and C, but not in the conflict between B and D.)
Let us apply these propositions to the doctrine of liberal
neutrality.

It is true that the liberal has a decidedly individualistic
account of what constitutes a conception of the good life,
and of what it is to build and work with such a conception.
It is true that this account is quite restrictive, and that, for
example, it would exclude any faith that was bound up with
an effort to establish a specific system of religious law. It is
true that the liberal enjoins neutrality only as between conceptions of the good life that fit this highly restrictive spec-
ification. But so what? The liberal has not arbitrarily plucked
his account of what it is to have a conception of the good
life out of the air. He has settled on that view of a subject
matter for his concern because of the fundamental principles
and values that underlie his position. He thinks that the
shaping of individual lives by the individuals who are living
them is a good thing; and he fears for the results if that
process is distorted or usurped by externally applied coercion. On the basis of *these* concerns and *these* fears, he iden-
tifies moral views *of this individualistic sort* as those between
which legislative neutrality is required.

Now communitarian conceptions of the good – involving
as they do an urge by people to implicate themselves in the
moral governance of others – are not in that class: they are
not in the class of views among which the liberal thinks there
is good reason to be neutral. On the contrary, the very reasons that persuade him that it is a good idea to be neutral
between individualistic conceptions of the good also persuade him that it would be a bad idea to be neutral between
communitarian and individualistic conceptions of the good.

To repeat. On the basis of certain deep concerns, the liberal
has identified a certain conflict (let's call it conflict A) that he
believes the legislator should be neutral in. The fact that a
contest of a somewhat different sort can be identified – let's
call it contest B – need cause him no embarrassment. For
contest B involves views on moral, political, and religious
matters among which the liberal is not prepared to enjoin

neutrality, and among which neutrality would be enjoined, if it were enjoined at all, probably for quite different reasons. (That may be too strong: perhaps there are some justifications for liberal neutrality which would also be justifications for neutrality between communitarian and individualistic views; if so, it would be simply inconsistent to enjoin neutrality in one contest and not the other; but the inconsistency does not arise in general – it would center around the particular justification that was being considered.) One is always neutral in a particular dispute for a particular reason, and one cannot suppose in advance that that consideration gives one a reason to be neutral in a dispute that is different.

Everything therefore depends once more on the particular line of justification that the liberal wants to make out for his position. The line of argument will determine, not only, as I argued in the first part of this chapter, the conception of neutrality we adopt, but also, as I have argued in these last pages, the conception of the contest to which neutrality applies. My parting shot is to stress again the desirability, indeed the inescapability, of articulating the deep concerns that underlie the liberal position. For without that, we will never be sure what the position is, and what areas of human life it is supposed to govern.

Chapter 8

Particular values and
critical morality

I

When someone is condemned for violating the moral norms of his community, one typical response – which I shall call the liberal response – is to subject those norms to critical evaluation, and ask whether they embody just and desirable standards for the regulation of human conduct.

The controversy over the Supreme Court's decision in *Bowers v. Hardwick*[1] provides a good example. In that case, the Court upheld a Georgia statute that prohibited sodomy and dismissed the respondent's argument that he had a fundamental right to engage in acts of consensual sodomy: "[T]o claim that a right to engage in such conduct is 'deeply rooted in this Nation's history or tradition' . . . is, at best, facetious."[2] The liberal argument for the respondent's position was that whether such a right is fundamental depends not on its historical roots, but on its importance for the fulfillment of basic human needs. Homosexual intimacy can be classed alongside other intimate activities as part of the sphere of autonomy necessary for the flourishing of human personality. Because people need to be able to relate to one another intimately and sexually, and because not everyone finds fulfillment in the same rigid categories of gender and sex, the law ought to be as tolerant as possible in this area, at least where consenting adults are involved and no one is suffering any harm.[3]

Liberals need not deny that the condemnation of homosexual activity represents a moral consensus in the community. But they insist that a community consensus is not self-validating. To validate it, one must see whether it measures up to abstract principles drawn out of the very idea of individual fulfillment and the respect people owe to one another. These principles are arrived at and formulated in a way that is supposed to be applicable to *any* society, applicable to the interaction of *any* beings like ourselves. If the communal consensus measures up to these principles, then it is considered just. But if it does not, the liberal test condemns the norms and the community that embodies them as oppressive and inhumane.

In recent years, this approach has elicited a series of responses that have become known under the general heading of communitarianism. A number of writers have argued that the standards against which liberals measure the societal norms place too much stress on individual rights, individual fulfillment, and individual respect, and too little emphasis on the social conditions that make individuality possible, and on communal concerns taken as important in their own right.[4]

Some communitarian writers have developed an even more radical critique. They have argued that there is something fundamentally misconceived about measuring the moral culture of a particular community against *any* set of abstract standards, whether those standards ascribe importance to communal values or not. The fissure in modern social thought, they say, is not merely between individualist values and communitarian ones; it is between particularity and abstraction – the concrete reality of the norms of a given society and the abstract principles with which liberals purport to evaluate them.[5]

Liberals pride themselves on being able to discern, amidst the variety of different ways in which humans live in this world, a number of basic needs, interests, vulnerabilities, and capacities that each of us possesses – features that are common points of concern, part of our *common* humanity, part of what any society should address. They say, for example, that we can all feel pain, develop affection, form families, make plans, fear and suffer loss, speculate about God, discipline ourselves, hold views, join together in clubs and associations, have fun, experience beauty, and so on. On the basis of some such list, liberals purport to give a general account of what a society must be like if it is to accommodate the sorts of beings we are.[6] By contrast, communitarians, such as Alasdair MacIntyre, stress the uniqueness and distinctiveness of our situation in a particular social structure:

> I am someone's son or daughter, someone else's cousin or uncle; I am a citizen of this or that city, a member of this or that guild or profession; I belong to this clan, that tribe, this nation. . . . As such, I inherit from the past of my family, my city, my tribe, my nation, a variety of debts, inheritances, rightful expectations and obligations. These constitute the given of my life, my moral starting point. This is in part what gives my life its own moral particularity.[7]

Liberals, of course, have never denied that *some* features of a person's moral life are distinctive in this way, depending on his particular history and on the particular life he has led. People have *special* rights (and duties) arising out of promises, acquisitions, roles, and relationships, as well as the *general* ones we call human rights (and the duties correlative to those): the promises that have been made to me are not the ones that have been made to you, and so our moral situations differ to that extent. But for liberals the potential for creating this particularity is embedded in our general human nature – for example, our capacity for making particular promises is bound up with our autonomy, as an overarching and universal human interest – whereas the suggestion in MacIntyre's account is that our natures may be, so to speak, particular and special all the way down. According to this view, there may be nothing more to be said about human nature, for the purposes of social and political evaluation, than that the nature and interests of each person are constituted by the concrete social setting in which he lives.

Michael Sandel has proposed something similar in his critique of modern theories of autonomy and commitment. According to Sandel, when liberals write about the particular commitments and relationships that people may have, they suggest that each person is capable of standing apart from the things in which he is involved. They identify the self with the entity that chooses them and can give them up if it wants, rather than with the content of what has been chosen.

> One consequence of this distance is to put the self beyond the reach of experience, to make it invulnerable, to fix its identity once and for all. No commitment could grip me so deeply that I could not understand myself without it. No transformation of life purposes and plans could be so unsettling as to disrupt the contours of my identity. No project could be so essential that turning away from it would call into question the person I am.[8]

Liberals insist, he complains, that society must be made safe for a self that is autonomous in this sense: a self not enriched by any of the constitutive commitments that make someone the particular person he is. The liberal view, he says, is that social norms are to be evaluated for their effect on this independent self, rather than taken in themselves to be part of the essence of the persons who have grown up and nurtured their identities within the social framework that they define.

According to Sandel, the "thin-ness" of this approach is ultimately self-refuting. Liberals imagine that they are vindicating the claims of moral agency, but, to the extent that moral agency is bound up with character and reflection, they are taking away the ground that it rests on.

> To imagine a person incapable of constitutive attachments . . . is not to conceive an ideally free and rational agent, but to imagine a person wholly without character, without moral depth. For to have character is to know that I move in a history I neither summon nor command, which carries consequences none the less for my choices and conduct.[9]

171

In the end, Sandel argues, the only agency in the world is particular, situated agency, and the only people for us to respect in society are particular situated people. We cannot judge laws and mores in the abstract by analyzing how they affect human interests considered independently of the societies that define them:

> [W]e cannot regard ourselves as independent in this way without great cost to those loyalties and convictions whose moral force consists partly in the fact that living by them is inseparable from understanding ourselves as the particular persons we are – as members of this family or community or nation or people, as bearers of this history, as sons and daughters of that revolution, as citizens of this republic. Allegiances such as these are more than values I happen to have or aims I "espouse at any given time." They go beyond the obligations I voluntarily incur and the "natural duties" I owe to human beings as such. They allow that to some I owe more than justice requires or even permits, not by reason of agreements I have made but instead in virtue of those more or less enduring attachments and commitments which taken together partly define the person I am.[10]

Thus, communitarians of this persuasion are not content with the abstract propositions that man is a social animal, and that communal bonds have an importance equal to or greater than the values associated with individuality. They argue also that the culture, language, traditions, and mores of each community make a *particular* claim on the allegiance of the members of that community, a claim that goes to those members' identities and cannot be comprehended purely in terms of the *general* functions that tradition and mores serve in the constitution of human life.

II

I shall begin my discussion of this form of communitarianism by employing a concept that philosophers have used to categorize different types of moral principles. This is the concept of *agent-relativity*.

A principle is agent-relative if it assigns different goals or aims to different agents; a principle is agent-neutral if it assigns exactly the same goal to different agents.[11] A simple example of agent-relativity is the principle of parental concern – the idea that parents should bear a special concern for their own children. The general principle is similar for all parents, but the specific object is different for each set. This couple is to be concerned with this child, that couple with that child, and so on. Parental concern is to be distinguished in this regard from another principle with which it coexists: the more diffuse principle that requires us all to be concerned for the well-being of children generally. This latter principle requires each of us to be concerned about the welfare of every child. As such, it is agent-neutral, because it gives each agent exactly the same object. Egoism provides another example of an agent-relative theory. Although it can be universalized as a theory for everyone ("Everyone ought to pursue his own self-interest"), it nevertheless gives each agent a substantively different goal (X's goal is X's interest, Y's goal is Y's interest, and so on). It is therefore distinct from the particularist egoism of the megalomaniac ("Everyone ought to pursue my interest"), and from altruistic utilitarianism ("Everyone ought to pursue the interests of all"), both of which are agent neutral.

It is important to recognize that not all agent-relative principles are the same in their logical character. There is an interesting distinction between those that are normative from the point of view of others and those that are not. Although the principle of parental concern instructs each parent to look out for his own child rather than the children of others, it still makes sense for one set of parents to be concerned about and to condemn another's dereliction of this duty. By contrast, a principle such as egoism – though it can be formulated universally – looks odd if it is made the object of interpersonal concern. There is something incongruous about one scrupulous egoist condemning someone else for not being sufficiently egoistic.[12] If egoism is indeed a duty, it is as though the duty itself, and not just its object, is the special and private concern of each agent.

What is *this* distinction based on? A couple of possibilities spring to mind. First, some agent-relative principles and concerns are located against a background of more diffuse concerns which are agent-neutral. For example, the principle of parental concern is backed up by (perhaps even largely derived from) the general concern for children that I mentioned earlier. Our fundamental purpose is the welfare of all children; but we think this is best promoted if parents look after their own. This agent-neutral background then explains why one set of parents may properly be concerned about the children of other parents, and about other parents' dereliction of the (agent-relative) duty that they owe their children. By contrast, other agent-relative principles stand alone without a background of diffuse concerns. Though egoism is sometimes defended against a utilitarian background in a sort of "invisible hand" way, usually it stands by itself as a fundamental position, with nothing to provide any foothold for one egoist to commend the egoism or condemn the selflessness of another.

Second, some agent-relative concerns are competitive whereas others are not, or not to the same degree. To the extent that individuals are locked into some sort of Hobbesian struggle, it would be self-defeating for one egoist to commend egoism to another. But when one's own goals do not compete with those of others, one can coherently be morally concerned about others following the aims assigned to them. That is usually the case with parental concern. Except where parents are competing for, say, scarce educational places for their children, their concerns are not usually inimical to one another, and so one parent's commendation of parental solicitude to another makes a lot more sense.

When agent-relative concerns are competitive (and sometimes even when they are not), there is a certain incongruity about the agent's characterizing his concern in universalized terms. When asked what he is doing, the egoist is unlikely to say, "I am following the universal principle that requires everyone to pursue his own self-interest." This seems too much like an outsider's description of what he is doing, rather than a description that captures it for him. The same may even be true of parental concern. There is something cold about a parent saying, of his concern for his child, that he is following the universal principle that requires each parent to look after his own children. A better way of capturing how it feels for him would be to say that he is simply attending to Sam's needs or whatever. It seems characteristic of many agent-relative concerns that when they are formulated in terms appropriate to a universalized principle, they lose something of the flavor of the agent's internal point of view. This, as we shall see, is quite important.

I want to use this philosophical apparatus to examine the view that I mentioned at the beginning of the chapter, about the particularity of communal bonds and communal mores. It is fairly clear that that view has a strong scent of agent-relativity about it (if we regard each community, for the time being, as an agent). By contrast with the agent-neutrality of liberalism, communal particularity assigns different aims to different communities. This community is rightly and properly concerned with its own distinctive moral heritage; that community with a moral heritage of *its* own that may differ from the first; and so on.

The question I want to explore, and on which my critique of this aspect of communitarianism will be based, is whether this is the kind of agent-relative concern that is capable of being normative from an outsider's point of view. I suspect that it is not, and I want to take that as a basis for suggesting that it is odd to say, from inside a community, "These are our norms and that is the reason why we are enforcing them." Just as the parent's point of view is better captured by saying, "This is Sam and that's why I'm concerned," than by saying, "I am a parent, and this is my child," so the internal point of view of a community is better captured by saying, "This is sodomy (or whatever) and sodomy is wrong," than by saying, "This is the norm that happens to be distinctive of our community." Moreover, if, in a culture like ours, taking a norm seriously means trying as hard as we can to see whether or not it is really right, then the communitarian attack on liberal evaluation starts to seem more like a betrayal of our heritage than a celebration of its particularity. That is what I shall argue.

III

I want to illustrate these points with three examples of values and concerns associated with communal particularity: (1) the survival of a particular language; (2) the particularity of patriotic obligations; and (3) the authority and enforcement of a particular set of communal norms or mores. Obviously, the third of these will be the main focus of our interest.

Language

Consider first the survival of a language that is on the point of dying out. Welsh will do as an example: it is a language struggling to maintain its position in Wales against the overwhelming competition of English, the language of authority and convenience in the United Kingdom at large.

It is obvious that every community – Wales as much as any other – needs a language, and preferably one that is rich enough to express the variety and depth of the ideas that are involved in a modern society and in its science, ethics, economy, culture, literature, and history. That much can be stated at the level of an abstract proposition. The need, understood in this way, could be filled by *any* language which satisfied those conditions and which was fully understood by the members of the society. English could certainly serve that purpose in Wales, except for the handful of native speakers of Welsh who are not fully bilingual. Indeed it would probably serve better. It is a richer language with a much larger vocabulary and expressive power. It makes available a literature orders of magnitude greater than that available in Welsh, it enables the people of Wales to interact freely and fully with their fellow citizens in the United Kingdom, and it offers them a much better prospect of being understood abroad.

So the case for preserving the *Welsh* language cannot be stated in terms of the abstract need which every community has for a language. It has to be stated in terms which refer to the fact that *this* language is special to *this* community, that it is part of the historic and cultural identity that the members of the community share and that makes them what they are. Understood in this way, it is not something which is "fungible," that is, fully replaceable by any functional equivalent, by any other language that would facilitate communication and social interaction as well.

Notice some points about this example. First consider what I referred to as the "abstract need" that each society has for a language. In fact there is no simple opposition between "abstract" and "particular" here. Though it is true, as a universal proposition, that every society needs *a language* that will satisfy functions A, B, and C, of course what is the case is that every society needs some language in particular and not merely the abstract idea of a language. So the special point about particularity in the case of the preservation of Welsh has got to be more than that: it has got to be, not only that Wales needs some language in particular, but that it needs *this language* in particular and that no other particular language will do even if it satisfies functions A, B, and C.

Second, though we have contrasted the abstract need for a language with the particular relation of Welsh to Wales, the claim we are making about the latter relation is nevertheless one that can be stated in abstract and universalized terms. After all, our point is not only about the importance of Welsh to Wales; it suggests also that Gaelic may have exactly the same importance to the people of the Scottish Highlands, that French has a similar importance for *Québecois* society and so on. Though the relation of a particular language to a particular people is special, irreducible, and non-fungible, it may nevertheless be a type of relation that other languages have to other peoples. Indeed something like this has to be the case, or else the particular claim that the Welsh were making would be quite unintelligible to outsiders. We can state this importance in a general way, in the words of Herder: "Has a nation anything more precious than the language of its fathers? In it dwell its entire world of tradition, history, religion and principles of existence; its whole heart and soul."[13] Though his point is about *a* nation (in the sense of *any* nation), it is about the intimate one-on-one relation of each particular nation to its own particular heritage.

Third, we must distinguish this claim about the specialness of a particular language to a particular community from a claim about the general importance of sustaining linguistic variety in the world and of preserving as many living specimens of language as we can. The latter is an outsider's claim. It is the claim, for example, of a linguistic scholar who regrets the demise of Latin even though he has never been to Rome, or sheds tears over the disappearance of Cornish despite the fact that he has no roots of his own in Cornwall. It is a claim comparable to that of the ecologist who is concerned about the preservation of species as such, and who tells us every year how many different types of moths have died out, or how many fewer species of birds there are, due to man's depredation of the environment. Behind both claims – the linguist's and the ecologist's – is the idea that the world is a poorer place (less colorful, less interesting, less diverse) when some type of thing dies out. That is probably true, but it does not capture the special concern of the insider about the particularity of his *own* language and culture.

The Welsh speaker worried about the imminent demise of his native tongue is not necessarily concerned for linguistic diversity at large in the world, and certainly his concern would not be satisfied if all Welsh school children were taught Latin instead. He cherishes the Welsh language because *it* is his heritage, not because of the richness or poverty of some taxonomic concern.

Clearly, then, the concern of a people for the survival of their own language is an "agent-relative" concern, in the sense we have defined. Though the Welsh case is matched by a similar case for Gaelic and another similar concern in the case of the *Québecois*, still the proposition that universalizes these relations makes it clear that each community focuses on a different object. Though community *X*'s concern for language *A* is similar to community *Y*'s concern for language *B*, it is *A* and not *B* (and not both) that *X* is concerned with, and *B* and not *A* (and not both) that is the focus of *Y*'s concern.

Certainly, *some* of the concerns about language that we have mentioned are agent-neutral. The concern that every society should have a language is a general and neutral concern, which might even be satisfied by giving each society the same language (English or whatever). The linguist's concern for the diversity of man's linguistic heritage is agent neutral as well. It gives the Welsh linguist the same aim as the English linguist: namely, that as many living specimens of language as possible should survive. Such concerns therefore are different in kind from the particular concern the Welsh have for their own native tongue.

It is true that a concern about one's own language is often made the basis of a claim against outsiders. The people of Wales not only appeal to each other to keep Welsh alive, they appeal also to the British government to help them in that endeavor. This seems to detract from the agent-relative aspect; after all, the important thing about an agent-relative principle is that the goals assigned to *me* are not any business of *yours*, and vice versa. But the claim is often a negative one ("Stop messing with our culture") rather than a claim for positive assistance. Or if it is a claim for positive assistance and facilitation, it is a claim made to the government not as an outsider but as an entity that must regard itself as in part a representative of distinctive Welsh interests. To that extent, the agent-relative character of the concern remains.

What about the distinction we drew in Section II, between agent-relative concerns that are normative from the point of view of outsiders and those that are not? Are the Welsh likely to be concerned if the Scots do not preserve Gaelic or if the

179

Québecois become lazy about their French? It seems unlikely that they would, except to the extent that their concern was based on the linguist's ideal of diversity. The Welsh of course are in a position to understand something of what it feels like for other peoples clinging to their respective traditions, and so it will be easy for them to empathize. But they are likely to say that if other peoples do not want to preserve their own heritage then that is a matter for them.

Patriotism

A second example that I want to use to develop the theme of particularity is patriotism. Patriotism is the love, devotion, and allegiance that people are supposed to bear to their own country; it is supposed to provide a moral basis for a willingness to stand up for one's country, a willingness to defend it, and in the last resort a willingness even to lay down one's life for its sake.

In a lecture given in 1984, Alasdair MacIntyre attempted to defend the thesis that patriotism is a moral virtue, against what he took to be the critique of liberal philosophy, that patriotism engenders an unhealthy indifference to the requirements of international justice, a chauvinistic repudiation of the universal norms of morality, and a dangerous blindness to the faults of one's own nation – the blindness connoted in the hackneyed phrase, "My country, right or wrong."[14]

The difficulty arises, MacIntyre argued, from the fact that the true patriot does not bear allegiance to his country because of something independently attractive about the norms and ideals that it stands for: the American patriot does not stand by the United States just because of its commitment to constitutional democracy, nor does the French patriot stand by his country because of its commitment to *civilisation*. If those ideals were the sole basis of allegiance, their partisans would be willing to support them wherever they were found and to abandon any particular allegiance whenever they were disserved. Instead, the true patriot stands by his country first and foremost because it is his country, and it is only in the light of this prior and particular allegiance that he sees any virtues (or for that matter any vices) that it has. The virtues of his fatherland are for him matters of particular pride, and its vices – if they can be recognized as such – are a matter for guilt and shame rather than an occasion for exercising the easy mobility of the liberal conscience. As MacIntyre put it, "The particularity of the relationship is essential and in-eliminable." The virtue of a person standing up for *this* country rather than *that* is determined by what the liberal would regard as the arbitrary accident of his birth:

> [P]atriotism requires me to exhibit peculiar devotion to my nation and you to yours. It requires me to regard such contingent social facts as where I was born and what government ruled over that place at that time, who my parents were, who my great-great-grandparents were and so on, as deciding for me the question of what virtuous action is – at least insofar as it is the virtue of patriotism which is in question.[15]

If it is understood in this way, patriotism has the feature of agent-relativity that we talked about earlier. Though we may state it as a universal principle – "Each person owes patriotic devotion to his fatherland" – it is a principle which generates concretely different requirements for different agents, depending, obviously, on what their fatherland is. Again the clash with liberal morality is the clash between an agent-relative and an agent-neutral theory: each patriot is necessarily a partisan of his own country's claims, whereas the liberal ideal requires of each of us loyalty to the same substantial principles of international morality and justice.

But the example of patriotism also illustrates the additional complication that we have noticed in the idea of agent-relative concern: how should we view one patriot's attitude toward the patriotism or lack of patriotism of another?

If we speak of a universal (albeit agent-relative) principle of patriotism, we seem to have it in mind that Germans can recognize, respect, and even encourage in the French the latter's devotion to France, just as the French can recognize, respect, and encourage Germans' devotion to *their* nation. On this rather chivalric model, French soldiers may even criticize Germans who fail to stand against France when the two countries are at war (in roughly the spirit in which one parent may criticize another for failing to look after his children).

But though that model has its attractions – mutual respect among enemies, for example – it can sometimes seem contrived and artificial. A psychologically more realistic model may have the French soldiers feeling the normative force of patriotism so far as their own allegiance to France is concerned, but feeling no disposition whatever to commend or encourage an analogous allegiance on the part of a foreigner, or to condemn unpatriotic foreigners when they fail to take their place in the opposite trenches. On this more chauvinistic model, it is as though the virtue, the duty, or the very normativeness of patriotism is made agent-relative, not merely its object.

On the chivalric model, we all recognize, for ourselves and our enemies, the force of the norm of devotion to one's own country, and we go our separate ways only as each of us finds out what that country is. But on the chauvinistic model, each of us feels the normativity of patriotism as essentially bound up with what is in fact its proper object for us. Patriotism turns out to be a different phenomenon for the Germans than it is for the French: for the former it is devotion-to-Germany, rather than devotion-to-one's-country (which just happens to be Germany), and for the latter it is devotion-to-France. I do not mean that a neutral observer would fail to see the similarity; I mean that in a sense you have to be neutral or take the stance of an outsider to grasp the analogy. From the internal point of view, one German would say of another that he had not grasped the particularity of patriotism as it applied to him if he thought of it simply as the analogue for his own case of what the Frenchman owes to France.

What then is different between patriotism and parental

devotion? For the latter case, we can make perfect sense of one parent commending another's devotion to his children, or criticizing another parent who fails to look after his family. As I suggested earlier, part of the answer must lie in the fact that patriotism normally operates in the context of international competition (or, of course, even war) whereas parenthood does not. It is part of the point of patriotism to stand up for one's country *against other countries,* whereas it is not part of the point of the agent-relativity of parenthood that one stand up for one's children *against* others.[16] That competitive context (not to mention the fact that true patriots are supposed to be slaughtering their putative analogues on the other side) gives the chauvinistic model more force. It explains why patriotism might be inculcated in a way that made its normativity seem special for the inhabitants of each country, rather than in a way that presented their allegiance as simply a counterpart of the allegiance of their enemies.

Community Standards

Different communities require different things of their members in the way of civility, decency, and morality. One community may permit polygamy, another may require monogamy. One may have a practice of strictly excluding fathers from the birth of their children, while another may encourage their participation and frown if they are absent. One society may condemn homosexuality as wicked and depraved, while another may be open to it as a valid type of human relationship. Together such norms will constitute the practices and the way of life that make each community the distinctive social entity that it is.

From time to time, a moral rule in a given community may be called into question. Some members may ask whether this is a good rule to have, or they may disagree about the exact way in which it should be enforced. For example, to the extent that there is a moral rule against homosexual intercourse in parts of the United States, those whose behavior it condemns and whose lives it makes unbearable may complain that it is unjust and inhumane. Even if they are unsuccessful in that, they may raise further questions about the mode of its enforcement, asking whether it is appropriate for such a norm to be embodied in law, for example, or permitted as a legitimate basis for discrimination in housing and employment.

When questions like these are raised, one possible response (which communitarian theorists seem to find increasingly attractive, at least in the abstract) is to say, "Of course this norm should be upheld, for it is part of what makes us the particular community we are." If the person questioning the norm is so impertinent as to plead for tolerance, the communitarian retort is blunt:

> Only a thoroughly demoralized community can tolerate everything. . . . A community without boundaries is without shape or identity; if pursued with single-minded determination, tolerance is incompatible with the very possibility of a community. For this reason tolerance as an ideal is incomplete. If community life is to survive, on either the local or national level, tolerance must at some point or another come to an end.[17]

On this approach, abandoning a communal norm because it offends some abstract principle of autonomy is like cutting off a part of our identity. We should not be persuaded to forsake our communal heritage on the basis of liberal theories of rights and justice that stand apart from the distinctive particularity of our communal way of life.[18]

This sort of response is my third illustration of communal particularity. Like the cases of linguistic heritage and patriotic devotion, the present approach seems to celebrate something as valuable and important *for us* (for our community in particular) rather than as something valuable and important for all communities across the board. The importance it accords to a given set of mores and to the way they constitute our communal identity is once more agent-relative, relative that is to the identity of the members of this particular community rather than to the abstract idea of community as such. We do not expect every society to enforce and uphold our norms; we know that the rules are different elsewhere. But we cherish and support our own because they make us who we are.

As with the other examples, it seems possible at first sight to universalize this agent-relativity. Instead of saying simply, "*These* norms make *us* who we are," we can say, "The distinctive norms of *any* community make it what it is," and we ought to be able to understand any society wanting to protect itself in this way. But the point I made earlier about patriotism applies even more clearly here. An outsider such as an anthropologist may be able to assert the universalized proposition, but it may be very difficult for it to be embraced *within* the membership of a given community (call it "community *A*"). Certainly it seems unlikely that the universal proposition could have any normative force inside community *A*, allowing the members of *A* to commend and encourage people in community *B* for remaining faithful to the (different and contrary) mores of *B*, or to criticize them for deviations from the mores of *B*. Inasmuch as a given set of moral rules constitutes the distinctive character of community *A*, it is presumably part of that communal identity to take those rules as seriously as possible, and not to entertain them simply as "something we happen to do around here."

Thus, suppose community *A* condemns homosexuality as wicked and depraved whereas community *B* does not. The members of *A* may know this about *B*, but the very norms that make them who they are will lead them either to condemn or, at the very least, to be bewildered and bemused by the contrary attitudes of that other society. They will not view *B*'s fidelity to its different norms as one parent views the discharge of parental duties by another. They will not say to themselves, "Oh good, community *B* is remaining faithful to its identity as we are to ours." As with my chauvinistic model of patriotism, the apparatus of approval and condemnation will be bound up with the contents of each moral code. Whereas in the parenting case it is merely the objects of the normative attitudes that are agent-relative, here it is the normative attitudes themselves.

The point needs to be qualified a little, but only in a way that makes its force even clearer. In a given community there may be *some* norms that *are* understood by its members as nothing much more than "the way we happen to do things around here." The norms for beginning and ending letters may be an example: the fact that we begin with "Dear John" rather than "John:" and sign off with "Yours sincerely" rather than "Good-bye for now." Other societies do these things in different styles and it is not a difference we take particularly seriously (indeed, it is part of our identity that we do not take such things especially seriously). The norms of letter writing serve their purpose even though those whose behavior they govern have thoroughly internalized the point that they are simply matters of convention. So we are in a position to think it perfectly appropriate for members of some other community to end their letters with exclamations like "Allah be praised!" or optatives like "May your loins be fruitful!" even though we would never do the same.

But the norms we treat like that are to be contrasted with others we do not treat in this way. Though we recognize that other societies have attitudes toward race, for example, that are different from ours, we do not in any sense endorse their practice of their norms on that matter, nor do we think their racism "appropriate for them." The very considerations that make us condemn racism around here also commit us to its condemnation in other societies.

Partly this is a matter of how seriously we take the norm of ours that is in question. Partly it is also a matter of how that norm is understood. A community like the United States cannot found itself on something it takes to be a "self-evident" truth – "that all men are created equal" – and then go on to say glibly, "But that's just what we happen to think around here; different attitudes toward equality are distinctive of and valid for different societies." A person who says anything like that from within our society betrays our norms (and hence our communal identity) in at least two ways. He does not keep faith with the *content* of our norm – namely, that it is *all men* (not simply all men who happen to live around here) who are said to have been created equal. Though the norm is our norm and distinctive of our community, it implicitly condemns racism in South Africa and China, and caste systems in England and India. Anyone who fails to grasp that doesn't understand *our norm*: he doesn't understand the significance of the word "all" or, for that matter, the implied reference to a Creator.

Moreover, the attitude that is tolerant of the differing practices of other communities on this point misses our sense that human equality is utterly basic to moral behavior. The distinctive thought of our community is predicated on the idea that one cannot go anywhere in serious moral thought except on the basis of some such assumption about the fundamental equality of human worth. We are aware that some other societies do not agree with this, but we cannot simply say, "That's appropriate for them" without appearing halfhearted about the status or the epistemology of our own shared commitments.

The same is true of many other distinctive norms. Take for example, the "norm" relied on by the majority in *Bowers v. Hardwick*. If there is a consensus condemning homosexuality in the United States, it is predicated on some thought about what is "natural" and "unnatural" in human relations and the use of one's body. One simply cannot have *those thoughts* and still believe that homosexuality is perfectly appropriate for a society whose norms permit it or that the ambit of our condemnation is limited by the boundaries of those who share the views of human nature that we have.

In my earlier discussion of patriotism, I suggested that what fueled the chauvinistic (as opposed to the chivalric) model was that patriotism was an inherently competitive virtue. I think something analogous goes on in the case of communal mores. As we develop our norms and practices, we do not say simply to one another, "Do this" and "Don't do that." We say things like, "This is the best way to live a human life" and "That is unnatural." In so doing, we make claims that leave no room for any other position. It is as though there were a competition to find out the best way of living life in which the mores of various communities were rivals and competitors. Each community puts forward a set of answers, and none can recognize even the local validity of the others' claims without detracting from the force and the confidence of its own.

Interestingly, these considerations distinguish both patriotism and communal morals from the language case. Though each society cherishes its own language, the claims that are made for any one language are not usually competitive with those made by any other. The French do not maintain that "*chien*" is a better word for dogs than the German "*hund.*" It is recognized on all sides that languages are simply conventional and that recognition does not at all subvert or undermine the quality of anyone's particular affection for the language of her people. But in morality, conventionalism does have that subversive implication for most of our serious positions. Our communal mores are claims we make about what is really right and really wrong on sex, justice, equality, and so forth, and their nature is to leave no room for the thought that they are merely conventional, and that contrary claims may be also right for those who make them.

None of this shows that our local moralities are "correct" in making the grandiose and universal claims that they do. But that they make such claims is beyond dispute. It is simply not possible to understand (for example) Christian ethics, Kantian ethics, or the morality of human rights, unless one sees that they are presented as statements of what is good and right for people *everywhere.*[19] Moreover, the communitarian is not in a position to criticize these ethics for their universalism or imperialism. If these ethics characterize our community then, according to the communitarian, there is no point of view from which we can criticize either their content or their pretensions. Particularity – including the particularity of our moral imperialism – is all there is.

IV

The conclusion for which I have argued so far may seem to be exactly the one that the communitarian wants to reach. If the members of a given community are too immersed in their own practices to endorse or approve the differing practices of other communities, then it looks as though the cosmopolitanism of liberal morality is simply doomed, to say nothing of its fabled principles of toleration and moral neutrality. There is no getting outside our most cherished moral positions, no "Archimedean point" from which they may be evaluated *ab extra* and approved, reformed, or discarded.[20] There is only our community, its mores, and we, the people whom they constitute.

We must be careful, however, how we interpret this conclusion. Communitarians seem to think it appropriate within our society to say of some widely accepted norm, "This is one of the norms that gives our community its distinctive character, and that is why it is appropriate for us to enforce it." But to describe a norm in this spirit is already to take an attitude toward it that is somewhat different from that of a person who actually subscribes to it. To subscribe to a norm like "Sodomy is wicked," is to be convinced of the wickedness of sodomy. To subscribe to a norm like "Racism is wrong," is to sincerely and wholeheartedly condemn racism. By contrast, describing the norm in terms of the contribution it makes to our communal identity means abandoning that essentially moralistic stance, and taking up a standpoint that is more external, more like the standpoint of an anthropologist who wants to know what distinguishes one community from another. It is to describe what we are doing in enforcing our norms in a way that brings out what it has in common with what a different community is doing in enforcing *its* norms. That already involves a substantial abstraction from the reality of what our most serious moral commitments mean to us.

The point can be elaborated in relation to a couple of arguments in recent political philosophy. In his book *Spheres of Justice*, Michael Walzer has argued that justice is a matter, for each society, of its being true to the social meanings that shape its institutions, its practices, and its understanding of the world:

> There are an infinite number of possible lives, shaped by an infinite number of possible cultures, religions, political arrangements, geographical conditions, and so on. A given society is just if its substantive life is lived in a certain way – that is, in a way faithful to the shared understandings of the members.... We are (all of us) culture-producing creatures; we make and inhabit meaningful worlds. Since there is no way to rank and order these worlds with regard to their understanding of social goods, we do justice to actual men and women by respecting their particular creations.... Justice is rooted in the distinct understandings of places, honors, jobs, things of all sorts, that constitute a shared way of life. To override those understandings is (always) to act unjustly.[21]

If this is true, it does not mean that we must go around saying to one another in society, "This is what this good or that practice means in our community, and so this is what justice must be based on." To say that is to describe from the outside, rather than participate in, the social understandings in question. The truth in Walzer's position must not preclude our making serious and categorical claims about what is just and what is unjust in relation to some good or practice. It is precisely in making such claims that we evince our subscription to the meanings that the good or practice has for us. In making the claim, we are *living* it.

The same point helps us see what has been going on in John Rawls's recent characterization of his own work on justice. When *A Theory of Justice* was first published it appeared to be making categorical claims about what was just or unjust in the way of social arrangements for *any* society. It was not qualified by any claim such as, "This is simply what we happen to think around here." The categorical tone seemed present from the opening lines of Rawls's book:

Justice is the first virtue of social institutions, as truth is of systems of thought. A theory however elegant and economical must be rejected or revised if it is untrue; likewise laws and institutions no matter how efficient and well-arranged must be reformed or abolished if they are unjust.[22]

And Rawls went on immediately to imply that any society, under modern conditions, should stand condemned if it (for example) subordinated liberty to economic prosperity or if it sacrificed the interests of some for the sake of the greater utility of others. He seemed to be arguing, in other words, about ideals that could be applied as universal standards of criticism. In more recent reflection, however, Rawls seems to say that the task of a theory of justice is more modest:

What justifies a conception of justice is not its being true to an order antecedent to and given to us, but its congruence with our deeper understanding of ourselves and our aspirations, and our realization that, given our history and the traditions embedded in our public life, it is the most reasonable doctrine for us.[23]

This makes it sound as though a conception of justice is expected only to capture the particularity of American (or perhaps Western) thought and practice, not to make any transcendent or overarching claim.

Much of the tension between these two approaches can be resolved by distinguishing the internal from the external point of view. From an external point of view, the priority of liberty and the rejection of utilitarian sacrifices can be seen as nothing but a part of our particular history and traditions. But from the internal point of view of those of us who have this history and share these traditions, the categorical tone of *A Theory of Justice* is entirely appropriate. To argue in that manner is precisely what it is to be faithful to our shared understandings. Paradoxically, we cannot keep this faith by saying out loud all the time that that is what we are doing.

The point is similar to one that has been made in recent discussions in meta-ethics. According to an emotivist, making a moral judgment is simply expressing one's emotions; a moral judgment does not have the character of a truth claim, on this account. But expressing one's emotions on some issue is different from *saying* one is expressing one's emotions on that issue. The latter describes what is going on from an external point of view, but it does not capture the content of what is being thought, felt, and said by the person doing the "emoting."[24]

By the same token, although in condemning racism or exploitation we are expressing and participating in the shared culture of our community, we are not taking the existence of that culture as our reason or as a basis for our condemnation. The reason why things like racism and exploitation are wrong, we say, is the indignity they offer to the human person. Though no doubt we would think differently had we been brought up somewhere else, it is no part of what we think on these matters that they should properly be sensitive to such differences.

In the end, the point is just an application of the Wittgensteinian dictum, "What *can* be shown, *cannot* be said."[25] In upholding social mores, we show the particularity of our culture, just as in expounding a moral view we show the emotions that we are expressing. The moral view that we are expressing gets muddled or distorted if what we say, as we expound it, is that it is an expression of our emotions. And likewise, the particular identity of our community on moral matters is obscured or betrayed, if we say that preserving that particularity is what we are doing as we uphold our social norms.

v

There is one last step to make in the argument. I have said that a communitarian betrays rather than participates in our communal identity by taking that particular identity as itself a ground for moral or political action. By asking what is really right and really wrong, the liberal is closer to participating in the spirit of our traditions than the communitarian who says that what matters to us is nothing more than that *these* happen to be *our* traditions.

So far I have left unexamined the question of the homogeneity of these mores that are said to be *ours*. If there are widely shared values and understandings in our culture, then we can respect that consensus (if that is what we want to do) only by subscribing to them and immersing ourselves in them, and not by stepping outside them and talking about their particularity. But is there such a consensus? What is this community and who is this "we" we keep talking about? Answers to these questions quickly indicate that the liberal approach is even closer than the communitarian to the spirit of such shared understandings as we have.

The Problem of Defining "Community"

When we speak of the moral norms of a community, it is tempting to think of a relatively simple moral consensus, one that forms a homogeneous, enduring, uncontroversial, and relatively unreflective basis for our lives, culture, and traditions. But there can be no doubt that such an image is unrealistic, at least for a community in the modern world. There is nothing that we can call the morality of a modern community that does not exhibit features like change, diversity, controversy, and self-consciousness. Any theory built on the particularity of our traditions or those of any other existing society must take account of that.

To the extent that they yearn for a body of mores that is more stable and homogeneous than this, communitarians are simply indulging in fantasy or nostalgia, and they are certainly not keeping faith with the way of life that we happen to share around here. The wishful thinking of modern communitarianism is something that a number of critics have noticed:

> Words like fraternity, belonging and community are so soaked with nostalgia and utopianism that they are nearly useless as guides to the real possibilities of solidarity in modern society.

Modern life has changed the possibilities of civic solidarity, and our language stumbles behind like an overburdened porter with a mountain of old cases. . . . Our task is to find a language for our need for belonging which is not just a way of expressing nostalgia, fear and estrangement from modernity. Our political images of civic belonging remain haunted by the classical polis, by Athens, Rome and Florence. Is there a language of belonging adequate to Los Angeles?[26]

One example of this difficulty is found in the way communitarians characteristically avoid the task of defining "community." What sort of entity is it that is supposed to have made us who we are, given us our character, endowed our lives with their particularity? For example, as we write these papers on the role played by "community" in our moral reasoning about the law, are we talking about some neighborhood association in Berkeley, or about the People and State of California, or about the United States as a whole? Or are our perspectives even wider than that? Are we talking about the common culture and civilization that makes it possible for a New Zealander trained at Oxford to write for the *California Law Review*?[27] We do not have to wait for an answer in order to recognize the following point: any plausible sense of community is going to refer to a life lived together by a number of people that is large enough to render it vanishingly improbable that they all hold the same moral views on any topic you care to mention. One does not have to embrace methodological individualism to see that any community worth our interest will comprise people of different ages, characters, experiences, genders, moral and intellectual powers. These differences are bound to color their view of how they ought to live.

The point is obvious enough when applied to America, or indeed to any of the States that compose it: there are literally thousands of moralities jostling and competing with one another in the marketplace of American ideas, and none of them can, without distortion or special pleading, be taken as "the" particular morality of this country or the way "we" do things around here.[28] One might want to argue that the morality of "our" community is what all these diverse positions have in common. But that is ludicrous: the common denominator (if one can be found) is likely to be held by nobody as a set of principles in its own right, particularly once one recognizes that people take their moralities whole, so to speak, and that any principle or value is colored by the others with which it is conjoined.

The same is true of any attempt to identify "our" morality with the morality embodied in our laws, our constitution, and the other formal aspects of our political life. It is notorious that these are subject to widely differing interpretations, and that those interpretations stem at least in part from the fact that people combine their constitutional understandings with other commitments they have (their religious and ideological beliefs, for example) which cannot be accommodated in any account of the consensus that makes "us" who "we" are.[29]

Even if from a distance the members of a community seem to share some moral orthodoxy, on closer examination one will certainly find differences of emphasis, interpretation, and understanding. This is not to say there is no such thing as a communal morality; it is to say only that any identification of a communal morality that precludes diversity and disagreement is simplistic and sociologically naive.

One could, I suppose, *define* "community" in a way that excluded diversity of moral view. On that definition, two people could not be said to belong to a single community if they held different moral perspectives. But such a definitional approach would be hopeless for social and political theory. For one thing, it would cut the term loose from any reference to a sociologically recognizable entity. Indeed it would effectively eliminate communitarian ideas as worthy of consideration in their own right. If a community just is all the people who hold a certain view, then appealing to the norms of the community is no different from simply referring to the norms themselves (and saying that people hold them). Saying that they are embodied *in a community* would be adding nothing to that.

It is sometimes thought that the Aristotelian tradition in political philosophy embraced an image of community that was united by a common view of ethics, that the polis comprised a group of people who shared the same norms and traditions, and that this was incompatible with the sort of diversity to which I have referred. In fact, as an interpretation of Aristotle, nothing could be further from the truth. When Aristotle wrote, in a famous passage, that "Nature . . . does nothing without some purpose; and for the purpose of making man a political animal she has endowed him alone among the animals with the power of reasoned speech,"[30] he did not mean that our power of speech was our ability to chant moral slogans in unison. On the contrary, he recognized that we can hope as a community to attain knowledge of goodness and justice only by conversation among people who bring different views, perspectives, and experiences to political life. If we accept the Aristotelian claim that no one individual can arrive at the truth about goodness on his own, it follows that the apprehension of goodness can never be a matter of simple unanimity either.[31] In this respect Aristotle's views (and those of other thinkers in his tradition such as Aquinas) are closer to those of someone like John Stuart Mill than to the modern communitarianism that condemns pluralism and yearns for moral homogeneity.[32]

These points are confirmed when we consider that, whatever a community is, it has to be something that endures through and therefore changes over time. A community has a life that is longer than any of its members, but longer too than that of any of the circumstances and problems to which its particular mores are a response. We cannot predict how the norms and shared meanings of a community change with changing circumstances (indeed it is arguably a condition of communal particularity that this is unpredictable), but change there will certainly be in any community worth taking seriously in the modern world.

It follows that it is impossible and wrongheaded to talk about *the* morality of a community, if what is meant by "morality" is a settled consensus on an identifiable set of first-level standards of conduct. As circumstances change, moral standards will be in flux, new ones overlapping with old ones, sometimes challenging them, sometimes shoring them up, and, of course, some held by some members or generations in the community and some by others. At best, talk of a community's morality can only be a reference to the particular features of the flux itself and the different ways in which people cope with change. There is no sense therefore in setting up an antithesis between communal morality, on the one hand, and changing standards on the other.

Again, it may be possible to *define* a sense of "community" so that it simply means a set of people who maintain exactly the same moral views over time. But if we take this approach, then, whenever moral change takes place, we will have to say that one community has been replaced with another.[33] Once again the definitional move is sterile. It leaves us with no argument at all for preserving one community (so defined) rather than another, especially once we recognize that moral change and controversy over time are a natural part of the life cycle of whatever it is that endures when successive generations of men and women make a life for themselves together.

Critical Morality as a Community Norm

It is an important feature of the morality or moralities of our modern society that there is a lot of self-consciousness about all this. Not only do different moral outlooks coexist and succeed one another, but it is distinctive of our society that we recognize this and that we evolve and develop various second-level standards and practices for coping with it (standards and practices which are themselves self-conscious, controversial and in flux). For example, even the most tightly knit religious group in America will be aware that it coexists with others, and that many of those others combine their religious faith with a commitment to such things as mutual toleration, the separation of church and state, and a self-denying refusal to embody specifically religious standards in positive law.

H. L. A. Hart has argued that the question of the enforcement of moral standards is a question in *critical* morality about the enforcement of the particular *positive* or *conventional* morality of the group.[34] But that need not be so: the question of enforcement is likely to be an issue addressed at the level of positive morality as well. For whatever our modern mores are, they are anything but unsophisticated; they are complex, they are articulate, and they deal with issues at a number of different levels. One does not have to repudiate our traditions and take off into Archimedean abstraction in order to raise questions about whether this or that local standard should be enforced. It is part of our particular heritage to address moral questions in this reflective and critical mode.

In general we should remember that men and women in a community are not the unthinking bearers of timeless convictions that communitarians make them out to be. Even when they are fully immersed in the practices of their community and intoxicated with its ethics, men and women see how the world goes and feel its pains and pleasures. They are creatures of experience, memory, thought, and above all imagination, and they are capable of entertaining and sharing with one another, in outrage or in hope, the possibility that things might go differently and indeed better than they are currently going in the circumstances they face.

To do that, they have to be capable of thinking that their social world might be different from what it currently is, and that they themselves (to the extent they are socially defined) might be different from the way they currently are. They have to be capable of saying, "Things would be better for us, or people like us, if different practices were adopted," and they have to be capable of acting on that thought. The modern fashion among communitarians is to condemn such imagination as inauthentic, to say with Michael Sandel that it leaves the self that is entertaining these thoughts with no essential social attributes, no social attributes that are beyond challenge from such imagination.[35] But whether communitarians like it or not, such a capacity is undoubtedly part of our heritage. And I think that, in their shoes, I should start to question my use of ill understood terms like "constitutive" and "essential" in this context, before I dreamed of denigrating it.

In many societies, the epitome of this reflective capacity is the development of traditions and practices of specialist reflection on local mores, ranging from rabbinical casuistry through the institutional practice of moral and political philosophy in the modern university.[36] These are our practices of "critical" morality, involving sustained, conscientious, and rational thought about moral ideas and social possibilities. They are part of what the communitarians have in mind when they attack those who apply "abstract" and "liberal" criteria to the evaluation of communal standards.

The charge of abstraction has at least two counts to it. In the first place, the worry is that "critical" moral thought is simply too distant from and too little immersed in the distinctive mores of our local traditions. In the second place, the charge is that the practice of "critical" morality is overly individualistic – setting the rational faculties of one philosopher against the wisdom and tradition of ages. Both criticisms are misconceived.

The first, as we have seen, would work only if there were a clear line between a grounded moral consensus on value, conduct, and virtue, on the one hand, and "critical" philosophical reflection on the other. But there is no such line. Critical reflection in one form or another is part and parcel of the moral consciousness of men and women in a modern community like ours. There is indeed a contrast between those who approach morality in a "liberal" spirit and those who approach it more conservatively, but there is no reason whatever to say that the latter take our communal particularity more seriously than their liberal opponents. Since our heritage is diverse and volatile, since it embodies in itself questioning and controversy, one does not betray communal values by taking the practice of critical reflection seriously. Indeed by immersing oneself in *that* practice a person keeps better faith with our traditions than someone who appeals plaintively and nostalgically to an imagined past of moral unanimity.

The other claim is that critical moral reflection is essentially individualistic, in its style and practice if not in its content and commitments. The image that accompanies this criticism is that of the solitary philosopher, alienated from the society that supports him, sitting in his armchair, garret, or ivory tower, setting up his individual reason as rational censor of the traditions of the community. The image is nicely carried in some phrases of Edmund Burke, condemning the moral innovations that accompanied the French Revolution:

> We are afraid to put men to live and trade each on his private stock of reason; because we suspect that this stock in each man is small, and that individuals would do better to avail themselves of the general bank and capital of nations, and of ages. ... Your literary men, and your politicians, and so do the whole clan of the enlightened among us, essentially differ in these points. They have no respect for the wisdom of others; but they pay it off by a very full measure of confidence in their own. With them it is a sufficient motive to destroy an old scheme of things, because it is an old one. As to the new, they are in no sort of fear with regard to the duration of a building run up in haste; because duration is no object to those who think little or nothing has been done before their time, and who place all their hopes in discovery.[37]

But the Burkeian attack was a travesty when it was made, and it is a travesty now. The *philosophes* were not individuals trading "each on his private stock of reason" with "no respect for the wisdom of others." They were themselves part of a philosophical and political community who shared ideas, not only with others in Paris, but with thinkers in England and America as well.[38] Moreover they understood themselves to be thinking and conversing as part of a tradition of republican and ethical thought that stretched back to antiquity. When Marx jibed that "the parties and masses of the old French Revolution performed the task of their time in Roman costume and with Roman phrases,"[39] he was paying unwitting tribute to the fact that the rational standards brought to bear on the institutions of the *ancien regime* were not the private stock of some atomized individual, but a heritage of critical thinking that has always been part of our tradition, an interwoven counterpoint to whatever we have had in the way of moral and political consensus.[40]

The same is true today. When moral philosophers, liberal or otherwise, subject the institutions and practices of their community to rational scrutiny, they do so as part of an intellectual community and as heirs of a tradition of thought that builds as firmly and faithfully on the wisdom of their predecessors (who took themselves to be doing the same) as any follower of Burke. One cannot read any of the classics of modern moral and political reflection without noticing the importance that is accorded to figures like Aristotle, Christ, Augustine, Hobbes, Locke, and Kant as forerunners and landmarks. These figures are not of course venerated; our practice has rather been to proceed by imagining ourselves in a sort of dialogue with them across the ages. Moreover, modern philosophers do not spend much time *saying* they are working in such a tradition, or validating their reflections explicitly in these terms. But the same points that were made in Section IV of the present chapter apply here as well. To be a part of this practice or this tradition is not to go around *saying* that you are a part of it, or to congratulate yourself on that fact. It is to engage in it, to actually do the thinking and the conversing with others, and to take that as seriously as it is possible to take it.

VI

I hope the strategy of this chapter has become reasonably clear. Modern communitarians criticize their liberal opponents for taking what they think of as an external or transcendent point of view on social mores. They criticize them for daring to expose the constitutive norms of our community to the harsh glare of abstract reason. They invite us to abandon the liberal stance, to step back inside the warmth and solidarity of the traditions and practices that make our community what it is, and to embrace them as a particular way of life to be lived rather than as an object to be rationally evaluated.

My argument is that if we do this, we should do it properly. If there are norms and practices that constitute "our" way of life, then we should embrace them wholeheartedly, and not in a way that leaves it open for us to peek out occasionally and say, "Every community needs boundaries," and "I am following the practices of my community," and so on. It is not and has not been the nature of our moral practices to go around saying that sort of thing about them. On the contrary, to congratulate oneself on following "the norms of my community" is already to take a point of view external to those norms, rather than to subscribe to the commitments they embody.

Second, I have argued that if we are to keep faith with our identity, we should immerse ourselves in our traditions as they are, not as we would nostalgically wish them to be. For us, as for the members of most modern societies, these are traditions of change, diversity, controversy, and reflection. They are traditions of philosophy as well as virtue, practices of thought as well as conduct, communities of reflection as well as moral solidarity.

No practice or tradition is self-validating, of course, and maybe by doing all this we are making an appalling mistake. Perhaps there are reasons for thinking that we would do better to abandon our heritage of critical reflection. Philosophical arguments are sometimes produced to that effect.[41] But they cannot be communitarian arguments: no one can deny that it is part of the particular heritage of our community to think critically and abstractly on moral matters. If we want to engage in the practices of our community, we do better to get on with that thinking and to take it seriously, than to yearn vainly and fatuously for traditions and a moral ingenuousness that we never really shared.

Chapter 9

Rights in conflict

This chapter is about conflicts of rights. It asks whether, in our moral thinking, we should regard rights as considerations that are capable of conflicting with one another, and, if they are to be thought of in this way, how such conflicts should be resolved. I do not have any definitive answers to these questions, partly because how we answer them depends on how we conceive of rights. However, I shall argue as follows: first, that if rights are understood along the lines of the Interest Theory proposed by Joseph Raz, then conflicts of rights must be regarded as more or less inevitable; second, that rights on this conception should be thought of, not as correlative to single duties, but as generating a multiplicity of duties; and third, that this multiplicity stands in the way of any tidy or single-minded account of the way in which the resolution of rights conflicts should be approached.

I

The issue is complicated by the lack of any consensus about the proper conception of rights. Not only do philosophers differ about what rights we have, they differ also on what is being said when we are told that someone has a right to something.

These disagreements have a direct bearing on our question about moral conflicts. Consider the conception of rights put forward by Robert Nozick. According to Nozick, rights are to be thought of as *side constraints* – limits on the actions that

are morally available to any agent. They are essentially negative in character, requiring each agent to *refrain* from performing actions of the specified type: they never require
anything other than an omission. And they are *agent-relative,*
in the sense that each agent is taken to be concerned only
with his own observance of the constraints. Since a constraint
presents itself to him simply as a limit on *his* conduct, he is
not required by a concern for rights to try to limit the conduct
of others to see that rights are respected by them, and so the
question of whether he should violate some rights himself
in order to prevent graver violations by others does not arise.[1]
On this conception, rights are more or less incapable of conflicting with one another. However, the price for this tidiness
is a severe limitation on the types of moral concerns that can
be articulated in the Nozickian framework.[2]

Consider now the conception of rights put forward by
Joseph Raz. According to Raz, a person may be said to have
a right if and only if some aspect of his well-being (some
interest of his) is sufficiently important in itself to justify
holding some other person or persons to be under a duty.[3]
Thus, when A is said to have a *right* to free speech, part of
what is claimed is that his interest in speaking out freely is
sufficiently important from a moral point of view to justify
holding other people, particularly the government, to have
duties not to place him under any restrictions or penalties in
this regard.

On this conception, basing duties on rights is quite a different matter from basing them on general utility. According
to a utilitarian, the government's duty to let someone speak
out is never inferred merely from the importance of the interest that the individual person himself has in the matter;
rather it is inferred from a calculus that relates the importance
of that interest to the importance of every other interest that
may be affected by the imposition of the duty. By contrast,
a theory of rights bases its commitment on the good to each
individual, taken one by one, of being able to speak his mind
freely. A's right to free speech is based on the importance
of A's interest in speaking, B's right is based on the impor-

tance of B's interest, C's on that of C, and so on. For the utilitarian, by contrast, free speech for A may be justified only through a calculus of the interests that A *and* B *and* C *and* everyone else have at stake in the matter.

Not all individual interests have sufficient importance to form the basis of rights. There are some interests such that the utilitarian mode of calculation is the only appropriate basis for determining morally the respect that they require. On Raz's conception, the idea of rights is a discriminating idea, sorting out those interests that merit special attention from those for which utilitarian calculation seems appropriate. It is the task of a substantive *theory* of rights to provide a rationale for this discrimination.

Unlike Nozick's view, Raz's conception provides no basis for any confidence that rights or the duties they generate will not conflict with one another. A theory of rights singles out certain interests on the basis of their moral importance. We know individual interests often conflict with one another – that is the stuff of moral and political life. It does not always happen: no doubt there is a set S1 of individual interests the members of which are perfectly compossible with one another and can all be served and promoted without posing any hard choices.[4] But it would be surprising – indeed, a massively improbable coincidence – if the set of interests associated with the special level of concern that rights indicate (call it S2) just *happened* to be coextensive with S1. It is unlikely, not only because we have no reason for thinking that these properties – compossibility and moral importance – are invariably associated but also because what we know of the human condition indicates that many of the areas in which moral conflicts occur are exactly the areas of life in which important individual interests are engaged.

Thus, different ways of constructing a conception of rights lead to different conclusions about the possibility of rights conflicting with one another. The negative and agent-relative structure of Nozick's theory precludes such conflicts, even before we ask about the content of Nozickian rights; whereas Raz's Interest Theory indicates that conflicts of rights, though not logically necessary, are in the circumstances of the real world more or less inevitable.

It is tempting to think that we have to decide who is right about rights – those who think of them as side constraints or those who adopt the Interest Theory – before we can answer the questions with which we began. That may be a mistake, born of the conviction that the phrase "moral rights" must have a single correct meaning. A more sensible approach may be to say that Nozick and Raz are identifying two quite different types of moral considerations (for all that they use the common term "rights" to describe them) and that, while there are interesting questions about which type of consideration is more important, there is no interesting question about which really captures the essence of *rights*.[5] Since we are interested above all in moral conflicts, we should focus on the Interest Theory, since the issue is not one that arises for the sort of moral concern on which Nozick's conception is focused. If someone wants to insist that the conflicts we are studying are not properly called conflicts *of rights*, that can be conceded. Though we shall call them "rights," the substantial point is that they are a distinct type of moral consideration and the conflicts they give rise to are important.

II

When we say rights conflict, what we really mean is that the duties they imply are not compossible. Two people, A and B, may be said to have rights which conflict if some interest of A is important enough in itself to justify holding some person, C, to be under a duty whose performance by him will not be possible if he performs some other duty whose imposition is justified by the importance of some interest of B. For example, if we think that A's interest in not drowning is sufficiently important to justify holding others to be under a duty to rescue him when he gets into difficulties, and if we think (for reasons of universalizability) that the same is true of B's interest in not drowning, then we will be faced with a conflict of rights whenever both are in difficulties and there are resources available to rescue only one.

Here is a common objection to the idea of rights conflicts. If we are unable to rescue both A and B then, since "ought" implies "can," it is not the case that we *ought* to rescue both A and B. The objection is fallacious. The conflict arises from the fact that we can and ought to rescue A together with the fact that we can and ought to rescue B. Each "ought" satisfies the requirement of practicability. The situation would not be nearly so awful from a moral point of view if one of the victims could not be rescued anyway (for example, because he was too far out to sea already); the tragedy of the conflict consists in the fact that we could rescue either of them, but not both. So while it would be a mistake to say that we ought to rescue both A and B, the principle that "ought" implies "can" does nothing to alleviate the fact that we are pulled morally in different and incompatible directions by the generalized duty to rescue.

This point is important for evaluating what critics sometimes say about welfare rights. Sometimes it is said that there is no human right to welfare (education, a decent standard of living, medical care, a job, holidays with pay, etc.) because these are not goods that can be secured in poor countries for everyone. "If it is impossible for a thing to be done, it is absurd to claim it as a right. At present it is utterly impossible, and will be for a long time yet, to provide 'holidays with pay' for everybody in the world. For millions of people who live in those parts of Asia, Africa, and South America where industrialization has hardly begun, such claims are vain and idle."[6] But for each of the inhabitants of these regions, it is *not* the case that his government is unable to secure holidays with pay, or medical care, or education, or other aspects of welfare, *for him*. Indeed, it can probably do so (and does!) for a fair number of its citizens, leaving it an open question who these lucky individuals are to be. For any inhabitant of these regions, a claim might sensibly be made that his interest in basic welfare is sufficiently important to justify holding the government to be under a duty to provide it, and it would be a duty that the government is capable of performing. So, in each case, the putative right does satisfy the test of practicability. The problems posed by scarcity and underdevelopment only arise when we take all the claims of right together. It is not the duties in each individual case which demand the impossible (as it would be for example, if we talked about a right to happiness); rather it is the combination of all the duties taken together which cannot be fulfilled. But one of the important features of rights discourse is that rights are attributed to individuals one by one, not collectively or in the aggregate.[7]

III

Many philosophers are reluctant to admit claims to the realm of rights if they seem likely to conflict with one another. One reason is that they are worried about the proliferation of rights claims. The more interests that are accorded rights status, the more potential for conflict there is. A no-conflict requirement is a good heuristic for keeping the number of valid rights claims down to a decent minimum.

A more interesting ground for opposition to the idea of rights conflicts has to do with the fact that much of the impetus toward rights in the first place stemmed from a deep unease about the way moral conflicts were resolved in the utilitarian tradition.

Utilitarianism is sometimes regarded as the one moral theory that manages to avoid the issue of conflict. Since it is "a single-principle conception with one ultimate standard" it does not face the problem of weighing different principles against one another in the way "intuitionistic" theories do.[8] However, a better way of looking at the utilitarian standard ("Maximize happiness") is to see it as a master rule designed precisely to resolve, rather than avoid, the myriad conflicts generated by its positive evaluation of every occurrence of happiness and its negative evaluation of every occurrence of suffering. The much vaunted coherence and completeness of the theory consists, not in the fact that its value-theory avoids conflicts, but in its unflinching commitment to a single simple principle for dealing with those conflicts when they arise.

To many theorists of rights, the utilitarian approach to conflict resolution is unpalatable. Utilitarian reasoning involves *trade-offs*: if there are two courses of action open to us, one harming A and the other harming B and C (with equal degrees of gravity), we are justified in harming A because his loss can be "traded off" in our moral computations against a commensurate benefit to B (the benefit of not being harmed), leaving the similar benefit to C (of not being harmed) as the determining factor for our decision. But justifying harming A in this way seems a callous and exploitative thing to do. It seems like a way of *using* him for the benefit of others. As such it seems to violate the Kantian injunction against the exploitation of humans as means rather than ends in themselves.

The idea of rights has been seized on as a way of resisting these trade-offs. Rights express limits on what can be done to individuals for the sake of the greater benefit of others; they impose limits on the sacrifices that can be demanded from them as a contribution to the general good. Though we may reasonably be required to accept some losses and frustrations in social life along the lines utilitarians suggest, rights are designed to pick out those interests of ours that are not to be traded off against the interests of others in this way. They are, to use Ronald Dworkin's image, our "trump cards," to be played in the last resort to protect the basics of our individual freedom and well-being.[9]

But if rights themselves conflict, the specter of trade-offs is reintroduced. For in identifying those interests that are not to be sacrificed to the utilitarian calculus, we may still be picking out interests that are incompatible with one another and so reproducing in the realm of rights the very issues that we tried to avoid in the realm of social utility. People, we may think, are likely to feel as used and as exploited when a "right" of theirs is traded off against the "rights" of others as they are when a similar choice is made under the blander guise of maximizing satisfaction.

Later I shall argue that brute trade-offs may not be the only option for a theorist who faces the sort of conflict we have been discussing. But even if it were, there are some points worth making to address the concerns outlined in the previous paragraph.

First, it is important not to saddle the proponent of trade-offs with responsibility for the actual existence of moral conflicts. Whether a given interest of A can be pursued or protected compossibly with a given interest of B is a matter of fact. If it can, then fine. But if it cannot, then a hard choice *has* to be made, on any account, and the only way of mitigating its hardness is to diminish the concern we feel about one or both of the options. It is not the fault of the theorist who proposes trade-offs that there are sometimes several drowning people and only one lifeguard. The theorist's sin (if it is one) is simply that of recognizing the dilemma for what it is, and of refusing in all honesty to say that a consideration loses the status of a right when it happens to conflict with another. Or to put it the other way round, people would still drown in these situations if we refused to countenance the idea of trade-offs; the only difference would be that we would no longer say that they had a right to be rescued.

The second point is more conciliatory. There *are* differences between the trade-offs involved in utilitarian theory and the sorts of trade-offs that might be adopted as a solution to conflicts of rights. The worry that some of us have about the calculus of utility is not so much that individual interests are traded off against one another: that, as we have just seen, may be inevitable (no matter how it is characterized). The worry is that, in the utilitarian calculus, important individual interests may end up being traded off against considerations which are intrinsically less important and which have the weight that they do in the calculus only because of the numbers involved. For example, a minority's interest in political freedom may be traded off against the satisfaction of the desires of a majority to be free from discomfort and irritation. Or a person's life may be sacrificed in the circus for the sake of a momentary thrill enjoyed by thousands.

On this account, what is wrong with utilitarianism is not that it contemplates trade-offs but that it combines the idea of trade-offs with a doctrine of the quantitative commensurability of all values. This means that each distinct value (every interest, every pleasure) can be expressed as an arithmetical function of every other, since all can be reduced to a single metric of satisfaction. So – for the utilitarian – there is an amount (maybe large, but certainly finite) of comfort which it is not worth sacrificing for the sake of someone's life, and there is a quantity of pleasure which is worth securing in a community even at the expense of the abject deprivation of an underclass. All that matters is that the numbers be large enough on the side of the lesser consideration. These are not merely puzzle cases conjured irresponsibly out of the philosophical imagination to embarrass the utilitarian.[10] They are direct consequences of the feature of utilitarian theory on which its proponents most pride themselves: that it is a monistic theory of value, with a single metric and a unified decision procedure, and that it gives no interest or value qualitative precedence over any other. The trade-offs contemplated by the rights theorist are unhappy enough, but probably inevitable: sometimes one life *must* be sacrificed so that a greater number of lives may be saved. But some of the trade-offs that can be based on utilitarian commensurability seem simply obscene, and the rights theorist should be perceived as resisting those, even though he is not necessarily resisting the idea of trade-offs as such.

IV

We saw earlier that talking about conflicts of rights is a way of talking about the incompatibility of the duties that rights involve. What we refer to as a trade-off of one right against another, then, need not involve the sacrifice of one of the *rights;* rather, it involves a decision not to do what is required by a particular *duty* associated with the right.

That distinction may seem specious until we recognize that – on the Interest Theory, at least – rights are unlikely to stand in a simple one-to-one relation with duties. We talk about rights when we think that some interest of an individual has sufficient moral importance to justify holding others to be under a duty to serve it. But if a given interest has that degree of importance, it is unlikely that it will justify the imposition of just one duty. Interests are complicated things. There are many ways in which a given interest can be served or disserved, and we should not expect to find that only *one* of those ways is singled out and made the subject matter of a duty. For example, if an individual's interest in speaking freely is important enough to justify holding the government to be under a duty not to impose censorship, it is likely also to be important enough to generate other duties: a duty to protect those who make speeches in public from the wrath of those who are disturbed by what they say; a duty to establish rules of order so that possibilities for public speech do not evaporate in the noise of several loudspeakers vying for the attention of the same audience; and so on.

Even a particular duty, thought of as associated with a right, itself generates waves of duties that back it up and root it firmly in the complex, messy reality of political life. The right not to be tortured, for example, clearly generates a duty not to torture. But, in various circumstances, that simple duty will be backed up by others: a duty to instruct people about the wrongness of torture; a duty to be vigilant about the danger of, and temptation to, torture; a duty to ameliorate situations in which torture might be thought likely to occur; and so on. Once it is discovered that people have been tortured, the right generates remedial duties such as the duty to rescue people from torture, the duty on government officials to find out who is doing and authorizing the torture, remove them from office, and bring them to justice, the duty to set up safeguards to prevent recurrence of the abuses, and so on. If these duties in turn are not carried out, then the right generates further duties of enforcement and enquiry with regard to *them*. And so on.

In the case of each of these duties, the argument for imposing it is traced back, via the complexities of political life, to the concern for an individual interest that underpinned the right in the first place: we say that the right protects a basic human interest and that in the current circumstances of human life one cannot be said to take that interest seriously if one is content to stop at the *previous* wave of duty and not worry about anything further. A conception of rights which regarded each right as simply a correlative reflection of some independently justified duty might not have this characteristic (though I am inclined to think that any *credible* theory of political rights will be susceptible to the sort of extrapolation sketched out in the previous paragraph). But certainly the rights contemplated in an Interest Theory will work like this, for our conception of the interest will operate as a normative resource base from which a whole array of moral requirements can be developed.

Someone may object that this account of the way rights generate duties depends on a particular view about the individuation of duties. For example, are the duty not to torture and the duty to punish torturers really distinct from one another? Or are they simply different facets of one and the same duty? As with most such issues, it is difficult to know what would count as resolving it, and in the end I do not think it matters. Whether we are dealing with a multiplicity of duties or whether we are dealing with the multiple facets of a single duty correlative to the right, the points I want to establish on the basis of this analysis remain the same.

A first point is that we are unlikely to be able to sustain any simple division between negative and positive rights of the sort that liberals have often tried to work with. Those who criticized the inclusion of "socioeconomic" rights in the Universal Declaration, for example, sometimes argued that these were "positive" rights – that is, rights correlative to duties positively to perform some action or render some service – whereas the traditional rights of liberal theory, such

as the right to free speech or freedom of religion were "negative" rights – that is, rights correlative to duties that required
only omissions of those whom they constrained.[11] The
chances were much less that "negative" rights would conflict, because a given agent could perform any number of
omissions at one and the same time.

If we accept, however, that rights mark the way in which
interests generate duties, then the picture is likely to appear
much less tidy than this. A duty to refrain from interfering
with someone's freedom is likely to be accompanied by a
"positive" (and therefore costly) duty on other agents to
protect people from such interference. And a duty positively
to provide people with welfare is likely to be accompanied
by various "negative" (and thus relatively costless) duties on
other agents to refrain from interfering with such provision
if it is already underway. One and the same right may generate both negative and positive duties: some will require
omissions while others will require actions and the expenditure of resources. This means that it is impossible to say
definitively of a given right that it is purely negative (or
purely positive) in character. Since what actually conflict for
us are the duties that rights generate from time to time, it
means that we are unlikely to be able to identify in advance
any set of rights – liberal or otherwise – and say confidently,
"*These* rights will never conflict in any of the requirements
that they generate."[12]

A second consequence takes us back to the point about
trade-offs. Once we accept that each right is to be thought
of as generating not just one duty but successive waves of
duty, then the whole language of trade-offs – the idea of
trading off A's right against B's – with its resonance of callous
amorality, may begin to seem less drastic. Rights conflicts
arise when a duty generated by one right is not compossible
with a duty generated by another. It is most unlikely that,
in a given case, *all* the duties generated by the rights in
question are incompossible. This means that even while we
are "trading off" one duty generated by A's right against
one duty generated by B's, we may nevertheless be perfectly

well able to fulfill *other* duties owed to A in regard to that
right. Consider a conflict between putative rights to medical
care held by A and B. A shortage of medical resources may
mean that A's primary needs go untreated for a while. But
his right to medical care (along with those of others who
have missed out) continues to impose other duties. It places
constraints on the sorts of production and trading decisions
we may make in the economy; if we have a choice, we may
not produce or import luxury goods at the expense of the
medical resources we are short of. It may require us to start
training more doctors. It may require us to set up an inquiry
into the state of health services. It may even require us to
compensate the victims of the trade-offs in other ways if we
can. All this may be owed to the bearer of a right, in virtue
of the moral importance of the interest that the right protects,
even though what appears to be our primary duty to him in
this regard cannot be discharged.

So an individual's right does not simply disappear from
view once it has been traded off against the rights of others
in the sorts of cases we have been imagining. It remains in
the picture and must be taken seriously as a residual source
of other duties and obligations. Since rights generate not
single duties but what I have referred to as successive waves
of duty, the trading off of one right against another, in a
situation of conflict, is never the end of the story. (Exactly
the same points can be made about our ability to satisfy *some
aspects* of the single multifaceted duty that a given right entails even when we cannot satisfy all of them, if we prefer
to speak of single-duty correlativity.)

V

A third point is less helpful. The existence of successive
waves of duty associated with a given right is likely to play
havoc with any tidy sense of the priority that the right has
over other moral considerations.

The discussion at the end of Section III suggested that a
theory of rights singles out certain interests whose promotion

or protection is to be given qualitative precedence over the social calculus of interests generally. We expressed concern about utilitarian commensurability, and we hinted at something like a "lexical priority" of rights over social utility: the interests identified as rights are to be attended to before any question of attending to other, less important interests arises.[13] Now, as John Rawls has pointed out, the idea of lexical priority seems ill suited to principles or moral considerations which are, so to speak, open-ended in the requirements they generate: "unless the earlier principles have but a limited application and establish definite requirements which can be fulfilled, later principles will never come into play."[14] We surely think that *some* attention is due to considerations of ordinary utility, and while it is reasonable to postpone that until the most striking of the requirements generated by rights have been satisfied, it is not reasonable to postpone it forever while we satisfy duty after duty associated with rights. Maybe there is no limit on the social convenience that should be sacrificed for the sake of the prohibition on torture. But is there equally no limit on the convenience that should be sacrificed for the success of the Commission of Inquiry that has been set up to bring torturers to justice and ensure that torture is made marginally less likely in the future? If the interest in not being tortured is the basis of the moral importance of the duty, and if at least one of the duties generated has priority over some other moral consideration, does that mean that *all* the duties generated by concern for that interest have the same priority? And if not, why not?[15]

One way of answering the last question might be to distinguish those duties whose infringement would lead directly to a palpable harm to the interest in question, from those whose infringement only makes it marginally less likely that the interest will be served. Given an assignment of moral weight to the former, the latter might be treated probabilistically, having some fraction of that weight or importance. But the quantitative image of weight seems unsatisfactory in a number of ways. Not all of the duties generated are related

216

instrumentally to the underlying interest in the way this approach requires: for some the connection may be symbolic (consider, for example, a retributive account of the duty to punish rights violators). Anyway, in a lexical ordering, this sort of move is unavailable: there cannot be fractions of lexical priority. If a duty to make it marginally less likely that an important interest will be harmed may be balanced legitimately against lesser considerations of utility, then the logic of the idea of weight suggests that ultimately *any* duty associated with the interest may be dealt with in that way.

VI

The same applies to any attempt to establish an ordering among rights themselves. Conflicts of rights can be placed initially in two categories: *intra*-right conflicts, that is, conflicts between different instances of the same right; and *inter*-right conflicts, that is, conflicts between particular instances of different rights.

Intra-right conflicts are exemplified by the demands made by a number of sick or injured people on a stock of scarce medical resources. If those people are thought to have a right to medical care, there must be some way of resolving the moral conflict that arises when it is found to be impossible to attend to the needs of all. So long as we focus on a single type of duty generated by the right (for example, the duty to provide emergency treatment), some maximizing approach seems to be in order: if we cannot save all, we should deal with them in a manner that enables us to treat as many as possible, even if this means that some are neglected.[16]

Now the existence of other duties generated by the same right both mitigates and complicates the rigors of the trade-offs that maximization may involve. It mitigates them in the sense that we may be able to discharge some duty to a given person even though we cannot discharge others. And it complicates them because we may not know how to balance a duty of one sort generated by a given interest that one person has, against a duty of another sort generated by the same or similar interest that another person has. Simple maximization of duty fulfillment will seem insensitive to the differences between the kinds of duties involved. In some cases, we can assign degrees of importance to different duties generated by the same right. If injuries differ in their seriousness or reparability, we can establish the sorts of priorities that, for example, a system of triage involves. Even so, once we concede that different duties generated by the same right have different degrees of importance, we begin to lose our sense of the qualitative precedence this right – as a source of duties – has over other considerations in morality.

Inter-right conflicts arise when the performance of a duty generated by one right turns out to be incompatible with the performance of a duty generated by a right of a different type: the more resources that we spend on hospitals, for example, the less we can spend on police protection. Once again, we should note that we are unlikely to face any unmitigated trade-offs: there will usually be *something* we can do to promote the interest in education, for example, even though many of the resources that schools are crying out for are diverted to provide citizens with better protection against murder.

When hard choices arise, however, it is less easy to see how they should be resolved. The idea that all rights should be put on a par seems implausible. Though we may think that any right should have precedence over considerations of ordinary utility, we may think also that some rights are more important than others. Maybe the right to life is more important than the right to free speech, which is more important, in turn, than the right to privacy, and so on. Once again, this sense of what is "more important" may be understood in terms of a lexical ordering: different rights have the same sort of priority over one another that rights generally are sometimes given over considerations of mundane utility.[17]

But if rights are thought of, not as correlative to single duties, but as generating successive waves of duty, then this ordering will have the same difficulty that we noted in the previous section. Suppose we rank the right not to be tortured ahead of the right to free speech because we think it wrong to torture people no matter how much free speech one could protect in that way. If we believe that, are we also committed to ranking the duty to investigate torture, the duty to compensate victims of torture, and all the other duties associated with that right ahead of any requirement associated with free speech? If police time and resources are limited, is it the case that *any* project associated with the prevention of torture, no matter how marginal, has priority over urgent action associated with the protection of political freedom? Most of us would not want to accept an order of priorities as rigid as this. Though the right not to be tortured is more important than many other rights, it does not follow that every duty associated with it is more important than any duty associated with any of the others.

The alternative to a lexical ordering is to think of rights as weighted quantitatively in relation to one another (so that we allow a right to life to be worth five rights to free speech, or whatever). Then the importance of different duties can be expressed as a fraction of the importance of the right from which they flow. The duty to investigate instances of torture will not have the same importance as the duty not to torture but a fraction of that importance, and it may be overridden by some duty connected with free speech on a particular occasion, even though in general free speech is less important than the right not to be tortured.

However, as before, the difficulty with this approach is that it makes it hard for us to sustain *any* sense of the qualitative priority that a given right may have over some other right or over other types of moral considerations. Remember that on the Interest Theory of rights, the imposition of duties is warranted by our sense of the importance of the underlying interest. If that importance can *sometimes* be quantified in relation to other moral considerations, why can it not *always* be so quantified? Once we concede that *some* of the duties associated with one right are commensurable with *some* of the duties associated with another, it is not clear how we can sustain a thesis of incommensurability in relation to *any* pair of the duties that they respectively generate.

VII

We seem to want to have our cake and eat it too. We want to retain some sense that rights have qualitative priority over considerations of utility and even in regard to one another. But we also want some way of expressing the fact that not all the duties generated by a given right have the same degree of importance.

Part of the difficulty stems, I think, from the fact that we have not fully articulated what we want to capture in the idea of a lexical ordering. It is tempting to think that because we know technically how to work with lexical priority we therefore understand when and why to deploy it. But we cannot just announce or "intuit" that the concern aroused by one type of interest has lexical priority over the concern aroused by another. We ought to be in the business of trying to *justify* such claims. One possibility worth exploring is that lexical priority expresses the fact that a pair of moral considerations are related *internally* to one another, rather than externally in the way that a purely quantitative account of their respective importance would imply.

An example of this sort of relation is Ronald Dworkin's theory of "rights as trumps." According to Dworkin, we say that a person has a right to some benefit if it is the case that any utilitarian argument in favor of denying him that benefit is likely in the real world to have been "corrupted" by the counting of what he calls "external preferences." (Dworkin argues that counting external along with personal preferences undermines any claim that the utility calculus has to be an adequate expression of the principle of equal concern. We shall not attempt to evaluate that controversial argument here.)[18] Since it is impossible in practice to disentangle external from personal preferences in utilitarian calculations, we introduce rights as a corrective. Now for rights set up in this way, the resolution of any conflict with considerations of utility is obvious: rights are to prevail over utility precisely because the whole point of setting them up is to correct for defects in the utilitarian arguments which are likely to oppose them. We do not stare at the utility calculus and then stare at the rights, and discover that the second are sufficiently important to "trump" the importance of the first. Instead, our sense of an internal connection between the two establishes the order of priorities.[19]

Another example of an "internal relation" argument may be drawn from John Stuart Mill's account of individual freedom. In *On Liberty*, one of the considerations in favor of freedom of thought and expression is that the challenge of opposing ideas is a useful way of shaking people out of the complacency with which received opinions are held.[20] This right to freedom of expression is widely believed to clash with the interest people have in avoiding the distress that arises when their cherished beliefs are contradicted. But, within Mill's framework, that conflict is easily resolved. Since the whole point of free expression is to challenge received opinion and shake up complacency, the discomfiture attendant on that challenge is to be given no weight at all against free speech; rather it is to be regarded as a good sign that free speech is fulfilling its function.[21] Once again, our conception of the interest's importance already tells us a lot about the sort of consideration to which it is appropriately opposed.

The interesting thing about such approaches is that they do *not* commit us to the troublesome view that all duties generated by a given right have the same moral priority. Take two duties generated by the right to free speech: the duty not to suppress a person's speech and the duty to punish suppressors. On Mill's view, the first has absolute priority over any duty to avoid moral distress because the value of a person's speaking freely is precisely the disruptive effect it has on moral complacency. The point of punishing suppressors of free speech, however, is not directly to shake up moral complacency (in the way free speech itself does); though its aim is to vindicate and protect an interest which does have this point, it does not in itself have this internal relation to moral complacency. So balancing the second duty against a concern about moral distress may not be as misconceived as balancing the first duty against that concern would be. Similarly with Dworkin's account. Whether utilitarian concerns ought to be allowed to weigh in the balance against a particular requirement depends on whether the sorts of considerations typically brought up against such requirements are antecedently likely to have been corrupted by external preferences. Now two requirements may differ in this regard, even when they are connected in other ways. We may have reason to think that utilitarian arguments for censorship are likely to have been corrupted by external preferences in a way in which arguments of convenience against punishing would-be censors are not. At least, that is a possibility, and it shows how duties generated by the same right may stand in different relations to the concerns that are likely to oppose them.

The examples discussed so far embody views about the priority that rights may have over lesser moral concerns. A similar approach may be sometimes available to establish priorities among rights themselves.

Consider the conflict that exists when one group of people (call them "Nazis") proposes to make inflammatory speeches calling for the suppression of another group of people (call them "Communists"). If we think there is a real danger that the Nazis' speeches will have the effect of inciting people to invade Communist gatherings and prevent Communists from speaking freely, we may have to think in terms of a conflict between the Nazis' right to free speech and the Communists' right to free speech. What we must do to secure the latter might be incompatible with what is called for by respect for the former. Now if we think in terms of a quantitative utilitarianism of rights, perhaps what we should do is work out the number of members in each group, work out the probability that the Nazis' speeches will have a rights-threatening effect, multiply through, and come up with a strategy that will produce the infringement of the smallest number of rights. Fortunately, that is not the only way of thinking about the issue. Instead of approaching free speech in terms of each individual's interest in expressing his views, we might think of it in a more systemic way – in terms of each person's interest in participating on equal terms in a form of public life in which all may speak their minds. On this account, the conflict between the Nazis and the Communists can be more easily resolved. To count as a genuine exercise of free speech, a person's contribution must be related to that of his opponent in a way that makes room for them both. Though they claim to be exercising that right, the Nazis' speeches do not have this character. The speeches they claim the right to make are calculated to bring an end to the form of life in relation to which the idea of free speech is conceived. We may ban their speeches, therefore, not because we think we can necessarily safeguard more rights by doing so, but because in their content and tendency the Nazis' speeches are incompatible with the very idea of the right they are asserting. What looked like a brute confrontation between two rival interests, independently understood, turns out to be resolved by considering the internal relation that obtains between our understanding of the respective rights claims.

The establishment of this sort of internal relation between moral considerations is an attractive way of justifying claims about lexical priority. Instead of announcing peremptorily that a certain interest just *has* absolute priority over some other interest, we express our sense of a particular priority in our conception of the interest itself. In thinking about it, and singling it out for moral attention, we are already thinking about the type of consideration with which it is likely to conflict.

However, this approach will not deal with all moral conflicts and there is no reason to want it to. Many conflicts – whether between rights and utility or among rights themselves – *are* best handled in the sort of balancing way that the quantitative image of weight suggests: we establish the relative importance of the interests at stake, and the contribution each of the conflicting duties may make to the importance of the interest it protects, and we try to maximize our promotion of what we take to be important. What we were looking for was something to capture our sense that this is not always the whole story – our sense that sometimes, or in some conflicts, the issue is one of qualitative precedence rather than quantitative weight. I think the idea of internal connections helps to capture some of that. And it does so in a way that means we do not have to give up the view that rights entail requirements of different sorts that are ordered in various ways in relation to other moral considerations. We can establish qualitative priorities in some places, without thinking we have to establish qualitative priorities everywhere.

Chapter 10

Welfare and the images of charity

I

The way we think about *charity* will determine in part the way we think about the welfare state. Charity is usually understood as a person giving part of his wealth to others who are less well-off than he is. The welfare state can be seen as an institutionalization of such giving, with the important qualifications that the donation is compulsory, collected as taxation, and that the nature and destination of the tax or "gift" is not under the direct control of the giver. The welfare state, to put it crudely, is a form of government-directed charity.

In this chapter I want to consider the way in which different images of charity are related to the justification of welfare provision. The moral legitimacy of welfare provision in the modern state is sometimes denied. Many of those who oppose it are particularly concerned about the element of *compulsion* it introduces into the sphere of philanthropy. There is, they say, no objection to the redistribution of wealth when it is a matter of voluntary transfers from rich to poor. But they complain that the moral quality of these transfers is destroyed and that serious issues of liberty and justice are raised when people are compelled under threat of punishment to transfer part of their wealth to the state so that it can be distributed to other citizens who are poor and needy. My hunch is that the force of this sort of complaint depends crucially on a particular view of what charitable giving is and what it amounts to. I am going to argue that if we adopt a somewhat different image of charity – one that is less familiar but, as I shall claim, more faithful to the underlying relation between charity and property rights – we will find the complaint about the morality of *compulsory* charity somewhat less convincing.

II

There have been many challenges to the desirability of compulsory welfare provision. Sometimes it is suggested that welfare provision has detrimental effects on the wider economy, reinforcing structural rigidities in the labor market and undermining the discipline and virtue of the working class. Sometimes it is suggested that welfare provision is insulting and demeaning to those who receive it, a suggestion that is coupled with another, heard more often from the political Left than the Right, to the effect that the apparatus of welfare provision involves an unacceptable level of intrusion into privacy and personal liberty and an enormous enhancement of the surveillance and supervisory roles of the state. Sometimes it is suggested that the form of welfare administration under the complex circumstances of modern industrial economy inevitably involves substantial derogations from principles of procedural justice associated with the rule of law. These challenges are all important and interesting, but they are not what I shall concentrate on in the argument that follows.

Very rarely in this literature do we find any suggestion that there is anything intrinsically *wrong* with giving resources to the poor. Even among libertarian philosophers, very few adopt what might be called the Nietzschean position that giving (even private charitable giving), like other forms of altruism, is ethically depraved or degrading for the strong and the powerful.[1] It is true that the late Ayn Rand, the libertarian novelist who has something of a cult following in the United States, toyed with this position. In her novel *Atlas Shrugged*, the heroine Dagny Taggart is required to subscribe to this oath before she enters John Galt's entrepreneurial utopia: "I swear by my life and my love of it that I will never live for the sake of another man, nor ask another man to live for mine." And she is told by John Galt that "it *is* against our rules to provide the unearned sustenance of another human being."[2] Rand believes that selfishness is a virtue and therefore that the good man is the one who does *not* respond selflessly to the abject predicament of others.[3]

Rand apart, the moral objection that must be taken most seriously is this. Charitable giving by the wealthy to the poor is not only morally permissible, it is indeed morally desirable. It is a good thing if those who have surplus wealth give it to what they regard as deserving cases. It is good not merely because generosity is a virtue and we ought to have as many virtues as possible: that line of thought leads toward the crazy view that we should be glad there are poor people about so that we have someone to be charitable to. It is good because of the moral force of the needs of those who are potential recipients of our charity. It is because we care for them, and not (merely) because we care for our own moral integrity, that we ought to take note of their plight and do whatever we can to ameliorate it. Indeed, we can be subject to moral criticism and moral pressure if we fail to do so. That much is conceded by almost all of the modern opponents of state welfare provision.

The mistake, they say, is to convert moral pressure into compulsion – to *force* people to do what everyone agrees it would be morally desirable for them to do. Murray Rothbard's view is typical. He recognizes that charity is a good thing, but writes, "[I]t makes all the difference in the world whether the aid is given voluntarily or is stolen by force."

[I]t is hardly charity to take wealth by force and hand it over to someone else. Indeed this is the direct opposite of charity, which can only be an unbought, voluntary act of grace. Compulsory confiscation can only *deaden* charitable desires completely, as the wealthier grumble that there is no point in giving to charity when the state has already taken on the task. This

is another illustration of the truth that men can become more
moral only through rational persuasion, not through violence,
which will, in fact, have the opposite effect.[4]

The argument is a powerful one – the more so because, of
course, the general point invoked at the end of this passage
is absolutely fundamental to the entire tradition of liberal
philosophy (and not merely its "New Right" wing). Most
liberals base their belief in toleration and civil rights in part
on the irrationality and immorality of *forcing* people to do
something *merely* on the ground that it is (believed to be)
morally desirable. Since this is so, Rothbard and other libertarians appear to have a powerful argument against their
opponents, at least in this tradition. The argument is that
the welfare state, with its apparatus of compulsory contribution, "poisons the springs of private charitable activity"[5]
just as the enforcement of a religious faith, a personal ethic,
or a scientific belief would, in the eyes of Locke, Kant, or
Mill, poison the basis of personal commitment, moral autonomy, and individual rationality.

It is easy to overlook this point, and spend one's energy
demonstrating that charitable giving is *morally right*, that
everyone *ought* to give something to those worse off than
themselves, and that those who would be the targets of coercion in a welfare state – those who would withhold charity
– are *morally in the wrong*. But this is not seriously in dispute.
The libertarian argument is that, even if charity is morally
desirable, indeed even if it is in some sense a duty, it is
nevertheless wrong to require people by the threat of legal
penalties and confiscation to give up their wealth for redistribution to the poor. This is the challenge that must be met
by defenders of the welfare state.

For this reason, it seems unlikely that an adequate defence
of welfare can be based on compassion alone. Compassion
dictates a concern that something should be done about the
plight of the poor, but it does not dictate an equivalent concern that something should be done against those who *fail*
to do anything to alleviate it. It is true that compassion has

sometimes underpinned political decisions about the use of force as well as moral decisions at a personal level. But as Hannah Arendt has pointed out, there are great dangers in appealing to compassion in politics to justify the use of violence – not least dangers relating to the introduction of an ethics of motive and feeling into an arena where only behavior and consequences can be subject to public scrutiny.[6] These dangers are sufficiently grave to warrant our looking for other arguments which are more apposite to the element of compulsion which the welfare state necessarily involves.

Other moral arguments for charity do not rely on feelings like compassion. In *Groundwork to the Metaphysics of Morals,* for example, Kant derived a duty of charity from the categorical imperative; that was the last of the four famous examples of its application.[7] But although this establishes that charity is a moral duty, it does not establish, in Kant's system, that those in need have any sort of *right,* in the political sense, to charitable assistance. The argument for charity in *Groundwork* has to do with the *internal* quality of an agent's willing: because an uncharitable maxim cannot be universalized, the will of the uncharitable man must be determined by something other than the idea of conformity to self-imposed universal law. The argument therefore gets no grip in *political* philosophy since political philosophy, concerned as it is with the *external* qualities of action, cannot take account of considerations based on internal features of the will.[8] It is true that some duties, like the duty of promise keeping, can be argued for in both spheres; but the content of the duty is subtly different, and anyway the point is that the moral argument by itself is not conclusive in both spheres. Thus a Kantian demonstration that an act is right is not by itself a demonstration of the permissibility of making it compulsory. (There is not space here to voice any wider concern about the tendency in modern theories of justice to treat Kant's moral philosophy as though it were his *political* philosophy and to ignore the distinctions that he insisted would have to be drawn between these two domains of practical reason.)[9]

So far this is merely negative: though many moral duties are properly enforceable, the fact that something (like giving to charity) is a moral duty does not by itself show that it ought to be enforced. Positive moral arguments have been developed too. The challenge to the welfare state that has been taken most seriously in recent political philosophy is that of Robert Nozick. In a famous passage in *Anarchy, State and Utopia*, Nozick suggests that taxing a man's income or wealth ("seizing his goods," as he puts it) in order to provide for the needy is morally on a par with forced labor. For those of us who are inclined to believe that forced labor in the service of the destitute, where there is no other way to provide for their needs, might not be a bad thing, Nozick insists that this in turn is morally on a par with slavery and other forms of interpersonal aggression.[10] Just as people have rights over their bodies that may not be violated even when doing so would be to the greater benefit of others, so Nozick believes individuals can acquire similar rights in relation to external objects by processes of appropriation and voluntary transfer. He accepts without question that philanthropy is morally desirable: it is an excellent way in which a person may exercise his rights.[11] But our goals and our aims, no matter how high-minded and philanthropic, are constrained by the rights of others. Just as I may not send *your* money to Ethiopia, or promise *your* blood to the Blood Transfusion Service, so a government, no matter how democratic it is, may not simply take the property of its subjects for charitable purposes if the subjects would rather use it for something else. Nozick believes that individual property rights over material objects "fill the space of rights, leaving no room" for general welfare rights like the right to a minimum subsistence.[12] Compelling a private property owner to contribute to a welfare scheme for others is a way of violating his moral rights; and there can be no justification for doing so since, on Nozick's analysis, there are simply no rights to welfare that could possibly be regarded as being in conflict or competition with the property rights in question.

III

It is important for the arguments we have been considering that the refusal to give should be sharply distinguished from aggressive actions of various sorts, such as directly *attacking* the supplicants who are pleading for assistance. The distinction is important because *everyone* agrees that it is permissible to use force to stop one person from attacking another. Indeed, in classical liberal philosophy, that is the *only* basis on which the use of force may be justified.[13] A promising line of attack, then, for the liberal defender of welfare provision might be to challenge that distinction.

One such challenge is laid down by Ted Honderich in *Violence for Equality*. Honderich maintains that there is in principle no moral difference between the withholding of assistance from a person with the result that he suffers (or continues to suffer) a certain degree of avoidable pain, misery, and deprivation, and an aggressive attack. The second is an *action* while the first is an *omission*; but, if the consequences are identical, that is no basis for a moral distinction between them, according to Honderich. So, if it is all right to use force to prevent the active infliction of a certain amount of harm, why is it not equally all right to use force to prevent the occurrence of the same harm as a result of an omission?[14]

This is an interesting argument and it raises a number of important issues in moral philosophy. Is our concern about aggression exhausted by our concern about the harm it causes to its victims? If the answer is "Yes," Honderich's challenge is sustained. But if the answer is "No" – if, for example, the *active* and *intentional* nature of the attack is the locus of the special concern that we feel in cases of aggression – then there might still be room for a moral distinction between harming people and not helping them, and the New Right argument would be safe for the time being. I do not want to go into the details of that question here.[15] Instead, I want to come at the same target from a slightly different angle.

IV

Consider what charity is and what it involves. The usual story is that charity involves a positive act of assistance, so that withholding charity can be seen as an omission – a mere failure to act. This image of charity is embodied in the biblical story of the Good Samaritan.[16] A man going down to Jericho fell among thieves, who stripped him and beat him up, leaving him half dead. He was lying there moaning by the roadside when a priest and a Levite came along. When they saw him they passed by on the other side of the road as, on Nozick's account, they had a perfect right to do. They did not put themselves out; they did not intervene; they did nothing. Then along came a Samaritan, and when he saw the plight of the victim, he stopped in his tracks, crossed the road, bandaged his wounds, took him to an inn nearby, took care of him, paid his bill in advance, and so on. The very image of charity, we may think: charity means putting oneself out, actively intervening for someone else's benefit.

But let me tell another story, which presents a different image of charity. A man wandering in the mountains is overtaken by a blizzard. He loses his way and is soon tired and hungry and in danger of perishing from exposure. Suddenly through the snow he sees a log cabin with a light burning in the window. He shuffles toward it, pushes open the door, and is about to take off his jacket, warm his hands by the fire, and begin serving himself some soup from the pot that is simmering on the stove, when out from another room come a priest and a Levite. "What do you think you are doing?" they shout, "Don't you know this is private property? Get out!" And grabbing hold of him, but using no more than what the law would deem to be reasonable force, they throw him out into the snow. Having done this, they go back to their own abundant supply of hot soup. Meanwhile our hero struggles on and, by a miracle perhaps, he spies another log cabin, again with a light burning and the door slightly ajar. He pushes it open, enters, takes off his jacket, warms his hands, and prepares to serve himself a cup of soup as before.

The owner of the hut – you guessed it, a Good Samaritan – comes in from the other room. When he sees what the weary traveler is doing – helping himself to his property – he does . . . nothing. He sits down on one side of the stove and watches while the weary traveler finishes his meal and prepares to bunk down on the floor for the night. Eventually when the traveler is asleep, the Samaritan retires to his own bed, and in the morning when the blizzard has cleared, they depart without a word, and go their separate ways.

What are we to say about this second story? Is this an instance of charity? Certainly, we should say that the priest and the Levite in the second story were uncharitable. They could have let the traveler stay there and finish the soup at very little cost to themselves. Instead, they chose to lay hold of him and throw him out into the snow. What could be more uncharitable than that? For us the significant point is that it was their lack of charity which involved the active expenditure of energy, whereas the charity of the Good Samaritan in the second story was entirely passive and inactive in character.

Can charity be inactive? Is it possible to be charitable by doing, as the Good Samaritan in the second story did, absolutely *nothing*. It may strain at the limits of ordinary usage (for that matter, so does talk of *"compulsory* charity"), but I cannot see that there is any objection, apart from a purely verbal one, to speaking in this way. Charity, as we noted earlier, involves *giving*, but giving – the exercise of the power of alienation of one's property – need not involve any active or onerous expenditure of effort. If you have physical possession of my typewriter already (you were carrying it home for me, say, as a favor), and I say, "Keep it – it's yours," the only action I have to perform is the purely symbolic or gestural one of saying that a gift has been made. To give you something, I do not have to put myself out for your sake or come actively to your assistance. The airiest waiver of my property rights is quite sufficient. [Even in those cases where the law requires the physical delivery of the subject of a gift, the requirement is no more than symbolic – and its main purpose is not to aid the recipient of the gift (to make it easier for him to pick up the object) but to mark the time at which ownership passes.]

For charitable giving to be merely a matter of forbearance, one condition must be met: the recipient of the charity must be capable of "helping himself." In other words, it must be the case that the *only* thing standing between the potential recipient and the use of the resources in question is the former's respect for the property rights of the potential donor. (If this condition fails, then the active assistance of the donor or somebody else may be necessary in order for the recipient to get over the physical obstacles in the way of his use of these resources.) This condition was satisfied in the second story, but not in the biblical story of the man who fell among thieves. That unfortunate fellow was so severely debilitated that he was incapable of helping himself. Nothing but the active assistance of another could be of any use to him. I shall return to this contrast at the end of the chapter. In much of what follows, I am going to assume that we are dealing with cases in which the condition I mentioned *is* satisfied. This means that the argument I shall develop is limited in certain ways: it is more easily applied to the issue of welfarist redistribution of property (that is, income and wealth) than to the provision of welfare *services*. Nevertheless I think this assumption provides a better starting point for thinking about the legitimacy of compulsory charity, for it enables us to focus on the direct connection that exists between discussion of that issue and justification of the system of property.[17]

We have, then, two models of charity. The first is a model of charity as active intervention, exemplified in the biblical story of the Good Samaritan. The second is a model of charity as passive forbearance, exemplified in my story of the Samaritan in the log cabin. My hunch is that it makes a difference which of these models is uppermost in our minds when we are evaluating the morality of *compulsory* charity, that is the morality of something like the welfare state.

Charity is compulsory when those who refuse voluntarily to be charitable are forced or compelled to be charitable. To evaluate the legitimacy of such coercion, we must consider what it is to refuse to be charitable, and what forcing such a recusant amounts to.

Corresponding to our two models of charity, we have now two images of what it is to refuse to be charitable, and, corresponding to them, two images of forcing someone to be charitable. On the first model, where charity itself is viewed as active intervention to help another, refusing to be charitable can be seen as an omission, as a passive refusal to intervene. Forcing someone to be charitable, then, means forcing him to undertake some action that he would not otherwise have performed, and that, as we have seen, is assimilated by Nozick to forced labor. On the second model, where charity is seen as mere forbearance, where it consists simply in passively allowing another to help himself to the resources that one owns, refusing to be charitable means the withholding of this forbearance; the uncharitable act is a positive act of intervention, the positive assertion of one's rights, in the face of someone else helping himself to one's goods. Being uncharitable, on this model, means *stopping* someone from doing something, rather than merely failing to assist him. So, on this second model, the enforcement of charity involves preventing someone from stopping someone else from doing something. Far from being forced labor, it is enforced idleness, or, more accurately, enforced forbearance.

The differences are clear. What moral significance do they have? One way of discussing this is in relation to the idea of coercion.

On the first model, the enforcement of charity is simple coercion: we force someone to do something he would not otherwise do. No doubt it is coercion in a good cause; the action we are forcing is a morally desirable one. But the fact remains that the enforcement of charity represents the *first* introduction of coercion into the situation – the first use of force – and that is a matter of concern to a liberal (particularly to the old-fashioned Kantian liberal who holds that force is presumptively illegitimate and can be used legitimately only to prevent coercion). On the second model, the enforcement of charity is not the first introduction of coercion but a response to the coercion involved in the refusal to be charitable. It is the priest and the Levite who first introduce force into the situation.

What about the traveler's use of the priest's and the Levite's resources in the second story? Is that not coercion? Is he not forcibly making use of another's property? I think the answer is "No." By drinking his soup and sleeping on his floor, the traveler lessens the options for action that are open to the owner. But lessening options is not definitive of coercion: when a person drinks his own soup and sleeps on his own floor, he lessens others' options – for they can now not make that use of those resources – but he can hardly be said to be coercing them. We may want to say that the traveler violates the rights of those whose resources he uses. (Whether we should say this will be considered in the following section.) But "coercion" is not a catchall term for any rights violation. Some violations of rights are coercive (those involving interpersonal force and threats); others are not. If the latter are wrong, they are wrong for a different reason than that which has led liberals to their special concern about coercion. It is the priest's and the Levite's intervention, then, not the traveler's helping himself, which is to be regarded as the first coercive act.

In some cases we may want to trace the coercion back a bit further. We may want to say that the initial predicament of the needy man was itself the result of coercion, if he was poor not through his own fault nor as a matter of natural fact, but as a result of coercive expropriation and exploitation by others.[18] (This is the case with the man who fell among thieves, and perhaps it is true of all the world's poor.) If so, then even on the first model, we could say that the enforcement of charity would be a response to preexisting coercion rather than a first use of force (though it is not necessarily a response to the coercive acts of those who are now being coerced). Many socialists have taken this line: compulsory redistribution is justified because the existing distribution itself was based on robbery and violence so that none of the "victims" of such redistribution now has any right to complain. (Often these arguments draw on something like Marx's account of capitalist accumulation in the first volume of *Capital*.)[19] But it is a perilous business making the justifiability of the welfare state rest on a particular theory about the origins of social disadvantage.[20] Many of us want to insist that welfare provision would be justified even if the poverty to which it was a response were *nobody's* fault, that is, even if it were not rooted in preexisting coercion. We want to say that welfare is justified by the *nature* of poverty and the fact that something can *now* be done about it, rather than by anything related to the origins of poverty.[21]

But if they adopt the second model of charity, liberals do not need to get embroiled in these difficulties. On this model, the enforcement of charity is always a response to coercion or the threat of coercion; it is never, on any account of the causes of social deprivation, to be taken as an illegitimate first use of force. Since the withholding of charity on this model is *already* coercive (remember we have in mind the priest and the Levite grabbing the weary traveler and throwing him out into the snow), the enforcement of charity can always be seen as a liberal response to that coercion.

V

I think this is a significant change of perspective on the idea of charity. It challenges the active light in which *giving* is usually seen; indeed, it threatens to relegate the *activity* of giving (as opposed to the forbearance which it essentially involves) to the level of mere symbolism. If this is our image of charity, then the donor should not be seen as putting himself out for the sake of another. Rather he is someone who refrains from making the effort to uphold his property rights against another's incursions.

By itself, however, this does not provide an unanswerable justification of compulsory charity. A defender of private property, such as Nozick, may respond along the following lines. It is true that, on the second model, the enforcement of charity does not represent an illegitimate *first* use of force. But it may still represent a first *illegitimate* use of force. For, however odious the behavior of the priest and Levite may seem to us, the fact remains that they were acting as they were entitled to act in defence of their property. Property owners are entitled to use (reasonable) force when goods they own are attacked by another; that is part of what being an owner involves. So when the state (or anyone else) stops them from doing that, it is stopping them from doing something that they are entitled to do, and it is therefore intervening in a way which is, from a moral point of view, at least as bad as the first use of force would be. Our intervention on behalf of someone who is attacking another person's property is to be accounted as much a violation of the latter's rights as the initial attack, notwithstanding the fact that the property owner was using force in defence of his rights already.

This argument presupposes that property rights are already settled at the time these incidents take place. When I set out the second version of the Good Samaritan story, I suggested that the first hut and the food it contained *belonged* to the priest and the Levite, and that the second hut and the food it contained *belonged* to the Samaritan, as though these were settled and straightforward matters of fact. If we accept that, and if we accept the traditional rule of common law that necessity is not usually a defence to a violation of property rights,[22] then the argument we have set out on Nozick's behalf is a good one. By focusing our discussion on the question of what to do about uncharitable *owners*, we have already conceded that the people we are discussing have rights they are *entitled* to enforce.

Discussions about the morality of charity usually do take place against the background of some such concession. We only begin talking about charity once it is clear who is the owner of what. But there is a difficulty with this supposition when we come to talk about *compulsory* charity. The difficulty arises as follows. It is sometimes said that the set of *property* rules comprises *all* enforceable rules about the use and distribution of resources, so that the justifiability of a system of property has not been settled until we have settled all questions about the use of force in economic matters. Certainly this is not self-evident, but whether it is true or not, the Nozickian response is embarrassed. Suppose it is true: then the last word on property has not been said until we have reached a conclusion about the enforceability of charity; so property rights cannot be set up as a moral obstacle to such enforceability. Suppose, however, that the claim about property rules is false: then the fact that someone is defending his property is not by itself conclusive against the legitimacy of interfering with him, for there may be other enforceable rules about resource use that a bare statement of his position as proprietor does not take into account. Either way, property rights may not be invoked to settle the question of whether the moral obligation of charity ought to be enforced.

We can see, then, why the Nozickian response is inadequate. The Nozickian supposes that the property rights of the uncharitable man are absolute and insists that *this* should be the basis of our thinking about the morality of the enforcement of charity. In so doing, he ignores the possibility that the issue may be stated the other way round. In considering whether or not to regard property rights as absolute, we may want to think about the morality of the enforcement of charity; and clearly, as we have seen, the model of charity that we employ here may make a difference to what we think.

VI

Let us return now to our second model of charity. The charity of the Good Samaritan consists in his *not* intervening when the weary traveler begins to make use of the goods that he desperately needs. If we had to force someone to be charitable in this sense, that would involve preventing him from intervening in those circumstances. What moral principle could justify such coercive prevention?

One possibility is the old-fashioned liberal approach that

we have already considered. The force used by an uncharitable man would be a first use of force, and liberals, who
want to eliminate force, would see a justification for intervening (forcibly) to prevent its initiation in this case. (This
principle – of using coercion only against or in anticipation
of prior coercion, of only coercing coercers – is the foundation
of Kant's political philosophy in *Metaphysical Elements of Justice*.[23]) Unfortunately, as it stands, this approach proves too
much. It would prohibit the use of force against *anyone* who
was making use of *any* resource, except those who were
actually coercing other *people* in the process (robbery with
violence, etc.). That would undermine not just property *in
extremis*, but the whole idea of property. It would undermine
the idea that in at least some cases sometimes an individual
A has such an interest in a resource (for example, an interest
established by its being the product of his labor) as to justify
coercively preventing B from using it even when B's use of
it would not involve coercing A, that is, even when it is not
in A's grasp. Kant attempted to get round this by basing
property on the interest persons have in exercising their wills
in a material world – an interest related so closely to the
interest protected by the principle of coercion as to justify
bringing the enforcement of property rights under the same
rubric.[24] For our purposes the important point is this. We
want a principle prohibiting the use of force to uphold property rights *specifically in cases of abject need* rather than a blunt
principle prohibiting all use of force in relation to resources
and therefore precluding the possibility of any theory of
property rights at all.

VII

Let me state such a principle and then make some suggestions as to how it might be justified. What I have in mind is
something along the following lines:

(P) Nobody should be permitted ever to use force to
prevent another man from satisfying his very basic

needs in circumstances where there seems to be no other way of satisfying them.[25]

As it stands, this is a rather vague principle. To flesh it out, we would have to incorporate some determinate conception of *very basic needs,* and we would have to say more about the subjectivity of the requirement that there must appear to be no other way of satisfying the needs in question. We may also want to add a proviso that the principle should cease to apply in circumstances where two people, both in desperate need, are competing for the use of the same resource. In those circumstances, perhaps each party may do *anything* to the other that he thinks reasonably necessary for his self-preservation.[26] At any rate, qualified or unqualified, I want to suggest that something like (P) is intimately involved in the justification of the modern welfare state.

How might (P) be justified? One might appeal to an almost intuitive revulsion from the obscenity of using force to stop a person from doing what he has to do to prevent his own death or abject debilitation. In some sense, the urge to survive should be respected as a primal human motivation, at least in the straightforward cases indicated by a *qualified* version of the principle – cases where no one else's survival is so immediately at stake.

There are deeper arguments too. They are Rawlsian or contractarian in character. The use of force in society should be restricted to cases where rules or prohibitions are being upheld which could have commanded free assent in good faith from those now subject to them in an "original position" of fair deliberation.[27] Now it is notoriously difficult to determine in a positive way what cases would satisfy this condition. It seems plausible to suggest that parties in an "original position" would agree to some rules of property – some prohibitions on using what others may have acquired interests in – but it is difficult to say which ones. Negatively, however, the contractarian approach may provide determinate answers.[28] A rule or prohibition is excluded if it could not have been agreed to in advance in good faith by those who are to be subject to it, and it is limited or qualified to the extent that those who are to be bound by it could not have given a bona fide undertaking to abide by it in its unqualified form. As we saw in Chapter 2, this negative use of the contract idea is quite common in liberal philosophy. Hobbes, for example, regards it as conclusive against any rule prohibiting self-defence that no one could undertake in good faith to obey such a rule. Even the limited self-knowledge that Hobbesian man has would indicate clearly to him the limits of consensual politics in this regard.[29] Locke used a similar maneuver against political absolutism. "[N]o Body can transfer to another more power than he has in himself"; therefore there cannot conceivably be a contractarian argument for a form of government in which the legislature is "absolutely Arbitrary over the Lives and Fortunes of the People."[30] More recently, John Rawls has argued that parties in his Original Position could not accept utilitarian principles of justice, since those principles may possibly demand sacrifices of them in society which they know they could not bring themselves to make.[31]

It seems to me that something along these lines is also true of a rule of property (no matter what it is based on) which prohibits the use of another's resources even in cases of pressing material need. Desperate hunger and deprivation *impel* the actions that they command, and for the people who are under that impulsion it is, in some sense, unthinkable that they should refrain from them. It is hard to tell a plausible story about a man dying of hunger who can bring himself voluntarily to refrain from consuming, say, a glass of milk belonging to another which is physically available to him. Certainly, it is hard to tell a plausible contractarian story about people who know what hunger and deprivation are like and who agree (other than in the disingenuous hope that the situation will never arise) to refrain from taking the milk should they ever be in this situation. If this is true, then the enforcement of such a prohibition cannot be justified in the contractarian tradition. It would be sheer force ungrounded in even the most hypothetical consent of those subject to it. Principle (P) then represents a determination to reject such sheer force in the economic sphere. What we know about material need and its relation to action requires us, on contractarian grounds, to prohibit the use of force in these cases.

This is much less than the full argument that would be necessary to support (P). Its elaboration is a matter for a book, not a paragraph. But even at this stage, we can see that it has the advantage of allowing us to tighten up the concept of *need* in the principle we are discussing. Something counts as a basic need for the purposes of (P) just to the extent that it is the sort of condition that is likely to drive a person to satisfy it and to push aside even the rules that he would otherwise be prepared to agree to. Liberal rules and prohibitions may be expected to check our desires but not our needs, on this approach to the concept.

VIII

In our second Good Samaritan Story, principle (P) justifies forcing the priest and the Levite to be charitable. They are using sheer force when they lay hands on the weary traveler who is helping himself to their food and throw him out into the snow, force in support of a rule which could not possibly have commanded the consent in good faith of the man now subject to it. So their use of force is impermissible; and of course impermissible uses of force are themselves proper subjects for coercion in a liberal regime.

But we are still some distance from a justification of anything like the modern welfare state. However charitable such regimes may be, they do not tolerate needy people helping themselves to the goods of those who are better off than themselves. A free-for-all of that sort would be socially chaotic and open to the worst sort of abuse. So, since welfare states cannot in general permit people to help themselves – or rather since they cannot rely on self-help as the dominant mode of satisfying the needs born of deprivation – how is principle (P) relevant to their justification?

The best way into this is to consider again the way in which a welfare system relates to a system of property. A system of property is a response to the fact that resources are scarce relative to the demands that people place upon them. It responds to this scarcity by specifying a set of social rules to determine authoritatively which of the competing demands are to be satisfied on which resource and when. (Different property systems set up these rules in different ways: private property allocates exclusive control of whole objects to specified individuals, whereas communist systems make the use of economically important resources a matter for collective decision.) What property does is to give preference to some of the demands placed on scarce resources over others (or to provide procedures for giving such preference). Since we cannot be sure that *all* people will abide even by rules which they would have accepted in a fair contractual position, and since we cannot reasonably expect that *anyone* will abide by such a rule unless he has an assurance that others will abide by it also, it is usually necessary for these rules and social decisions to be backed up by force.[32]

Now principle (P) requires that force not be used to stop people from satisfying their desperate needs. It therefore constrains the operation of a property system as we have described it. The force intrinsic to a property system must not be used when violations of its rules are occasioned by abject deprivation. At first sight, it does not appear as if the system of property we have in a welfare state recognizes such a constraint. As I have already said, we do not allow needy people to help themselves and even the staunchest egalitarian would not welcome the sort of disorder that self-help in matters of property would generate.

But the welfare state recognizes the constraint in another way. In providing (or purporting to provide) subsistence for everyone, it ensures (or purports to ensure) that the situation prohibited by principle (P) will never arise. The welfare state is a way of ensuring that no one should ever be in such abject need that he would be driven to violate otherwise enforceable rules of property. Or, to put it another way: the welfare state provides us with an assurance that if somebody *is* violating property rules, abject need is most probably *not* his motive. It provides us therefore with an assurance that we can resort to force if necessary to uphold the rules of property against him without risking any violation of (P). So when I discover burglars breaking into my house, I do not have to worry (as I call the police or rush at them with a frying pan) that I am using coercion against those in desperate need. Or, if somebody is defrauding a corporation of its income, the fraud squad need have no qualms that this is the only way that he can feed himself or his children. They can be assured that, for this particular villain, there was always an alternative: he didn't *need* to interfere with someone else's property rights.

None of this can be achieved by magic and the effect of a welfare guarantee is still to limit existing property rights (or rather to produce a set of property rights more limited than they might otherwise be). We limit them however not by placing direct constraints on their enforcement (so that they cannot be enforced against the demands of abject need), but by making them liable to the redistributive taxation that is necessary to guarantee subsistence for all. Everyone must do his bit to see that (P) is not violated; and we do this by ensuring redistributively that the conflict between social force and individual need will never arise. If some property owner resists paying the welfare tax, his resistance amounts to a refusal to do his part in what is necessary to uphold this principle. Since (P) is a principle about the use of social force, his refusal to support it is a proper subject for coercion. In *this* sense, my argument has been, we are justified in forcing him to be charitable.

IX

We have come a long way from the story of the Good Samaritan. But I think one can see what a difference a variation in the image of charity makes to our understanding of the welfare state. If charity is seen as active intervention for the sake of another, then the morality of its enforcement is problematic. But if charity is seen as passive forbearance from the enforcement of property rules, then it is much easier to accommodate, with the help of the principle I have been describing, in a liberal account of the justification of a compulsory welfare state. Compulsory charity is the enforcement of passive forbearance in the face of a needy person helping himself to resources. The welfare state is a way of ensuring that the dilemmas generated by such conflicts between social rules and individual deprivation need never arise.

The argument I have outlined is a limited one: it establishes only that *some* compulsory welfare provision may be morally justified. This has been denied, as we saw in Section II, by philosophers such as Robert Nozick. Rebutting that denial, however, is far from making a case for the sort of extensive and genuinely redistributive provision with which we are familiar. In conclusion, I want to discuss three respects in which my argument might be thought more limited than an argument for welfare provision ought to be.

First, I have considered only the issue of provision for subsistence. In some countries, the welfare state goes beyond that and guarantees not just a minimum but some sort of *reasonable* standard of living to all citizens. The extent of this further provision remains controversial, and I have said nothing here to address that controversy. It is not easy to see how principle (P), as I have outlined it, could be extended to cover this more extensive provision; for the argument quickly becomes quite weak as the degree of deprivation and the impulsion which that generates diminishes. It is worth noting, however, that it is neither necessary nor sufficient for a need to be covered by (P) that it be a need related to survival. It is not sufficient because if the existence of the need is unknown to those who have it, then a contractarian argument need take no account of the possibility that they may be impelled to act on it even in the face of property rules. It is not necessary, because man, being a social animal, is capable of being driven or impelled by needs whose substance and the desperation of whose felt quality is socially rather than biologically determined. The goods, for example, that are necessary for basic interaction with others may vary from society to society; but it may well be true that in each society those goods are so important to the social side of human existence that men and women will be driven to strive for them even in the face of social rules that say they must not. However, even if the argument can be expanded along these lines, I am by no means confident that it can be made to cover all that is distributed and redistributed under the auspices of the modern welfare state. We should confront the possibility that perhaps that extra provision is *un*justified. Or perhaps there are other good arguments – arguments based directly on a theory of just distribution – to justify it, say, in its redistributive aspect. I have made various comments in this chapter on the inadequacy of certain types of argument for welfare provision; but that is not supposed to indicate that the present argument is the *only* way in which that provision may be justified.

Second, I have not attempted to do justice to the variety of modern welfare provision. In speaking mainly about redistribution, and in focusing on the second image of charity, I have ignored the question of the provision of social *services* – such as medical care, education, transport, legal aid, and so on. These all seem to be cases of helping the weak in an *active* sense, and they are difficult to accommodate in an argument which has focused mainly (though, as we saw in the previous section, indirectly) on the idea of the needy helping themselves. To the extent that some of the beneficiaries of our welfare services could not conceivably help themselves to others' resources (they would simply perish if we did not actively care for them), then my argument does not show why forcing people to help them is justified. This is by no means an incidental feature of contractarian arguments: a contractarian views a society as a scheme of reasonable cooperation, rather than a scheme in which some make unreciprocated sacrifices for the good of others.[33] The very weak and the elderly are vulnerable in modern society precisely because they *cannot* say that the receipt of assistance from others is the price of their continuing to abide by the scheme of social cooperation; their weakness leaves them no credible alternative that they can threaten. Still, the contractarian tradition is not without its resources here, and a couple of epicycles may be sketched to try and accommodate these cases. First, to the extent that humans are motivated sympathetically by others' needs, there may be parallel arguments for provision for those who are the objects of such sympathy. The best example is the case of parent and child: just as I cannot undertake in good faith not to drink a glass of milk belonging to another when I am hungry, so a parent cannot undertake in good faith not to seize a glass of milk belonging to another for his hungry child. He is as much impelled by the needs of his baby as I am by my needs. Second, though this is weaker, people may be impelled by the specter of need rather than need itself, so that an able-bodied person cannot give a sincere undertaking now to refrain from others' property in cases where this is the only way he thinks he will be able to take care of the needs of his later self. Neither of these arguments is tight, but they give an indication of the sort of lines along which a contractarian would have to argue to accommodate cases where active assistance rather than passive forbearance is required.

Third, my argument says nothing to the issue of transfers of resources *between* societies – for example, from the U.S. to Ethiopia. The victims of famine can hardly come here and help themselves to our grain. Our provision for their needs, then, cannot be regarded as the price we pay for being justified in enforcing the security of our silos. Our grain stores could lie open and they would still starve to death. Again, this is what we should expect on the contractarian approach. Arrangements made within a society may have a different basis in political morality from arrangements made between societies.[34] It may well be, however, that as the world gets "smaller" and more interdependent, the confinement of contractarian arguments to a nation-state framework will become obsolete. If that is the case, then perhaps a version of my argument will eventually be applicable to international transfers as well.

Chapter 11

John Rawls and the
social minimum

I

The idea of a social minimum – a level of material well-being beneath which no member of society should be allowed to fall – has played an important role in the development and operation of welfare programs in modern societies.[1] At a theoretical level, there are at least two ways in which this idea may be conceived. From the point of view of distributive justice, it may be thought of as an approximation to an egalitarian principle of distribution. People are entitled in principle to an equal share of the goods available for distribution in society. It is not possible to guarantee that everyone's share is equal all of the time, but by committing ourselves to maintaining a certain minimum, we go at least some way toward fulfilling the requirements of justice. On this approach, the social minimum represents in some sense a social *dividend.* Ideally it will be set at a level so high that it will not fall far short of the average or indeed the highest levels of income and wealth. Certainly, as an approximation to an equal dividend, we would expect the minimum to rise as the wealth of the society increases. Alternatively, the social minimum might be conceived in terms that are more needs-based than distributive. Instead of saying that people are entitled to an approximately equal share of social wealth (whatever that turns out to be), we might say that, humans being what they are (and society what it is), a certain minimum provision is necessary for people to lead decent and tolerable lives. Spec-

250

ification of this minimum will not be in terms of a dividend of social wealth, but in terms of what is seen as objectively necessary for the satisfaction of certain needs. By comparison with the distributive approach, this latter conception of the social minimum will seem somewhat static: there will be no necessary reason for the minimum to rise as the amount of wealth available in society for distribution increases. However it need not involve an absolutely inflexible standard. What is objectively necessary for a tolerable life changes over time and from society to society; but those changes will be accounted for in the theory of need rather than in terms of a purely quantitative assessment of the level of wealth available for distribution.[2]

The main difference between the two conceptions lies in the way the minimum is fixed. In one it is fixed as a notionally equal distribution of social wealth; the idea is that nobody's share should be much greater than anybody else's. In the other, it is fixed on the basis of an assessment of the resources that basic human needs require. These differences in conception are likely to have a considerable impact on the way in which welfare systems operate when they are organized around the idea of a social minimum, and on the net amounts that beneficiaries ultimately receive. For this reason, it is a matter of some importance to see which has a better grounding in philosophical considerations of justice.

This chapter does not attempt any overall answer to that question. Instead I have undertaken the more modest task of seeing which has the better grounding in a Rawlsian theory of justice.[3] That may seem a redundant enterprise, for it is well known that Rawls himself opted for the first of the two approaches I have outlined – the distributive conception, deriving a social minimum from the egalitarian (or neo-egalitarian) difference principle. It is implicit in his argument that a theory of needs, though it can tell us what kinds of goods are the appropriate subject matter for justice, cannot by itself determine what quantity of these goods each person is entitled to have. I think Rawls is wrong to take this view – and wrong in the sense that it is not a view ultimately supported by the arguments with which the difference principle is defended. In showing that the second or needs-based conception has greater support in the theoretical foundations of the Rawlsian enterprise than Rawls himself asserts, I hope also to be able to cast some light on our general understanding of social minimum approaches as a response to the problem of need.

II

Let me begin with an outline of Rawls's own views on the matter.

One of the theories of justice on the agenda for consideration in Rawls's original position is the following "mixed" conception which I shall call the "social minimum" conception of justice. It comprises the following principles, ranked lexically:

(1) The principle of the greatest equal liberty.

(2a) The principle of fair equality of opportunity.

(2b) The social minimum principle, that is, the principle of average utility subject to a constraint that a certain social minimum of well-being be maintained for every individual.[4]

This conception differs from Rawls's own favored principles of justice as fairness only in the substitution of 2b – the social minimum principle – for Rawls's

(2b*) The difference principle, that is, social and economic inequalities are to be adjusted so that they are of the greatest benefit to the members of the least favored social group.[5]

What is the difference in effect likely to be between these two principles? In considering this, we must remember that principles of justice are not intended to cover "distributions of particular goods to particular persons": they are used to evaluate the design, development, maintenance, and reform of the basic institutions of society, not to determine payouts at the individual level. The moral evaluation of individual payouts is to be "procedural" in relation to the rules whose justice has already been assessed.[6] Bearing this caveat in mind, however, the difference between the effects of the two principles may be elucidated as follows.

The difference principle (2b*) requires us to attend to the position of the least favored group whenever social inequalities are in question, no matter what their level of well-being may be. The social minimum principle (2b) by contrast requires us to attend to their position only if there is a danger of members of that group falling below the level of a certain specified minimum. If all groups in a society are clearly at or above that minimum, further inequalities may be justified according to principle (2b) on purely utilitarian grounds irrespective of which groups they benefit.

The effect of the social minimum approach will depend on historical and socioeconomic contingencies. But its tendency may well be to legitimize somewhat greater inequalities than would be permitted in a society the design of whose institutions was governed by Rawls's principles. For example, it has been argued by many "New Right" theorists that a free market economy unconstrained by any egalitarian concerns over and above the maintenance of a social minimum is likely to be more prosperous than an economy in which the position of the less favored groups is in all circumstances the object of solicitous attention by an interventionist state.[7] Even if that attention benefits the least favored groups, it might still drastically reduce the efficiency of the economy as a whole and *a fortiori* the prosperity of upper and middle class social groupings.

The contrast can be illustrated with an imaginary case. If we define an acceptable social minimum for the sake of argument as a net monthly income of $800 (problems in defining the minimum will be dealt with in detail later), the difference between the two principles might yield a choice between two types of economies which yielded the results shown in the accompany table:

	Economy governed by principle 2b, the social minimum	Economy governed by principle 2b*, the difference principle
Best-off 20%	$6,000	$4,000
Middle 60%	$2,500	$2,000
Worst-off 20%	$900	$1,200

The figures refer to lowest monthly income for any member of the percentile mentioned. Other things being equal, the first type of economy is more prosperous than the second, though the worst-off 20 percent do not benefit from that prosperity. The extra prosperity can be attributed perhaps to a structure of industrial and managerial incentives which does not have to be oriented, as incentives in a Rawlsian society do, to the well-being of the poorest section in society. But (again, other things being equal) Rawls's approach to justice would dictate the choice of the less prosperous economy if these were the only options and insofar as this was a matter for social choice. He believes that the parties to the original position would not in the end be attracted by the prospect of greater average prosperity offered by a social minimum approach.

Why would the social minimum conception be rejected in the original position? No explicit answer is given in Chapter 3 of *A Theory of Justice*, where the choice of economic principles is discussed; but there is a sort of answer implicit in Rawls's general argument for justice as fairness. To the extent that the social minimum conception might permit greater inequalities, the parties in the original position would be gambling with their own and their descendants' futures by accepting it. They would be undertaking a somewhat greater risk of faring badly by doing so (in our example, the risk is that they end up some $300 closer to the poverty line in monthly income); and that is true *ex hypothesi* since the difference principle is calculated specifically to minimize the worst possible outcome that members of any group will face. Since the parties in the original position are supposed to be risk-averse, they would not undertake the greater risk of faring badly that the social minimum approach involved. We will explore the difficulties with this argument in Section III.

A more explicit argument is offered in Chapter 5. Rawls says that the difficulty with the social minimum conception lies in the setting of the minimum level: "How is the social minimum to be selected and adjusted to changing circumstances?" He is inclined to consider only two possible ways in which this question might be answered. Either it is answered "intuitionistically," in which case a determinate conception of justice has not been properly articulated. Or it is answered by covert and perhaps unconscious reference back to what the difference principle would dictate: "[H]ow do we know that a person who adopts this mixed view does not in fact rely on the difference principle?" He concedes that judgments about a social minimum "may match some other standard," but fails to explore what that standard might be, and insists rather unsatisfactorily that the matter is left "unsettled."[8]

Though Rawls rejects the social minimum as a principle of justice, he does not of course reject the idea that a just society will guarantee a certain minimum standard of living for its citizens. It is important to distinguish between the idea of a social minimum as a social policy (adopted pursuant to principles of justice) and the idea of a social minimum as a principle of justice, specifying the provision of some determined standard of well-being for all citizens as one of the first principles by which social and economic institutions are to be assessed. Rawls's social minimum fits into the former category; the principle of justice that I am considering into the latter. In the final section of this chapter, I shall comment on the way Rawls thinks a social minimum policy can be implemented. At this point I want to say a word or two about the way in which the social minimum for a Rawlsian society will be calculated. The basic formula is obvious:

> Once the difference principle is accepted . . . it follows that the minimum is to be set at that point which, taking

wages into account, maximizes the expectations of the least advantaged group.

Rawls acknowledges that this formula seems very generous:

> Now offhand it might seem that the difference principle requires a very high minimum. One naturally imagines that the greater wealth of those better off is to be scaled down until eventually everyone has nearly the same income. But this is a misconception, although it might hold in special circumstances.

The minimum, he says, is likely to fall short of equality, first because some resources must be put aside in the form of "real capital accumulation" for the benefit of later generations and second because there may come a point at which raising the minimum toward equality "interfere[s] so much with economic efficiency that the prospects of the least advantaged in the present generation are no longer improved but begin to decline."[9]

The first reason of course is not a good one, since it does not explain why wealth less savings should not be distributed equally according to the difference principle. But if there is anything in the second argument, it may well be that the discrepancy between the minimum level determined by the difference principle and the minimum level determined cardinally by a social minimum principle of justice would not be all that great. (Accordingly I have tried not to exaggerate the difference in the artificial example used above.) The possibility of this sort of convergence may well explain Rawls's belief that a social minimum could not be specified for a principle of justice in a nonintuitionistic way apart from resort back to the difference principle.

III

In the rest of this chapter, I want to set out an alternative and more plausible approach that could be taken to the problem of setting the social minimum. This approach, I shall argue, is one that Rawls himself ought to have recognized. I want to show also that my approach undermines both the explicit and the earlier implicit argument against the social minimum conception.

To see what this approach is, let us go back to Rawls's argument for risk aversion in the original position. It is often thought that Rawls is claiming merely that it would be *irrational* for the parties in the uncertainty of the choice situation they face to gamble on coming out on the right side of any inequalities they license.[10] Certainly, Rawls does say something like this in relation to the cautious or conservative strategy of "maximin" for the original position: "the original position has been defined so that it is a situation in which the maximin rule applies."[11]

But it is not clear that this is achieved by the *uncertainty* that Rawls has built into the definition of the original position. Even behind a "veil of ignorance" of the kind he imposes, it may still make sense to gamble. Actuarially, it has to be a good bet for an economically rational man to gamble on coming out on the right side of inequalities justified on average utilitarian grounds. He does not need to know the probabilities: all he needs to know is that no more equal distribution would yield the same or a greater balance of average utility, that is, total utility divided by the number of persons among whom it is to be shared. In the absence of determinate knowledge of the probability of his being in any of the various social groups, the rational gambler will assume that he has an equal chance of turning out to be anybody and weigh the prospects of each position for himself accordingly. As Rawls himself acknowledges:

Let n be the number of persons in a society. Let their levels of well-being be $u_1, u_2, \ldots u_n$. Then the total utility is Σu_i and the average is $\Sigma u_i/n$. Assuming that one has an equal chance of being any person, one's prospect is: $1/nu_1 + 1/nu_2 + \ldots + 1/nu_n$ or $\Sigma u_i/n$. The value of the prospect is identical with the average utility.[12]

If there is irrationality here, it has nothing to do with the formal structure of the gamble under uncertainty; formally it is impeccable.

The irrationality resides, Rawls argues, in the application of classical gaming rationality to the choice situation faced by the parties in the original position. In a classic gaming situation, such as an evening (or a lifetime) of poker, one plays hand after hand; and the initial assumption that the cards will be distributed equiprobabilistically is warranted, not by any feature of each deal (the shuffle, after all, guarantees nothing but ignorance of the distribution), but by the stochastic features of a succession of deals during the course of the evening's (or lifetime's) play. In the original position, by contrast, the game (if we can call it that) is played once and once only, and the play that is made will decisively and perhaps irrevocably determine one's life prospects thereafter. The one-off character of the gamble is crucial to Rawls's argument against it.

Rawls suggests that in order to justify the gambling approach, one would have to assume

> either that men move from one social position to another in random fashion and live long enough for gains and losses to average out, or else that there is some mechanism which insures that legislation guided by the principle of utility distributes its favours evenly over time.

But, he goes on:

> clearly society is not a stochastic process of this type; and some questions of social policy are much more vital than others, often causing large and enduring shifts in the institutional balance of advantages. . . . The pervasive and continuing influence of our initial place in society and of our native endowments, and of the fact that the social order is one system, is what characterises the problem of justice in the first place. We must not be enticed by mathematically attractive assumptions into pretending that the contingencies of men's social positions and the asymmetries of their situations somehow even out in

the end. Rather we must choose our conception of justice fully recognizing that this is not and cannot be the case.

So Rawls's attack on the rationality of risk taking in the original position is based in the first instance on doubts about the applicability of classic gaming rationality in the situation of a *one-off* bet which has drastic consequences for one's prospects if one loses.[13]

Whether he is right or wrong about this depends, I suspect, on quite deep philosophical issues about the reality of probabilities. Briefly, if we treat probabilities realistically we will insist that *there exists a correct solution* to the problem of rationality for a one-off bet, whereas if we adopt an antirealist or constructivist position we will be less confident about how to handle these cases.[14]

However, this is not Rawls's main argument against the adoption of utilitarian principles in the original position. The considerations about maximin and gambling in the original position are put forward in the spirit of "intuitive remarks favoring the two principles . . . intended only to clarify the structure of the choice problem in the original position . . . [and to] depict its qualitative anatomy."[15] Despite the claims that Rawls makes in various places, the original position device does not in the end present the theory of justice as "a part, perhaps the most significant part, of the theory of rational choice."[16] His main argument is in effect a moral one, not a rational choice one: it is that the parties in the original position *should* not take the risks involved in accepting a utilitarian principle, not that they could not or would not do so.

The original position, it must be stressed, is conceived as a situation not only of choice, but of *contract, undertaking*, and *commitment*. Some critics have argued that the assumption of a veil of ignorance, covering all features that might distinguish one person from another, derogates both from the contractual aspects of the original position and the plurality of the parties assumed to be in it.[17] That criticism is misplaced in this respect at least: the issue facing the parties in the original position is not simply "What principles would you choose?" but rather "What principles would you be prepared to commit yourself to?" Rawls is adamant about this and insists that the main argument for his principles and against any principle of average utilitarianism concerns the nature of the commitment that is being undertaken:

> [W]hen we enter an agreement we must be able to honor it even should the worst possibilities turn out to be the case. Otherwise we have not acted in good faith. Thus the parties must weigh with care whether they will be able to stick with their commitment in all circumstances. . . . They cannot enter into agreements that may have consequences they cannot accept. They will avoid those they can adhere to only with great difficulty. Since the original agreement is final and made in perpetuity, there is no second chance. In view of the serious nature of the possible consequences, the question of the burden of commitment is especially acute. A person is choosing once and for all the standards which are to govern his life prospects.[18]

The issue concerns what Rawls terms "the strains of commitment": the problem of assuring that one enters only into obligations that one is confident one can discharge.[19] If this problem is taken into account, Rawls believes that the parties will reject average utilitarian principles out of hand, not because they are unsure as to whether they represent a good bet, but because they cannot be confident that they will be in a position to pay up and honor their losses, as it were, if the gamble turns out badly for them.

Suppose that as a party in the original position I opt for average utilitarian principles; but then through bad luck when I emerge from behind the veil of ignorance I turn out to be one of the least advantaged in a society where the weak are exploited as slaves for the sake of the greatest average happiness. Despite the undertaking I gave in the original position, it is unlikely that in this desperate situation, I will be able to give a wholehearted commitment to the institutions of the society that exploits me. At best, I will give it the sullen and apathetic allegiance of somebody who has no choice. Starved, oppressed, and exploited, I will have no sense of the justice of my society, I will not be bound to it by anything approximating continuing consent, and I will look forward enthusiastically to the overthrow of my utilitarian masters (and their replacement by a Rawlsian regime). Perhaps this is a general truth about social psychology: in desperate circumstances, people are more likely to regard the institutions of their society with hostility particularly if it is widely believed that the institutions are responsible for their circumstances. Since the parties in the original position know the general facts of human psychology, and since they intend to commit themselves honorably and in good faith and not to enter into undertakings they cannot fulfil, they will act, Rawls suggests, to minimize the possibility of their being in this position. They will refrain on moral grounds, in terms of the constraints of right that they are under, from undertaking even good bets – bets which offer, in classical terms, an excellent chance of doing well – if those bets have desperate poverty as a possible unlucky outcome.

Is Rawls's assumption here about human psychology justified? Do people lose their sense of justice and are they inclined to hostility toward their social system when they discover their interests have been neglected or sacrificed for the sake of others? Does the fact that these sacrifices have a principled justification affect the tendency of those who are sacrificed to withdraw their allegiance from the system that requires them? These are the important questions that need to be asked about Rawls's attack on utilitarianism.

But there are also questions to be asked about his favoring the difference principle over the principle of the social minimum. Is it the mere fact that the situation of the least favored group could be improved but has not been that would excite their disaffection? Or would that depend on the actual level of well-being they enjoyed? Are they more disposed to disaffection at a lower level of welfare than at a higher level (the degree of inequality with other classes being equal)? The argument for the difference principle seems to assume that the answer to this last question is "No." But that assumption seems far from obvious. I would have thought that a party to the original position would feel more confident about being able to honor his undertaking, even in the face of massive inequality, if he had a guarantee that his basic needs would be taken care of than if he did not. And that suggests something more like a social minimum than a difference principle approach.

The most likely conclusion in the original position is that the parties are aware of the problem of the strains of commitment but are (like us) uncertain about the answers to any of the questions we have been asking. If that is their situation, what should they do? The answer is obvious. Being aware of the problem of the strains of commitment, they should opt for a principle which fixes a social minimum just above that level of immiseration – whatever it is – which turns out, on the basis of the facts of social psychology, to be the level beneath which sacrifices of well-being cannot normally be expected from individuals without serious disaffection and discontent. We do not know a priori what that level is, but we have some idea how to go about fixing it. In designing institutions for our society, we will ask our psychologists and sociologists something like: "How badly off can a person be before he will begin withdrawing his allegiance from (say) utilitarian principles of justice which he has undertaken to respect?" Or, more crudely: "How badly off do people have to be before they get desperate?" If we can get answers to these questions, we can set a social minimum accordingly. In advance of knowing what the answer is, I think it is clear that the parties to the original position should select at least *this method* of setting the minimum. If they know it is going to be set in this way, and that the level arrived at is going to be guaranteed, then they can be sure they are bargaining in good faith in the original position and taking due account of the strains of commitment.

Rawls may be right that this social minimum approach would in the end yield results identical in effect with the difference principle. But that depends on the following pessimistic assumption about human nature: that a member of the worst-off group in any society will always withdraw his allegiance from its institutions if they impose *any* avoidable sacrifices on him, no matter how well off he is. Some weight may be lent to this claim by theses of relative deprivation and by historical claims that events like the French Revolution were occasioned not by the immiseration of the poor but by the thwarted ambitions of those who were already well-off and rising.[20] Even so, I think it is unlikely to be true. In any case, what is important for our purposes is that the *approach* to inequality on the social minimum conception would still be quite different from the Rawlsian difference principle approach. Any coincidence would be purely contingent.

We have therefore answered Rawls's challenge to produce a basis for determining a social minimum which is neither intuitionistic nor dependent in the last resort on a covert appeal back to the difference principle. What is more we have found reason to think that this conception of justice is more consonant with Rawls's argument for the difference principle than the difference principle itself.

IV

In *A Theory of Justice* and in his publications since then, Rawls has been at pains to stress that the original position and the social contract are not to be taken literally as historical assumptions or even as foundational justificatory devices. That they cannot play the latter role was emphasized also by a number of Rawls's critics.[21] The choice situation of the original position is to be seen as a heuristic device helping us to "uncover the fundamental ideas (latent in common sense) of freedom and equality, of ideal social co-operation, and of the person" in the search for a deep basis of agreement among people like us as to how our society should be organized.[22] This suggests that it ought to be possible, as it were, to "translate" claims that have been expressed in terms of social contract and the original position into terms that refer more directly to the problems of social cooperation that we face and the deep values with which we are disposed to face them. I shall now try to do that in regard to the claims about the social minimum that we have been discussing.

The assertion to be "translated" is that the parties in Rawls's original position would embrace the principle of a social minimum on the ground that any commitments they enter into must be ones they are sure they can abide by and that there is a level of deprivation such that no one can be confident of his ability to support, operate, and respect institutions that impose that level of deprivation on him where he can conceive of any practicable alternative. What is the direct force of this assertion?

The underlying idea can best be expressed in terms of a series of claims about *need*. Often "need" is used simply as a cognate of "necessary for"; in this broad sense, its relevance for a theory of justice is problematic, since one may have needs relative to ends of all sorts, only a few of which are morally compelling. Sometimes, "need" is used in a way that connotes, not merely necessary instrumentality, but a certain subjective or appetitive state or condition. To need something is to suffer a lack, but in the sense I am talking about it is also to *suffer* a lack – to experience it as a burning frustration and as a crippling and overwhelming debility. If, in Anscombe's phrase, "the natural sign of wanting is trying to get," the natural sign of this sort of needing may be desperate and reckless activity oriented to getting whatever it is the lack of which is so sorely felt.[23] There is a subjective urgency about claims of need which goes along with the desperation of certain deprivations and the violence of the actions likely to be undertaken to supply them.[24] There are reasons for thinking that the existence of this sort of need poses special problems for a society committed to respect for the humanity of its members.

Modern societies depend largely on the willingness of (most of) their members to bear with and work within the basic institutions that structure them. This is a truth independent of any social contract hypothesis, though of course it is the foothold in social experience that contractarian theories step up on. No society can long tolerate a situation in which significant numbers of people are so seriously disaffected that they are tempted to violate and subvert its basic structure whenever they think it conducive to their self-interest to do so. Any society therefore must pay attention to the likely causes of disaffection and of the withdrawal of the active allegiance and voluntary forbearance on which social organization depends.

Need in the sense I have been describing is undoubtedly one of these causes. In the despair that characterizes it, the defiance it excites, and the single-minded violence that it may occasion, it poses a simmering threat to the viability of the societies it afflicts. There is therefore a prima facie reason why any society should avoid the situation in which significant numbers of people are in need.

No doubt, the threat posed by need is one that may successfully be resisted by structures of power that are sufficiently ruthless and resilient. If we raise our fences high enough or deploy enough razor-edged barbed wire, the granaries can be kept secure from the depredations of the hungry. (Bruce Ackerman has even suggested – in a spirit I find utterly incompatible with the liberal approach to social obligation – that in thinking about justice we should imagine in the first instance that we have the technology to remove disobedience as a problem from whatever principles we select.)[25] It may be possible to "educate" or "socialize" a people in such a way that even when they are starving they will repress the urge to action that their hunger impels. What this suggests is that we might want to view the impulsion of need in the same way as we view any other violent antisocial force that has to be held in check. Pathologically impelled action is a familiar enough concern after all; and any society must equip itself to cope with those who (as John Locke put it) act "as a Lyon or a Tyger, one of those wild Savage Beasts with whom Men can have no Society nor Security."[26] The violence of need, as much as any violent impulsion that overwhelms voluntary restraint, can be met with the combined force of the community, if we are sufficiently committed to the arrangements that evoke it. If my argument is to go through, reasons must be given for distinguishing need from other (pathological) causes of reckless action in politics.

The reason I think is the following. To put it paradoxically, the reckless impulsion of action by need is a *normal* human phenomenon (unlike the pathological compulsions with which we compared it in the previous paragraph): it is the normal condition of a human who lacks certain things; it is the state that beings like us normally, naturally, and perhaps properly get into when the wherewithal for their health, flourishing, or survival is lacking. Let me appeal to the reader's own feelings on a couple of examples. Surely any of us, asked in advance whether he would like therapy to remove the urge to grab others' surplus food should he be desperately hungry, would repudiate the offer as an insult. But faced with a similar offer, in advance, of therapy to cope with the unlikely event that one became pathologically disposed to rape, who among us would not embrace it? The threat to society from need is to be distinguished from other compulsive threats in that it involves humans responding normally and desirably to a certain sort of circumstance. The psychological condition that poses this threat – despite its impelling and overwhelming character – is a condition which is not in the circumstances incompatible with what our most basic ethical convictions tell us to cherish and respect in our humanity.

All societies require legitimation, and societies like ours seek to associate that requirement with underlying principles of respect for the humanity of their members. That rules out the coercive option in the face of the threat posed by need. Since this is so, these societies must pay special attention to the avoidance of the circumstances which generate the type of need that we have been talking about. The least this requires is a calculation of the minimum level of material well-being required before people are plunged into the despair and impulsion of abject need, and a determination to secure that level as far as possible for every citizen as a first charge on the resources and services of the society. Whatever other principles of social distribution and economy are adopted, this seems a necessary condition for their tolerable application in a society which seeks the support and not merely the subjection of its citizens.

I do not believe a similar argument can be made for the Rawlsian difference principle. That is, I do not think we can argue in the same way for treating the situation of the least-favored group in society as a first charge on its resources *irrespective of their actual level of well-being.* And this – still translating out of contract-ese – is what is wrong with Rawls's position. Unless relative deprivation threatens social allegiance as much as abject deprivation (and Rawls's own remarks on the problem of envy suggest that he does not believe this) some other basis must be found for the extra egalitarianism of the Rawlsian difference principle.[27]

V

The principle of the social minimum may seem a little severe as a principle of justice. Is this *all* that the poor are entitled to? No more than is necessary to keep them from revolt? A welfare state oriented primarily, as radical cynics have always maintained, to the preservation of social stability?[28] Rawls's own principle has been criticized for allowing too much inequality.[29] But the principle of the social minimum goes further and abandons equality as a substantive concern altogether. I want to conclude with some comments on this issue.

The first thing to note is that the form of contractarian argument I have been using is negative rather than positive.[30] The argument has been that an economic system without a social minimum is not a system that could possibly be agreed on in the original position: the strains of commitment rule it out as a possible subject for agreement. I have insisted that this form of argument takes us only as far as a social minimum and that, despite what Rawls says, it does not rule out all economic systems which fail to give primary concern to the position of those least advantaged by social inequalities. But that does not mean that there are not *other* reasons of justice for focusing on the welfare of the least advantaged. Except in circumstances of the utmost scarcity, the principle of a social minimum does not define a complete conception of economic justice. I have assumed without argument that its role is to constrain a broader principle of average utility, regarding the gamble represented by the utilitarian option as a starting point for the problem of the strains of commitment. We should remember that, despite their bad reputation at the moment in ethics, utilitarian principles historically have been unfriendly to economic inequality.

Second, we should note that the argument is not purely a cynical one. As we saw in the previous section, it depended at a crucial point on avoiding a certain cynicism toward need and the disaffection it evokes. The threat of need can be handled in either of two ways: by supplying the need or by neutralizing the threat that it poses. On the cynical view, a capitalist regime will adopt whichever strategy is the most efficient in handling the threat. But on the view we have taken here, the second strategy is ruled out as being incompatible with the principle of respect for humanity which underlies a liberal society. Moreover, even if my approach here matches the stragety that might be adopted by a prudent defender of capitalism in certain circumstances, it is important to see that the case for that strategy is not merely cynical and self-serving, but moral as well. There are moral as well as prudential reasons for seeing to it that no one is led to threaten the stability of his own society by the desperate predicament in which it places him.

The third point is related to the second. Though many apologists for capitalism are willing to concede that there may be a prudential argument for the setting up of a welfare state, an increasing number in recent years have repudiated the idea that there is any *moral* justification for compulsory provision. Robert Nozick, for example, denies that justice grounds any general right to be at a certain level of material well-being. The main moral objection, he says, to the idea

that people might have rights, for example, to a certain minimum level of well-being

> is that these "rights" require a substructure of things and ma-
> terials and actions; and *other* people may have rights and en-
> titlements over these.... There are particular rights over
> particular things held by particular persons.... No rights exist
> in conflict with this substructure of particular rights.... The
> particular rights over things fill the space of rights, leaving no
> room for general rights to be in a certain material condition.[31]

This is a moral challenge even to the most minimal provisions
that might be made for dealing with abject need. Although
the conclusions of my argument are modest, it is worth re-
membering that even those modest conclusions are being
denied.

Fourth, it should be noted that the upshot of my argument
does not necessarily mean the simple "tacking on" of a welfare system to other economic institutions insensitive to
need. The principles of justice are to govern what Rawls
refers to as "the basic structure" of society. Though that
structure consists of many institutions – taxation arrangements, the system of property, the welfare state institutions,
the regulation of the market, monetary institutions, and so
on – those institutions unite to form a *system* so far as their
impact on the fortunes of members of society are concerned.
(This, as we saw, was stressed most strongly by Rawls in
his argument against the gambling approach in the original
position: we must not think that each institution represents
a discrete game in a series where our luck is likely to even
out.)[32] Indeed, what we have learned from fifty years of the
operation of the modern welfare state is that problems like
poverty or low income cannot be handled by one institution
alone. Phenomena like the poverty trap and the unemployment trap suggest that there has to be a systematic approach
to such problems, coordinating the tax system, the system
of social security, various aspects of incomes policy, and the
system of emergency benefits. A welfare system tacked on

as an afterthought to a structure of other institutions that have not also been made sensitive to the problems we are aiming to solve may well turn out to be worse than useless. The system as a whole must be oriented toward social justice, not particular institutions one by one. It seems, then, that the differences between the application of the two principles – Rawls's difference principle and the principle of the social minimum – are likely to be apparent across the board of social and economic institutions and not merely in the benefit levels secured by the operation of the welfare state.

The final point to emphasize is that, on this approach, a social minimum is intended to secure not just the simmering acquiescence of an underclass, but enough active support to constitute an entire social structure and sustain it through the ordinary vicissitudes of political life. The Rawlsian doctrine I have been explicating is about the strains of *commitment*, not just the strains of submission. Contractarianism is not just a theory about how governments should behave, it is a theory about the basis on which governance is constituted. The claim is that there can *be* no society, government, or authority except to the extent that people play a willing part in a common enterprise. Apart from such engagement, authority is nothing but intimidation, on the liberal view. We should bear these points in mind when we think about what a social minimum requires. If people's circumstances are such that they are unable to sustain a sense of themselves as active citizens of this society – charter members, so to speak – or if they lack a sense that this society is theirs too, organized in their name to respect and promote their interests, then the threshold of social concern is set too low. My appeal to the notion of a minimum, rather than to Rawls's difference principle, expresses the idea of a determinate level at which this sense of constitutive membership kicks in. It is not, however, intended to *minimize* either the level of provision or the critical force of the liberal conception to which that provision is a response.

Chapter 12

Social citizenship and the defense of welfare provision

I

From the Second World War until very recently, most Western societies treated an expanding public sector as the norm. Citizens in those countries grew used to a consistent expansion in the state's provision of goods and services, and in particular goods and services associated with the welfare state like education, health, social security, and employment.[1] The 1945 election of the Labour party in Britain is often seen as a watershed in this regard – an emphatic popular endorsement of state planning as a promoter of the collective good through the pursuit of welfare policies and the creation of institutions like the National Health Service.[2] It is striking how common this process has been among advanced industrial democracies. In most OECD countries, including the United States, the proportion of national income allocated to welfare services has increased steadily (in some instances dramatically) since the late 1940s, frequently absorbing as much as 50 percent of gross domestic product, and there has been a dramatic expansion in public employment and in the number of citizens receiving their primary income from the state in one form or another.[3]

Since the mid-1970s, however, this orthodoxy has suffered

In its original form, this was written by me and my colleague at Edinburgh, Desmond King. I am grateful to him for consenting to its reproduction here in a slightly edited form. Dr. King is now Fellow and Tutor in Politics at St. John's College, Oxford.

a serious material and ideological challenge. Materially, the post-1973 economic crisis rapidly undermined any expectation that economic growth would continue to supply the wealth needed to sustain extensive public provision of welfare services. As a result, most developed countries have had to initiate some control of welfare spending (however modest or unsuccessful), and in many of them "bringing welfare spending under control" has become a major political imperative. In the United States and Britain particularly, such policies have received ideological support from the most striking political development of the late 1970s and 1980s, the growth of the so-called New Right. The New Right has many forms (both intellectual and political) but the core features of the movement include: a critique of the economics of state intervention, particularly Keynesianism; an economic and moral critique of the welfare state; and an advocacy of free market mechanisms in all areas of public policy including meeting welfare needs in society. New Right theorists and politicians have sought to bring about a reversal in the post–1945 expansion of the public sector, as manifested primarily in the growth of the welfare state.

New Right theorists are troubled by the welfare state for both economic and moral reasons. Economically, the provision of public welfare is thought to erode incentives and thus distort the market for labor by providing people with a guaranteed source of income during difficult circumstances, making their search for work (especially for low-paying jobs) less diligent than it would be if such income were not available. Further, the welfare state is said to be economically damaging by virtue of its size (for example, crowding out private activity) and by virtue of its negative impact on individual savings as a basis for investment.[4]

In addition, the welfare state has regularly been cited as a source of moral corruption through its effect on the family. Since it provides support when families break down, it is said to encourage familial disintegration or to encourage some people not to enter into families at all. Some critics complain that it saps the authority of the male breadwinner and even encourages feminism.[5] As well as the effect on morals, there is also the effect on values such as liberty. New Right theorists claim that the bureaucracy of welfare institutions reduces individual freedom and enhances state power. Collective provision limits the role of market processes, which are said to be both the embodiment of economic freedom and the most powerful guarantors of political liberty.[6] Moreover, being financed out of taxation, welfare provision involves interference with private property and direct coercion of those individual taxpayers who would rather not contribute to compulsory charity in this way.[7]

Despite the influence enjoyed by the New Right challenge in, for example, the public policies of the Thatcher and Reagan administrations in the 1980s, it is striking how little the welfare state has actually been eroded. There have certainly been cuts but they have not turned out to be as draconian as many feared (or as many hoped). In part, the maintenance of high levels of welfare spending reflects the impact of the economic recession: high unemployment has obviously raised the volume of direct income support from the state. Still, on the whole, the main institutions – in Britain, for example, the National Health Service, the education system, and the supplementary benefit system – remain largely intact, and it is noticeable that politicians (even those on the Right like Margaret Thatcher and her followers) have felt constrained to assure voters that these institutions are "safe in our hands." Some commentators argue that this is not just a superficial whim of the electorate. It is an indication of the extent to which welfare provision is now conceived as a core element of *citizenship* in Western society.[8]

One way of putting the point is to say that the publicly guaranteed provision of goods and services associated with the post-war expansion of the state is no longer seen as a contingency of public policy, as something that might be changed or abolished whenever the administration changes its political hue. Instead, collective provision for welfare is associated now with an idea of social citizenship, and is taken to be comparable in status and importance to other aspects of citizenship such as the right to own property and the right to vote. This perception implies that if governments try to cut the welfare state, they will confront resistance based on a belief that people have rights embedded in welfare services which no one ought to tamper with. Welfare rights are integral to the modern sense of citizenship – so the argument goes – and therefore cannot simply be abrogated or whittled away at the whim of a particular government.

That this is a widely held opinion cannot be doubted. But in this chapter, I am going to attempt to *evaluate* it. I want to consider whether there is any normative justification for treating welfare provision and citizenship as linked in this way. I should perhaps emphasize that there are other defenses of the welfare state apart from those that can be developed through the citizenship idea.[9] The focus of the present argument does not imply any disparagement of these other approaches, but it is the citizenship argument I am concerned with. The argument is one that has enjoyed considerable prominence recently, in Britain and elsewhere,[10] and warrants, I think, a more thorough and searching examination, particularly in normative theory, than it has received up till now.

II

The principal theorist of the concept of "social citizenship" is the British sociologist T. H. Marshall. In an essay entitled "Citizenship and Social Class," published originally in 1949, Marshall argued that social provision constituted one of three sets of rights associated with citizenship in modern Britain, the others being civil and political rights.[11] He began by defining citizenship in the following general terms:

Citizenship is a status bestowed on those who are full members of a community. All who possess the status are equal with respect to the rights and duties with which the status is endowed. There is no universal principle that determines what those rights and duties shall be, but societies in which citizenship is a developing institution create an image of an ideal citizenship against which achievement can be measured and towards which aspiration can be directed. The urge forward along the path thus plotted is an urge towards a fuller measure of equality, an enrichment of the stuff of which the status is made and an increase in the number of those on whom the status is bestowed.... Citizenship requires a ... direct sense of community membership based on loyalty to a civilization which is a common possession. It is a loyalty of free men endowed with rights and protected by a common law. Its growth is stimulated both by the struggle to win those rights and by their enjoyment when won.[12]

What are these rights and how have they evolved? In his 1949 essay Marshall distinguished three layers of citizenship rights. The first layer comprises *civil rights*, rights concerning individual freedom which are associated with the sphere of civil society: "liberty of the person, freedom of speech, thought and faith, the right to own property and to conclude valid contracts, and the right to justice."[13] Civil rights are associated principally with the institutions of the legal system, such as the courts. They are rights held by discrete individuals and firms which they may come to law to vindicate. The second layer comprises *political rights*, that is, democratic rights of participation: "the right to participate in the exercise of political power, as a member of a body invested with political authority or as an elector of the members of such a body."[14] The institutions of representative democracy (Parliament and the electoral system) are central to the realization and maintenance of this second layer of rights. Third, there are *social rights*. By these, Marshall meant economic and welfare rights, rights to a minimum standard of welfare and income: they range "from the right to a modicum of economic welfare and security to the right to share to the full in the social heritage and to live the life of a civilised being according to the standard prevailing in the society."[15] Welfare state policies and institutions – the education system and the social services – are the main components of this third layer. The general idea is that by providing civil rights, society mitigates the impact of force, violence, and conflict in relations between people. By providing political rights, society recognizes individual men and women as capable of participating in the government of the whole community as well as in the governance of their own individual lives. Finally, by securing minimum standards of economic well-being the state offsets the vagaries of market processes and corrects the gross inequalities of distribution that markets both presuppose and amplify.

The first thing to note about these three types of citizenship rights is that they are not mutually exclusive as categories. Free speech, for example, can be regarded as both a civil right and a political right. This point has particular relevance to some of the items on the social agenda. Take the case of education. Education is a facility important both for individual life chances and for participation in other citizenship activities, such as voting or seeking redress through the courts.[16] That overlap is crucial to many traditional arguments about citizenship, as we shall see below. Like many citizenship ideas, it indicates a tight reciprocity between the duties individuals owe to the community and the duties the community owes to them. As Marshall put it, "we have here a personal right combined with a public duty to exercise the right."[17] In its contribution to a person's own well-being, free education is a social good; in its contribution to his participatory status and capabilities, it is a political right and, indeed, a political duty. Much the same can be said about the other aspects of welfare provision like health, social security, and employment.

Thus, the fact that Marshall's categories are not rigid should not worry us. Sometimes it is the very fluidity of the boundaries that provides the best case for the idea of social citizenship. One of the strongest arguments in favor of welfare provision is the empirical one that securing basic social standards does in fact promote the existence and responsible exercise of other rights indisputably embodied in citizenship. We will explore this argument in Section IV.

Consideration of the way in which these various elements

of citizenship have evolved plays an important part in Marshall's argument. In each case the evolution can be considered in two dimensions: in relation to the content of the element in question; and in relation to its status as something enjoyed universally in a society. For example, when the concept of political citizenship emerged, it was first confined to a minority of the inhabitants of the society; only recently has it been extended to all. Of these two aspects of evolution, it is the second which is of interest to us in this article – the gradual universalization of social provision, to the point where it is available equally to all.

Marshall suggests that the three kinds of citizenship rights were originally part and parcel of a single core: "in early times these three strands were wound into a single thread," in which there was a "fusion of political and civil institutions and rights."

> [A] man's social rights, too, were part of the same amalgam, and derived from the status which also determined the kind of justice he could get and where he could get it, and the way in which he could take part in the administration of the affairs of the community of which he was a member.[18]

However, this earlier "amalgam" is by no means a direct equivalent of citizenship according to contemporary conceptions. Modern citizenship began in the twelfth century, according to Marshall, but it is the eighteenth, nineteenth, and twentieth centuries that are crucial for the transformation of civil, political, and social rights successively into universal rights.

Civil rights were established, in Britain, between the Revolution and the first Reform Act. During the eighteenth century the rule of law was established, mainly through the "work of the courts, both in their daily practice and also in a series of famous cases in some of which they were fighting against parliament in defence of individual liberty."[19] A civil right also developed in the economic sphere, the right to work, that is, the right to economic freedom as a complement to the rule of law, resultant, in no small degree, on the development of markets. Thus, individual freedom, as embodied in civil rights, became a universal feature of citizenship with the emergence and growth of the bourgeoisie. *Political rights* emerged in the nineteenth century, according to Marshall, as the franchise was steadily extended (to some extent as a consequence of working-class pressure for equal citizen rights) and the status of citizenship expanded to include the right to vote and other rights of democratic participation. Not until the present century, however, were political rights universalized through the institution of a franchise based on the equality of individuals as an attribute of citizenship. By the 1920s in Britain, civil and political rights reflected the status each man and woman enjoyed as a citizen. Formally, at least, all citizens enjoyed equal rights in civil and political life, and these rights were understood to be part and parcel of what it was to be a member of a society like our own.

Social citizenship is largely a twentieth-century phenomenon. Twentieth-century rights to education, health, and an assured income are in many ways diametrically opposed to earlier practice in this area. For example, the 1834 Poor Law implemented an exclusionary principle of citizenship, since according to Marshall, it

> treated the claims of the poor, not as an integral part of the rights of the citizen, but as an alternative to them – as claims which could be met only if the claimants ceased to be citizens in any true sense of the word. For paupers forfeited in practice the civil right of personal liberty, by internment in the workhouse, and they forfeited by law any political rights they might possess.[20]

The Factory Acts also initially narrowed the meaning of citizenship by applying to children and women exclusively, though "by the end of the nineteenth century, such arguments had become obsolete, and the factory code had become one of the pillars of the edifice of social rights."[21]

In the twentieth century these social rights have undergone

enormous expansion as state responsibility for education, health, welfare, safety, and employment has been increasingly taken for granted. For Marshall this expanded responsibility constitutes social or welfare rights and transforms them into legitimate attributes of citizenship. These developments were stimulated in part by growth in money incomes, by the introduction of direct taxation, and by mass production and consumerism which fueled demands for reductions in inequality.[22] Welfare state institutions directly counter market processes by providing citizens with a minimum income, a basic standard of social services (health and education), and respite against economic uncertainty.[23]

Marshall's account of the development of the rights of citizenship has been the subject of controversy in two ways: there have been disputes about its descriptive plausibility and disputes about its normative claims. The second set of issues is my central concern, and I will deal with them in the sections that follow.[24]

III

In saying that welfare provision is part and parcel of citizenship in the modern state, Marshall was describing both how it has evolved and how it is viewed by the people who enjoy it. But I think he was also doing more than this: he was talking about the way in which welfare provision *ought* to be viewed, and intimating a normative argument about how it might be defended.

At a minimum, to associate welfare provision with citizenship is to make a proposal about how welfare should be handled in society. For example, as we have seen, it is to endorse the replacement of the Poor Law approach with provision for need that is given universally, that is provided without supplication or stigma, and that avoids as far as possible the invidious operation of official discretion.[25] However, associating it with citizenship is not just a way of making this proposal; it is also a way of defending it. The suggestion is that we *ought* to associate welfare with citizenship because our concept of citizenship will be radically impoverished if we do not. Citizenship, on this account, *demands* welfare provision; we cannot have an adequate notion of citizenship without it.

Is there any justification for this claim? In normative terms, does our concept of citizenship provide us with a reason for continuing to assure health, education, social services, and income support to everyone in our society? Is there anything in the idea of social citizenship to trouble the theorists of the New Right in the normative arguments they are making against the welfare state?

One way into these questions is through Marshall's focus on equality. We have already mentioned that, for Marshall, citizenship is about expanding and enriching society's notion of equality by extending its scope through civil, political, and social rights. The development of universal rights of citizenship has pushed forward the meaning of equality by broadening the scope of its application. Marshall stresses that it is not "absolute equality" he is aiming at nor is it any rigid equality of wealth:

> The extension of the social services is not primarily a means of equalizing incomes. In some cases it may, in others it may not. The question is relatively unimportant. . . . What matters is that there is a *general enrichment of the concrete substance of civilized life, a general reduction of risk and insecurity, an equalization between the more and the less fortunate at all levels.* . . . Equalization is not so much between classes as between individuals within a population which is now treated for this purpose as though it were one class. Equality of status is more important than equality of income.[26]

To talk about equality in this context is to talk about a progressive enlargement and enrichment of people's life chances. Citizenship does this principally by altering existing patterns of social inequality, and making it less likely that extremes can be sustained: "the preservation of inequalities has been made more difficult by the enrichment of the status of citizenship. There is less room for them and there is more and more likelihood of their being challenged."[27] But, again, what if someone simply denies that this is an *enrichment* of the notion of equality, or that the value of equality, so enriched, is attractive? Does the notion of citizenship give us any substantial basis for rebuttal?

There are two ways in which it might help. First, we might be able to show that citizenship as it has been traditionally understood is a concept which requires social provision and enriched equality for its effective realization. Or second, even if that is not the case, we might be able to show that a *new* concept of citizenship which *does* include a guarantee of social provision is more attractive as an ideal than one which does not. The first line of argument takes us from a familiar value to one that is in dispute, asserting an empirical connection between welfare provision and the possibility of effective participation by everyone as a citizen. The second line of argument challenges us directly to adopt the disputed conception of citizenship as our modern social ideal. Instead of asserting an empirical connection between welfare and citizenship, it challenges us to adopt a new account of citizenship of which the guarantee of welfare rights is partly constitutive.

I will explore the first line of argument in Section IV, but most often it is the second line that Marshall is hinting at. His thesis seems to be that social rights derive from a widely shared notion of ideal citizenship within a given society. He implies, in other words, that there is a public conviction about the appropriateness of social welfare as a characteristic of the status of equal citizenship. Certainly his evolutionary argument appears to advance such a position. He contends that "societies in which citizenship is a developing institution create an image of an ideal citizenship against which the achievement can be measured and towards which aspiration can be directed."[28] The ideal emerges in the struggle for rights. As rights have been extended to more and more members of society through processes of conflict and demand (for example, working-class pressure for universal suffrage), those to whom such rights have historically been denied have developed a sense (sometimes realistic, sometimes utopian) of the sort of citizenship they aspire to enjoy. It would not be remarkable if such an ideal expanded historically from civil through political to social rights as Marshall depicts.[29] Indeed, citizenship demands retain a dynamic aspect likely to expand into other areas in the future.[30]

The limitation of this view, however, is that it requires us to impose some sort of teleology or purpose on what may in fact be a purely accidental and contingent process of social evolution. It also makes welfare provision vulnerable to the course which that evolution happens to take. What if society lurches away from the welfare state, under the impact of New Right policies and ideologies? Does that show that the ideal of citizenship now no longer involves social rights? Or that it never really did? Or does it show that, as a society, we have abandoned or betrayed this ideal of citizenship? And how might we decide between those interpretations?

In Sections V and VI, I shall explore two different ways in which social citizenship might be vindicated as a distinct ideal. One of the arguments is relative to the actual course of development in our society, whereas the other purports to be more absolute. In Section V, I argue that Marshall's idea of social citizenship captures something that has, whether we like it or not, become embedded in the expectations of ordinary people, and that it can now not easily be altered without grave disruption to people's lives. In Section VI, I develop a Rawlsian argument about what it is to be a *member* of a modern society. Whatever course social development has actually taken so far, a society can not now claim to treat its citizens as equals or as members unless it provides socioeconomic structures that they could all have agreed to live under. I argue that a society without welfare provision would not be a structure that satisfied this condition.

But before exploring these arguments for social citizenship as a distinct ideal, let us see how far we can get with the notion of citizenship as it has been traditionally understood.

IV

Marshall, it will be remembered, distinguished between the political rights and the social rights associated with citizenship. But we know these are not rigid categories, and an obvious starting point for our inquiry is to ask whether there are any deep or important connections between the two.

The most familiar notion of political citizenship that we have is of the citizen as a participator – particularly a participator in republican or democratic politics. In classical political thought, a citizen was a full member of a city, a polis, or a republic. He was not merely subject to its laws and under its protection – these were often characteristics of noncitizens as well (resident aliens, for example). His citizenship consisted in the fact that he could hold public office, that he could join in the making of the laws, and (as a juror) in their application, and that he could be called on to discharge patriotic duties such as the defense of his polity against external attack. The classic definition was that of Aristotle: "A citizen is one who has a share in both ruling and being ruled."[31] The idea of citizenship is connected, then, with the view that political power should be exercised, not by a specialist elite who have made politics their vocation, but by ordinary members of the polity, acting either together or in rotation. Citizenship does not necessarily imply democracy: roughly, a democracy is a republic in which all adult men and women are citizens. In ancient Athens slaves and women were excluded from citizenship, and in the ideal polity that Aristotle proposed, many workers and artisans would be excluded as well. In Britain (to the extent that it has ever had a genuine notion of the citizen, as opposed to the subject) citizenship was restricted until the late nineteenth century to men, and to men who held more than a specified amount of property. But citizenship in Britain is now universal: every adult participates in ruling to the extent that each can vote for representative legislators in elections, and any adult may be called to serve on a jury or nominated for election to public office.

It may be thought that this idea of citizenship is *simply* a matter of political rights and that no conclusions can be drawn about the social or economic position that the citizen, as such, ought to be in. In fact, the tradition of Western thought about political citizenship completely contradicts this. Almost all the great theorists of that tradition – Aristotle, Cicero, Machiavelli, Rousseau, Burke, de Tocqueville, Mill, and, in the twentieth century, Hannah Arendt – have believed that in order to be a citizen of a polis, in order to be able to participate fully in public life, one needed to be in a certain socioeconomic position. Or they certainly believed that a *well ordered* city or republic would be one in which political participants were in a certain socioeconomic position. People, it was said, could not act as citizens at all, or could not be expected to act well in the political sphere and to make adequate decisions, unless some attention was paid to matters of their wealth, their well-being, and their social and economic status.

Two things have always been thought particularly important in this connection: the absence of great inequality, and the possession by all of some modicum of wealth (for example, a property qualification). I want to discuss them both.

Among theorists of citizenship, there has always been a consensus that some sort of rough equality among citizens is desirable. We find this in the Greek thinkers. Although Plato did not develop a theory of citizenship in *The Republic,* he did stress there the danger of the struggle between rich and poor as a source of political instability, and in his later and less utopian work, *The Laws,* he suggested that no citizen should be permitted to own an amount of wealth above a norm set at a level five times greater than the property of the poorest citizen.[32] Aristotle agreed that extremes of riches and poverty were likely to be a destabilizing factor, though he shied away from the imposition of any egalitarian norm, stressing instead that it was important for the polis to educate citizens to the virtue of moderation and persuade them that acquisitiveness was a vice.[33]

In later political thought, Machiavelli argued that political solidarity was greatest among those who shared a reasonably austere style of life (the example he appealed to was Sparta), and he suggested that republican institutions could survive in a territory only if the richer members of the gentry were liquidated.[34] Rousseau, too, insisted that extreme inequality was dangerous: it was the cause "of mutual hatred among the citizens, of indifference to the common cause, of the corruption of the people, and of the weakening of all the springs of government." Society must be arranged, he said, so that no citizen is rich enough to buy another, and no one poor enough to be bought.[35]

I am not citing these writers because I think they are sages to whose authority we should submit on matters of citizenship; their works are not, as it were, sacred texts. But there is a long tradition of thinking about citizenship, and in our thought about modern institutions we should take advantage of whatever insights and arguments they offer. The theme linking inequality and instability is an important one. If those who are radically unequal share in the exercise of political authority and the determination of the laws, there will be a constant and understandable tendency for one group of citizens to enviously challenge the existing distribution of property, for another group of citizens to jealously defend that distribution, and for both the challenge and the defense to be fired up by considerations of intense personal advantage as well as, and perhaps at the expense of, whatever sense of justice there is on either side. In modern terms, reductions in inequality may enhance social integration and therefore promote stability.

Put more positively, the suggestion is that we need a certain spirit of fraternity among citizens. They must regard one another as friends and work on a basis of goodwill and mutual understanding. Such goodwill and understanding are required if civic politics is to be undertaken in good faith, and if debate and disagreement are to be possible without suspicion and paranoia creeping in. That sort of solidarity and mutual trust may depend in turn on rough equality as much as on a sense of community and belonging, for the more inequality there is, the more cleavages we will find in things like consumption patterns and life-style, and, in a sense, the less comprehensible citizens are likely to be to one another. (It is partly these ideas that are being appealed to, when concern is voiced about "two nations" in British society.)

Besides stability and solidarity, other arguments for equality in the civic tradition have focused on the need for citizens to be economically independent of one another. They rest on the premise that a citizen should be one who is in a position to bring his *own* judgment to public issues, rather than one who responds as a member of a faction or retinue or as a mere mouthpiece for another. As independent individuals, citizens have some hope of reaching agreement on the common good; and no citizen would ever be interested in purchasing the vote or opinion of another unless he wanted to promote some sectional or peculiar interest of his own. There are, therefore, good civic reasons for ensuring, on the one hand, that no one is in a position to do this, and, on the other, that no one is so economically vulnerable that he would be tempted to betray his civic obligations for the food and shelter he needs to live. These concerns have been amplified in modern political theory with an awareness of how easily the opinions, preferences, and perceived interests of the poorer groups can be manipulated by those who have economic power over them – those with whom they must come to terms if they are to secure a living.[36]

So far I have presented this as an attack on inequality. It does not follow that citizens should be rigidly equal in their wealth and income; these are arguments against *extremes* of inequality, arguments for narrowing the range between rich and poor, not arguments for making everyone the same or leveling all differences. Moreover, although extreme inequality as such undermines civic life because of the lack of fraternity between rich and poor, it also corrupts the individuals who are at either end of the social scale. Luxury and wealth corrupt the rich – that was Machiavelli's concern about the gentry. And poverty and vulnerability corrupt the poor, according to the republican tradition. A defense of welfare on the basis of citizenship will naturally focus mainly on this last concern: the predicament of poverty, and the insistence, by almost every writer in this tradition, that those who are poor cannot be citizens, that, in Aristotle's words, "you could no more make a city out of paupers than out of slaves."[37]

The view that the poor cannot be citizens is based in part on the way in which desperate need is conceived to interfere with the processes of reflection and deliberation that civic politics requires. It is trite to say that hunger is something of a distraction so far as politics is concerned. Perhaps it is more telling to reflect that people who are completely unsure about food and shelter in the coming days for themselves and their families will be worried sick and obsessed with this issue all the time, in a way which leaves very little mental space for any general and long-term reflection on issues that go beyond their present material predicament. Similar concerns were voiced by the English Idealists (T. H. Green and others) when they argued that political participants could not develop into moral citizens, capable of contributing to the common good, if they were absorbed all the time by the pressure of material need.

Now, of course, we should take care not to exaggerate these points. We do not need to agree with Hegel that such a situation is one of "savagery and unfreedom," nor should we go so far as Hobbes, who suggests that the drive for elementary survival is psychologically irresistible and simply short-circuits all the apparatus of rational deliberation and consent on which political structures depend. We do not even have to agree with Hannah Arendt that the domination of politics by questions of need signals the entrance of violence and terror into the political realm. However, there *is* something to Arendt's conviction that civic politics in a republic cannot be expected to survive very long if there is constant clamoring for bread, constant demands for "action now, not words" to meet the predicament of those who may perish while politicians talk. To clamor for "action now, not words" to meet a social problem is, in effect, to dismiss as instantly irrelevant any articulate consideration of the means whereby the social problem may be addressed and any reflective discussion of the way those means might fit with the other goals and priorities of the republic. It is, in other words, to dismiss as irrelevant *politics* as the republican tradition understands it.[38]

Plato and Aristotle more or less took it for granted that the poverty of the masses, if given a political voice, would drive them to rapacious greed rather than to a concern for justice. The hidden assumption of that view is not that the masses are inherently depraved, but that poverty itself interferes with the articulate deliberation that a political concern for justice necessarily involves. Those who are in desperate need cannot be expected to take time to reflect on the issue of what resources they are justly entitled to; they are too taken up with literally getting a living to concern themselves with that. If articulate reflection about justice is, as Aristotle believed, the essence of politics, need must somehow be banished from the forum before political activity can take place.

The point is one that can be taken conservatively or liberally. At the very least, it seems to imply that hungry people must not be let loose in the political forum, for their needs will impel them to make demands that subvert and short-circuit the leisurely course of civic deliberations. This implies that citizenship should be the privilege of those who are economically secure. But that may not be enough to meet the concern, for, as Arendt quite rightly points out, the compassion which desperate need kindles in others can often be as violent and antipolitical in character as the original needs themselves. This sometimes leads her to the odd suggestion that citizens must steel themselves to resist the siren charms of compassion, and that they must bind themselves to resist any concern with the economic predicament of those languishing in poverty outside the doors of the assembly. Politics, she claims, must not concern itself with the life process.[39] But that is fatuous, first, because people cannot always succeed in distancing themselves in that way, and

second, because it implies that citizens should be unconcerned with the conditions that make their civic life possible.
A more sensible and liberal solution is to say that the removal
of need from society is one of the great and urgent tasks of
civic life, because as long as it remains, whether the poor are
admitted to the assembly or not, there is always the danger
that – directly or relatedly through compassion – the clamor
for bread *now* will subvert the processes of politics.

Apart from the threat posed by need itself, there is also
concern among republican theorists about the sort of life the
poorest members of society are likely to lead. Aristotle wrote
that "the best state will not make the labourer a citizen,"[40]
and Plato spoke in *The Republic* of the "stunted natures" of
the working classes – "their minds being as cramped and
crushed by their mechanical lives as their bodies are de-
formed by manual trades."[41] In ancient thought the concern
was that the long hours of work necessary to secure a living
for those who had no independent means would not leave
them the time or the leisure to acquaint themselves with and
deliberate on the issues that citizens ought to be addressing.
In modern political thought, this has combined with concern
about the effects of the division of labor and the way it contracts a person's mind and strength to the performance of
just one task.[42]

Inevitably, these lines of thought direct the republican tradition toward the idea of a property franchise. The property
owner is independent of others, and he can hold independent views. Unlike the propertyless members of the proletariat, he does not have to come to terms with and submit
himself to people in another class in order to secure a living.
He can live off his own resources or the income which they
generate.[43] To get a living he does not have to work long
hours and preoccupy himself exclusively with one task; his
independent income gives him time and leisure to reflect on
broader political issues.

As well as these considerations, there are several other
arguments for restricting the class of citizens to property
holders. One is the narrow, pragmatic view favored by

Locke, that the tasks of the citizen in the modern state may not involve much more than periodic consent to taxation; and consent to taxation is morally required only from those on whom the fiscal burden falls. But Locke had a relatively impoverished notion of civic participation. More interesting are the arguments of Edmund Burke, to the effect that only property holders have something solidly and permanently at stake in the commonwealth, or (if one is unconvinced by that argument, thinking perhaps that *everyone* has something solid at stake in the commonwealth, namely his life and well-being), only property holders can be expected to have a proper sense of caution, prudence, responsibility, and permanence in their thought and action in public affairs.[44]

The theme of the ethical importance of property owning is also taken up by Hegel in the *Philosophy of Right*. Owning property, he said, allows the individual's will to transcend and supersede "the pure subjectivity of personality."[45] People have all sorts of schemes and good ideas whizzing about in their heads, constantly changing and replacing one another. But once they have property to work on, the objects themselves start to register and embody the effects of their schemes and purposes in a more or less inerasable form, and so they have to start taking seriously the business of settling upon some particular purpose or project. You cannot always be changing your mind once you are working on external objects, for you will soon learn that the whimsicality of subjective thinking can wreck and undermine everything when it is applied in the real world. Along Burkean lines, then, there is an emphasis on a sense of permanence, a sense of responsibility, and a concrete sense of purpose which property owners can be expected to have, and which those who are propertyless are likely to lack.

Enough has been said, I hope, to indicate that the traditional notion of citizenship is not independent of social and economic concerns. Everyone in the civic republican tradition – that is, everyone who has ever thought seriously about citizenship in a political sense – has reached certain conclusions about what the economic situation of the citizen ought to be. However, one may still think that we are miles away from social citizenship in T. H. Marshall's sense. Indeed, if anything, we seem to be going in the opposite direction: instead of just taking welfare rights away from the poor, the tendency of this tradition is to take political rights away from them as well!

The interesting thing, though, is that each of the arguments we have been considering can be pushed in either of two directions. On the one hand, as we have seen, they can be used as arguments for restricting citizenship to those who happen to be in a certain socioeconomic position, those who own property, those of independent means, or those who are economically secure in some other sense. On the other hand, they can be used as a basis for exactly the opposite conclusion: if we want to have universal citizenship, in a political sense, for our society, then we should do it properly and see that *everyone* is put in the socioeconomic position that we have reason to believe citizens ought to be in. In other words, if we take the idea of universal suffrage seriously, then we should not be content simply to give everybody a vote; we should set about the task of giving them the economic security, which, on the arguments we have been considering, is the necessary precondition for the responsible exercise of the franchise.

It is true that the arguments we have been considering are not in themselves considerations in favor of universal suffrage. In the modern democratic age, we think we have independent arguments for that: ethical ideas about equal respect, utilitarian ideas about the necessity to get governments to promote the general interest, neo-Aristotelian ideas about participation being part of human nature, not just the nature of a few, arguments about what political obligation presupposes, and so on. My thesis is a conditional one. *If* we accept any of these independent arguments for universal suffrage, *then*, taking seriously the arguments I have outlined about fraternity, economic independence, security, and responsibility, we will have powerful reasons for associating political citizenship with at least some of the welfare rights

Marshall spoke about when he referred to citizenship in a social sense.

V

So far I have explored the connections between what Marshall called political citizenship and what he calleld social citizenship. The other arguments I want to discuss appeal, however, to a broader notion of citizenship than this. Often when we say "X is a citizen of the United Kingdom," what we mean is that he is a fully fledged *member* of this community, entitled to live here and make a life here. We may not be implying any theory about political participation; we may be saying, rather, that this is where he belongs. What is the normative force of this idea? Is there anything in the concept of membership or belonging that lends support to Marshall's conception of social citizenship?

Let me start modestly with a discussion of what it is to belong to a society *like our own*. Then in Section VI, I will consider whether any normative argument can be drawn out of the concept of belonging itself, quite apart from the history of the particular community with which it is associated. The argument I want to consider in the present section goes roughly like this.

Over the past fifty years in Britain, we have taken it on ourselves collectively to provide for much of the basic welfare of the members of society. Over that period, people who live here have become familiar with that provision: they are familiar with the way welfare is provided and they are familiar with the way it is paid for, out of taxation. Both taxpayers and potential recipients have taken all this on board, and organized their expectations and the structure of their lives accordingly. There is disagreement at the margins: about the precise array of goods and services on offer, and about the extent and incidence of taxation. But the broad idea that this is what our society does for its members and this is how it does it, has caught on and is used as a primary point of reference for the way people organize their lives. To launch an attack, then, on *the very idea* of welfare provision, as some New Right thinkers have done, is to challenge the way people have grown accustomed to think about themselves. It is to attack their basic sense of what it is to live here, to make a life here, to belong here. It is, in that way, to attack their sense of citizenship.

Notice a few things about this argument. It does not proceed, as the previous one did, from an antecedent notion of citizenship to the demand that there should be welfare provision. Instead it proceeds from the contingent fact that welfare guarantees have been established in this society (for whatever reason) to the claim that they are now part of what we understand by citizenship. The suggestion is that what it is to be a member is not something fixed in stone for all time, but is expandable, as new ways develop in which the state can offer various benefits that accrue from collective organization, and in which members can become participants in schemes to offer various social, cultural, and economic guarantees.

Second, the concept of citizenship here is somewhat broader than that used in the previous discussion. Now it means not only political participation, but all aspects of what it is to be a *member* of a society. Many political scientists argue that participation in politics is not what people think is most important (though some regret that this is so). The present argument is realistic, then, in focusing on a sense of citizenship that connects more comprehensively with people's sense of their social selves and of the organization of their lives.

The third thing to note is that, insofar as it has any normative force, this argument is primarily a conservative argument, with a small "c" (and we shall have to consider shortly whether it is not *too* conservative). According to this approach, the reasons for keeping welfare guarantees in existence once they have become established are not confined to the reasons there were for establishing them in the first place. Once a certain form of provision is established, people build their expectations around it; they would not build their expectations around a mere demand that welfare provision *ought* to be established. But when people do start building their expectations, the fact of institutional establishment takes on a moral significance of its own.

The point can be expressed in terms of security. When Jeremy Bentham wrote about security as one of the ends of law, he said that "security consists in receiving no check, no shock, no derangement to the expectation founded on the laws, of enjoying such and such a portion of good: the legislator owes the greatest respect to this expectation which he has himself produced."[46] Security of expectation, he argued, is the basis of people's ability to plan their lives: "It is hence that we have the power of forming a general plan of conduct; it is hence that the successive instants which compose the duration of life are not like isolated and independent points, but become continuous parts of a whole."[47] Similar points have been made in the New Right context as well by F. A. Hayek and others, stressing the need for stable and predictable laws.[48]

As Bentham stated it, the point was mainly about property. Though there are good utilitarian reasons for redistributing property (the theory favors equality on the basis of the diminishing marginal utility of resources), there are also powerful utilitarian reasons for resisting redistribution. Bentham believed it was possible to calculate in advance that both the property owner who suffers a shock to his expectations and those who are frightened or made anxious by the example of what is happening to him will suffer more, directly and indirectly, than the beneficiaries of redistribution could possibly gain, even taking into account diminishing marginal utility. Everything that Bentham says about property expectations can be applied to welfare expectations, once they too have become established. Indeed, once they are established there is as much a case for regarding them as part of the overall property scheme as there is for regarding, say, home ownership in this way. In each case, someone has a recognized legal claim over certain of the resources available in society, and that claim forms the basis of his expectations and his ability to plan his life. (This is why a number of American writers have argued, for example, that welfare entitlements should be given protection under the Fifth Amendment to the U.S. Constitution, which prohibits the taking of private property for public use without just compensation.)

Many welfare benefits are awarded on a discretionary basis and this raises the issue of whether it is possible to describe them strictly speaking as *rights*. Though Marshall uses the terminology of rights, there is not space to consider here in any detail the issue of whether legal entitlement is the appropriate vehicle for welfare provision. Some welfare benefits are in fact distributed as a matter of entitlement (for example, education and child benefits in the U.K.) but even those that are discretionary can still give rise to strong expectations amongst the members of a community. The fact that some aspects of welfare are discretionary does not prevent people from forming expectations about them, and organizing their lives in often quite important ways on the basis of those expectations. Though people may know that there is discretion in the award of welfare payments, still they expect that discretion to be exercised in their favor, at least if theirs is (to their mind) a clearly needy case, and they will be shocked, taken aback, and outraged if it is not. That is the key to my argument.

To violate these expectations is not merely to disappoint people. It is also to radically disrupt their personal planning. Social security expectations crucially affect the risks people think they can run in making their decisions. I have in mind here things like forming and breaking marital or quasi-marital relationships, conceiving children, moving away from close-knit communities, making employment decisions, taking certain attitudes to one's employer, starting a small business, opting for higher education, and so on. In all these areas, people are taking chances, entering into gambles if you like, on certain assumptions and against the background of certain conditions. Attitudes to social risk play a large part in establishing individual identity in society, and beliefs about welfare provision are crucial to those attitudes. My sense of what it is to be a member of this community is going to be centrally linked to my awareness of the conditions under which I am to think about making a life for myself in this community and about taking the various risks that that involves.

Clearly, people will be willing to take much greater risks when they know there is a safety net – a limit to the catastrophic losses they may incur. They can say to themselves, "I will go into this new relationship, or I will take the risk of college education rather than a minimum wage job, or I will start this new business, knowing that if things work out badly at least I will not starve." Many of these risks are long-term, and the willingness to undertake them is based on long-run expectations. So we can see immediately the force of the argument that would say it is unfair to change the terms of the gamble – by abolishing the safety net – halfway through.

Some New Right theorists have seized on this aspect of welfare provision as the very thing they are objecting to: welfare provision, they say, encourages people to run irresponsible risks, so that they become less prudent in their decisions about families, strike action, education, and so on. As I mentioned at the beginning of this chapter, they claim that the mitigation of risk undermines market discipline and other forms of discipline in society. I do not want to get into that argument except to say that attitudes toward risk in *any* society are going to be relative to institutional expectations. The New Right view thus presupposes already that there is some independent argument for choosing markets-without-safety-nets as the baseline in terms of which personal responsibility is to be assessed. That presupposition may be questioned. I should also add that there are arguments on the other side – particularly feminist and modernist (as well as economic) arguments – for increasing mobility and choice in modern society for everyone in it. Mitigating the risks of choice is one way of doing this.

But eventually we come back to the point about conservatism. Suppose the New Right theorists are even half right, and we do suffer harm as a society – in terms of market distortion and the erosion of incentives – because welfare guarantees are available. Is it my contention that no established expectations can *ever* be overturned, no matter how socially harmful they are?

The question is a good one, and the argument I have put forward should not be regarded as absolute. There are all sorts of traditional privileges in society, which are the center of people's established expectations, but which nevertheless are socially harmful and ought to be abolished. For example, one of the issues at stake in the American Civil War was not whether slavery was wrong but whether it was right to violate all the expectations and life plans that had become bound up with the institution. The danger is that people can organize their lives around harmful systems as well as good ones; and then the force of a conservative argument would be to perpetuate the evil. Indeed, if this had been accepted as a general argument in 1945, social provision in its modern form might never have been established.

The force of this objection should not be exaggerated, however, in the present context. It is important for the case of social rights that we are talking, not about an institution like slavery, but about benefits and privileges that are universal. That is part of the significance of drawing attention to their status as elements of "citizenship." Since this is so, we need to be quite clear about what is being said when they are alleged to be socially harmful. Is it alleged that *everyone* would be better off if welfare benefits were withdrawn, if the risks people run were not socially underwritten, and if unmitigated market discipline were allowed to operate? Or is it merely that *some* would be better off and their gains would outweigh others' losses? We may be dealing here with a clash between the common good and the greatest good, familiar to all involved in the modern discussion of utilitarianism. The fact that a conservative argument protects a universal entitlement in the face of *aggregate* social utility is hardly a devastating objection, unless more is said.

Second, a conservative argument does not imply absolute and slavish adherence to the expectations of the past. It implies rather that if one wants to make changes in the basis of people's expectations, one must do so slowly, over decades or even generations, rather than (say) in the space of one parliament. Otherwise one is not sufficiently respecting the people one is dealing with – the people who have to live their lives in the environment one is manipulating – and their need for a settled sense of the basis on which they can make their plans and choices.

Third, it should be noted that, although the objection is an important one, it does nothing to diminish the *concern* which is at the basis of my argument: it does not deny that people do form expectations, and that their lives may be disrupted and disoriented if these are shattered, by even well intentioned reform. The argument I am making is not a cast-iron defense of welfare provision, but it uses the notions of citizenship, membership, and belonging – as they relate to our society – to sound a serious note of caution about any attempt to roll back the welfare state. The virtue of the social citizenship argument, on this interpretation, is to draw attention to certain costs, which might otherwise be underestimated, attendant on any such antiwelfare initiative. Moreover, we must bear in mind that the argument made here is not necessarily an argument for a massive welfare state or a welfare state expanding inexorably toward socialism. The argument concerns public provision of a minimum level of welfare as a universal entitlement, defining a threshold below which people will not be allowed to fall without diminishing their sense of and their capacities for citizenship. That is something one ought to be very wary about disrupting, for it is most unlikely that the alienation, disappointment, and disorientation that would result from the abrogation of minimum support would have no effect on other aspects of social action, stability, and integration.

VI

The argument I have just made is a relative one: the sort of welfare provision established in Britain, for example, helps to constitute citizens' sense of what it is to be a member of that society. Some writers, however, have taken the citizen-ship-membership-welfare link even further, arguing that welfare provision is not just an incident of particular conceptions of community and membership in particular countries, but something partly constitutive of *the very concept* of community and membership. If there is any force to this argument, it provides a universal rather than a merely relative case for welfare based on citizenship. Though some of Marshall's arguments seem oriented toward the relative approach – this is where *we* (for example, in Britain) have got to in the evolution of citizenship – some of his arguments, as we have seen, imply that a more absolute case can be made. They imply that there is a trans-societal *ideal* of social citizenship toward which the evolution of modern citizenship in various countries is taking us.

To make this case, it is not enough to establish that welfare provision is, in fact, a characteristic of all societies. The "constant conjunction" of citizenship and welfare in the modern world does not establish that one is *implied* by the other. It may be mere coincidence; or it may be that all societies have accepted other arguments for welfare provision that have nothing to do with citizenship. Moreover, we should remember that the New Right proposal, that universal practice should be altered in this regard, is one which is also made in all modern societies. One does not have to be a firm believer in the fact/value gap to see that a normative argument for resisting that proposal cannot be inferred directly from the very state of affairs that New Right critics are proposing to challenge.

Nor are we likely to get very far with purely conceptual or linguistic analyses of ideas like "citizenship," "membership," and "community." We can stare at the words for as long as we like, but the dictionary will not do our moral thinking for us. Anyone who thinks that such terms can be linked *definitionally* to the pursuit of ends such as the provision of welfare, should go back to Max Weber's dictum that "the state cannot be defined in terms of its end. There is scarcely any task that some political association has not taken in hand."[49] Equally one might say with Weber that there is no task that has not sometime been neglected by political associations or communities. Societies have neglected welfare provision in the past, or administered it grudgingly and shamefully, and there are proposals from people on the Right that they should neglect welfare provision in the future. I suppose one can insist that such societies are not really entitled to be called "*communities*" in some substantively defined sense; but that is just rhetoric and it begs the morally more important question of why people should be interested in the application of *that* definition, rather than some other.

In his book *Spheres of Justice*, Michael Walzer claimed that "every political community is in principle a 'welfare state','"[50] and insisted that the very idea of a community connotes some distribution according to need:

> Every political community must attend to the needs of its members as they collectively understand those needs; . . . the goods that are distributed must be distributed in proportion to need; and that distribution must recognize and uphold the underlying equality of membership.[51]

If Walzer is right about this, then citizenship in the sense of membership has a direct implication of welfare provision. Unfortunately, his argument falls into both the traps I have mentioned. First, he takes the fact that welfare provision is a universal feature of all societies as a basis for the normative claim that proposals to end welfare provision are misguided:

> There has never been a political community that did not provide, or try to provide, or claim to provide, for the needs of its members as its members understood those needs. And there has never been a political community that did not engage its collective strength – its capacity to direct, regulate, pressure and coerce – in this project.[52]

That claim, if true, is no doubt interesting; but it does not in itself imply any reason not to try something new in this regard. As it happens, Walzer's factual claim is false. He himself cites the example of Athens as a society which recognized and understood a much wider range of poverty-related needs than it attempted to cater for. It was well understood, for example, that *all* widows were potentially in need of economic assistance, but there was state provision only for the widows of fallen soldiers. Athens certainly recognized the importance of economic support for political citizenship: public money was paid out to make it possible for poorer citizens to miss a day's business to come to the Assembly or serve on juries, and this charge often amounted to more than half the public revenue of the city. This was in recognition of some of the arguments I mentioned in Section IV. But beyond that, it is simply wrong to say that Athens catered for all the needs, or even all the pressing needs, that it recognized its members to have.

There are two moves Walzer uses to deal with such counterexamples. On the one hand, he argues that certain societies do not count as communities in the appropriate sense. Thus, "the indifference of Britain's rulers during the Irish potato famine is a sure sign that Ireland was a colony," not part of the British community; and he says also that his principles, such as the principle that if distribution *is* undertaken it is distribution according to need, "probably don't apply to a society organized hierarchically, as in traditional India, where the fruits of the harvest are distributed not according to need but according to caste."[53] The question then arises: what moral reason is there for having a community rather than a colony or caste society in this sense? Walzer gives no answer. But it's the answer to this question that will contain the real argument for welfare.

Second, and connected with that, Walzer stresses the vagueness of welfare provision as a concept applying to all communities: "the idea of need and the commitment to communal provision do not by themselves yield any clear determination of priorities and degrees."[54] That is something, Walzer believed, that every society works out for itself in terms of its own history, politics, and social understandings.

(It is not for the philosopher to second-guess from his arm-chair the process of the evolution Marshall has described.) But then, Walzer is really moving back toward the relativist position we have already considered in Section V:

> The ancient Athenians, for example, provided public baths and gymnasiums for the citizens but never provided anything re-motely resembling unemployment insurance or social security. They made a choice about how to spend public funds, a choice shaped presumably by their understanding of what the common life required. It would be hard to argue that they made a mistake. I suppose there are notions of need that would yield such a conclusion, but these would not be notions acceptable to – they might not even be comprehensible to – the Athenians themselves.[55]

In fact the main interest of Walzer's book has been in his relativist suggestion that different standards of distribution are morally appropriate to the social understandings established in different societies. For my purposes the important point is that, in this and similar passages, there is no longer any sense of an argument that membership and community, as such, imply a commitment to welfare provision in anything other than a notional sense.

Are there then no substantive conclusions we can reach about membership, only the relativist conclusions with which we ended the previous section? I think that there is one other approach that may be promising.

The work of John Rawls has been very influential in recent political philosophy, for its revival of contractarianism as a method of argument, and for the liberal egalitarianism of its conclusions.[56] Rawls's argument is usually considered in terms of justice and injustice. A just society, he argues, will be one in which people enjoy equal basic liberties and in which inequalities of wealth and power are tolerated only if they contribute positively to the well-being of the least ad-vantaged group. Though Rawls is agnostic about whether these principles are capable of legitimating a market economy and the institutions of capitalism, there is no doubt at all that they require social redistribution and the establishment of something recognizable as a welfare state.[57] Rawls's theory has been subject to many criticisms by New Right philosophers. Some, like Anthony Flew, accuse him of distorting the very notion of justice;[58] others, like Nozick, take him to task for ignoring the primacy of property entitlements and for assuming that society simply has at its disposal goods that it may distribute in accordance with Rawlsian principles;[59] still others, like Hayek, extend a cautious welcome to Rawls's work mainly because they have misunderstood its tendency.[60]

For my purposes, the interest lies not only in the welfarist and redistributivist *conclusions* of Rawls's discussion, but also in the way they are presented. I believe Rawls's work can be understood as a discussion of what it is to be a citizen or member of a given society. A person is a mere *subject* of a regime and not a citizen, if its rules and policies will be applied to him whether he likes it or not and whether they serve his interests or not. They are applied without reference to his consent. Since Locke, the liberal tradition has always been that we should try to think of subjects as though they were founding members of the society in which they live. Even though they cannot actually choose a regime to live under, nevertheless in our attempts to evaluate and legitimize their society, we should at least ask what sort of order they *would* have chosen if they had had the choice. This is the tradition Rawls pursues. For Rawls, being a member of a society is not just a matter of living in and being subject to a social framework; it is also a matter of how that framework is justified. A person is a *member* of a society if and only if the design of its basic institutions fairly reflects a concern for his interests along with those of everyone else.

As we all know, the way Rawls chooses to express this idea is through the myth of the social contract. A society is just, and the people living in it are members rather than subjects, if one can show that its institutions satisfy certain principles. If they are based on principles that would not or could not have been agreed to in advance by those who would have to live with them, then they cannot be regarded as just, for they do not embody sufficient respect for the persons they apply to. Thus understood, the social contract myth attractively expresses the idea of a veto. You cannot be voted into a contract; everyone has to agree, everyone has to be convinced, and everyone has to gain.

Rawls is the first to concede that in fact nothing like the "original position" has ever taken place: the social contract is a moral perspective or a thought experiment, not a historical speculation:[61]

> No society can, of course, be a scheme of cooperation which men enter voluntarily in a literal sense; each person finds himself placed at birth in some particular position in some particular society, and the nature of his position materially affects his life prospects. Yet a society satisfying the principles of justice comes as close as a society can to being a voluntary scheme, for it meets the principles which free and equal people *would assent to* under circumstances that are fair. In this sense, its members are autonomous and the obligations they recognize self-imposed.[62]

If people learn to think about their society in this way, then they can say to one another "that they are cooperating on terms to which they would agree if they were free and equal."[63] Or, if they are critical, they can say that what is wrong with their society is that it would *not* pass this test of agreement by everyone under conditions of fairness. Thus terms that *would* be agreed to can be used as a basis for evaluating both present arrangements and proposals for change in the future.

Rawls believes that people in his original position would choose a mix of principles. They would choose a principle of equal political liberty; and they would choose a principle of fair equality of opportunity and what he calls "the Difference Principle" to govern the distribution of social and economic goods. The Difference Principle is my concern here. Rawls argues that it would be impossible in the original position to secure general agreement for a set of social institutions that did not make collective provision for the plight of the members of the worst-off group. Social institutions that did not include the securing of a social minimum, the familiar apparatus of welfare provision, and perhaps more substantial methods of redistribution as well, would not command unanimous agreement in the original position. People would not be willing to accept an economic system or a system of property unless it had all this built into it. Those who feared they might fall into the worst-off group would be reluctant to accept anything less than this, because they would be unsure of their ability to *live with* anything less. Agreeing to terms of cooperation that did not include such guarantees would impose what Rawls refers to as "strains of commitment" on the parties:

> [T]hey cannot enter into agreements that may have consequences they cannot accept. They will avoid those that they can adhere to only with great difficulty. Since the original agreement is final and made in perpetuity, there is no second chance. In view of the serious nature of the possible consequences, the question of burden of commitment is especially acute. . . . Looking at the question from the standpoint of the original position, the parties recognize that it would be highly unwise if not irrational to choose principles which may have consequences so extreme that they could not accept them in practice.[64]

In other words, the Rawlsian argument takes us from what he refers to as "a general knowledge of human psychology" to speculations about the sorts of social arrangements people can live with. Faced with great deprivation and inequality, people cannot be expected to live quiet and satisfied lives. They therefore cannot in good faith undertake or agree to live with such deprivation and inequality. So a political theory which gives any weight to the question of what people would agree to has an argument against the acceptability of such neglectful arrangements.

Rawls's argument thus connects with my concerns in two ways. First, a political theory treats people as citizens, in the sense of members (as opposed to subjects), only if it concerns itself with what social arrangements those people would agree to. Second, Rawls argues that people would agree only to principles that focused concern on the plight of the poorest members of society. His principles certainly require a welfare state; indeed they may require much more. They therefore provide the backbone of a powerful argument connecting citizenship or membership as such with at least basic welfare provision.

As Rawls presents it, *no one* would sign up for an economic system without welfare provision. That is because one of the features of his original position is that the people taking this perspective must pretend to be ignorant of their wealth, class, and talents, and Rawls argues that no one would take the risk of turning out to be poor and untalented in a society that lacked a safety net. However, it is worth noting that the argument can be made out even without Rawls's controversial "veil of ignorance." All one needs is a veto and the requirement of unanimous agreement. Those who happen to be poor or untalented may be expected to veto the adoption of any social system that does not attempt to ameliorate their plight. If they have to live under such a system, they will be unable to give it their support and they will be driven by their need to subvert it where they can. Knowing this, they will be unable in good faith to agree to such a system from the standpoint of the original position. If nevertheless they find themselves in a society which lacks a safety net, or which lacks a basic welfare system, they are perfectly entitled to say to one another, "This society does not treat us as members, as citizens, or as people who belong here, for it is operating a system which could not possibly have commanded our consent." The warning of the social citizenship argument, on this interpretation, is that the cost of rolling back welfare provision may be the acceptance of exactly this sort of alienation.

If an argument like this can be made, then there is a reason for having welfare rights in a society whether it has a tradition of such institutions or not. Social rights of citizenship are a necessary condition for genuine and meaningful consent to economic and political arrangements. It is true that in his more recent work, Rawls has drawn back a little from the apparent universalism of *A Theory of Justice*. He now maintains that the principles of justice and the reasoning that leads to them do not represent moral conclusions valid for all times and places but rather moral conclusions whose validity is in some sense relative to the "social and historical conditions" which have produced what he calls "an overlapping consensus" about the basic values of a democratic society.[65] Rawls appears to be adopting a deep philosophical relativism about social and political thought. But the relativism that distinguished my argument in Section V was more concerned with existing institutional arrangements like the welfare state and their effect on people's expectations. It is therefore a more "surface-level" relativism than that with which Rawls is toying. The argument I have made in this section may be relative in Rawls's terms – that is, it may only make sense to people who have been brought up in a certain sort of culture with a certain history of arguing about freedom, equality, and democracy. All the same, some of the societies with this history have had satisfactory welfare arrangements; others have not. The Rawlsian argument reaches deeply into the underlying values of our culture to show that welfare provision is necessary if we are to keep faith with those values.

VII

In this chapter, I have sought to explore different arguments which might underlie, and give normative substance to, the notion of social citizenship. My analysis has been framed with reference to two possible views of the relation between welfare provision and citizenship: an idealistic argument whereby social welfare is presented as an attribute of citizenship in a statement about the most desirable form of social organization, and an empirical argument about the necessity of welfare for effective citizenship in a traditional sense. The first branch of the argument in turn divided in two: one branch arguing from the impact of expectations of existing welfare provision, the other not being so directly relative to existent social institutions. The arguments are separate but they are not meant to be mutually exclusive: I have presented them here as overlapping, complementary ways of teasing out the normative implications of citizenship.

The importance of this discussion lies in its relevance to contemporary political and social discourse. In an effort to rebut New Right arguments and policies, some scholars and politicians have drawn on social right and citizenship arguments to defend the policies and institutions of the welfare state. I have tried to evaluate the strength of such claims through an examination of their analytical basis and to suggest various ways in which those claims might be understood. Above all, I think it important that the idea of citizenship should remain at the center of modern political debates about social and economic arrangements. The concept of a citizen is that of a person who can hold his head high and participate fully and with dignity in the life of his society. Although, as we have seen, there are many competing conceptions of what it is to be a citizen in the modern state, and although, as our argument has shown, none of these conceptions is particularly straightforward, nevertheless the underlying idea must not ever be lost sight of when we are considering in our political and philosophical discussions what life in this society is to be like for its poorest members.

Chapter 13

Homelessness and the issue of freedom

There are many facets to the nightmare of homelessness. In this chapter, I want to explore just one of them: the relation between homelessness, the rules of public and private property, and the underlying freedom of those who are condemned by poverty to walk the streets and sleep in the open. Unlike some recent discussions, my concern is not with the constitutionality of various restrictions on the homeless (though that, of course, is important).[1] I want to address a more fundamental question of legal and moral philosophy: how should we think about homelessness, how should we conceive of it, in relation to a value like freedom?

The discussion that follows is, in some ways, an abstract one. That is intentional. One of my aims is to refute the view that, on abstract liberal principles, there is no reason to be troubled by the plight of the homeless, and that one has to come down to the more concrete principles of a communitarian ethic in order to find a focus for such concern. I shall argue that homelessness is in fact a matter of the utmost concern in relation to some of the most fundamental and abstract principles of liberal value. That an argument is abstract should not make us think of it as thin or watery. If homelessness raises questions even in regard to basic principles of freedom, it is an issue that ought to preoccupy liberal theorists as much as more familiar worries about torture, the suppression of dissent, and other violations of human rights. That the partisans of liberty in our culture have not always been willing to see this (or say it) should be taken as an indication of the consistency and good faith with which they espouse and proclaim their principles.

I

Some truisms to begin with. Everything that is done has to be done somewhere. No one is free to perform an action unless there is somewhere he is free to perform it. Since we are embodied beings, we always have a location. Moreover, though everyone has to be somewhere, a person cannot choose any location he likes. Some locations are physically inaccessible. And, physical inaccessibility aside, there are some places one is simply not allowed to be.

One of the functions of property rules, particularly so far as land is concerned, is to provide a basis for determining who is allowed to be where. For the purposes of these rules, a country is divided up into spatially defined regions or, as we usually say, places. The rules of property give us a way of determining, in the case of each place, who is allowed to be in that place and who is not. For example, if a place is governed by a private property rule, then there is an individual whose determination is final on the question of who is and who is not allowed to be in that place. Sometimes that individual is the owner of the land in question, and sometimes (as in a landlord-tenant relationship) the owner gives another person the power to make that determination (indeed to make it, for the time being, even as against the owner). Either way, it is characteristic of private ownership that some particular legal person has this power to determine who is allowed to be on the property.

The actual rules of private property are, of course, more complicated than this and they involve much besides this elementary power of decision.[2] To get the discussion going, however, it is enough to recognize that there is something like this individual power of decision in most systems of private ownership. I say who is allowed to be in my house. He says who is to be allowed in his restaurant. And so on.

The concept of *being allowed* to be in a place is fairly straightforward. We can define it negatively. An individual who is in a place where he is not allowed to be may be removed, and he may be subject to civil or criminal sanctions for trespass or some other similar offense. No doubt people are sometimes physically removed from places where they *are* allowed to be. But if a person is in a place where he is not allowed to be, not only may he be physically removed, but there is a social rule to the effect that his removal may be facilitated by the forces of the state. In short, the police may be called and he may be dragged away.

I said that one function of property rules is to indicate procedures for determining who is allowed and not allowed (in this sense) to be in a given place, and I gave the example of a private property rule. Not all rules of property are like private property rules in this regard. We may use a familiar classification and say that, though many places in this country are governed by private property rules, some are governed by rules of collective property, and those divide further into rules of state property and rules of common property (though neither the labels nor the exact details of this second distinction matter much for the points I am going to make).[3]

If a place is governed by a *collective* property rule, there is no private person in the position of owner. Instead, the use of collective property is determined by people, usually officials, acting in the name of the whole community.

Common property may be regarded as a subclass of collective property. A place is common property if part of the point of putting it under collective control is to allow anyone in the society to make use of it without having to secure the permission of anybody else. Not all collective property is like this: places like military firing ranges, nationalized factories, and government offices are off-limits to members of the general public unless they have special permission or a legitimate purpose for being there. They are held as collective property for purposes other than making them available for public use. However, examples of common property spring fairly readily to mind: they include streets, sidewalks, subways, city parks, national parks, and wilderness areas. These places are held in the name of the whole society in order to make them fairly accessible to everyone. As we shall see, they are by no means unregulated as to the nature or time of their use. Still, they are relatively open at most times to a fairly indeterminate range of uses by anyone. In the broadest terms, they are places where anyone may be.

Sometimes the state insists that certain places owned by private individuals or corporations should be treated like common property if they fulfill the function of public places. For example, shopping malls in the United States are usually on privately owned land. However, because of the functions such places serve, the state imposes considerable restrictions on the owners' powers of exclusion (people may not be excluded from a shopping mall on racial grounds, for example) and on their power to limit the activities (such as political pamphleteering) that may take place there.[4] Though this is an important development, it does not alter the analysis I am developing in this chapter, and for simplicity I shall ignore it in what follows.

Property rules differ from society to society. Though we describe some societies (like the United States) as having systems of private property, and others (like China) as having collectivist systems, all societies have some places governed by private property rules, some places governed by state property rules, and some places governed by common property rules. Every society has private houses, military bases, and public parks. So if we want to categorize whole societies along these lines, we have to say it is a matter of balance and emphasis. For example, we say that China is a collectivist society and that the United States is not, not because there is no private property in China, but because most industrial and agricultural land there is held collectively whereas most industrial and agricultural land in America is privately owned. The distinction is one of degree. Even as between two countries have basically capitalist economies, New Zealand (say) and Britain, we may say that the former is "communist" to a greater extent (that is, is more a system of common property) than the latter because more places (for example, all river banks) are held as common property in New Zealand than are held as common property in Britain. Of course, these propositions are as vague as they are useful. If we are measuring the "extent" to which a country is collectivist, that measure is ambiguous as between the quantitative proportion of land that is governed by rules of collective property and some more qualitative assessment of the importance of the places that are governed in this way.[5]

II

Estimates of the number of homeless people in the United States range from two hundred and fifty thousand to three million. A person who is homeless is, obviously enough, a person who has no home. One way of describing the plight of a homeless individual might be to say that there is no place governed by a private property rule where he is allowed to be.

In fact, that is not quite correct. A private proprietor may invite a homeless person into his house, and if he does there *will* be some private place where the homeless person is allowed to be. A technically more accurate description of his plight is that there is no place governed by a private property rule where he is allowed to be whenever *he* chooses, no place governed by a private property rule from which he may not at any time be excluded as a result of someone else's say-so. As far as being on private property is concerned – in people's houses or gardens, on farms or in hotels, in offices or restaurants – the homeless person is utterly and at all times at the mercy of others. And we know enough about how this mercy is generally exercised to figure that the description in the previous paragraph is more or less accurate as a matter of fact, even if it is not strictly accurate as a matter of law.[6]

For the most part the homeless are excluded from *all* the places governed by private property rules, whereas the rest of us are, in the same sense, excluded from *all but one* (or maybe all but a few) of those places. This is another way of saying that each of us has at least one place to be in a country composed of private places, whereas the homeless person has none.

Some libertarians fantasize about the possibility that *all* the land in a society might be held as private property ("Sell the streets!").[7] That would be catastrophic for the homeless. Since most private proprietors are already disposed to exclude him from their property, the homeless person might discover in such a libertarian paradise that there was literally *nowhere* he was allowed to be. Wherever he went he would be liable to penalties for trespass and he would be liable to eviction, to being thrown out by an owner or dragged away by the police. Moving from one place to another would involve nothing more liberating than moving from one trespass liability to another. Since land is finite in any society, there is only a limited number of places where a person can (physically) be, and such a person would find that he was legally excluded from all of them. (It would not be entirely mischievous to add that since, in order to exist, a person has to be *somewhere*, such a person would not be permitted to exist.)

Our society saves the homeless from this catastrophe only by virtue of the fact that some of its territory is held as collective property and made available for common use. The homeless are allowed to *be* – provided they are on the streets, in the parks, or under the bridges. Some of them are allowed to crowd together into publicly provided "shelters" after dark (though these are dangerous places and anyway there are not nearly enough shelters for all of them). In the daytime and, for many of them, all through the night, wandering in public places is their only option. When all else is privately owned, the sidewalks are their salvation. They are allowed to *be* in our society only to the extent that our society is communist.

This is one of the reasons why most defenders of private property are uncomfortable with the libertarian proposal, and why it remains sheer fantasy.[8] However, there is a modified form of the libertarian catastrophe in prospect with which moderate and even liberal defenders of ownership seem much more comfortable. This is the increasing regulation of the streets, subways, parks, and other public places to restrict the activities that can be performed there. What is emerging – and this is not just a matter of fantasy – is a state of affairs in which a million or more citizens have no place to perform elementary human activities like urinating, washing, sleeping, cooking, eating, and standing around. Legislators voted for by people who own private places in which they can do all these things are increasingly deciding to make public places available only for activities other than these primal human tasks. The streets and subways, they say, are for commuting from home to office. They are not for sleeping; sleeping is something one does at home. The parks are for recreations like walking and informal ball games, things for which one's own yard is a little too confined. Parks are not for cooking or urinating; again, these are things one does at home. Since the public and the private are complementary, the activities performed in public are to be the complement of those appropriately performed in private. This complementarity works fine for those who have the benefit of both sorts of places. However, it is disastrous for those who must live their whole lives on common land. If I am right about this, it is one of the most callous and tyrannical exercises of power in modern times by a (comparatively) rich and complacent majority against a minority of their less fortunate fellow human beings.

III

The points made so far can be restated in terms of freedom. Someone who is allowed to be in a place is, in a fairly straightforward sense, free to be there. A person who is not allowed to be in a place is unfree to be there. However, the concept of freedom usually applies to actions rather than locations: one is free or unfree to do X or to do Y. What is the connection, then, between freedom to be somewhere and freedom to do something?

At the outset I recited the truism that anything a person does has to be done somewhere. All actions involve a spatial component (just as many actions involve, in addition, a material component like the use of tools, implements, or raw materials). It should be obvious that, if one is not free to be in a certain place, one is not free to do anything at that place. If I am not allowed to be in your garden (because you have forbidden me) then I am not allowed to eat my lunch, make a speech, or turn a somersault in your garden. Though I may be free to do these things somewhere else, I am not free to do them there. It follows, strikingly, that a person who is not free to be in any place is not free to do anything; such a person is comprehensively unfree. In the libertarian paradise we imagined in the previous section, this would be the plight of the homeless. They would be simply without freedom (or, more accurately, any freedom they had would depend utterly on the forbearance of those who owned the places that made up the territory of the society in question).

Fortunately, our society is not such a libertarian paradise. There are places where the homeless may be and, by virtue of that, there are actions they may perform: they are free to perform actions on the streets, in the parks, and under the bridges. Their freedom depends on common property in a way that ours does not. Once again, the homeless have freedom in our society only to the extent that our society is communist.

That conclusion may sound glib and provocative. It is meant as a reflection on the cold and awful reality of the experience of men, women, and children who are homeless in America. For them the rules of private property are a series of fences that stand between them and somewhere to be, somewhere to act. The only hope they have so far as freedom is concerned lies in the streets, parks, and public shelters, and in the fact that those are collectivized resources made available openly to all.

It is sometimes said that freedom means little or nothing to a cold and hungry person. We should focus on the material predicament of the homeless, it is said, not on this abstract liberal concern about liberty. That may be an appropriate response to someone who is talking high-mindedly and fat-

uously about securing freedom of speech or freedom of religion for people who lack the elementary necessities of
human life.[9] But the contrast between liberty and the satisfaction of material needs must not be drawn too sharply, as
though the latter had no relation at all to what one is free or
unfree to do. I am focusing on freedoms that are intimately
connected with food, shelter, clothing, and the satisfaction
of basic needs. When a person is needy, he does not cease
to be preoccupied with freedom; rather, his preoccupation
tends to focus on freedom to perform certain actions in particular. The freedom that means most to a person who is
cold and wet is the freedom that consists in staying under
whatever shelter he has found. The freedom that means most
to someone who is exhausted is the freedom not to be prod-
ded with a nightstick as he tries to catch a few hours of sleep
on a park bench.

There is a general point here about the rather *passive* image
of the poor held by those who say we should concern ourselves with their needs, not their freedom.[10] People remain
agents, with ideas and initiatives of their own, even when
they are poor. Indeed, since they are on their own, in a
situation of danger, without any place of safety, they must
often be more resourceful, spend more time working out how
to live, thinking things through much more carefully, taking
much less for granted, than the comfortable image we have
of the autonomous agent in a family with a house and a job
in an office or university. And – when they are allowed to –
the poor do find ways of using their initiative to rise to these
challenges. They have to; if they do not, they die.

Even the most desperately needy are not always paralyzed
by want. There are certain things they are physically capable
of doing for themselves. Sometimes they find shelter, by
occupying an empty house, or sleeping in a sheltered spot.
They gather food from various places, they light a fire to cook
it, and they sit down in a park to eat. They may urinate
behind bushes, and wash their clothes in a fountain. Their
physical condition is certainly not comfortable, but they are
capable of acting in ways that make things a little more bear-

able for themselves. Now one question we face as a society – a broad question of justice and social policy – is whether we are willing to tolerate an economic system in which large numbers of people are homeless. Since the answer is evidently, "Yes," the question that remains is whether we are willing to allow those who are in this predicament to act as free agents, looking after their own needs, in public places – the only space available to them. It is a deeply frightening fact about the modern United States that those who *have* homes and jobs are willing to answer "Yes" to the first question and "No" to the second.

IV

Before going on, I want to say something about the conception of freedom I am using in this chapter. Those who argue that the homeless (or the poor generally) are less free than the rest of us are often accused of appealing to a controversial, dangerous, and question-begging conception of "positive" freedom.[11] It is commonly thought that one has to step outside the traditional liberal idea of "negative" freedom in order to make these points.

However, there is no need to argue about that here. The definition of freedom with which I have been working so far is as "negative" as can be. There is nothing unfamiliar about it (except perhaps the consistency with which it is being deployed). I am saying that a person is free to be someplace just in case he is not legally liable to be physically removed from that place or penalized for being there. At the very least, negative freedom is freedom from obstructions such as someone else's forceful effort to prevent one from doing something.[12] In exactly this negative sense (absence of forcible interference), the homeless person is unfree to be in any place governed by a private property rule (unless the owner for some reason elects to give him his permission to be there). The familiar claim that, in the negative sense of "freedom," the poor are as free as the rest of us – and that

318

you have to move to a positive definition in order to dispute that – is simply false.[13]

That private property limits freedom seems obvious.[14] If I own a piece of land, others have a duty not to use it (without my consent) and there is a battery of legal remedies which I can deploy to enforce this duty as I please. The right correlative to this duty is an essential incident of ownership, and any enforcement of the duty necessarily amounts to a deliberate interference with someone else's action. It is true that the connection between property and the restriction of liberty is in some ways a contingent one: as Andrew Reeve notes, "even if I am entitled to use my property to prevent you from taking some action, I will not necessarily do so."[15] But there is a similar contingency in any juridical restriction. A repressive state may have laws entitling officials to crush dissent. In practice they might choose to refrain from doing so on certain occasions; but we would still describe the law as a restriction on freedom if dissidents had to take into account the likelihood of its being used against them. Indeed we often say that the unpredictable element of official discretion "chills" whatever freedom remains in the interstices of its enforcement. Thus, in exactly the way in which we call repressive political laws restrictions on freedom, we can call property rights restrictions on freedom. We do not need any special definition of freedom over and above the negative one used by liberals in contexts that are ideologically more congenial.

The definitional objection is sometimes based on a distinction between freedom and ability.[16] The homeless, it is said, are in the relevant sense *free* to perform the same activities as the rest of us; but the sad fact is that they do not have the *means* or the *power* or the *ability* to exercise these freedoms. This claim is almost always false. With the exception of a few who are so weakened by their plight that they are incapable of anything, the homeless are not *unable* to enter the privately owned places from which they are banned. They can climb walls, open doors, cross thresholds, break windows, and so on, to gain entry to the premises from which the laws of property exclude them. What stands in their way is simply what stands in the way of anyone who is negatively unfree: the likelihood that someone else will forcibly prevent their action. Of course, the rich do try to make it impossible as well as illegal for the homeless to enter their gardens: they build their walls as high as possible and top them with broken glass. But that this does not constitute mere inability as opposed to unfreedom is indicated by the fact that the homeless are not permitted even to *try* to overcome these physical obstacles. They may be dragged away and penalized for attempting to scale the walls.

A second line that is sometimes taken is this: one should regard the homeless as less free than the rest of us only if one believes that some human agency (other than their own) is responsible for their plight.[17] However, the idea of someone else's being responsible for the plight of the homeless is an ambiguous one. It may well be the case that people are homeless as a result of earlier deliberate and heartless actions by landlords, employers, or officials, or as a result of a deliberate capitalist strategy to create and sustain a vast reserve industrial army of the unemployed.[18] That *may* be the case. But even if it is not, even if their being homeless cannot be laid at anyone's door or attributed to anything over and above their own choices or the impersonal workings of the market, my point remains. Their homelessness *consists* in unfreedom. Though it may not be anyone's fault that there is no place they can go without being dragged away, still their being removed from the places they are not allowed to be is itself a derogation from their freedom, a derogation constituted by the deliberate human action of property owners, security guards, and police officers. To repeat, their having nowhere to go *is* their being unfree (in a negative sense) to be anywhere; it is identical with the fact that others are authorized deliberately to drag them away from wherever they choose to be. We do not need any further account of the *cause* of this state of affairs to describe it as, in itself, a situation of unfreedom.

Third, someone may object that a person is not made unfree if he is prevented from doing something wrong – or something he has no right to do. Since entering others' property and abusing common property are wrong, it is not really a derogation from freedom to enforce a person's duties in these respects. Ironically, this "moralization" of the concept of freedom certainly *would* amount to a shift in the direction of a positive definition.[19] It was precisely the identification of freedom with virtue (and the inference that a restriction on vice was no restriction at all) that most troubled liberals about theories of positive liberty.[20]

In any case, the "moralization" of freedom is confusing and question-begging in the present context. It elides the notions of a restriction on freedom and an unjustified restriction on freedom, closing off certain questions that common sense regards as open. It seems to rest on a sense – elsewhere repudiated by many liberals – that all our moral and political concerns fit together in a tidy package, so that we need not ever worry about trade-offs between freedom (properly understood) and other values, such as property and justice.[21] The more honest course is to acknowledge that freedom is not the sum of all goods. To say – as I have insisted we should say – that property rules limit freedom, is not to say they are *eo ipso* wrong.[22] It is simply to say that they engage a concern about liberty, and that anyone who values liberty should put himself on alert when questions of property are being discussed.

Above all, by building the morality of a given property system (rights, duties, and the current distribution) into the concept of freedom, the moralizing approach precludes the use of that concept as a basis for arguing about property. If when we use the words "free" and "unfree," we are already assuming that it is wrong for A to use something that belongs to B, we cannot appeal to "freedom" to explain why B's ownership of the resource is justified. We cannot even extol our property system as the basis of a "free" society, for such a boast would be nothing more than tautological. It is true that if we have independent grounds of justification for our private property system, then we *can* say that interfering with property rights is wrong without appealing to the idea of freedom. In that case, there is nothing question-begging about the claim that preventing someone from violating property rights does not count as a restriction on his freedom. But the price of this strategy is high. It not only transforms our conception of freedom into a moralized definition of positive liberty (so that the only freedom that is relevant is the freedom to do what is right), but it also excludes the concept of freedom altogether from the debate about the justification of property rights. Since most theorists of property do not want to deprive themselves of the concept of freedom as a resource in that argument, the insistence that the enforcement of property rules should not count as a restriction on freedom is, at the very least, a serious strategic mistake.

V

I think the account I have given is faithful to the tradition of negative liberty. One is free to do something only if one is not liable to be forcibly prevented from or penalized for doing it. However, the way I have applied this account may seem a little disconcerting. The issue has to do with the level of generality at which actions are described.

The laws we have usually mention general *types* of actions, rather than particular actions done by particular people at specific times and places. Statutes do not say, "Jane Smith is not to assault Sarah Jones on Friday, November 24, on the corner of College Avenue and Bancroft." They say, "Assault is prohibited," or some equivalent, and it is understood that the prohibition applies to all such actions performed by anyone anywhere. A prohibition on a general type of action is understood to be a prohibition on all tokens of that type. Jurists say we should value this generality in our laws; it is part of the complex ideal of "The Rule of Law." It makes the laws more predictable and more learnable. It makes them a better guide for the ordinary citizen who needs a rough and ready understanding (rather than a copious technical knowledge) of what he is and isn't allowed to do as he goes about his business. A quick checklist of prohibited acts, formulated in general terms, serves that purpose admirably.[23] It also serves moral ideals of universalizability and rationality: a reason for restraining any particular act ought to be a reason for restraining any other act of the same type, unless there is a relevant difference between them (which can be formulated also in general terms).[24]

All that is important. However, there is another aspect of "The Rule of Law" ideal that can lead one into difficulties if it is combined with this insistence on generality. Legal systems of the kind we have pride themselves on the following feature: "Everything which is not explicitly prohibited is permitted." If the law does not formulate any prohibition on singing or jogging, for example, that is an indication to the citizen that singing and jogging are permitted, that he is free to perform them. To gauge the extent of his freedom, all he needs to know are the prohibitions imposed by the law. His freedom is simply the complement of that.[25]

The difficulty arises if it is inferred from this that a person's freedom is the complement of the *general* prohibitions that apply to him. For although it is possible to infer particular prohibitions from prohibitions formulated at a general level ("All murder is wrong" implies "This murder by me today is wrong"), it is not possible to infer particular permissions from the absence of any general prohibition. In our society, there is no general prohibition on cycling, but one cannot infer from this that any particular act of riding a bicycle is permitted. It depends (among other things) on whether the person involved has the right to use the particular bicycle he is proposing to ride.

This does not affect the basic point about complementarity. Our freedoms *are* the complement of the prohibitions that apply to us. The mistake arises from thinking that the only prohibitions that apply to us are general prohibitions. For, in addition to the general prohibitions laid down (say) in the criminal law, there are also the prohibitions on using particular objects and places that are generated by the laws of property. Until we know how these latter laws apply, we do not know whether we are free to perform a particular action.

It is *not* a telling response to this point to say that the effect of the laws of property can be stated in terms of a general principle – "No one is to use the property of another without his permission." They *can* be so stated; but in order to apply that principle, we need particular knowledge, not just general knowledge.[26] A person needs to know that *this* bicycle belongs to him, whereas *those* bicycles belong to other people. He needs that particular knowledge about specific objects as well as his general knowledge about the types of actions that are and are not permitted.

The conclusions about freedom that I have reached depend on taking the prohibitions relating to particular objects generated by property laws as seriously as we take the more general prohibitions imposed by the criminal law. No doubt these different types of prohibitions are imposed for different reasons. But if freedom means simply the absence of deliberate interference with one's actions, we will not be in a position to say how free a person is until we know everything about the universe of legal restraints that may be applied to him. After all, it is not freedom in the abstract that people value, but freedom to perform particular actions. If the absence of a general prohibition tells us nothing about anyone's concrete freedom, we should be wary of using only the checklist of general prohibitions to tell us how free or unfree a person or a society really is.

These points can readily be applied to the homeless. There are no general prohibitions in our society on actions like sleeping or washing. However, we cannot infer from this that anyone may sleep or wash wherever he chooses. In order to work out whether a particular person is free to sleep or wash, we must also ask whether there are any prohibitions *of place* that apply to his performance of actions of this type. As a matter of fact, all of us face a formidable battery of such prohibitions. Most private places are off-limits to us for these (or any other) activities. Though I am a well paid professor, there are only a couple of private places where I am allowed to sleep or wash (without having someone's specific permission): my home, my office, and whatever restaurant I am patronizing. Most homeless people do not have jobs and few of them are allowed inside restaurants. ("Bathrooms for the use of customers only.") Above all, they have no homes. So there is literally no private place where they are free to sleep or wash.

For them, that is a desperately important fact about their freedom, one that must preoccupy much of every day. Unlike us, they have no private place where they can take it for granted that they will be allowed to sleep or wash. Since everyone needs to sleep and wash regularly, homeless people have to spend time searching for nonprivate places – like public restrooms (of which there are precious few in America, by the standards of most countries) and shelters (available, if at all, only at night) – where these actions may be performed without fear of interference. If we regard freedom as simply the complement of the general prohibitions imposed by law, we are in danger of overlooking this fact about the freedom of the homeless. Most of us can afford to overlook it, because we have homes to go to. But without a home, a person's freedom is his freedom to act in public, in places governed by common property rules. That is the difference between our freedom and the freedom of the homeless.

VI

What then are we to say about public places? If there is anywhere the homeless are free to act, it is in the streets, the subways, and the parks. These regions are governed by common property rules. Since these are the only places they are allowed to be, these are the only places they are free to act.

However, a person is not allowed do just whatever he likes in a public place. There are at least three types of prohibitions that one faces in a place governed by rules of common property.

(1) If there are any general prohibitions on types of actions

in a society, like the prohibition on murder or the prohibition on selling narcotics, then they apply to all tokens of those types performed anywhere, public or private. These prohibitions apply to everyone: though it is only the homeless who have no choice but to be in public places, the law forbids the rich as well as the poor to sell narcotics, and a fortiori to sell narcotics on the streets and in the parks.

(2) Typically, there are also prohibitions that are specific to public places and provide the basis of their commonality. Parks have curfews; streets and sidewalks have rules that govern the extent to which one person's use of these places may interfere with another's; there are rules about obstruction, jaywalking, and so on. Many of these can be characterized as rules of fairness. If public places are to be available for everyone's use, then we must ensure that their use by some does not preclude or obstruct their use by others.

(3) Some of the rules that govern behavior in public places are more substantive than that: they concern particular forms of behavior that are not to be performed in public whether there is an issue of fairness involved or not. For example, many states and municipalities forbid the use of parks for making love. It is not that there is any general constraint on lovemaking as a type of action (though some states still have laws against fornication). Although sexual intercourse between a husband and wife is permitted and even encouraged by the law, it is usually forbidden in public places. The place for that sort of activity, we say, is the privacy of the home.

Other examples spring to mind. There is no law against urinating – it is a necessary human activity. However, there is a law against urinating in public, except in the specially designated premises of public restrooms. It is an activity which we are free to do mainly at home or in some other private place (a bathroom in a restaurant) where we have an independent right to be. There is no law against sleeping – again a necessary and desirable human activity. To maintain their physical and mental health, people need to sleep for a substantial period every day. However, states and municipalities are increasingly passing ordinances to prohibit sleeping in public places like streets and parks.[27] The decision of the Transit Authority in New York to enforce prohibitions on sleeping in the subways attracted national attention a few years ago.[28]

Such ordinances have and are known and even intended to have a specific effect on the homeless which is different from their effect on the rest of us. We are all familiar with the dictum of Anatole France: "[L]a majestueuse égalité des lois . . . interdit au riche comme au pauvre de coucher sous les ponts."[29] We might adapt it to the present point, noting that the new rules in the subway will prohibit anyone from sleeping or lying down in the cars and stations, whether they are rich or poor, homeless or housed. They will be phrased with majestic impartiality, and indeed their drafters know that they would be struck down immediately by the courts if they were formulated specifically to target those who have no homes. Still everyone is perfectly well aware of the point of passing these ordinances, and any attempt to defend them on the basis of their generality is quite disingenuous. Their point is to make sleeping in the subways off-limits to those who have nowhere else to sleep.[30]

Four facts are telling in this regard. First, it is well known among those who press for these laws that the subway is such an unpleasant place to sleep that almost no one would do it if they had anywhere else to go. Second, the pressure for these laws comes as a response to what is well known to be "the problem of homelessness." It is not as though people suddenly became concerned about *sleeping* in the subway (as though that were a particularly dangerous activity to perform there, like smoking or jumping onto a moving train). When people write to the Transit Authority and say, "Just get them out. I don't care. Just get them out any way you can," we all know who the word "them" refers to.[31] People do not want to be confronted with the sight of the homeless – it is uncomfortable for the well-off to be reminded of the human price that is paid for a social structure like theirs – and they are willing to deprive those people of their last opportunity to sleep in order to protect themselves from

this discomfort. Third, the legislation is called for and promoted by people who are secure in the knowledge that they
themselves have some place where they are permitted to
sleep. Because *they* have some place to sleep which is not
the subway, they infer that the subway is not a place for
sleeping. The subway is a place where those who have some
other place to sleep may do things besides sleeping.

Finally, and most strikingly, those who push for these laws
will amend them or reformulate them if they turn out to have
an unwelcome impact on people who are not homeless. A
city ordinance in Clearwater, Florida, prohibiting sleeping in
public, was struck down as too broad because it would have
applied even to a person sleeping in his car.[32] Most people
who have cars also have homes, and we would not want a
statute aimed at the homeless to prevent car owners from
sleeping in public.

Though we all know what the real object of these ordinances is, we may not have thought very hard about their
cumulative effect. That effect is as follows.

For a person who has no home, and has no expectation
of being allowed into a private office building or a restaurant,
prohibitions on things like sleeping that apply particularly
to public places pose a special problem. For although there
is no *general* prohibition on acts of these types, still they are
effectively ruled out altogether for anyone who is homeless
and who has no shelter to go to. The prohibition is comprehensive in effect because of the cumulation, in the case of
the homeless, of a number of different bans, differently imposed. The rules of property prohibit the homeless person
from doing any of these acts in private, since there is no
private place that he has a right to be. And the rules gov-
erning public places prohibit him from doing any of these
acts in public, since that is how we have decided to regulate
the use of public places. So what is the result? Since private
places and public places between them exhaust all the places
that there are, there is nowhere that these actions may be
performed by the homeless person. And since freedom to
perform a concrete action requires freedom to perform it at

some place, it follows that the homeless person does not have the freedom to perform them. If sleeping is prohibited in public places, then sleeping is comprehensively prohibited to the homeless. If urinating is prohibited in public places (and if there are no public lavatories) then the homeless are simply unfree to urinate. These are not altogether comfortable conclusions, and they are certainly not comfortable for those who have to live with them.

VII

I have said the predicament is cumulative. I have argued that if an action X is prohibited to everyone in public places and if a person A has no access to a private place in which to perform it, then action X is effectively prohibited to A *everywhere*, and so A is comprehensively unfree to do X. However, people may balk at this point. They may argue:

> Surely prohibition is an intentional notion, and nobody is intending that A not be permitted to do X. We do intend that he should be prohibited from X-ing in public, but we don't intend that he should be prohibited from X-ing in private. That's just the way the distribution of property turns out. We don't intend as a society – and certainly the state does not intend – that there should be *no* place where A is permitted to do X. It just happens that way.[33]

We have already seen that this point about intention cannot be sustained at the level of individual acts. If a homeless tramp tries to urinate in a rich person's yard, the rich person may try to prevent that, and he is authorized to do so. There is no doubt about the intentionality of this particular restraint on this particular violation of property rules. The point of the present objection is that the rich person doesn't intend that there should be nowhere the tramp is allowed to urinate (indeed, he probably hopes that there is somewhere – provided it is not in his backyard). Similarly for each proprietor in turn. No one intends that the tramp should never be allowed to urinate. That just happens, in an invisible hand sort of way, as a result of each proprietor saying, in effect, "Anywhere but here." Though each particular unfreedom involves an intentional restraint, their cumulation is not in itself the product of anyone's intention.

The objection can be conceded. We can tie judgments about freedom and unfreedom this closely to intentionality if we like. On that approach, all we can say about the home-less person's freedom is that he is unfree to urinate in place X *and* he is unfree to urinate in place Y *and* he is unfree to urinate in place Z *and* ... so on, for each place that there is. We refrain from the inference: "So he is unfree to urinate (anywhere)." However, even if we are scrupulous about not making that generalization, still there is *something* we can say at a general level about his predicament. We can say, for example, "There is no place where he is free to urinate." The logic of such a quantified sentence (that is, "There is no place p such that he is free to urinate at p") does not commit us to any cumulation of unfreedoms, and it is an accurate state-ment of his position. Anyway, even if no one has intended that there be no place this person is free to urinate, it cannot be said that his predicament, so described, is a matter of no concern. It is hard to imagine how anyone could think free-dom important in relation to each particular restraint, but yet have no concern about the cumulative effect of such re-straints. Moreover, even if our concern about the cumulation is not directly expressed in terms of freedom because freedom is taken to be an intentional notion, it is at least freedom *related*. If we value freedom in each particular case because of the importance of choice and of not being constrained in the choices one makes, then that value ought to direct some attention to how many choices a person has left after each constraint has been exercised. From any point of view that values freedom of action, it ought to be a matter of concern that the choices left open to a person are being progressively closed off, one by one, and that he is nearing a situation where there is literally nowhere he can turn.

The fact that no one intended his overall predicament may

mean that there is no one to *blame* for it. However, each private proprietor will have a pretty good idea about how others may be expected to exercise their rights in this regard. It would be quite disingenuous for any of them to say, "I thought some of the other owners would let him use their property." Moral philosophers have developed interesting models of joint and collective responsibility for outcomes like these, and those models seem quite applicable here.[34] Also, those who impose a ban on these activities in public places certainly do know very well what the result of *that* will be: that the homeless will have almost nowhere to go, in the territory subject to their jurisdiction. Indeed the aim – again, as we all know – is often to drive them out of the jurisdiction so that some other city or state has to take care of the problem. Or even grant that *this* is not intentional; still the intentional infliction of harm is not the only thing we blame people for. "I didn't mean to" is not the all-purpose excuse it is often taken to be. We blame people for recklessness and negligence, and certainly the promoters of these ordinances are quite reckless whether they leave the homeless anywhere to go or not. ("Just get them out. I don't care. Just get them out any way you can.")[35]

In any case, our concern about freedom and unfreedom is not principally a concern to find someone to blame. An intentional attack on freedom is blameworthy in part because the freedom of those who are attacked matters. If freedom is sufficiently important to sustain moral blame against those who attack it, it ought to matter also in other cases where blame is not the issue. Sometimes we can promote freedom, or make people more free, or organize our institutions so that there are fewer ways in which their freedom is restricted, and we may want to do this even in cases where we are not responding with outrage to the moral culpability of an attack on liberty. Freedom is a multifaceted concern in our political morality. Sure, we blame those who attack it deliberately or recklessly. But we are also solicitous for it and do our best to make it flourish, even when there is no evil freedom hater obstructing our efforts. Blame, and the intentionality that blame is wrongly thought to presuppose, are not the only important things in the world.

VIII

I have argued that a rule against performing an act in a public place amounts *in effect* to a *comprehensive* ban on that action so far as the homeless are concerned. If that argument is accepted, our next question should be: "How serious is this limitation on freedom?" Freedom in any society is limited in all sorts of ways: I have no freedom to pass through a red light or to drive east on Bancroft Avenue. Any society involves a complicated array of freedoms and unfreedoms, and our assessment of *how free* a given society is (our assessment, for example, that the United States is a freer society than China) involves some assessment of the balance in that array.

Such assessments are characteristically qualitative as well as quantitative. We don't simply ask, "How many actions are people free or unfree to perform?" Indeed, such questions are very difficult to answer or even to formulate coherently.[36] Instead we ask qualitative questions: "How important are the actions that people are prohibited from performing?" One of the tasks of a theory of human rights is to pick out a set of actions it is thought particularly important from a moral point of view that people should have the freedom to perform, choices it is thought particularly important that they should have the freedom to make, whatever other restrictions there are on their conduct.[37] The Bill of Rights, for example, picks out things like religious worship, political speech, and the possession of firearms as actions or choices whose restriction we should be specially concerned about. A society that places restrictions on activities of these types is held to be worse, in point of freedom, than a society that merely restricts activities like drinking, smoking, or driving.

The reason for the concern has in part to do with the special significance of these actions. Religious worship is where we disclose and practice our deepest beliefs. Political speech is where we communicate with one another as citizens of a republic. Even bearing arms is held, by those who defend its status as a right, to be a special assertion of dignity, mature responsibility, civic participation, and freedom from the prospect of tyranny. People occasionally disagree about the contents of these lists of important freedoms. Is it really important to have the right to bear arms in a modern democratic society? Is commercial advertising as important as individual political discourse? These are disputes about which choices have this high ethical import. They are disputes about which liberties should be given special protection in the name of human dignity or autonomy, and which attacks on freedom should be viewed as particularly inimical to a person's identity as a citizen and as a moral agent.

On the whole, the actions specified by Bills of Rights are not what is at stake in the issue of homelessness. Certainly there would be an uproar if an ordinance were passed making it an offense to pray in the subway or to pass one's time there in political debate.[38] There has been some concern in America about the restriction of free speech in public and quasi-public places (since it is arguable that the whole point of free speech is that it take place in the public realm).[39] However, the actions that are being closed off to the homeless are, for the most part, not significant in this high-minded sense. They are significant in another way: they are actions basic to the sustenance of a decent or healthy life, in some cases basic to the sustenance of life itself. There may not seem anything particularly autonomous or self-assertive or civically republican or ethically ennobling about sleeping or cooking or urinating. You will not find them listed in any Charter. But that does not mean it is a matter of slight concern when people are prohibited from performing such actions, a concern analogous to that aroused by a traffic regulation or the introduction of a commercial standard.

For one thing, the regular performance of such actions is a precondition for all other aspects of life and activity. It is a precondition for the sort of autonomous life that is celebrated and affirmed when Bills of Rights are proclaimed. I am not making the crude mistake of saying that if we value autonomy, we must value its preconditions in exactly the same way. But if we value autonomy we should regard the satisfaction of its preconditions as a matter of importance; otherwise, our values simply ring hollow so far as real people are concerned.

Moreover, though we say there is nothing particularly dignified about sleeping or urinating, there is certainly something deeply and inherently *un*dignified about being prevented from doing so. Every torturer knows this: to break the human spirit, focus the mind of the victim through petty restrictions pitilessly imposed on the banal necessities of human life. We should be ashamed that we have allowed our laws of public and private property to reduce a million or more citizens to something approaching this level of degradation.

Increasingly, in the way we organize common property, we have done all we can to prevent people from taking care of these elementary needs themselves, quietly, with dignity, as ordinary human beings. If someone needs to urinate, what he needs above all as a dignified person is the *freedom* to do so in privacy and relative independence of the arbitrary will of anyone else. But we have set things up so that either the street person must *beg* for this opportunity, several times every day, as a favor from people who recoil from him in horror, or, if he wants to act independently on his own initiative, he must break the law and risk arrest. The generous provision of public lavatories would make an immense difference in this regard – and it would be a difference to freedom and dignity, not just a matter of welfare.

Finally we need to understand that any restriction on the performance of these basic acts has the feature of being not only uncomfortable and degrading, but more or less literally *unbearable* for the people concerned. People need sleep, for example, not just in the sense that sleep is necessary for health, but also in the sense that they will eventually fall asleep or drop from exhaustion if it is denied them. People simply cannot bear a lack of sleep, and they will do themselves a great deal of damage trying to bear it. The same,

obviously, is true of bodily functions like urinating and de-
fecating. These are things that people simply have to do; any
attempt voluntarily to refrain from doing them is at once
painful, dangerous, and finally impossible. That our social
system might in effect deny them the right to do these things,
by prohibiting their being done in each and every place,
ought to be a matter of the gravest concern.[40]

It may seem sordid or in bad taste to make such a lot of
these elementary physical points in a philosophical discussion of freedom. But if freedom is important, it is as freedom
for human beings, that is, for the embodied and needy or-
ganisms that we are. The activities I have mentioned are both
urgent and quotidian. They are urgent because they are basic
to all other functions. These actions *have* to be performed, if
one is to be free to do anything else without distraction and
distress. And they are quotidian in the sense that they are
actions that have to be done every day. They are not actions
a person can *wait* to perform until he acquires a home. Every
day, he must eat and excrete and sleep. Every day, if he is
homeless, he will face the overwhelming task of trying to
find somewhere where he is allowed to do this.

IX

That last point is particularly important as an answer to a
final objection that may be made. Someone might object that
I have so far said nothing about the fact that our society gives
everyone the *opportunity* to acquire a home, and that we are
all – the homeless and the housed – equal in *this* regard even
if we are unequal in our actual ownership of real estate.

There is something to this objection, but not much. Certainly a society that denied a caste of persons the right
(or juridical power) to own or lease property would be
even worse than ours. The opportunity to acquire a home
(even if it is just the juridical power) is surely worth having.
But, to put it crudely, one cannot pee in an opportunity.
Since the homeless, like us, are real people, they need some

real place to be, not just the notional reflex of a Hohfeldian power.[41]

We also know enough about how the world works to see that one's need for somewhere to sleep and wash is, if anything, greatest during the time that one is trying to consummate this opportunity to find a home. The lack of liberty that homelessness involves makes it harder to impress, appeal to, or deal with the people who might eventually provide one with a job and with the money to afford housing. The irony of opportunity, in other words, is that the longer it remains unconsummated, for whatever reason, the more difficult it is to exploit.

In the final analysis, whether or not a person really has the *opportunity* to obtain somewhere to live is a matter of his position in a society; it is a matter of his ability to deal with the people around him and of there being an opening in social and economic structures so that his wants and abilities can be brought into relation with others'.[42] That position, that ability, and that opening do not exist magically as a result of legal status. The juridical fact that a person is not legally barred from becoming a tenant or a proprietor does not mean that there is any realistic prospect of that happening. Whether it happens depends, among other things, on how he can present himself, how reliable and respectable he appears, what skills and abilities he can deploy, how much time, effort, and mobility he can invest in a search for housing, assistance, and employment, and so on.

Those are abstract formulations. We could say equally that it is hard to get a job when one appears filthy, that many of the benefits of social and economic interaction cannot be obtained without an address or without a way of receiving telephone calls, that a person cannot take *all* his possessions with him in a shopping cart when he goes for an interview but he may have nowhere to leave them, that those who are homeless become so because they have run out of cash altogether and so of course do not have the up-front fees and deposits that landlords require from potential tenants, and so on.

Everything we call a social or economic opportunity depends cruelly on a person's being able to *do* certain things – for example, his being able to wash, to sleep, and to base himself somewhere. When someone is homeless they are, as we have seen, effectively *banned* from doing these things; these are things they are *not allowed to do*. So long as that is the case, it is a contemptible mockery to reassure the victims of such coercion that they have the *opportunity* to play a full part in social and economic life. The rules of property are such that they are *prohibited* from doing the minimum that would be necessary to take advantage of that opportunity.[43]

X

Lack of freedom is not all there is to the nightmare of homelessness. There is also the cold, the hunger, the disease and lack of medical treatment, the danger, the beatings, the loneliness, and the shame and despair that may come from being unable to care for oneself, one's child, or a friend. By focusing on freedom in this chapter, I have not wanted to detract from any of that.

But there are good reasons to pay attention to the issue of freedom. They are not merely strategic, though in a society that prides itself as "the land of the free," this may be one way of shaming a people into action and concern. Homelessness is partly about property and law, and freedom provides the connecting term that makes those categories relevant. By considering not only what a person is allowed to do, but where he is allowed to do it, we can see a system of property for what it is: rules that provide freedom and prosperity for some by imposing restrictions on others. So long as everyone enjoys some of the benefits as well as some of the restrictions, that correlativity is bearable. It ceases to be so when there is a class of persons who bear *all* of the restrictions and nothing else, a class of persons for whom property is nothing but a way of limiting their freedom.

Perhaps the strongest argument for thinking about homelessness as an issue of freedom is that it forces us to see people in need as *agents*. Destitution is not necessarily passive; and public provision is not always a way of compounding passivity. By focusing on what we allow people to do to satisfy their own basic needs on their own initiative, and by scrutinizing the legal obstacles that we place in their way (the doors we lock, the ordinances we enforce, and the nightsticks we raise), we get a better sense that what we are dealing with here is not just "the problem of homelessness," but a million or more *persons* whose activity, dignity, and freedom are at stake.

Chapter 14

Can communal goods be human rights?

I

There is talk today of a "new generation" of human rights. An idea which was associated in the first instance with civil and political liberties ("first generation" rights), and which was used after the Second World War to express popular aspirations to economic and social well-being ("second generation" rights), is now being invoked as a vehicle for claims about the importance of the environment, peace, and economic development, particularly in the Third World.[1] No one doubts that these are worthy aims. But instead of merely saying that Third World countries need to develop their economies, instead of saying that peace is essential in a nuclear world, and that we must maintain and respect the ecosystems on which human life depends, the proclamation is being made that these are *human rights* – things to which people are *entitled* in the same way they are entitled to democratic freedom or the right not to be tortured.

Opinions differ among commentators in the human rights field and in international law about the desirability of expressing such claims in this new terminology.[2] Many feel there is a danger of debasing the currency of rights, while others worry that the subject matter of the new rights is insufficiently defined. However, the most interesting debates have focused on the communal and nonindividualistic character of the new rights. Economic development, peace, and the integrity of the environment are not conditions which

339

are predicated of individuals; they apply to whole societies or, in the case of peace, to whole regions or even to the world. Of course, it is not difficult to show that the achievement of certain communal aspirations is a necessary condition for the fulfillment of other aims that are traditionally regarded as human rights – the rights of individuals do not flourish in times of war or famine. Moreover, the idea that whole societies may have rights has been around for some time. The U.N. Covenant on Civil and Political Rights, 1966, opens with the claim that "All peoples have a right of self-determination"; and Article 27 provides that "In those States in which ethnic, religious or linguistic minorities exist, persons belonging to such minorities shall not be denied the right, in community with the other members of their group, to enjoy their own culture, to profess and practise their own religion, or to use their own language." Though the claim is expressed in terms of the rights of persons, the rights are such that they can only be exercised in solidarity with others. So claims of this sort are not unfamiliar. What is striking about recent developments, however, is the deliberate and sustained shift of focus to the rights of communities. Such claims are being pushed into the foreground, forcing us to reconsider many of the assumptions we have traditionally made about the analysis of human rights.

In this chapter, I do not propose to say much about the importance of these communal aspirations. I shall take that as given. The questions I want to consider are more abstract ones that arise with this shift of focus from the individual to the community. Is the language of human rights essentially individualistic? If so, is it coherent to deploy that language to express the aspirations of whole peoples? Should we not use other normative language for such claims? (And the meta-questions: Is this anything more than a quibble about words? What would be lost if we were to abandon the language of rights for this purpose? What would be lost if we didn't?) Again, if the language of rights is individualistic, is anything gained (or lost) in talking about individual communities, rather than individual men and women, as bearers of rights?

I will proceed as follows. In Section II, I shall discuss the view that first and second generation rights, at any rate, are individualistic, and I shall compare them with the third generation rights that we are interested in. Sections III and IV will concentrate on the sorts of goods that are involved in these third generation claims; they will distinguish between public goods (in the economists' sense) and what I shall call "communal goods." In Section V, I shall argue that communal goods, though they may be important, should not be regarded as the subject matter of individual rights. In Section VI, I shall ask whether it is sensible to talk of group rights. Finally in Section VII, I shall say a word or two about what I termed the meta-questions – why any of this should matter.

II

The claim is often made that the traditional rights of liberal theory are excessively individualistic in their emphasis, and that the so-called second and third generation rights help to correct this individualistic bias. In fact, this indictment (if that is what it is) is remarkably difficult to sustain.

The 1789 Declaration of the Rights of Man and the Citizen, along with similar manifestoes like the United States Bill of Rights, and (much more recently) the European Convention on Human Rights, embody this first generation of rights claims. They include rights to free speech, freedom of association, the protection of private property, liberty in personal affairs, freedom to take part in democratic elections, and personal security against torture, assault, arbitrary imprisonment, and the like. They are alleged to be narrowly individualistic in at least two senses. First, they protect individual interests which, as it were, divide people from the community. As Marx put it in "On the Jewish Question": "None of the so-called rights of man goes beyond egoistic man . . . man separated from other men and the community

... man treated as an isolated monad withdrawn into him-self."[3] Second, they are rights which do not call for positive and collective action by the state; on the contrary, since all they call for on the part of the state is *in*action (the govern-ment must *not* torture its subjects, must *not* pass laws ab-rogating free speech, etc.), they are perfectly compatible with the laissez-faire state of classical individualist liberalism.

I believe both these points are misleading, and it may be worth briefly saying why, before discussing the sense in which rights talk really *is* individualistic.

The first point is acknowledged to be false even by Karl Marx, the great critic of first generation rights. It is certainly true that what he called "the rights of *man*" (freedom, prop-erty, security, and equality) are rights which afford protection to individuals in their purely private concerns. But this is emphatically not the case with what he called "the rights of *the citizen*" in the 1789 manifesto, for all that the two sets of rights are usually lumped together under this heading of first generation rights. The right to vote, to hold public officials accountable, to participate in the execution of the public power, even arguably the rights of freedom of speech and association, cannot plausibly be regarded as the rights of "an isolated monad withdrawn into himself." They are rights which bring people together to act collectively and in concert, rather than rights which drive them back into the narrow preoccupations of their privacy. As Marx put it, these rights are "political rights that are only exercised in community with other men. Their content is formed by participation in the common essence, the political essence, the essence of the state."[4] Admittedly, he went on to say that the rights of the citizen are tainted by being made subservient to an economy dominated by private interests; participation in public life in a capitalist society has no real content so long as the public is not in control of the processes of production.[5] He also hinted (elsewhere) at a thought better expressed by Hannah Arendt when she wrote that the polling booth is too small to be taken seriously as a focus for public life: "It has room for only one."[6] But the basic point remains. In their form, at least, democratic rights, the rights of the citizen, express a vision of political community, not a nightmare of privatized individualism.

Reflection on the rights of the citizen also undermines the other claim about individualism – the claim that first generation rights call only for inaction, rather than collective intervention, by the state. In fact, rights to democratic participation require much more than mere omissions by the state. They require officials to approach their task in a certain spirit, and they require the establishment of political structures to provide a place for popular participation and to give effect to people's wishes, expressed by voting and other forms of pressure. (One way of emphasizing this is to say that many participatory rights have the character of Hohfeldian *powers*, rather than claim rights to negative freedom: each voter has the power to make a difference – a very little difference but formally no smaller than that made by anyone else – to the appointment of legislators and the passage of legislation.)

Even with regard to those first generation rights which are not participatory, it is seldom merely *inaction* that is called for. As I argued in Chapter 1, we set governments up according to traditional liberal theory, not only to *respect* our rights (what would be the point of that?), but to protect, uphold, and vindicate them. That involves positive collective action, action which makes use of scarce manpower and resources. It involves the operation of a police force, law courts, and so on, which are certainly not inconsiderable expenditures on the part of the state and of society collectively.

So the familiar view that first generation rights are purely individualistic, either in their content or in their application, is not in general true. What *is* true is that these rights protect individual interests – whether they are individuals' private interests (in property, security, or whatever) or individuals' interests in participating on equal terms with others in public life. Though all of them appeal for collective action, and though some of them help to constitute a collective life, they are not themselves direct expressions of communal goals or values. They are expressions of the more important interests that individuals may have, as far as communal life is concerned.

Now, in fact, exactly the same is true of most of the claims associated with second generation human rights. Second generation rights include those embodied, for example, in Articles 22 through 27 of the Universal Declaration of Human Rights, 1948 – rights to social security, work and leisure, minimum free education and health care, and so on. In their content, they are no less individualistic than first generation rights (each person is claiming social security or health care, etc., for himself). Some are claims to personal benefits; others are claims to the wherewithal to participate in the social, economic and cultural life of the community. Though it is true that they are also claims to be benefited *by* the resources, manpower, and collective action of the community, that is something which, as we have seen, is no less true of first generation rights as well. First *and* second generation rights, then, both stand in complicated relation to the idea of community and collective action; but at bottom both express the importance of individual interests in relation to those ideas.

The possibility I want to explore is that the same cannot be said for third generation rights – the claims that are being made about the importance of peace, development, and the integrity of the environment. The very terms themselves seem to mark these things out as goals to which whole communities will aspire, rather than attributes which individual men and women may or may not attain. We are in danger of distorting our appreciation of these goals if we try to understand them entirely in terms of the individual interests they may serve.

III

We should ask, then, whether there is a type of good, or a type of aspiration, whose importance is best not expressed in the language of individual rights. If so, do the goods or aspirations referred to in the third generation rights fall into this category?

I start from the idea that rights purport to secure goods *for individuals:* that is an elementary consequence of their logical form. A right is always somebody's right, and we never attempt to secure things *as a matter of right* unless there is some individual or unless there are some individuals whose rights we conceive to be in question. So the language of rights differs crucially from moral locutions like *"It would be a good thing if* such-and-such" or "Such-and-such *ought to be the case."* The language of rights is not simply another way of expressing the moral desirability of some object or state of affairs. Rights express moral desirability *to* or *for* or *from the point of view of* some individual, whereas those other locutions are used to express moral desirability *sans phrase.* This suggests that goods whose moral desirability cannot adequately be expressed in terms which refer to benefits secured to, for, or from the point of view of some individual should not be commended in the language of rights; if they are to be commended at all, the other more impersonal locutions should be used.

Goods whose moral desirability cannot adequately be expressed in individual terms may be called "nonindividualized" goods. One can imagine a moral "fanatic" or "idealist" (to use R. M. Hare's terms) pursuing values which made no reference at all to the good or well-being of individual human beings.[7] Some ecologists take the view that the survival of the earth and its main ecosystems might be worth promoting even at the expense of human welfare. And one can imagine an aesthetic theory in which the existence of things of beauty was thought to be of value quite apart from human appreciation of them.[8] It would be very odd for anyone to attempt to express these views in the language of rights. More interesting, however, are moral considerations which *are* related to human well-being but whose desirability nevertheless is incapable of being adequately characterized *individualistically.* It may be thought, for example, that the value of goods like *community, fraternity,* or *culture* is distorted if we try and characterize them in terms of benefit to individual people. These are a subset of nonindividualized goods, and I shall call them "communal goods." The thesis I want to consider is the following: if there are any communal goods, if there are goods which, though they have consequences for human well-being, are nevertheless nonindividualized in this strong sense, the language of rights should not be used to commend them.

To clarify this thesis, it is worth comparing it with what two recent theorists of rights – Neil MacCormick and Joseph Raz – have said on the subject. Both have insisted that the language of rights should not be used to express the moral desirability of what they call "collective" goods. Now it is always unwise to proliferate terminology, but I have chosen the term "communal goods" rather than "collective goods" for the thesis I want to consider, because both Raz and MacCormick use the term "collective goods" to express a somewhat different idea – the idea of what economists refer to as "publicness." Both Raz and MacCormick believe that *public* goods, in the technical sense, cannot sensibly be made the subject matter of individual rights. I think they are mistaken about that. I shall examine their arguments in this section, before moving on, in Section IV, to show that it is not publicness, as such, which is at issue.

In his article "Rights in Legislation," MacCormick offers the following as one of the "features which must be included in any characterization of rules which confer rights":

> *they concern the enjoyment of goods by individuals separately,* not simply as members of a collectivity enjoying a diffuse common benefit in which all participate in indistinguishable and unassignable shares. [I]t is correct to say that such rules of law must be concerned with classes of individuals, but the benefit secured is secured to each and every individual severally upon satisfaction of the 'institutive' or 'investive' conditions.[9]

In a later piece he glosses this with the claim that

> what [rights] do is secure individuals . . . in the enjoyment of some good or other. But not by way of a collective good col-

lectively enjoyed, like clean air in a city, but rather an individual good individually enjoyed by each, like the protection of each occupier's particular environment as secured by the law of private nuisance.[10]

Of course, universalizability guarantees that if any individual has a right to some good then all individuals (or all like him in the relevant respect) have a right to a good like that too. MacCormick's point is that if rights secure goods for everyone, they do so on an individual-by-individual basis, so that even when X, Y, and Z all have a right to G, the securing of G to X is a separate matter from its being secured to Y, and separate again from its being secured to Z.

Raz has made somewhat similar claims, though he talks about right-based moralities rather than rights as such. He says that right-based moralities are "usually individualistic moral theories" and goes on to say that a theory is individualistic if it "does not recognize any intrinsic value in any collective good." A collective good, he says, is an "inherent public good" by which he means a good which is nonexcludable and noncontingently so.[11] (MacCormick's example, clean air, is not a case Raz would use because, though we lack the technology to control air distribution, this limitation on our technical ability is only a contingent one.) The examples he uses of inherent public goods are what he calls "general beneficial features of a society":

> It is a public good, and inherently so, that this society is a tolerant society, that it is an educated society, that it is infused with a sense of respect for human beings etc. Living in a society with these characteristics is generally of benefit to individuals. ... Different people benefit from the good qualities of the society to different degrees. But the degree to which they benefit depends on their character, interests and dispositions, and cannot be directly controlled by others. ... Naturally one can exclude individuals from benefiting from such goods by excluding them from the society to which they pertain. But that does not affect the character of the goods as public goods which

depends on non-exclusivity of enjoyment among members of the society in which they are public goods.[12]

Raz's thesis then is that goods which are inherently nonexcludable cannot be the subject matter of individual rights.

Why do MacCormick and Raz believe that public goods cannot be the subject matter of rights? Before answering this question, I shall say something about the definition of the term "public good." Though "public good" is a technical term, it is associated in the economic literature with a cluster of criteria (which seem to operate in a sort of "family resemblance" way) rather than a single criterion. For our purposes, the two most important criteria are nonexcludability and jointness of production. A good is *nonexcludable*, relative to a group, if it is the case that, if it is to be supplied to any member of the group, it cannot be denied to any other member of the group (the benefit of a lighthouse is a good example). A good is *jointly produced* to the extent that it cannot be produced by a private individual or firm acting alone, but can only be produced by the cooperation of all or most members of the group (clean air in a residential suburb is an example). Both are matters of degree – in each case so far as feasibility is concerned, and, in the case of joint production, so far as the number of people involved in production is concerned. Though these features are often associated (in the case of clean air, for instance), they are theoretically quite distinct: it is possible for a good to be nonexcludable but privately produced (a privately built lighthouse warning ships away from dangerous reefs is the best example); and it is possible for a good to be jointly produced but excludable (a system of public honors, for example). Both Raz and MacCormick say in the passages I have quoted that it is nonexcludability they are focusing on. But, when Raz gets around to offering an argument, it turns out to be concerned not with the nonexcludability aspect of publicness but with *jointness of production*. I want to examine this argument, before going on to consider whether there are any good arguments for the thesis based on nonexcludability itself.

Raz's recent work on rights is based on the following very plausible definition: " 'x has a right' means that, other things being equal, an aspect of x's well-being (his interest) is a sufficient reason for holding some other person(s) to be under a duty."[13] The individual interests which are the basis for rights must be important enough to warrant imposing the duties on others that would normally be necessary to promote them. Given this conception, Raz believes theories of rights will find it difficult to accommodate what he calls "collective" goods. Although it is true that individuals have interests in the existence of such goods, these goods can be produced only by the collective action of all members of the society, and Raz thinks it is unlikely that a single individual's interest could justify the imposition of the widespread duties that would be required for their provision. Denise Reaume has produced a lucid summary of the argument:

> Consider, for instance, the public good of a cultured society. Such a society requires the existence of a certain "critical mass" of cultured individuals – people who write music and literature and who paint and sculpt, together with consumers of these products. If no such critical mass existed, the person who claimed the right to cultured society would be claiming that her interests justified the imposition of a duty on others to create such a body. . . . The point is, firstly, that the provision of such a public good requires the widespread participation of many people, and secondly, that it requires interference with important choices about how to live one's own life. When these features are made explicit the plausibility of Raz's argument becomes apparent. It is difficult to see how one person's desire to live in a cultured society can justify such an imposition on so many others. The ultimate answer to this question will depend upon substantive moral arguments about the weight to be assigned to the various interests at stake, but it is Raz's intuition that substantive arguments capable of justifying such a right will not be forthcoming.[14]

This does not mean that one's interest in the matter is politically irrelevant. As Raz puts it, "my interest that my society shall be of this character is *a reason* to develop it in such a direction" (my emphasis). But it is a reason to be weighed in the social calculus alongside other reasons; unlike, for example, the individual interest in not being tortured, it is not sufficient in itself to yield the conclusion that one's fellow citizens or one's government are under duties in this regard.[15]

Reaume goes on to note, I think correctly, that in the end this is not an argument about public goods at all, but about the relative moral weight of interests. Many private goods are very costly to produce or maintain. And many of the things we are certain that people have rights to (like freedom of political association, for example) may impose immense costs on governments and therefore indirectly on the mass of one's fellow citizens. Since we believe nevertheless that sometimes people do have rights to such goods, the mere fact that the costs of providing "collective" goods may be onerous and widespread cannot be a reason for denying that they are a plausible subject matter for rights. Indeed, as Reaume notes, the costs of providing the kinds of collective goods in which Raz is interested may in fact be quite low, since they have the feature that the interest others have in their existence provides a reason for them to participate in their production. People enjoy participating in the production of a cultured society, for example. So, basing an argument purely on the costs involved in supplying jointly produced goods is not a convincing strategy.[16]

Let us return now to nonexcludability. Is there any reason to believe that goods with this feature cannot be the subject matter of rights? Neither Raz nor MacCormick attempts an argument to this effect, but one might be constructed along the following lines.

Goods which are nonexcludable cannot be secured to individuals one at a time; securing G to X involves, in effect, securing it also to Y and Z. One can imagine then that in law certain difficulties will arise in regard to the *enforcement* of rights to these goods. A case brought by X to secure G for himself will necessarily raise the issue of its being secured to everyone else and in that sense prejudice any action brought by Y or by Z to secure G for themselves. These problems are familiar in relation to legal rules of locus standi for public nuisance and other public wrongs. The traditional position in law is that before one's claim can be heard, one must have a *special interest* in the matter of a public nuisance, or in seeking an injunction to restrain a public wrong, over and above the interest that members of the public have in it generally.[17] Certainly, there have been significant developments in the area of group and representative actions to cope with the collective action problems that these stipulations can sometimes generate. But they are fraught with the difficulties I have in mind: namely, the possibility of a conflict between a plaintiff's own interest in the matter (the enthusiasm he has for the action, the terms on which he is prepared to settle, and so on) and the interests of others who are affected in the same way he is.[18] The point is that rights to nonexcludable goods are not independently justiciable, or not easily independently justiciable; and this might provide a reason for thinking that the language of rights, where the importance of the good in question is always pinned down to a particular individual, is not the most appropriate language in which claims to nonexcludable goods should be expressed.

I have some sympathy with this line of argument, but it suffers from two important drawbacks. First, the implicit contrast between private and public goods in this regard does not have very much significance in real life. Nowadays the pursuit of almost all important individual rights involves *test case* litigation. When a question about a right (even to an excludable private good like the right not to be tortured) comes before a tribunal like the European Court of Human Rights, it comes in reality as a test case for the similar rights of countless individuals who stand to be affected in the same way, and the judgment handed down to the individual plaintiff is almost always taken by the relevant authority as determining how it should treat thousands of other nonplaintiffs involved in similar situations. Ordinary private legal rights (in tort and contract, etc.) continue to be pursued individually, with the terms of settlement affecting none but the parties to the action; but even there the doctrine of precedent ensures an impact beyond the bounds of particular litigation. In the field of rights, then, strictly individual justiciability is in practice, if not in theory, a bit of a myth.

Second, I believe the argument depends on something like the Choice Theory of rights. The Choice Theory was made popular in modern jurisprudence (though it has since been repudiated) by H. L. A. Hart.[19] For our purposes, we can state it as the thesis that to be a right holder is not necessarily to be in a position to *benefit* from another's duty, but it is to be in a position of *control* over another's duty. X has a right against W, on this account, only if it is *for* X to claim performance of the duty from W or to waive it – in other words, if it is *for* X to determine, by his choice, how W ought to act in this regard. From the point of view of the Choice Theory, the problem with rights to nonexcludable goods is not that other plaintiffs may be denied what they have a right to by the first plaintiff's action (in fact, quite the contrary). The problem is that they may be deprived of the opportunity to waive their right or settle their claim on other terms. If having a right is essentially a matter of being in a position to control somebody else's duty by one's choice, it is important that one right holder's choice be insulated from the impact of choices made by others with rights to the same thing. This certainly cannot be done in the case of nonexcludable goods: once X insists on having G, his fellow claimants Y and Z are deprived of any real choice in the matter. If G is nonoptional as well as nonexcludable, they cannot avoid benefiting from it if it is provided for X. But even if G is optional, its nonexcludability means that there is very little they can do with the choice their right nominally gives them, and therefore that qua choice it is worth very little. If X insists on the performance of the duty to provide G owed to him, then the duty that Y and Z are theoretically in a position to waive must be carried out whether they want it or not. Nonexcludable goods therefore queer the pitch for the operation of other people's rights according to the Choice Theory.

However, the Choice Theory is not a popular theory of rights, and none of this appears as a difficulty if we are not committed to it. If we say that the essence of having a right is simply standing to benefit from the performance of another's duty (or if we say, with Raz, that to have a right is for it to be the case that one's interest justifies holding someone else to have a duty), then the fact that X's insistence on his right benefits Y as well is, at most, an interesting and welcome side effect. There seems no reason whatever to hold that X may not have or exercise rights in cases where this is likely to happen.

So far, we have seen no reason to say, with Raz and MacCormick, that public goods cannot be the subject matter of individual rights. I think there are also good positive reasons for saying that public goods *can* be the subject matter of individual rights.

The idea of a public good (in either of the senses we have been discussing) is not necessarily a collectivist or communitarian one. It need not be a good *to the public* in any sense over and above its worth to particular individuals. It is simply the idea of a good whose provision to individuals has a certain shape, so far as incentives and production are concerned. Clean air, for example, is a public good (it is practicably nonexcludable and jointly produced), but still its importance can be fully captured by an account of its worth to individual breathers. Streetlighting is a public good (in the sense of nonexcludability), even though the basis of its desirability may simply be that it enables private individuals to see their way home by themselves to their private houses. The point of providing goods like these may be perfectly expressible in terms of a concern for individual interests. If we think that each individual's interest in receiving some benefit (like clean lungs, for example, or being able to see his way home) is sufficiently important to be the basis of a duty to provide that benefit, and if the provision of a public good is the only practicable way of doing that, then there can be no objection to saying that the individual has a right to that public good. If we do not believe this, but we believe that individual interests taken in the aggregate justify its provision, our case for the public good will be utilitarian rather than rights-based. Either way, we do not have to step outside the traditional confines of individualistic political morality to demand and extoll the worth of public goods. Of course, like many excludable goods, the provision of public goods may require collective action. But, as we saw in Section II, this does not distinguish them from the subject matter of first and second generation rights.

It seems then that if the novelty of third generation claims is simply that they concern public goods, there should be no difficulty at all in expressing them as human rights, no problem accommodating them to the idiom of that particular discourse.

Certainly, many of the goods extolled as third generation rights have some of the characteristics associated with publicness. Peace and the integrity of the environment are both nonexcludable so far as their benefits are concerned, and, arguably, those benefits are jointly produced (in the sense that no private individual or firm *could* produce them even if it had an incentive to do so). The nature of economic development is a little less clear in this respect, but there are obviously some nonexcludable aspects to it and some aspects of jointness in its production. My point is that it does not really matter whether economic development is a wholly public or a partly private good. Either way, there is no logical difficulty in expressing it as the subject matter of a right, if individuals' interests in the benefits that flow from it are felt to be sufficiently compelling.

IV

A public good may still be a good consumed and enjoyed by individuals: its publicness may consist simply in the fact that, if any individual is to benefit from the good, then no individual can be excluded from such benefit. There is, however, a deeper sense than this in which a good may be said to be publicly enjoyed or consumed.

Consider the good of *conviviality* at a party – the good atmosphere, high spirits, and lively conversation among the guests. However intangible it may seem, this is a good that almost every host strives to realize; his choice of guests and choice of wine are often directed to precisely this end. If he succeeds, a considerable benefit will accrue to all concerned. But it is a benefit they will have enjoyed *together*, not merely in the sense that to be enjoyed by one guest it cannot practicably be denied to the others (like the pleasure of hearing the host's efforts on the piano), but in the sense that its enjoyment is primarily a property of the group rather than each of the individual guests considered by himself. A party is convivial when people derive benefit from the active enjoyment of one another's company, not when each of them sits around experiencing the pleasures of the evening – the food, the wine, the music – as a purely personal enjoyment. Of course, it is possible to get all sorts of goods at a party; but if one comes away having enjoyed it and knowing that others did not, one has not participated in the sort of good I am talking about. Conviviality or good atmosphere is a *communal* good experienced as such by people only to the extent that they are participant members of a group to which the benefit of the good accrues at a collective level.

When we say that conviviality is a good enjoyed *by the group*, and that this enjoyment is not reducible to the sum of the enjoyments of individuals, are we, in effect, attributing conscious states to the group itself? That would make most people metaphysically uneasy. However, I don't think we need that; I don't think we need to deny that the only centers of consciousness involved are individual ones, in order to say that a good may be enjoyed by a group. We can accept that the only experiences taking place, to constitute this enjoyment, are experiences in the minds of individuals, but we can also insist that, in cases like this, the individual experiences are unintelligible apart from their reference to the enjoyments of others. For me to enjoy conviviality is partly for me to be assured that others are enjoying it too. This is not just a matter of sympathetic identification with others. What I identify with is not someone else's private enjoyment, but an enjoyment of theirs in turn constituted partly by a similar reference to the pleasures (similarly constituted) of me and the others. Thus the enjoyment I experience is not just a satisfaction or a warm glow that can be predicated of me alone; it is something which in its felt character looks beyond its embodiment in me to its embodiment in others. And the enjoyment in them that it looks toward is similarly not confined to their individuality, but refers back and forth to others, and so on.

An analogy with personal identity may illuminate the point. We think of human individuals as entities persisting through time, and we think of their experiences as states which exist through time. It is possible, however, in a Humean spirit to think of individuals and their experiences as simply bundles of momentary states – or, at any rate, bundles of states which, if not momentary, are of considerably shorter duration than the enduring experiences they compose.[20] When we say, for example, that an individual enjoys an opera, we may agree with Hume that his enjoyment is composed of short or momentary "bits" of experience. But, if we say this, we will also want to insist that the enjoyment of the opera is not merely an *aggregation* of "bits" of experience, each of which is entirely self-contained; we will insist that the felt quality of each of these bits is such as to refer backward and forward to all of the others, giving the enduring composite (if that is what it is) a unity which a mere series of self-contained experiential moments would not have. The frisson felt in the opening chords of *Tristan und Isolde* has the character it has partly because it is *the beginning* of something which is set to go on for five hours (or whatever), just as the thrill of the *liebestod* has partly to do with the fact that it resolves a tension that seems to have been building forever. My suggestion is that, in the case of conviviality, the experiences of individuals may stand in the same sort of relation to the enjoyment of the group, as momentary bits of experience stand to an individual's enjoyment of the opera. In both cases, we should take care that our enthusiasm for atomistic reduction – for reducing wholes to their constituent parts – does not blind us to the fact that the parts refer essentially in their felt character to their status as fragments of a whole.

So far I have concentrated on what something like conviviality *is*, and how it is related to individual experience. The aspect of communality becomes even more marked when we try to understand the *value* or *importance* of such things. A purely reductive analysis would make the value of conviviality a function of the values of the individual experiences of which it was composed. That would be an unsatisfactory account since, as we have seen, each of these experiences refers beyond itself to the wider group, and the account given by any of the individuals concerned of the value of the experience *to him* would make immediate reference to its value and importance for the others. An account, then, of the value of these things that was sensitive to what it was like to enjoy them would have to focus on their communal character.

Of course, someone might *insist* – in a Benthamite mood – that intrinsic value is to be predicated only of the pleasurable character of individual sensations; accordingly he might insist that the value of conviviality is nothing but the sum of individual pleasures. There is no knockdown argument against such hard-nosed hedonism. What one can say, though, is that it would cut the hedonistic account loose from its traditional basis in individuals' own estimations of the value of their experiences; for it seems to me unlikely that you will find anyone who has enjoyed the conviviality of a party saying that the importance of its enjoyment to him was nothing but the self-contained satisfaction that he got out of it, considered on his own.

Once we see that some goods, like conviviality, are to be understood as essentially communal goods, it is easy to think of other, perhaps more serious, examples from political philosophy. Examples include community-wide goods like fraternity, solidarity, the close integration of *gemeinschaft*, Rousseau's general will, Marx's notion of the "species-being"

357

of co-operative production, and so on. In each case, something is said to be valuable for human society without its value being adequately characterizable in terms of its worth to any or all of the individual members of the society considered one by one. If fraternity, for instance, is thought to be important, it is not because of what each *individual* comrade gets out of it; rather, what each individual comrade gets out of it will make essential and ineliminable reference to what all comrades together enjoy. We might also want to include under this heading the importance to a community of its traditions and its language. We can say that Welsh people, for example, do not benefit *as individuals* from the preservation of their language. Though each may get a warm glow of pride when he sees a road sign in Welsh, his own sense of that experience will refer immediately beyond itself to the fact that this is something whose nature and value make sense only on the assumption that others are enjoying and participating in it too. A number of the examples mentioned by Raz also fall into this category: the value of a cultured society, a tolerant society, and a society where there is a general sense of respect for persons. One does not have to be communist in order to recognize that *some* of the things worth pursuing in this world have this communal character.

I hope it is clear now why publicness, in the technical sense, is not sufficient to characterize the communality of certain values. It is true that many of the things I have just been talking about are public goods – a shared language, for example, is jointly produced and largely nonexcludable. But those are not what make its enjoyment communal, for, as we have seen, jointness of production and nonexcludability are perfectly compatible with the idea that the importance of some good (like clean air or streetlighting) can be characterized completely in terms which make reference only to the private purposes and satisfactions of atomized individuals. Fraternity, solidarity, conviviality, a shared language, culture, and traditions are not like that. Though they are certainly nonexcludable, no account of their *worth* to anyone can be given except by concentrating on what they are worth to everyone together.

V

It is, as I have said, widely believed that certain communal goods are important, and that governments have a duty to promote and protect them. Is there anything wrong with expressing this as a claim about *rights* – a claim that people have *a right* to these goods? I think there is.

In Section III, I pointed out that a claim of right does two things: it specifies a good, and it specifies a person – a beneficiary, a right-bearer – for whom, or for whose sake, that good is to be brought about. But a theory of rights is supposed to do more than merely provide a list of goods, a list of duties to promote those goods, and a list of associated beneficiaries. What is distinctive about a right is that the benefit to the individual is seen as the *ground* of the duty, as a "sufficient reason" for it, in Raz's phrase. An individual has a right to G when the importance of his interest in G, considered on its own, is sufficient to justify holding others to be under a duty to promote G.

But if there are communal goods and if there is a duty to promote them, it cannot be a duty grounded in benefits accruing to any one individual or to a class of individuals considered severally. The duty to realize such goods must be grounded in an adequate characterization of their desirability, and that is their worth to members of the group considered together and not as individual recipients of benefit. It is because X, Y, and Z enjoy the good together, and because the participation of each in that enjoyment is oriented toward the understanding that the others are participating in it too, that the good is worth pursuing. So since no adequate account of its desirability can be pinned down to either X or Y or Z, there can be no *point* in saying that it ought to be pursued as X's or Y's or Z's right.

It is true that most human rights are not seen as idiosyncratic to the individuals who have them; they are regarded as universalizable across all individuals. First and second generation rights are seen as things which anyone and everyone can claim. The important thing is that the basis of the claim is distinct in the case of each individual. It is the importance of *my* interest in liberty that grounds *my* right to freedom from arbitrary arrest and it is the importance of *your* interest in liberty that grounds *your* right to freedom from arbitrary arrest. The underlying argument is universalizable, but the universal quantification is across individuals taken one by one.

This point is brought out by contrasting it with the shape of utilitarian justifications. A utilitarian justifies the claim that X should not be imprisoned by reference to the importance not just of X's interest in the matter but Y's and Z's and everyone else's as well. Utilitarians, unlike rights theorists, are not prepared to justify the imposition of social duties by reference to the interests of just one individual. The account of communal goods that I have given is not a utilitarian account. But the claim that a communal good should be promoted shares with utilitarian claims a commitment to a form of justificatory discourse that does not proceed to the establishment of social duties from any conception of the importance of the interest of a single individual, taken on his own. The importance of promoting a communal good stems from its worth to members of the community in question taken together. It would be odd, then, to claim such a good as an individual right (or even as a right of all individuals). Such a claim would mislead one's audience about the way in which the importance of the good was to be understood.

VI

I do not know whether the new generation of human rights claims – peace, economic development, and the environment – fit into the category of communal goods. They have aspects that are enjoyed individually, even though they may be provided publicly: each individual benefits if the environment is unpolluted, the economy is thriving, and bombs are not falling. Those benefits may be all we want to stress when we say that such things are human rights. But I suspect that some of them are valued also as communal goods, in the sense I discussed in Section IV. Peace, especially, may be valued as a communal good; and other things that have been talked about as rights – like the importance of a people's language and the integrity of their traditions – also fall into this category. To the extent that they do, it is inappropriate to express convictions about the worth of these things and the importance of promoting them as claims about the rights of the individual.

Can they, however, be expressed as claims about the rights *of the community* or *of the whole people* to whom they pertain? This leads to the general question: is there anything wrong with moving from talk about the rights of *individual* men and women to talk about *the rights of groups?* Groups are different from individuals, and group talk differs from individual talk. Is there any logical or ontological reason for the hesitation some people feel about extending the language of rights in this direction? Or even if there are no (onto)logical objections, are there other reasons why this would be an unwise move to make?

There are two reasons for thinking that it is perfectly all right to talk about the rights of groups and the rights of communities.

One is that we do this already. We attribute rights to corporations, associating the capacity to bear rights with the attribution of *legal* personality rather than natural individuality. If ICI and Hoffman-La Roche are allowed to be right-bearers, it seems a bit harsh to deny that status to the community of French-speaking Canadians or the people of Malawi; certainly it would be pedantic to do so on purely verbal grounds.[21]

We should be cautious, though, about this argument from corporate personality. The fact that we do something in legal discourse may not always be a good indication that it is wise to do it in political morality. The issue here is whether *human* rights should or can include the rights of groups, not simply whether groups can have ordinary legal rights. Also, we must not pretend that the idea of corporate personality is perfectly well understood. It is not. Talk of the rights of corporations makes sense (if it does) in the context of a complicated and articulated theory of what corporate personality amounts to. If Jeremy Bentham and H. L. A. Hart are right in their suggestion that the meaning of terms like "corporation" can be elucidated only by *paraphrasis* – that is, by a consideration of the whole context in which they appear – then we cannot talk glibly about an analogy with the human rights of groups unless we are prepared to transplant something like the whole apparatus and context of company law into the area of ethnic and national communities.[22] The clearest objection to an analogy in this area is that positive law provides strict and clear criteria for determining the identity of a corporation and for tracing the impact of corporate rights and responsibilities on the rights and responsibilities of natural individuals. For example, legal rules provide a basis for determining whether a given company is the same as a company that existed in the past, and for determining whether a given individual is a shareholder or officer of that company. There may be no such criteria and no such agreed on rules for the groups, peoples, nations, and communities alluded to in third generation rights talk. A couple of problematic examples may be given. The Irish people have a right to self-determination; but does that mean that a majority in the Irish Republic can determine the fate of those in the North? The Welsh have a right to their language; but what if a large number of people living in Wales want to opt out of their Welshness and assert their identity as British? The problems can quickly become viciously circular in cases where the identity of the group is exactly the issue at stake in the asserted content of the alleged group right. Talk of individual rights has at least this advantage over talk of group rights: the identity of natural individuals is seldom disputed in the controversies in which their rights are thought to be involved.[23]

The second reason for thinking that talk of group rights

might be unexceptionable is this: particular groups may often stand to some larger entity in a similar relation to that in which individual men and women stand to the state. Just as the state may bear too heavily on some individual, so a whole society or a federation may bear too heavily on some constituent group. The issues, in other words, may have the same sort of shape, and we may think it perfectly appropriate to state those issues using the same sorts of concepts. Just as an individual – say, Joseph Raz – has rights against the British government – rights whose function is to place limits on the purposes the government can pursue or to constrain the means it may use to pursue its purposes, or to impose limits on the losses Raz can be asked to bear and the sacrifices he can be called upon to make – so we may say that the Welsh people have rights against the United Kingdom, rights which preclude the government from pursuing goals of linguistic homogeneity, or which constrain its strategies for road traffic control by requiring road signs in Wales which are unintelligible to English drivers, or which impose limits on the losses Welsh poetry can be expected to suffer at a time of general retrenchment on arts spending, and so on. In both cases, rights appear to do the same sort of job.

We may not even have to contrast the right-bearing group with an overarching federation or a formal institution like the United Kingdom. Just as we say that individuals have rights which constrain all their fellow citizens, so we may say that peoples and nations have rights which constrain all other peoples and nations in the world, or rights which constrain the world community as a whole.

All this seems fine. Still there are differences between the individual/state relation and the group/federation relation. The most important difference is that the group is itself composed of individuals who will, on any account, be the bearers of rights. The problem with the idea of group rights is that it involves the attribution of rights to entities which are composed of, and may therefore be making demands on, other entities which are also right-bearers, in their own right. The idea is unexceptionable so long as we concentrate on relations between the group and some higher entity like a federation, or between the group and coordinate entities like other groups. Problems may arise, however, when we consider relations between the group and its own members. To go back to our Welsh example, what happens if the rights of the Welsh community, considered as a group, make demands on individual men and women living in Wales? What happens if it limits their freedom to choose an English education for their children, or denies them the opportunity to enjoy the same culture as fellow citizens living in other parts of the United Kingdom?

The problem here is essentially that stated by Ronald Dworkin in his discussion of the claim that *society* has rights which must be balanced against those of the individual:

> It is true that we speak of the "right" of society to do what it wants, but this cannot be a "competing right" of the sort that may justify the invasion of a right against the Government. The existence of rights against the Government would be jeopardized if the Government were able to defeat such a right by appealing to the right of a democratic majority to work its will. A right against the Government must be a right to do something even when the majority thinks it would be wrong to do it, and even when the majority would be worse off for having it done. If we now say that society has a right to do whatever is in the general benefit, or the right to preserve whatever sort of environment the majority wishes to live in, and we mean that these are the sort of rights that provide justification for overruling any rights against the Government that may conflict, then we have annihilated the latter rights.[24]

If the whole point of rights for individuals is to place limits on the pursuit of some communal goal, it will hardly do to characterize that goal as a community right which may then conflict with, and possibly override, the rights of individuals.

The difficulty is a real one, but it is important to see that it is not a reason for ruling out group rights altogether. To begin with, the problem only arises if one adopts Dworkin's theory of rights as "trumps" over what he calls "collective

justifications", such as utilitarian policies.²⁵ That approach is
more idiosyncratic than the popularity of the "trumps" image
might suggest. Dworkin's argument is essentially that we
come to our understanding of rights via our concern about
shortcomings in our calculation or conception of social goals.
(For example: "The concept of an individual political right,
in the strong anti-utilitarian sense . . . , is a response to the
philosophical defects of a utilitarianism that counts external
preferences and the practical impossibility of a utilitarianism
that does not."²⁶ It would be absurd to set up rights as a
response to the defects in some communal goal and then
define the communal goal, in turn, as a right which competed
on equal terms with the rights we had just set up. But if one
adopts a different approach to rights – for example, a theory
that defines each individual right in terms of the inherent
importance of the interest it protects rather than in terms
relative to some conception of a social goal – then the problem
does not arise.²⁷ The clash between the rights of a group,
such as the Welsh people, and the rights of some individual
Welshman would simply be a clash between the importance
of different sorts of interests. We have to cope with such
clashes in any plausible political theory anyway.

Second, even if one accepts Dworkin's theory of rights,
still the problem only arises when the individual's right
clashes with the very communal goal in relation to which the
individual right has been defined. If the individual right is
defined as a trump over general utility, and the group right
involves the pursuit of some group interest *other than* the
general utility of its members – for example, a nonutilitarian
group interest such as the integrity of a certain culture – then
the problem does not arise. The Dworkin theory does not
imply that individual rights are trumps over *all* communal
goals; or, if that is what he believes, he has yet to argue for
it.²⁸ Particular rights, for Dworkin, are defined as trumps in
relation to particular group interests; for example, civil and
political liberties are trumps in relation to general utility via
the argument about external preferences. There may be no
objection to saying that civil liberties must be balanced

against the group's right to national glory, for example, if conceptions of national glory do not involve the reference to external preferences which was our reason for saying civil liberties were rights in the first place. Everything depends on whether there is an internal relation between the individual right and the collective goal.[29] If there is not, then there is no problem; if there is, there may be.

So there need be no general incompatibility between talk of the rights of a group and talk of the rights of constituent members of the group. We do have to be careful in cases where the group right expresses a collective aim whose limitation is the specific point of treating certain individual rights as trumps. For example, the whole point of insisting that a person may marry whom he pleases (if she will have him) might have been to place limits on the extent to which a culture can be permitted to stifle its members' individuality; if so, it would be self-defeating to say that the cultural goal of ethnic integrity is a right of the group and that the individual's right to marry freely must be balanced against it. For this and similar cases, what Dworkin says is correct: the group right cannot be asserted against the individual right by anyone who professes to take the latter seriously. But even in these cases, the group right may still be asserted against other respondents – the members of other groups or the overarching federation. Though the impact of the group right on the federation may eventually trickle down to the group's members, still the interests of theirs that are eventually affected may not be the same as the interests in terms of which their rights were originally defined. In other cases, where the rights of the individual and the aims of the group are defined quite independently of each other, we need have no worries of this kind about formulating the latter as group or community rights (though of course our earlier worries about group identity and membership still remain).

The only other difficulty I can think of is that group rights may not be justifiable on the same basis as individual rights. For example, someone may think (following Hart's original view) that the whole point of human rights is to protect

individual freedom.[30] Since few of us think that groups have
an interest in freedom, we may doubt whether group rights
can be accommodated to this theory. There are two answers
to this. First, as Raz has shown in *The Morality of Freedom*,
there are many more and deeper connections between communal goods and individual autonomy than at first appear.
Even if we say that individual autonomy is the be-all and
end-all of human rights, still, as Raz argues, some of what
I have termed communal goods are not merely instrumental
to, but even partially constitutive of, individual autonomy.[31]
Second, it is hard nowadays to find any merit in the claim
that all rights must in the end derive from the same justification. Individual rights exist when the interests of some
person, taken by themselves, justify the imposition of duties
on others. There may be many such justifications – that is,
many different ways and bases on which this sort of importance can be attributed to an individual interest. We might
as well embrace this pluralism, and take advantage of the
opportunity it offers to extend the language of rights to claims
made on behalf of other human entities as well.

The verdict on group rights, then, is a mixed one. Where
the identity of a right-bearer is in dispute, there are often
problems with rights talk; and this is obviously going to be
more of a problem for group rights than for the rights of
individual men and women. But in cases where the identity
of the group is not seriously disputed, talk of group rights
is quite intelligible and may be a useful vehicle for the expression of third generation claims. In these cases, the only reasons for caution will concern possible conflicts between the
rights of groups and those individual rights that are understood as trumps over the goals of the community.

VII

How can one tell whether I am right about any of this? And
does it matter? Some may say this is all a waste of breath.
The language of human rights, they may say, is simply the
language we use to express the things we think are impor-

tant. It has become the language for expressing our most urgent aspirations: no more and no less than that. Why worry about its logic or its grammar? If someone says the integrity of the environment is a human right, we all know (roughly) what he means.

I am sure that is true. Nothing is more pathetic than the image of a philosopher (or any other pedant) shouting "You can't say this!" or "You can't say that!" while the chanting crowds trample him cheerfully under foot. Verbal stipulation is a thankless task at the best of times, and particularly so in an area where passions run as high, and misunderstandings are as common, as they are in the area of human rights. I do not think anything is seriously lost if politicians and diplomats at the United Nations or wherever go around saying that communal goals are individual rights or talking about group rights in cases where a philosopher might think it inappropriate.

The reason (if there is one) for taking these points seriously has to do with the aims of an adjacent but somewhat separate enterprise. Political theorists are still interested (perhaps naively) in constructing coherent and philosophically attractive *theories* of human rights – theories which try to articulate with some rigor what the form and foundations of human rights claims might be, what their presuppositions are, and what their relation is to other types of normative claims. The aim of such theorizing is *not* to discipline ordinary users of the concept, or to serve as a basis for correcting politicians' grammar. It is part of the general enterprise of political philosophy: to probe the depths of our commitments, make sense of them, and systematize them as far as we can. This is not a task to everyone's taste; and philosophers should certainly not be exasperated if working politicians excuse themselves from it. But it is an assumption of our culture that the task be performed,[32] and I believe also that many ordinary and political users of the language of human rights assume, or at least hope, that somewhere out there, someone is trying to make coherent sense of all their talk.

At any rate, the definitions of rights that I have been appealing to are part of that enterprise, and what has been going on here is some preliminary reflection on how the emergence, at a political level, of these third generation rights claims might be related to the deeper academic task of making philosophical sense of the aims, aspirations, and principles of politics.

Chapter 15

When justice replaces affection:
The need for rights

I

Why do people need legal rights? In a world crying out for a greater emphasis on communal responsibility, what is the point of an institution that legitimates the making of querulous and adversarial claims by individuals against their fellows? If human relations can be founded on affection, why is so much made in modern jurisprudence of formal and impersonal rights as a starting point for the evaluation of laws and social arrangements? In answering these questions, I shall take as my starting point a disagreement between the philosophers Kant and Hegel regarding the role of rights in marriage.

In his work on the philosophy of law, Immanuel Kant likened marriage to a contract between two people for "lifelong reciprocal possession of their sexual faculties."[1] He was quick to add that, though it is a contract, it is "not on that account a matter of arbitrary will"; rather, it is a matter of necessity for anyone who wants to enjoy another person sexually. In sexual relations, Kant says, one party is used as an object by the other, and that prima facie is incompatible with the basic "Law of Humanity" prohibiting the use of any human agent as a mere means to the satisfaction of one's desires. The situation can be rectified "only . . . under the condition that as the one Person is acquired by the other as a *res*, that same Person equally acquires the other reciprocally, and thus regains and re-establishes the rational

Personality."² Kant went on to say that the reciprocity of rights that this solution presupposes leads to a requirement of monogamy, because in a polygamous regime, one of the partners may be giving more to the other than the other is to her.³ The contract has got to be a matter of *equal* right in order to satisfy the fundamental test of respect for persons.

Sometimes it seems that Kant was not content with this contractualist characterization of marriage. In one place, he went further and argued that the rights involved are like rights of property:

> The Personal Right thus acquired is at the same time, real in kind. This characteristic of it is established by the fact that if one of the married Persons run away or enter into the possession of another, the other is entitled, at any time, and incontestably, to bring such a one back to the former relation, as if that Person were a Thing.⁴

Many have thought that such views are better ignored in the overall assessment of Kant's philosophy of morals.

The Kantian conception of marriage as a purely contractual arrangement was adamantly repudiated by Hegel – "shameful," he said, "is the only word for it."⁵ Hegel conceded that marriage *originates* in a contract between two people and that therefore, in its dependence on their say-so to get it underway, it has some of the contingency and "arbitrariness" that are associated with contractual relations.⁶ But, according to Hegel, rights and contract do not tell us the full story about the institution. For one thing, the public character of the marriage celebration (whether the ceremony is religious or civil) – the procedures of notification, licensing, witnessing, solemnization, registration, and so on – attest to a significance that goes far beyond a mere meeting of the wills or "the mutual caprice" of the prospective partners.⁷ For another thing, the parties celebrate their marriage not merely as a quid pro quo but in order to attain a union of desire, affection, interest, and identity that goes far beyond anything that could possibly be specified even in the fine print of a contract. There is a world of difference, on this view, between the Kantian "contract for reciprocal use" and the "love, trust, and common sharing of their existence as individuals" which is what married partners commit themselves to.[8] As Hegel puts it, if marriage begins in an agreement, "it is precisely a contract to transcend the standpoint of contract," that is, to transcend the standpoint of "individual self-subsistent units" making claims against one another, which is how contracting parties are normally understood.[9]

There are two distinct aspects to this critique. On the one hand, Hegel is attacking Kant's specific use of *contract* to characterize the marriage bond; the suggestion is that *this* legal concept is inappropriate in the particular context (though I imagine he would take even greater exception to Kant's use of the terminology of property). On the other hand, he is also attacking the broader target of Kant's pervasive legalism: the temptation, to which Kantians so often succumb, to reduce social institutions of all kinds to some formal array of legalistic rights and duties. Here it is not so much the idea of *contract*, but the more general idea of *a right*, that is out of place. This is the aspect of Hegel's critique that I will focus on, because I think it raises interesting and farreaching issues about liberal rights-based approaches to social and communal relations.

Few of us disagree with Hegel's basic point: claims of right should have little part to play in the context of a normal loving marriage. If we hear one partner complaining to the other about a denial or withdrawal of conjugal *rights*, we know that something has already gone wrong with the interplay of desire and affection between the partners. The same is true if people start talking about their *right* to a partner's fidelity, their *right* to be relieved of child care or domestic chores once in a while, their equal *right* to pursue a career, their *right* to draw equally on the family income, and so on. In each case, the substance of the claim may be indispensable for a happy and loving marriage in the modern world. It is its presentation *as a claim* – that is, as an entitlement that one party presses peremptorily, querulously, and adversarially against the other – that would lead to our misgivings. We certainly look for all these things in a marriage, but we hope to see them upheld and conceded, not as matters of right, but as the natural outcome of the intimate and mutual concern and respect brought to bear by the partners on the common problems they face. Even if such rights were acknowledged as the ground rules of the relationship in some sort of formal agreement drawn up by the partners, there would still be something unpleasant about their *asserting* them as rights or, as the phrase goes, *"standing on their rights"* in the normal functioning of the relationship. Such behavior would be seen as a way of blocking and preventing warmth and intimacy, replacing relatively unbounded and immediate care and sensitivity with rigid and abstract formulas of justice.

The point can be generalized. To stand on one's right is to distance oneself from those to whom the claim is made; it is to announce, so to speak, an opening of hostilities; and it is to acknowledge that other warmer bonds of kinship, affection, and intimacy can no longer hold. To do this in a context where adversarial hostility is inappropriate is a serious moral failing.[10] As Hegel put it in an Addition to the *Philosophy of Right:* "To have no interest except in one's formal right may be pure obstinacy, often a fitting accompaniment of a cold heart and restricted sympathies. It is uncultured people who insist most on their rights, while noble minds look on other aspects of the thing."[11]

II

Is there not anything, then, to be said for the Kantian position? I think there is this. Though marriage is certainly more than rights and correlative duties, and though one will not expect to hear claims of right in a happily functioning marriage, nevertheless the strength and security of the marriage commitment in the modern world depend in part on there being an array of legalistic rights and duties that the partners know they can fall back on, if ever their mutual affection fades. That is the idea I will consider in this chapter.

I want to explore this idea against the background of some criticisms that have been made of rights-based liberalism. In recent years, liberal theories have come under attack from socialists and communitarians for their implausible suggestion that the bonds of social life should be thought of as constituted primarily by the rights and rights-based relations of initially atomistic individuals.[12] I will consider how much of that attack would be mitigated or refuted if liberals were to concede that the structure of rights is not constitutive of social life, but is instead to be understood as a position of fallback and security in case other constitutive elements of a social relationship ever come apart. To go back to the marriage example, I will suggest that there is a need for an array of formal and legalistic rights and duties, not to constitute the affective bond, but to provide each person with secure knowledge of what he can count on in the unhappy event that there turns out to be no other basis for his dealings with his erstwhile partner in the relationship. The importance of rights ought to be much easier to defend from this somewhat less inflated position.

The argument is not merely a strategic retreat for liberals. Liberals are entitled to ask their communitarian critics how this important function of security is to be performed in a community that repudiates rights and legalism, and under the auspices of a theory that gives individual rights no part to play at all. Is it to be supposed that the intimate and affective relations that characterize various forms of community will never come apart, that affections will never change, and that people will never feel the urge to exit from some relationships and initiate others? If so, communitarianism in the modern world presents itself as naive or desperately dangerous, and probably both. Or is it supposed that a society will be pervaded by such a strong background sense of affection and responsibility that we can afford to allow people to change their intimate relations as they please without any attempt to articulate formally the terms on which they are to do so? That, for example, in the marriage case, we can somehow count on goodwill to provide for the continued care of a person's partner or children if they need it? Again, if this is the view that communitarians rely on, they are dangerously underestimating both the possibility for things to go wrong between human beings and the need for some sort of background guarantee, on which in the last resort one can rely in the face of that possibility.

Before continuing it may be worth saying a word or two about *communitarianism*. The new communitarianism is by no means a rigidly defined body of thought; the term refers rather to a trend in modern critiques of liberal political philosophy. In the work of writers like Roberto Unger, Michael Sandel, Alasdair Macintyre, and Charles Taylor, liberal theories have been attacked for their individualism, for the way they parade the desires and interests of the human individual as the be-all and end-all of politics, at the expense of notions like community, fraternity, and a shared social good.[13] It is not that liberals ignore those values altogether; but it is alleged that they give them only an instrumental significance or treat them merely as particular moral causes which individuals may or may not espouse. Partly it is a matter of perspective on society. For liberals, the point of reference is the "unencumbered" individual, free to shrug off his communal allegiances whenever he chooses. The relatively unaffectionate and formalistic language of rights and contract theory is said to be an expression of his essential detachability from affective commitments; its formalism expresses the facts deemed most important about his moral status, without reference to any content or community. Communitarians, on the other hand, take as their point of reference the shared lives of people who regard themselves as, in Sandel's words, "defined to some extent by the community of which they are a part"[14] – people who cannot imagine a standpoint of ethical judgment over and above their particular communal identity.

It is important to stress that community here is not an *abstract* idea; one's communal identity depends on the particularity of one's past. As Macintyre puts it, "I am someone's son or daughter, someone else's cousin or uncle; I am a citizen of this or that city, a member of this or that guild or profession."[15] Apart from the particularity of these attachments, there is said to be no standpoint for abstract political thought, communal or individual. The discourse of communitarian politics, then, will be informal and engaged rather than impersonal and abstract. Political thought will be a matter of the discovery and recognition of the particular social selves we are, rather than the deliberate choice and articulation of abstract principles of right. There are also other strands in the communitarian literature – notably a strand of civic republicanism[16] that is by no means so clearly incompatible with the traditional liberal point of view – but these are the ones I shall deal with in this chapter.

III

I chose marriage as my starting point because I wanted to illustrate two things. The first is the claim I have already outlined. The function of matrimonial law, with its contractual formulas and rigid rights and duties, is not necessarily to constitute the marriage bond; its function is to provide a basis on which ties of love can be converted into legal responsibilities in the unhappy situation where affection can no longer be guaranteed.

I also want to develop a second point. The structure of impersonal rules and rights not only provides a background guarantee; it also furnishes a basis on which people can initiate *new* relations with other people even from a position of alienation from the affective bonds of existing attachments and community. Impersonal rules and rights provide a basis for new beginnings and for moral initiatives which challenge existing affections, driving them in new directions or along lines that might seem uncomfortable or challenging to well-worn traditional folkways. Not only do these initiatives make life bearable for alienated individuals by allowing them to start out in new directions, but they also provide a dynamic

for social progress by challenging the existing types of relationships with new ones.[17] If we value these initiatives for
either or both of these reasons, we have to ask: "Under what
conditions are they possible in human affairs?" The traditional liberal reply is that people must be free from legal
coercion and social pressure so they can try out new exper-
iments in living.[18] But other conditions may be necessary
besides negative freedom. Can new initiatives be taken in a
social vacuum? Once men and women repudiate the existing
affections of their community, are they in a position to develop new types of relationships without any help from social
structures at all? If the answer is no, then there is a reason
to ensure that *some* social structures should be established
on a basis which distances them somewhat from existing
communal affections. That may be the job of legal rules and
legal rights: to constitute a nonaffective framework for actions
which are novel from a communal point of view. Without
some such impersonal framework, the creative human desire
for new initiatives faces a terrifying vacuum. If it is not to be
stifled by existing community, it must take its chances in a
world beyond community. That would be a world unstructured by *any* basis for security and expectation.

Let me illustrate this with an example. At a superficial
level, Shakespeare's *Romeo and Juliet* is a noble and lament-
able tragedy of star-crossed "death-marked" love:[19] the fates
bring the lovers together and, at the end, it is the fates who
cruelly divide them. But *Romeo and Juliet* can also be read as
a deeper text about the dangers that beset a new and un-
foreseen initiative – in this case a romantic initiative – in
circumstances where the only available structures for social
action are those embedded in the affections and disaffections
of the existing community. The bonds which tie together the
members of the respective clans of Capulet and Montague,
and which divide the clans from one another, are such as to
rule out of the question the union that the new lovers seek.
Driven by their need for each other, Juliet and Romeo seek
to create a marriage outside those inhibiting constraints.

The tragedy is that this cannot reliably be done in that

social world, for there is no framework of public or impersonal law, standing apart from communal attachments, of which people can avail themselves in circumstances like these. Even the apparent voice of the state – Prince Escalus – is presented as head of a third clan and himself deeply implicated in the disaffection between Capulet and Montague.[20] The lovers have to take their chances in a world outside the public realm. The arrangements they make are of necessity clandestine. There is no public and hence no visible and reliable way of coordinating actions and expectations. There is no way of counting on any but their own resources in a world where formally and publicly their relationship does not exist. Secret letters go astray. Another marriage is contracted for Juliet as though this one did not exist.[21] Communications break down, actions are misread, and timing fails as the lovers try to act in a world that provides no structure or landmarks for coordination. Their only hope of success is for Juliet to assume "the form of death" to the social world in which she was brought up, and to resurrect herself in the giddy space of a world beyond the city walls.[22]

On the superficial reading, the lovers are cursed by wretched bad luck in the final act. If only Friar Lawrence's letter had got through, if only Balthazar had seen Friar Lawrence before riding to talk with Romeo, if only Juliet had awoken a moment or two before Romeo took the poison – the tragedy might have been averted, and everyone might have lived happily ever after. On the deeper reading, misunderstanding, lack of coordination, failure in planning and communication, mistiming, and eventual catastrophe are more or less inevitable. For action, there is, as Romeo discovers, "no world without Verona walls."[23] There is nothing outside the structures of their warring clans that these two can rely on – no points of salience, no common framework of expectations, and no public knowledge – just their own meager resources and those of their understandably pusillanimous allies. Man is a social animal; only a god can live outside a state. We do not have the resources in ourselves to coordinate our activity without some social structures.[24]

There are two morals one can draw from this. The first is cautionary: "Don't fall in love with someone from a hostile clan", or in other words, "Don't ever try to act outside the structures of your community." But the second moral, and the one I want to draw, is addressed not to young lovers, but to those of our colleagues who call for a return to a particularist communitarian form of politics: "Don't urge us to identify the structures for social action too closely with the affections of existing communities. For in a human world, the limits of those affections may sometimes leave people with nowhere to go, and no reliable basis on which they can take new initiatives or constitute bearable lives for themselves."

What this indicates is the importance of a structure of rights that people can count on for organizing their lives, a structure which stands somewhat apart from communal or affective attachments and which can be relied on to survive as a basis for action no matter what happens to those attachments. In this regard, we are not just talking about a structure of claim-rights, but also a structure of what Hohfeld called "powers," or what Hart called secondary rules of change: some basis on which individuals or groups can reconstitute their relations to take new initiatives in social life without having to count on the affective support of the communities to which they have hitherto belonged.[25] We need not parade this as the most desirable basis for social action. The Veronan equivalent of marriage by a judge in a civil ceremony, which ought to have been available to Romeo and Juliet when their families failed to provide the necessary support, would seem a cold and arid setting for a wedding compared to the lavish ceremony which a loving community might have offered. That the liberal can concede. The point is that the civil ceremony would have been better than nothing – better, that is, than the lovers being driven by the disaffection of their families to take their chances in an outside world devoid of public structures on which they could in the last resort rely.[26]

379

I have used the marriage example to illustrate these points, but I do not want to give the impression that marriage is my sole concern.

Another example concerns welfare rights. It is common to hear laments about the loss of face-to-face charity and caring, whether by individuals or in family groups, and its replacement in modern society by more impersonal systems of state agencies and formalized welfare entitlements. Certainly, there is an important debate to be had about the nature and extent of our provision for need in society. However, it may be worth pointing out why the replacement of face-to-face caring by more impersonal structures is not altogether the disaster that some people make it out to be.

Consider care for the elderly. Age brings with it a certain amount of dependence. As one gets older, one's capacity to secure an income diminishes while one's needs increase. There have been societies, perhaps ours in an earlier age, or China both now and in the past, where the old have been able to count on the support of their adult children as their needs increase and their capacities diminish. That mode of caring strikes us as an attractive one, for it is based on ties of kinship, affection, and love, and it reciprocates in an almost symmetrical way the care that the parent once lavished on his children.

Moreover, it has the advantage of being personal. The care is between this particular old person and his children (who can be sensitive to the detail of his needs), rather than between old people and young people in general. Still, there are good reasons in the modern world why many old people feel less than confident about relying on their children's support. One problem is demographic: even in kin-oriented societies such as China, there are proportionately fewer working adults to support an increasing population of the aged. Other problems go deeper into modern life. People's lives and careers are complex, shifting, and often risky and demanding. They cannot always guarantee a secure base for themselves, let alone provide an assurance of security for their parents. People are torn by motives in modern life which, though not intrinsically hostile to the provision of this care, make it somewhat less certain that this will be something they want to provide.

To insist, then, in a communitarian spirit, that care for the aged should remain the responsibility of the family, we would have to accept either or maybe both of two costs. We would have to place limits on the *other* demands that adult children would be permitted to respond to, the risks they could run, and the mobility they could seek. (I suspect, by the way, that in the present state of things, this would involve limiting once again the capacity of *women* to move and flourish outside the home. A great many of the concerns about communitarianism articulated in this chapter are above all *feminist* concerns.) Or, if we were not prepared to do that (and maybe even if we were), we would have to accept the cost of exposing the elderly to a certain amount of insecurity and uncertainty in addition to the other burdens of their age. Neither in this country nor in Europe have people been willing to accept those costs.

Instead, we have opted for less personal, less affective modes of care. People are encouraged to purchase an income for their old age in the marketplace, so they can count on a pension check from a finance house even if they cannot rely on the warm support of their children. As a fallback position, the impersonal agencies of the state guarantee an income, either to all the elderly, or to those who have not made or have not been able to make impersonal provision for themselves. Thus, although we may not care for them on a face-to-face basis, we both provide impersonal structures to enable them to care for themselves and respond collectively and impersonally as a society to the rights that they have to our support. Our choice of this impersonality is well described in an English context by Michael Ignatieff in his book, *The Needs of Strangers:*

As we stand together in line at the post office, while they cash their pension cheques, some tiny portion of my income is transferred into their pockets through the numberless capillaries of the state. The mediated quality of our relationship seems necessary to both of us. They are dependent on the state, not upon me, and we are both glad of it.... My responsibilities towards them are mediated through a vast division of labour. In my name a social worker climbs the stairs to their rooms and makes sure they are as warm and as clean as they can be persuaded to be. When they get too old to go out, a volunteer will bring them a hot meal, make up their beds, and if the volunteer is a compassionate person, listen to their whispering streams of memory. When they can't go on, an ambulance will take them to the hospital, and when they die, a nurse will be there to listen to the ebbing of their breath. It is this solidarity among strangers, this transformation through the division of labour of needs into rights and rights into care that gives us whatever fragile basis we have for saying that we live in a moral community.[27]

It is not that a system of rights is the only imaginable way in which needs could be dealt with in a caring society. We could set things up in a way that encouraged old people to rely on the warm and loving support of their families. But even if we did that, I think we would still want to set up a system of rights as a fallback – as a basis on which some *assurance* of support could be given, without risking the insecurity, resentment, and indignity of leaving the elderly completely at "the uncertain mercy of their sons and daughters."[28]

V

These points suggest some more general reflections about the distribution of resources and well-being. There is a passage in the work of Karl Marx, and a tradition of Marxist thought, which criticizes philosophers who emphasize justice and individual rights in their accounts of social reform. In his "Critique of the Gotha Programme," Marx heaped derision even on egalitarian theories as proposals for the distribution of social wealth. He regarded all such proposals as "obsolete verbal rubbish"[29] so far as capitalism was concerned, and as too utopian and naive for the early stages of socialist construction. He was, however, prepared to predict that a time would come when people would lose their concern for justice and rights altogether:

> In a higher phase of communist society . . . after labour has become not only a means of life but life's prime want; after the productive forces have also increased with the all-round development of the individual, and all the springs of co-operative wealth flow more abundantly – only then can the narrow horizon of bourgeois right be crossed in its entirety and society inscribe on its banners: From each according to his ability, to each according to his needs![30]

The suggestion here is not that in a communist society people would have a *right* to the satisfaction of their needs. On the contrary, in a communist society we would be able to do away with rights altogether, and goods and services would be supplied naturally to needs and wants as they arose without the mediation of rigid individual entitlements. On the basis of this sort of talk, rights and rigid formulas of law have been regarded by many Marxists as essentially bourgeois forms destined to disappear with the rest of bourgeois society, including the restricted conditions of production which make that society possible. Bourgeois philosophers are engaged, they say, in asking precisely the wrong questions when they worry about what rights people would have in an ideal society.[31]

Some communitarians have echoed this theme. Sandel takes John Rawls to task for insisting on the primacy of distributive justice when Rawls himself acknowledges that justice makes sense only relative to circumstances in which resources are scarce and human sympathies limited. Sandel says it is easy to imagine small-scale communities in which neither of those conditions obtained: communities in which claims of justice and right would be replaced by spontaneous affection. In such a community, he says,

> Individual rights and fair decision procedures are seldom invoked, not because injustice is rampant but because their appeal is preempted by a spirit of generosity in which I am rarely inclined to *claim* my fair share. Nor does this generosity necessarily imply that I receive out of kindness a share that is equal to or greater than the share I would be entitled to under fair principles of justice. I may get less. The point is not that I get what I would otherwise get, only more spontaneously, but simply that questions of what I get and what I am due do not loom large in the context of this overall way of life.[32]

I do not want to embark on a discussion of how farfetched the Marxian idea of the "abolition of scarcity" is. We should note, however, that for the purposes of this argument, scarcity refers simply to the existence of opportunity costs in the use of resources, and many economists would regard the idea of the "abolition" of opportunity costs as incoherent rather than merely improbable.[33] Nor do I want to make any comment on the changes in human sympathies that Sandel and Marx are relying on, except to say that as long as goods are scarce in the sense just outlined, anything other than a situation in which each person's altruistic affections and strategies overlap perfectly with those of everyone else is going to be a situation in which competition for resources and hence the circumstances of justice continue to prevail.

If anything, the competition may be more intense if we all become altruists. History indicates that passionate altruists struggle much more ferociously for their ideals than those who are merely self-interested. And surely perfect uncompetitive altruism is unlikely (to say the least!) in a world in which, we are told, concern for others will be situated concretely in the particularity of each person's life rather than given abstractly as a general formula like the principle of utility.[34]

Even if we grant Sandel and Marx their assumptions, an unrepentant liberal might want to insist that there is *still* a place for rights in Marx's prosperous higher phase of communism and in Sandel's affectionate *gemeinschaft*. It matters to people that they and their loved ones have enough to eat, it matters to them that they have access to some of the resources necessary for the pursuit of their own projects and aspirations, and it is likely to go on mattering sufficiently for them to want some greater *assurance* of that than the affections of their fellow citizens can provide. Even if we concede that distribution can be conducted on the basis of spontaneous cooperation in circumstances of plenty, and even if we concede the desirability of its taking place on that basis, people will want some assurance that the circumstances that make this possible are going to continue. I cannot imagine that in any conceivable society this is something they will be able to take for granted; everything we know warns us of the dangers of such trust and complacency, touching though it is. (Again the background question is: are the socialists and communitarians asking us to think concretely or in terms of abstract possibilities?) So rights once again have at least a fallback function to perform. People might want to have some sense of what they *could* claim as their due in the unhappy though no doubt unlikely case that goods become scarce, or affections turn out to be limited after all.[35]

VI

Interestingly, it is not only welfare rights that perform this fallback function. A similar analysis is possible in the area of market relations – the area that liberals and their critics see as the domain *par excellence* of individual rights – as Marx described it, "a very Eden of the innate rights of man . . . the exclusive realm of Freedom, Equality, Property and Bentham."[36] At first sight, it is tempting to say about markets, not what we have said so far about rights – that they involve fallback positions for social relations constituted by affection or community – but rather that markets are social relations that are actually constituted by structures of contract and individual right, relations in which there is no prominent component of affection or community at all. We know, of course, that this is sociologically naive: a market cannot exist without an ethic of fidelity and without some underpinning for its property entitlements.[37] Still, the ethics, the ideology, and the force that make markets possible are not much more than what is presupposed by the idea of rights anyway, and the point is that they do not necessarily include any of the more robust and substantial commitments and affections associated in the modern mind with the idea of community.

Certainly the higher levels of the capitalist market – secondary capital markets, commodity markets, international trade and so on – have this character of being mainly rights-constituted (though even there the network of individual rights is mediated by more or less rigid codes of professional honor among the traders). Similarly, in more mundane contexts, we buy and sell in department stores with little more to bond us to our market partners than reciprocal self-interest and the laws of contract. In these cases, then, it is true that rights do not *underwrite* affective arrangements; rather, they *make possible* an enormous variety of arm's-length dealings between people who are in almost all other respects strangers to one another.

The point can be put in terms of an analogy with the *Romeo and Juliet* argument. If we were limited to the structures of *gemeinschaft*, if there were a sense that economic transactions and economic cooperation had always to be based on substantial and affectionate solidarity, the result would indeed be a warm and caring society, but also a desperately primitive and impoverished one. Human life would not be solitary, but many of the devices by which we have succeeded in mitigating its poverty, its nastiness, its brutishness, and its brevity would be limited or unavailable.[38] The division of labor, national and international trade, commercial research and development, and above all the coordination of the activity of millions of different centers of production, distribution, and exchange would be impossible. Those who wanted to take an initiative and deal with strangers or strike bargains with those they neither cared for nor expected to care for them would, like Shakespeare's lovers, have to step outside the world of social structures and rule-governed expectations altogether, and take their chances in an environment where there was nothing to count on but the unstructured self-interest of others. They would be stuck, as it were, in a perpetual black market.[39] Ground rules of rights and contract, on the other hand, conceived independently of communal bonds, make it possible for us to initiate dealings every day, directly or indirectly, with thousands of people we barely know, and to take advantage of their situation and abilities as they take advantage of ours, with the confidence that there are rules available to facilitate, structure, and secure these dealings even when there is no affection to base them on.[40]

Having said all that, it should be noted that there are many transactions, which we would call market transactions, that are not solely or explicitly constituted by rights and contracts. Transactions in the local store, for example, may be governed by implicit friendship and goodwill as much as by self-interest and legal obligation. Someone may ask, "Why can't all economic transactions be like that?" I think I have already given an answer, but it is important to stress that, even if they were, there would *still* be a role for rights to play. My grocer can deal with me in an informal, friendly way, sometimes giving me credit when I need it, or ordering some trivial item that I want, only if he has confidence that in the last resort he would be able to recover the money I owe if I abused his friendship, and that no one else can take unfair advantage of the "goodwill" he has accumulated. He may hope (just like the partners to a normal marriage) that he never has to invoke these formal guarantees, but that is consistent with the proposition that his assurance of their existence is one of the reasons he is able to act as informally as he does. Once again, we find that, far from destroying or replacing affective ties, fallback rights may be their precondition, at least in an imperfect world.

VII

I want to conclude by saying something about the individualism of this analysis. Someone might accept the need for formal legalistic structures as fallbacks to underpin social relations that are constituted on other terms. But he may still question why it is necessary for those *in extremis* arrangements to be presented as the rights *of an individual*. Surely groups and communities need something they can fall back on as well.

The point is a good one as far as it goes. *Romeo and Juliet* is not so much about the need for *individual* rights (though it can be expressed in those terms) as about the needs of *a couple*, needs that would of course be unintelligible apart from their involvement with one another. Similarly a village or local community, an ethnic group, or a family, may need to know what they can count on, and how they can organize their relations with other groups once their affectionate bonds to their neighbors or to the larger society have been broken. In these contexts, we may want to talk about the rights of groups, or we may think that other less individual-oriented legal terms are appropriate.[41] In other contexts, one affectionate or communal bond may be backed up by another. When a marriage fails and a woman is violently assaulted by her husband, she may find greater security in the communal atmosphere of a Woman's Refuge than in the austere individualism of the law courts.

Still there is some point to stressing that a set of legal rules conceived as fallbacks will have to include rights for individual men and women whatever else it includes. For any given social relation, there is always the possibility that it may disintegrate completely, leaving a naked individual bereft of any substantial bond to others, wanting to know where she stands. To recognize this possibility is not necessarily to embrace sociological individualism. It may still be true that the individual is the creation of the social, not the other way round, and that man, as Marx put it, is "an animal which can develop into an individual only in society."[42] All one needs to accept is that, as it were, individual *fallout* from social relations is possible. Indeed, if it is the case that the precipitated individual is going to be an incomplete and alienated being, confused, frightened, and truncated as a result of the social rupture, then the case for his protection and security in these unhappy circumstances is if anything more substantial.

Of course, modernists among us accept something more positive than this: though an individual standing apart from all social relations is unimaginable, nevertheless it is a good thing that modern men and women feel able to distance themselves from, reflect on, and consciously embrace or repudiate any or all of the relations that constitute their history.[43] Though we live in and for communities of one sort or another most of the time, our communal attachments are never so remote from our capacities as conscious, articulate, thinking, choosing, creating beings that we cannot subject them to scrutiny and consideration. Rights as fallbacks give us the vantage point from which that can be done. The point is not simply the liberal one about the importance of individuals autonomously shaping their lives. It is also that these processes of individual thought, reflection, and change are the source of many of the new beginnings in the world, including new communal beginnings. We should be careful not to undermine the possibility of that.[44]

In recent communitarian literature, Michael Sandel and others have condemned this image of the individual. Sandel says it seems to "rule out in advance any end whose adoption or pursuit could engage or transform the identity of the self."[45] The modern liberal self is said to stand apart from its attachments, particularly those attachments which might involve "more or less expansive self-understandings" to take in one's connections with others as well.

One consequence of this distance is to put the self beyond the reach of experience, to make it invulnerable, to fix its identity once and for all. No commitment could grip me so deeply that I could not understand myself without it. No transformation of life purposes and plans could be so unsettling as to disrupt the contours of my identity. No project could be so essential that turning away from it would call into question the person I am.[46]

Communal bonds, says Sandel, can never be *constitutive* of a liberal self, so long as the self retains this facility for questioning them. He calls instead for a conception of the person that is capable of being identified completely and essentially with some communal history or commitment (taking for granted that we know what "completely" and "essentially" mean in this context).

The critique appears an attractive one, for it associates flexibility of attachments with shallowness. "To imagine a person incapable of constitutive attachments is . . . to imagine a person wholly without character, without depth."[47] The sense we get is that one who knows he can alter his attachments – the liberal individual – cannot possibly feel as intensely or wholehearted about them as one who knows he cannot. But that is a mistake, based at best on a simplistic view of the relation between the metaphysics of the self and the phenomenology of commitment, and at worst on the mere rhetorical power of ill understood terms like "essence," "identity," and "constitutive." To retain the capacity to review our commitments, we do not always have to be *holding something back* from them. Having the capacity to reflect means *being able to make an effort* when one needs to, to wrench away and construct the necessary psychological distance. It does not require a continuous reserve of commitment and energy which *could* have been associated with one's attachment but is not, and it certainly does not mean sitting back all the time in the isolated citadel of the self treating the attachment as a curious and contingent event in which one has no real interest. In modern experience, intensity, wholeheartedness, and the sense of having identified comprehensively with a project or relationship are as much features of the commitments that people *choose*, the ones they could give up *if* they wanted to, as of the commitments people *discover* they have and find they cannot question. Many moderns would say more so. To repeat a point I have made a number of times: having something to fall back on if an attachment fails may be a *condition* of being able to identify intensely with one's attachments, rather than something which derogates from that intensity.

At any rate, these reflections at least make clear the nub of the controversy between communitarians and their modernist opponents. The debate is not between those who see social life as constitutively communal and those who do not. Nor is it between community and the values of bare individualism. It is between those who, on the one hand, yearn for communal bonds so rigid that the question of what happens when they come apart will not arise or need to be faced, and, on the other hand, those who are, first, realistic enough to notice the tragedy of the broken bond and ask "What happens next?"; and, second, optimistic enough to embrace the possibility of the construction of new bonds and new connections, and ask "How is that possible?" Those are the battle lines; in this chapter I have tried to indicate the role legal rights may play in that controversy.

Chapter 16

Rights and majorities:
Rousseau revisited

I

The distinction between political theory and political philosophy often seems artificial. The two terms pick out much the same discipline pursued under the auspices of different academic departments. But one topic where there has been a considerable divergence of emphasis between political theorists and political philosophers – or between those who study political morality in philosophy departments and those who study it in departments of political science – is the topic of fundamental rights. Those who believe in rights hold that individuals and minorities have certain interests that they can press, certain claims they can make against the rest of the community that are entitled to respect without further ado. Of course this view is controversial: some believe that individuals and minorities have rights in this sense, others do not, and even among those who do considerable disagreement exists about the nature of those rights. The divergence I am going to explore in this chapter, between political philosophers and political theorists, involves two different ways of characterizing that controversy.

For philosophers, the controversy has usually been characterized as a choice between individual rights and some version of utilitarian theory. They have taken the controversy to be one about justification. Is utilitarianism, as it claims to be, an adequate theory of political justification, or does it need to be supplemented (or indeed replaced) by an independently grounded theory of individual rights?

For political theorists, the contrast is characteristically not with utilitarianism but with majoritarian democracy. Political theorists are interested in forms of political decision-making, and they take the argument to be about political legitimacy. Is there nothing that cannot be made legitimate by a majority decision? Or should we recognize limits, based on individual rights, on what a majority can commit a society to do?

The contrast between justification and legitimacy may appear bewildering at first, since both are used here in a normative sense.[1] To ask whether a decision is justified is to ask whether it is, on the merits, the right decision; it is to look at the reasons weighing in favor of the course of action decided on. To ask whether a decision is politically legitimate is to raise a more procedural question; it is to ask whether it was taken in the way such decisions ought to be taken.[2] We need a distinction between justification and legitimacy, particularly in a democratic context, because we need some way of distinguishing between the reasons voters have for voting as they do, and the reasons officials have for implementing a certain decision after the votes have been counted. I may vote in a popular initiative for California to have a higher speed limit because I think saving lives matters less than fast cars; that is what I think about justification. But I believe the speed limit should stay as it is if most people in the state disagree with me; that is what I think about legitimacy. The fact that the majority approves of something is not a good reason for someone to vote in its favor (indeed, if everyone voted on the basis of reasons like that – "I vote for what the majority thinks" – voting would collapse as a practice). Reasons for supporting a given proposal are logically distinct from reasons for acting in politics on the basis of the fact that people support that proposal. Both are normative, but they capture different stages or levels of normativity in relation to political decision-making.[3]

Rights, then, can be seen – and are seen characteristically by philosophers – as an issue in the theory of justification.

And they can be seen – and are seen characteristically by political theorists – as located in the theory of legitimacy. In this chapter, I shall develop some ideas about the relation between these two ways of conceptualizing the issues. What is the relation between rights versus utility, on the one hand, and rights versus democracy, on the other?

II

An obvious way to begin is to ask about the connection between utilitarianism and majoritarian democracy. Do they in any sense amount to the same thing? When philosophers say that rights are "trumps" over utility (to use Ronald Dworkin's term), and political theorists say that rights are "trumps" over majoritarian democracy, are they in effect identifying the same target, the same suit, as it were, to be trumped?[4]

If you screw up your eyes and suspend a few critical questions, you can see a kind of connection. Suppose the votes cast on some issue represent individual preferences. Several alternative courses of action can be taken, and as good democrats we decide to adopt the course that attracts the greatest number of votes. That can sound a bit like trying to maximize satisfaction in the constituency, under a familiar utilitarian formula. In both cases, the fact that a course of action promotes the satisfaction of some preference counts in its favor; and when it becomes apparent that not all preferences can be satisfied, we opt to satisfy as many as we possibly can, given the choice that we face. As democrats, we follow the will of the majority; as utilitarians, we try to promote the greatest happiness of the greatest number. The two may amount to the same thing if votes are a reliable guide to individual happiness.

Something along these lines laid the basis for the utilitarian theory of democracy put forward by Jeremy Bentham in his later years. Throughout his career, Bentham had adhered to the principle of utility, which he described in 1789 as "that principle which approves or disapproves of every action

394

whatsoever, according to the tendency it has to augment or diminish the happiness of the party whose interest is in question ... if that party be the community in general, then the happiness of the community: if a particular individual, then the happiness of that individual."[5] But Bentham was also a psychological egoist, and he assumed that people always act to further their own satisfactions: they seek their own happiness and avoid their own pain. For a long time, he failed to face up to the implications of this egoism so far as those who made decisions in the name of the community were concerned. Considered in the abstract, a legislator's decisions affect the whole society, and so the standard of social utility is the appropriate criterion of justification. But considered from the legislator's point of view, the political choice represents an opportunity to augment or diminish his own happiness, and that is what Bentham's psychological theory predicts will matter to him. We should expect then that a legislator will always approve or disapprove of laws that affect the whole community according to their tendency to promote not the community's but his own happiness, for that is the happiness of the party whose interest is – psychologically – in question.

The cruelest of Bentham's biographers have suggested that he confronted this difficulty only after years of having what he took to be his eminently sensible utilitarian proposals for legislative reform trashed by the legislators to whom they were sent. Slowly it dawned on him that maybe these people were not particularly interested in promoting the general happiness along the lines he suggested (though there were other explanations available that did not, in all modesty, occur to Bentham). Eventually he turned his mind to consider what political structures would have to be like in order to establish some reliable coincidence between the personal interest of the legislator and the general happiness of society (and some greater receptivity to proposals like his own).[6]

About 1817, almost thirty years after the publication of *An Introduction to the Principles of Morals and Legislation*, Bentham began writing in favor of representative democracy based on what he called "virtually universal" suffrage. He rejected direct democracy on the Athenian model on the grounds that legislation required special skills, but opted for democratic accountability through general elections on the ground – reminiscent of Aristotle – that though it takes an expert cobbler to make a shoe, the only person who can judge whether it pinches is the person who wears it.[7] The idea was that each voter would express his opinion, based on experience, on whether this legislator's continuing in office was likely to benefit him, and the sum of these opinions based on voters' self-interest would be a rough-and-ready guide to whether the legislator's actions would in fact promote the aggregate interest of the community. Since the legislator was interested in remaining in office, he would have a personal incentive to act in a way that would benefit those with the power to decide his future.

It is a rough-and-ready theory indeed, and its difficulties are plain enough. For one thing it faces problems of implementation exactly like those that evoked it in the first place. Representative democracy is a no more convincing deus ex machina than a benevolent legislator. If people are egoists, why expect constitution writers to opt for a system of representative democracy? (Remember Bentham was writing some fifty years before the Second Reform Bill.) And if, by some happy chance, a representative system is set up, why expect people to sustain it or to do what is necessary to prevent its corruption?[8]

Other difficulties concern the democratic process itself. If decision-making is egoistic and prospective, the utilitarian argument relies on the assumption that each voter is a good judge of his own future self-interest. But on any account (including Bentham's) people are not reliably prudent. Their decisions about savings reflect this, and one imagines that electoral decisions will be similarly distorted in favor of over-consumption.[9] Moreover, an electoral outcome can correspond only very roughly to a social utility function. Voting cannot possibly be made to reflect the intensity of the satisfaction or dissatisfaction anticipated by individuals with respect to some law. Yet intensity of satisfaction is a crucial dimension in the Benthamite hedonic calculus.[10]

Deeper difficulties also arise. As a predictive theory, Bentham's psychological eogism is almost certainly false. People, whether they are voters or politicians, do not make decisions purely on the basis of self-interest. They are occasionally (I think, often) motivated by their sympathies for others, their own perception of what would be conducive to the general good, or adherence to some other moral ideal. This sounds as though it ought to make things better, since it mitigates the centrifugal force of egoism in politics; but in fact it makes things worse for the Benthamite theory of democracy. So long as each voter decides on the basis of his own interest, some chance exists that a majority decision might correspond roughly to the aggregate happiness of society. But if large numbers are voting each on the basis of what he thinks the aggregate happiness demands, then the whole thing falls apart. If some are voting that way and some are voting selfishly, adding those votes to one another is like adding chalk and cheese. And if all are voting selflessly on the basis of their personal perceptions of the general welfare, we have no aggregative reason for thinking that the majority decision tells us anything new at all. Aggregation over individual votes makes some sort of sense from the utilitarian point of view if votes represent individual preferences. But it makes no sense at all if votes represent utilitarian opinions.

III

Maybe we should set up an ideal-typic contrast between two different models of democracy or democratic decision-making. The first model is the Benthamite model, which I have just outlined and criticized. The important points about the Benthamite model are that individual votes represent individual satisfactions, and majority vote counting approximates a social welfare function with individual satisfactions as its arguments.

I wish to contrast that with something I shall call the Rousseauian model of democratic decision-making. The reference, of course, is to the discussion of the "general will" in books 2 and 4 of *The Social Contract*.[11] I am going to simplify my discussion in a way that will outrage students of Rousseau's writing, but the detail of his work is not what matters here. For my purpose, the important feature of Rousseau's conception is not his distinction between democratic laws and democratic government, or his preference for direct democracy over representative institutions, but his views about what citizens are doing when they cast their votes in a democratic polity.

> When a law is proposed in the people's assembly, what is asked of them is not precisely whether they approve of the proposition or reject it, but whether it is in conformity with the general will which is theirs; each by giving his vote gives his opinion on this question, and the counting of votes yields a declaration of the general will. When, therefore, the opinion contrary to my own prevails, this proves only that I have made a mistake, and that what I believed to be the general will was not so.[12]

Ignore for the moment the presumption in the final sentence that the majority must be right. The important point is that when voting the Rousseauian citizen is expressing an opinion about what the general will requires (which on Rousseau's view means what conduces to the common good of all in society), an opinion that it makes sense to assess as correct or mistaken.[13] If the individual vote is different from the majority verdict, one of them, at least, must be wrong. On the Benthamite model, by contrast, an individual's vote and the majority verdict can differ without any contradiction whatever. All it shows is that the individual in question is not among the "greatest number" whose satisfactions are to be advanced.

That is the contrast I want. Bentham's voter is taken to be expressing a preference of his own; his vote represents a possible individual satisfaction. Rousseau's voter is not supposed to express his personal preference; rather he affirms his personal belief about the best way to promote the general good. The Benthamite political system sums votes as utilitarianism sums satisfactions, while the Rousseauian political system counts votes to determine the preponderance of opinion. What we have is the divergence that Rousseau pointed to when he distinguished between the general will and the will of all: "the general will studies only the common interest while the will of all studies private interest, and is indeed no more than the sum of individual desires."[14]

A further question concerns what the general good, the proper object of individual voting, amounts to on the Rousseauian account. Are people supposed to be thinking utilitarian thoughts, thoughts about the greatest happiness of the greatest number, as they struggle to express the general will? Or are they, as Rousseau sometimes suggests, supposed to be turning their attention to the common good, that is, to rules or practices that benefit everyone? The idea of the general good, and accordingly that of the general will, is vague enough to cover either of these criteria and a number of others besides. I want to leave this question open at this stage.[15]

It would be wrong to pretend that the ideal types of decision-making defined here are ever to be found in pure form. But they represent extremes on a spectrum. Given that democracies make social decisions functions of individual decisions, a theory of democracy is Benthamite to the extent that it takes individual decisions to represent personal satisfactions or interests and Rousseauian to the extent that it takes individual decisions to represent opinions or beliefs about the general good.

I have made a long detour away from the subject of rights. The question with which I began is whether the notion of rights as trumps over utility is in the end the same as the notion of rights as trumps over democracy. My answer is that they can be assimilated only to the extent that democratic decision-making is seen as a Benthamite process, and even then the assimilation is fraught with difficulty. If democracy is conceived in a Benthamite way then right-based reasons for concern about certain utilitarian justifications may cash out into right-based reasons for concern about certain democratic outcomes. But if democracy is more Rousseauian, then the idea of trumping democracy will be quite different from the idea of trumping utility, and we shall have to say rather more complicated things about the relation between them.

IV

It is time I said more about the idea of individual rights. In the first instance, the idea of rights is a claim about political justifications, in particular a claim that there are limits on what can be justified. In social and political life, individuals and groups inevitably will suffer disappointments, frustrations, losses, setbacks, defeats, and even harms of various sorts. No one can get everything he wants. Rights imply limits on the harms and losses that any individual or group may reasonably be expected to put up with; they indicate that certain losses and harms are not to be imposed on any individual or group for any reason. These are harms and losses that may not be traded off against a larger mass of lesser considerations in the way the utilitarian calculus allows. It follows, clearly enough, that rights mark constraints on the ends we may pursue and the means we may adopt in politics. Even for the sake of the greater happiness or the pursuit of some other noble goal, we must not impose the losses or inflict the harms that are specified. The job of rights is to stake out these limits.

So far, that is an abstract conception. It gains content when someone tells us what the limits are. And it becomes a theory when we are given an indication of why these losses and harms are not to be imposed, and why the reasons we might have for wanting to impose them are inadequate. The modern analysis of rights made an enormous leap forward when it was realized that talk about natural rights or human rights is not a way of giving those answers but a way of promising to give them.[16] As Richard Rorty put it, "to say that certain people have certain rights is merely to say that we should treat them in certain ways. It is not to give a *reason* for treating them in those ways."[17] The reasons will be rooted in some account of what is required as a minimum if individual men and women are to have any prospect of flourishing or any chance at all of a decent life. A theory of rights will identify certain human interests – some related to freedom, others perhaps to other aspects of well-being – and show the moral importance of those interests receiving a guaranteed level of protection and satisfaction. Different theories will do this in different ways, and they will identify different, though usually overlapping, sets of interests as the proper objects of this special concern.

Rights are not a simple matter. We are used to thinking of them in terms of relatively simple slogans: "Free speech," "The free exercise of religion," "Due process," "Life, liberty, and property," "No cruel and unusual punishment," and so on. But, as the history of judicial debate on these matters strikingly illustrates, moral principles cannot be interpreted and applied as easily as these formulations suggest. As the criterion of human flourishing and a decent life is complex and subtle, so the idea of what is required as its minimum condition must reflect that complexity and subtlety. Most important, it is something on which people, even with the best will in the world, are likely to disagree. We must not confuse the enthusiasm that exists for certain slogans (the amendments to the 1787 U.S. Constitution, for example) with any deep consensus about what rights we have or what they really involve. Use of simple phrases and well-known formulations is perhaps inevitable in the politics of human rights, but it is in the deeper concerns and in the arguments that support the formulations that we will find the substance of a particular theory. That substance may be controversial even when the slogans are not. Certainly the more or less universal acceptance of a human rights slogan as something to pledge allegiance to tells us little or nothing about the depth or the detail of political or moral consensus.[18]

When considering the tasks involved in the articulation of a theory of rights, and in its application to the real world, the notion that a right reflects a solid and unquestioned consensus becomes ludicrous. In a theory of rights, one has to give an account of the moral importance of some interest, and one has to address the relation between that account and other justificatory theories that might be deployed against it. There is possible moral conflict between rights and other considerations, or among rights themselves. People can certainly disagree about these matters without abandoning the idea of rights, and certainly without lapsing back into preoccupation with self-interest. We may be tempted to see trenchant and apparently irresolvable disagreements about rights as nothing more than disguised conflicts of interest. But the complexity of the subject gives excellent reason for resisting that temptation.

Above all I want to emphasize that the fact that a moral argument is subtle, complicated, difficult, and controversial does not mean it cannot be about rights. Though rights talk is customarily contrasted with other styles of moral reasoning, for example, the sort of trade-off calculations that a consequentialist engages in, it still has a special complexity, and with it a controversial character of its own. We cannot evade these difficulties in any theory of justification: political life is messy in the moral demands that it generates.

These complexities and controversies give rise to serious questions about what we should do politically when advocates of rights disagree. So long as rights are merely an aspect of justificatory debate, complexity and controversy can thrive. Some will say that a certain social practice or decision violates rights, others will say that it does not, and they will argue back and forth in journals and classrooms, in newspapers and caucuses, about what respect for rights requires. The real problem arises when some issue of rights is what we have to make a social decision about. For then we have to ask: should this decision be made by a majority, as other social decisions are made? Or should it be made using some other principle of political legitimacy?

V

I said earlier that political theorists think of rights, not merely as an aspect of the theory of political justification, but as part of the theory of legitimate decision-making. Certain decisions, they say, are not to be taken on a majoritarian basis: there are certain things a majority must not do.

Sometimes these views about legitimacy follow straightforwardly from theories of justification. Thinkers such as Madison, Tocqueville, and John Stuart Mill, for example, held that if something done by a despot or an elite would count as tyranny, it would still be tyrannical when done in the name of a majority: "the power to do everything, which I should refuse to one of my equals, I will never grant to any number of them."[19] Some actions are so wrong that not even the principle of majority rule can legitimate them.

Sometimes the conception of legitimacy is more procedural, however, and based on a concern for the decision-making process itself. John Hart Ely, for example, argues that rights are best understood as constraints designed to sustain, enhance, and facilitate the processes of representative democracy.[20] Between these poles of substance and procedure is a set of ideas about what is required to sustain the allegiance of all groups in society: what guarantees must be offered in order to prevent their secession or rebellion?[21]

Whatever the foundation of rights may be in a theory of political legitimacy, the following question arises: how are we actually to prevent the decisions that rights prohibit? If we believe that there can be no justification for imposing certain harms or losses on individuals, or if we believe that imposition of certain harms or losses must be prevented to protect the integrity of the democratic process or to sustain the allegiance of all sections of society, how are these results to be brought about? To say that rights impose limits on political legitimacy is so far mere talk. How can that talk be translated into appropriate political outcomes?

In the United States, it is natural to think immediately of institutionalizing rights as legal constraints on political decision-making. The Bill of Rights lays it down as a matter of principle that certain laws are not to be passed and certain official actions are not to be tolerated. The courts have taken it upon themselves to declare when these principles are violated and to nullify the application of any law or official action that falls foul of them. These determinations are now accepted as authoritative within the political system and in the country at large. Rights-based constraint on democratic decision-making is now established as a working political practice.

It is perhaps more difficult to see that this form of institutionalization is not the only or the inevitable upshot of the arguments about legitimacy. We tend to think that those who express concern about the dangers of the tyranny of the majority or about the threat to individual or minority rights *must* be proposing something like a Bill of Rights enforced by judges as the institutional prescription. The tendency is understandable given the ambiguity of the word "rights," which is used sometimes to characterize moral arguments and sometimes to depict arrangements of positive law. But it is not a necessary move at all. Institutional solutions other than a Bill of Rights may be entertained: for example, Madison opted for checks and balances and the separation of powers, rather than a Bill of Rights in any shape or form.[22]

Consider also the noninstitutional alternatives. John Stuart Mill proclaimed adherence to a principle of individual liberty that he said was "entitled to govern absolutely the dealings of society with the individual in the way of compulsion and control," and he expressed his fear of "an increasing inclination to stretch unduly the powers of society over the individual both by the force of opinion and even by that of legislation."[23] But his remedy was not to set up institutional checks and balances or embody his harm principle in a Bill of Rights. Instead, the aim of his work was to educate public opinion about the importance of respecting individual liberty:

The disposition of mankind, whether as rulers or as fellow citizens, to impose their own opinions and inclinations as a rule of conduct on others is so energetically supported by some of the best and some of the worst feelings incident to human nature that it is hardly ever to be kept under restraint by anything but want of power; and as the power is not declining, but growing, *unless a strong barrier of moral conviction can be raised against the mischief*, we must expect, in the present circumstances of the world to see it increase.[24]

Mill's analysis of the main threat to individuality is similar:

The combination of all these causes forms so great a mass of influences hostile to individuality that it is not easy to see how it can stand its ground. It will do so with increasing difficulty *unless the intelligent part of the public can be made to feel its value* – to see that it is good there should be differences, even though not for the better, even though, as it may appear to them, some should be for the worse.[25]

Admittedly, the target of Mill's concern was as much the tyranny of public opinion as majoritarian legislation, and so far as the former is concerned only moral restraint can have any effect. But Mill seems to have believed, and I think quite properly, that a change in public opinion was also necessary to protect individual interests from legal and political attack. "Unless a strong barrier of moral conviction" can be raised in favor of the idea of individual rights, "unless the intelligent part of the public can be made to see its value," then individual liberty and with it social progress would be swept aside by the legal and social pressures of mass society.

VI

Something like the consensus that Mill was seeking to create or evoke is probably necessary anyway, even if institutional constraints are the main line of defense. The point is the same as one noted earlier about Bentham's theory of democracy. Institutional constraints and Bills of Rights do not appear magically out of the air; they have to be politically agreed on and instituted like every other legal and political arrangement. Once instituted, they must be accepted, respected, and enforced; otherwise they will be what Madison referred to as "a mere demarcation on parchment," which, as the constitutional experience of most of the regimes in the world demonstrates, is no protection whatever against tyranny and oppression.[26]

It is tempting to say that institutional constraints of right, and constitutional provisions generally, must command unanimous support, for it is their job to set the terms on which majoritarian competition is subsequently to take place. In pure theory, that looks attractive. The constitutional framework can be presented as the terms of a social contract based on the consent of all, and then, within that framework and according to those terms, subsequent political disagreements can be resolved by procedures, such as majority rule, that are agreeable to everyone.[27]

In practice we know it is impossible to secure unanimous agreement on anything, and certainly not on a topic as divisive as individual rights. Even so, to be institutionalized and sustained, a Bill of Rights must command some consensus, at least at a superficial level. Certainly it will need wide public support, directly or indirectly, to be enacted and to last for more than one or two administrations. This is reflected in the demanding provision made for constitutional amendment. Once we see that the decision to institute constraints of right is itself a political decision, we see the possibility and indeed maybe the necessity for the majority, at least on some occasions, willingly to embrace restraints on its collective power.

It follows that any theory that holds that the majority will always abuse its power cannot be used as an argument in favor of a Bill of Rights. This theory would be too pessimistic, for it would preclude the possibility of a majority ever initiating and sustaining institutional constraints on itself, except by accident. A theorist who is at all optimistic about the possibility of protecting rights in a democratic system has to rest his hopes in the last resort on being able to convince a sufficient number of his fellow citizens, at least on occasion and probably continually, that respect for rights is important.

VII

I distinguished earlier between Benthamite and Rousseauian conceptions of democratic decision-making: a Benthamite voter votes according to his own interest, while a Rousseauian votes what he thinks the general good requires. In Section III, the question of what the phrase "the general good" means in the Rousseauian model was left unresolved.

Whatever the general good is supposed to mean for Rousseau or anyone attracted to this model of democracy, it must surely represent an adequate basis of justification. When voters turn their minds to the general good, when they try to express through their votes the general will, they must aspire to make political decisions that are just. This means, among other things, that they aspire to make political decisions that strike a proper balance between the interests of the various members of society. If the issue affects interests that may appropriately be dealt with in an aggregative way, they will seek a utilitarian verdict. But if it concerns interests that have the special importance associated with rights, then they will aim for a decision that is sensitive to that special importance.

In other words, if the philosophical theorist of rights is correct at the level of political justification, then social utility cannot always be the appropriate object of the general will. Some things must not be done, even in the name of social utility, and each person's thinking about the general good, each person's Rousseauian decision-making, will, it is hoped, reflect that consideration.

This is an important difference between Benthamite and Rousseauian conceptions of democracy. In Benthamite democracy, individual votes represent nothing more than individual satisfactions; they express nothing at all about the proper balance that is to be struck between the individual and society. Any concerns about that balance have got to be, as it were, external to the voting process. But in Rousseau's model, votes already deliver an opinion about the proper balance between the two. Weighing is intrinsic to what is going on in the individual voter's decision. There might, therefore, be some greater difficulty in justifying external institutional constraints of right in a Rousseauian democracy, because rights should already be taken account of by citizens as a matter of course in their thought and deliberation.

It is no good saying, in a hard-headed spirit, that Rousseau's model is too idealistic, and that pragmatically it makes more sense to assume that people will vote and behave politically as Bentham predicted. As I indicated in Section VI, that cannot be true all the time or there would be no hope of ever actually institutionalizing the constraints of right that this very model cries out for. We know anyway, from our own experience of politics, that it is *not* true much of the time. People often vote on the basis of what they think is the general good of society. They are concerned about the deficit, or about abortion, or about Eastern Europe, in a way that reflects nothing more about their own personal interests than that they too have a stake in the issues.[28] Similarly, the way they vote will usually take into account their conception of the special importance of certain interests and liberties. At least some of the time, people vote in a way that is sensitive to the idea of rights as they understand them, rather than merely on the basis of what they take to be their own self-interest. If one wants to be a hard-headed "realist" in politics, one should follow the evidence where it leads, and not simply assume selfish motivations when experience reveals that they are in play only part of the time.

In particular, though it is certain that voters behave sometimes in a Benthamite fashion and sometimes in a Rousseauian fashion, we have no evidence to support any correlation of this pattern with the distinction between those areas where we have and those areas where we do not have institutional constraints of right. There is no evidence to suggest that the issues covered by the Bill of Rights, for example,

are issues on which people would otherwise be most likely
to vote in a Benthamite way. My hunch is that the contrary
is true. When they are given the chance, these are the issues
on which voters are least likely to be Benthamite, precisely
because these are areas where we as a society have had some
measure of success in "raising the strong barriers of moral
conviction" that Mill talked about. Voters and their representatives are deeply aware that these are matters they
should not be deciding purely by consulting their own
interests.[29]

VIII

For voters to ask themselves in Rousseauian fashion what
the general good of the society requires is one thing; it is
quite another for them to agree about that. Even if "the
general good" were interpreted in a utilitarian way, we
should expect disagreement because people have varying
beliefs, different information, and differential capacities to
engage in complex consequential calculations. Indeed, one
of the hopes held out for the Benthamite model of democracy
is that voting outcomes would provide information about
aggregate welfare that would otherwise be unavailable to a
student of social utility.

I hope the argument in Section IV established that voters
are also likely to disagree about individual rights, even if
they all take them seriously, even if they all turn their minds
conscientiously in that direction. The contents of particular
rights, relations between rights and other moral considerations, and relations among rights themselves generate issues
of moral reasoning that are unlikely to yield any easy consensus through political deliberation. On any particular issue
of right, several conflicting conceptions are bound to emerge,
each attracting adherents who try to persuade the others as
the debate goes along.

It is possible that these disagreements are driven by underlying conflicts of interest, but that is unlikely to be the
case in any straightforward sense. People disagree about the

proper scope of free speech in modern society, even when their own interests are not at stake. Or, if their interests are at stake, those interests cannot be understood in Benthamite terms because they are informed by the perceived importance, at a social and political level, of certain values and principles that define their social role. Think, for example, of a journalist protecting his sources, or arguing for a particular conception of First Amendment freedoms.

The abortion debate provides a striking example. The moral issues involved in the question of whether abortion should be permitted and facilitated are almost intractably contentious, because they involve deep and challenging questions about the way we value life and its relation to the way we value autonomy and individual control. No one but a moral idiot thinks the issue is easily resolved, so we do not have to appeal to any underlying conflict of interests to explain the depth and intensity of this particular disagreement over rights. True, some have tried to frame the issue as a conflict of interest between the sexes. But that is simplistic. When more perceptive accounts have been given of the motivations of the contestants, the interests they have at stake are revealed as deep and clashing world views, about the ideal forms of individuality, procreation, sexuality, life-style, and social structure. Though it is easy to categorize the prochoice and pro-life activists as "interest groups," it is pretty clear that the issue between them is more a Rousseauian disagreement about the basic principles of social life than a Benthamite clash of different and incompatible claims to satisfaction.[30]

IX

When society divides on the existence, meaning, or limits of some individual right, as it almost always does, what is to be done? What ought to happen in a democracy, when the voters, having asked themselves Rousseauian questions and addressed them conscientiously, come up with different answers? Presumably the rival views will attract different degrees of popular support, and there may be one view that attracts more support than any of the others. Is this the one that should prevail?

The question is hard to answer. At least one of the traditional arguments in favor of majority rule does not work in Rousseau's model. But it is also important to see that the traditional objection to majority rule, the worry about the tyranny of the majority, does not apply either.

The traditional argument in favor of majority rule that does not work in a Rousseauian context is, of course, the Benthamite argument. As long as votes represent individual satisfactions, then a rough utilitarian argument favors trying to satisfy as many of them as possible. Since each vote represents a possible satisfaction, and since the aim is to maximize satisfaction, then each vote provides in itself an independent reason for action. But if votes offer opinions about the general good, including opinions about how satisfactions should be pursued and distributed in society, then no such maximizing reason for acting in accordance with the preponderance of opinion exists. A view that something should be done is not in itself a reason for doing it. Someone might suggest that acting in accordance with the greatest preponderance of opinion is at least a way of maximizing the amount of satisfaction that people get from having their opinions acted on. But the people concerned may well regard *those* satisfactions as in themselves quite trivial in comparison to the issues, including the issues of satisfaction, that form the subject matter of their opinions.

Rousseau's own comments on the matter are sketchy and unsatisfactory. In one passage he argues that unanimity is the mark of the general will and that "the more . . . that public opinion approaches unanimity, the more the general will is dominant; whereas long debates, dissensions and disturbances bespeak the ascendance of particular interests."[31] But as we have just seen, this is a mistake given the difficulty of even the most fundamental issues to which public opinion must speak. Rousseau did acknowledge that unanimity is no guarantee that citizens are genuinely addressing themselves to issues of the general good. "Fear and flattery," he said, "can change voting into acclamation; people no longer deliberate, they worship or they curse."[32] The "will-of-all" can also be unanimous.

Rousseau's settled position appears to have been this: *if* there is disagreement, and *if* in spite of that disagreement you can be sure that citizens are nevertheless addressing the issue of the general good, then, "the votes of the greatest number always bind the rest." He went on immediately to say that "this is a consequence of the [original social] contract itself."[33] But that remark is obscure. I can see nothing in Rousseau's earlier analysis of the social contract to which it could be a reference.

The only convincing argument in favor of majority rule consistent with Rousseau's thinking is the argument developed by Condorcet: if voters are independently addressing a question that is susceptible to a right and a wrong answer, and if the average probability of each voting for the correct answer is greater than 0.5, then the probability that the answer determined for the group by a majority procedure will be correct tends to certainty as group size increases.[34] Recently Condorcet's theorem has been presented as an explanation for Rousseau's conviction that the general will would usually emerge from majority voting.[35] But the application of the theorem must be tempered by Condorcet's own view that, independently, as group size increases, the average individual competence is likely to decline and to have fallen well below 0.5 before one reaches even the size of a citizen assembly in a small Rousseauian polis.[36] And, of course, the theorem implies that if average competence is below 0.5, then the chances of the majority being right decline to zero as group size increases.

Maybe something about the dynamics of argument can sustain average competence at a level where Condorcet's theorem produces favorable results. When a proposal is first mooted, some people will be for it and others against it. At this stage the distribution is random; there is no reason to think that the side that happens to have the largest number of supporters is correct. But suppose a debate now ensues, and people on both sides try to convince their opponents with arguments. If the issue is one where rational argument is possible, and if the people involved in the debate are susceptible to rational argument and immune to mere rhetoric ("fear and flattery" as Rousseau puts it) and not motivated by particularistic interest, we would expect that at the end of the debate the chances of a given person arriving at a correct answer would be greatly enhanced. We should not think that this violates the independence condition on Condorcet's theorem. Provided that the probability of each individual reaching a correct decision can be determined independently at the end of the deliberation and before the votes are cast, what that probability is a result of does not matter in the least.[37]

Though there are no knockdown arguments in favor of majority rule in a Rousseauian polity, it is important to see that the traditional objections to, and misgivings about, majority rule are almost entirely inappropriate in this context. The justificatory burden is to that extent lighter.

The most common misgiving is that in democratic decision-making, minorities or individuals may suffer oppression at the hands of a majority. That is an acute danger where the votes of those who compose the differing factions represent the particular interests or satisfactions of the voters. In that case, for a majority to prevail means nothing more than that the interests of the minority are sacrificed to those of the larger group. But nothing similar need happen between majorities and minorities in the Rousseauian case. There, each vote represents an individual opinion on a matter of common concern including, where appropriate, an opinion on the proper balance to be maintained among the various individual and minority interests. Nothing tyrannical happens to me merely by virtue of the fact that my opinion is not acted on. Provided that the opinion that is acted on takes my interests, along with everyone else's, properly into account, the fact that the opinion is not mine is not in itself a threat to my freedom or well-being.

Of course, if I disagree with the majority, I will not think that all interests have been properly taken into account or that the general good is being correctly discerned. And I may think consequently that a serious threat to my interests is posed. But that need not be the subject of the disagreement. If all parties are approaching the decision in a Rousseauian spirit, the issues on which they disagree need not reflect differential levels of concern for their own respective interests. It is true that *A* may differ from *B* and *C* about the proper regard that is due *A*'s interests; but *A* may also differ from *B* and *C* about the proper regard that is due *B*'s interests. He may think that *B* and *C*, the majority, are underestimating the importance of some interests they have but he lacks.

An example may help. Many women dissent from the feminist position on gender equality and independence, and some men do not. Suppose those of both sexes who are sympathetic to the feminist position happen to be in a minority. Then some members of the minority, the "feminist" men, may describe the disagreement by saying that some people in the majority, nonfeminist women, are not paying sufficient regard to their own interest in freedom and well-being.

The more important point is this. Even if the issue on which *A*, the minority, differs from *B* and *C* is the proper level of respect due *A*'s interest, there is no reason to take *A*'s view of the matter any more seriously or think it any more likely to be correct than the opinion shared by *B* and *C*. Again, with the proviso that all are approaching the matter in a Rousseauian spirit. The majority is not necessarily right, but on a matter concerning the rights of minorities it is not necessarily wrong either. Indeed, as I remarked in Section VI, the majority could not always or typically be wrong about such matters, or we would have no hope of ever getting political respect for the rights of minorities.

What respect, then, is owed to minority opinion in a Rousseauian polity? The provocative answer is none at all, so far as political action is concerned. If there is some sort of argument for the legitimacy of majoritarianism and if votes really do represent opinions on the proper balance of interest in society and not interests themselves, then the majority view should simply prevail, and the minority regard their view as defeated. Since it is defeat in a debate about a matter of common concern, not in a struggle of interests, they should be able to reconcile themselves without too much difficulty.

But that response is a little glib. Respect is owed to minority opinions as opinions. They should be aired in debate, and be given an effective opportunity to win supporters. And they should not be suppressed after the debate, either, because the citizenry may have to consider the matter again sometime and because liberal respect is owed to people simply as the proponents of opinions. Both from the point of view of the general good, and from the point of view of respect for persons, dissident thinking should be tolerated. But toleration is not the same as allowing an opinion to prevail to any extent. It is one thing to allow an opinion to exist and do its work in argumentation, quite another to allow it to be decisive or even to operate as a vector in political action.

Again the difference in significance between minority opinions as Rousseau conceives them and minority interests in a Benthamite democracy is striking. In a Benthamite world, proponents of rights want minority interests to prevail and to be decisive to a greater extent than the utilitarian calculus would allow. If I have a right to emigrate, then my interest in choosing whether or not to emigrate is to prevail even though social utility might be promoted by denying it. In this respect, rights are like vetoes; or to put it another way, they make individuals dictators on the issues they cover. In a Rousseauian democracy there may still be rights, but since they are the subject matter of individual opinions, they should never be identified with the individual opinions. There is no case then for allowing minority *opinions* to prevail, though individual opinions may and probably will make a case, a moral case, for allowing certain minority *interests* to prevail. In both types of democracy, of course, individual voting must be protected; in the Benthamite model, individuals must be allowed to assert their interests, and in Rousseauian democracy, individuals must be allowed to voice their opinions. But in addition, in the Benthamite model, certain individual voices must be allowed to prevail despite the fact that they are in the minority; in the Rousseauian model such a requirement is not needed.

X

I started thinking about these issues by pondering a question almost everyone interested in constitutional law asks sooner or later. When the people of a state, several million of them, have addressed an issue, directly or through their representatives, and passed a law on something they take to be a matter of public importance, what is the justification for allowing a handful of judges to second-guess their deliberations and strike down their law? Many of the usual justifications turn out to be unsatisfactory.

It is because the courts are a forum of principle, we are told, and they sustain and uphold the importance of principle in our political process.[38] But does anyone deny that a voter or a legislator is as capable of acting on principle as a judge? For example, does anyone seriously think that the legislators of Texas were not, at least by their own lights, acting on principle when they passed the laws that were struck down in *Roe* v. *Wade?*[39] They disagreed with the principled reasoning of a majority in the Supreme Court of course, but in an area as troublesome as abortion, it is ludicrous to infer from the fact of disagreement that only one body could be alive to issues of principle.[40]

Much the same can be said about the claim that review by a tiny elite is necessary to protect individual and minority rights. That sounds plausible only so long as it is reasonable to think that proper regard will not be paid to individual rights in the democratic and representative processes. If we view the political process in a Benthamite light we will jump quickly to that conclusion. But if we accept that voters and legislators are as obsessed with rights as everyone else in this country, we may incline to a more Rousseauian outlook. If voters and legislators are capable, as they undoubtedly are, of sometimes focusing their deliberations on the general good, and on some sense of the proper balance that should be held among individual interests in society, and if those deliberations sometimes inform their political decision-making, then by instituting a practice of judicial review, we are allowing the opinions of the people on a certain matter to be overridden by the opinions of nine judges on exactly the same matter for no better reason than ... well, what?

Is it that the judges are wiser and have a better understanding of the general good and of this proper balance than the people or their representatives? Don't say that they know more about the law. One of the issues at stake here is whether there should *be* a body of judicial doctrine on these matters. We allow majority voting by judges without regard to their comparative wisdom. What is the justification for denying the benefit of a similar decision procedure to the mass of others who may have thought as honestly and as high-mindedly about the issues as the judges have?

A third, unconvincing response is to point to the defects in the democratic and representative process. There are all sorts of concerns about electoral systems, political corruption, difficulties in voter registration, districting, and in general the looseness that exists between the popular will and its representation in state and federal legislatures. The concerns are legitimate, of course. But it is hard to see why giving a veto to a handful of judges is the appropriate remedy; that is, it is hard to see why that is not a way of making matters worse. We cannot justify one defect in the democratic system simply by pointing to others.

A fourth argument is one we have touched on already. Even if judicial review is not an appropriate way of ameliorating defects in the democratic process, it may nevertheless be a way of keeping the process open and ensuring that all have access to the public forum. Rights such as free speech, for example, do not necessarily cut across the ordinary processes of democracy. Rather they embody democratic values in themselves, and they help to ensure that our system remains true to its own procedural aspirations.[41] The argument is an interesting one. We have already seen it urged in favor of rights in a theory of legitimacy. However, for the reasons I have been outlining, it does not necessarily make a case for judicial intervention. It is true that the processes of democracy must be sustained and policed, but this is something with which citizens and their representatives should be concerned. Just as they are capable of considering matters of principle that go beyond their own personal interests, so they are capable of taking care of the integrity of the democratic process in a way that goes beyond the particular purposes for which that process is being used from time to time. Respect for democratic capacities does not stop at the threshold of procedure. A concern for the fairness and integrity of the process is something that Rousseau's citizen will exhibit along with everything else. He does not need a judge to do it for him.

As far as I can see, the only argument that justifies the role of courts in Rousseau's conception of politics is to see them essentially as participants in, and facilitators of, democratic political debate. Though we talk easily enough about democracy and the emergence of a majority view, we should remember that political debate is not always something that simply happens. Sometimes the impetus comes from the people and arises out of their experience and concerns. But often what happens is that a subject is raised first by some small interest or pressure group and only becomes a real issue for national political debate when the rest of the community is forced to take notice of it. This may happen through skillful politicking, or as a result of symbolic protest or mass demonstrations that are difficult to ignore. That, for example, is how the Campaign for Nuclear Disarmament and other peace groups in Britain and Europe forced the issue of nuclear weapons onto the political agenda. In a system with something like a Bill of Rights, it may also come about through litigation. An issue that might otherwise have remained a marginal minority concern can be imposed on the attention of society as a whole by being brought before a court connected to some human right that in the abstract at least enjoys widespread support.

The clearest illustration of this process is the campaign in the 1950s and 1960s for civil rights and desegregation in the United States. Without a Bill of Rights, the issue of school desegregation might have remained an irritant in the local politics of the South. By bringing it before the Supreme Court and by raising questions in that forum about whether segregation was compatible with the constitutional guarantee of "equal protection," civil rights leaders were able to initiate a campaign and a debate that changed the face of racial politics in America. There is no doubt that, as Ronald Dworkin puts it, the debate "would not have had the character it did but for the fact and symbolism of the Court's decisions."[42]

But although it is true that their decisions sometimes drive citizens to confront issues they may have wished to avoid, the Supreme Court's role in this process should not be exaggerated. I think that Dworkin is wrong when he argues that judicial review "forces political debate to include argument over principle," as though principles would naturally be absent from debate without the Court's intervention.[43] We have already seen that people are perfectly capable of thinking in principled terms; they do not need judges to teach them to do it. Or, if there is a case for saying that principles have tended to drop out of electoral politics, it is mainly a self-fulfilling prophecy. If we say to each other often enough that courts are the forums of principle, and legislatures and elections are simply processes in which interests confront one another in an unprincipled way, then we may end up with legislators and voters who answer to this denigration of their political capacities. If we insist that politics is about principle at every stage in the process, then the case for giving special authority to the courts to look after individual rights looks much less convincing.

XI

The upshot of my argument is that we should revise the way we think about rights to accommodate the prospect that voters and representatives in a democratic system will approach their responsibilities in a Rousseauian spirit. If we accept that as a possibility, we should recognize that rights may already be weighed in majoritarian decision-making. If so, the standard opposition between the democratic process and rights as external institutional constraints would have to be discarded. The concept of rights as trumps makes sense, at the level of justification, in relation to aggregate utility, and it also makes sense at the level of decision-making in relation to Benthamite democracy. But at that latter level it does not make sense in relation to Rousseauian democracy, for there everything relevant to political justification may already have been considered. Trumps cannot trump trumps, and trumps may already have been played in Rousseauian democratic deliberation.

We do not know, of course, and often we cannot tell, when political decision-making is Benthamite and when it is Rousseauian. Often it will be mixed, and sometimes in the minds of individual voters the two modes are hopelessly entangled. I have insisted (Section VII) only that electoral and legislative decision-making is sometimes Rousseauian, and that it is not uniformly or predictably Benthamite in those cases where external constraints of right are usually imposed. So long as this is the case, we should not think of individual rights and majoritarian democracy as necessarily antithetical to one another.

Let me end with a final comment in the spirit of Rousseau. We should perhaps take more seriously than we do the element of insult involved when a people or its representatives are told that they are incapable of making good laws, or that

420

the laws they make must be subject to review by a judicial elite. People fought long and hard in this country as well as in Europe for the right to participate in politics on roughly equal terms. It cannot be that they were fighting purely in a Benthamite spirit to have their interests taken into account along with everyone else's, though of course that was important. They were also fighting to be allowed a say in the shaping of a good society, of the community in which they in common with others were to make their lives – to have their opinion count for something on such matters. They wanted to be able to address the great questions of the general good, including the question of the balance of individual rights and the integrity of the process in which they were protected, and not have those issues snatched away from them on the grounds that they were not fit to deal with them. They wanted to embark on the great art of legislation, not to be confined by constitutional constraints to petty, pork-barrel politics.

It is sobering to detect the similarity between many of the arguments in favor of external constraints of right and the arguments that were traditionally advanced for aristocracy and against democratic forms of government. Plato, for example, despaired deeply of the capacity of the common people and their chosen leaders to understand and address the issue of justice.[44] If, despite our democratic pretensions, we see politics as a Benthamite contest, if we remove issues of right from the jurisdiction of the people and pass them to judges, it is presumably because we share this ancient pessimism. What I have wanted to argue is that there is nothing in the idea of rights to warrant this animus against democracy.[45]

Notes

1. John Stuart Mill, *On Liberty* (Indianapolis, 1955), Ch. 3, pp. 72, 70.

2. For a courageous defense of such a picture by one who knows what it may cost, see Salman Rushdie, "In Good Faith" (1990) in his collection *Imaginary Homelands: Essays and Criticism 1981–1991* (London, 1991), esp. pp. 393 ff.

3. Cf. Mill, op. cit., Ch. 2, p. 40: "Our merely social intolerance kills no one, roots out no opinions, but induces men to disguise them or to abstain from any active effort for their diffusion. With us, heretical opinions do not perceptibly gain, or even lose, ground in each decade or generation; they never blaze out far and wide, but continue to smolder in the narrow circles of thinking and studious persons among whom they originate, without ever lighting up the general affairs of mankind with either a true or a deceptive light."

4. Chapter 13, "Citizenship, Social Citizenship, and the Defense of Welfare Provision," was originally coauthored with Desmond King. The views expressed and the character of their exposition are his as much as mine.

5. The theoretical pursuit of liberal ideas in this second sense is sometimes called "left"-liberalism. I am happy to embrace that label, and I shall argue later in this chapter that it is a mistake to think that liberalism shades into communitarianism as it moves to the left. The main effect of any move to the left in liberal thought is usually a diminution of inconsistency in the

422

way ideals like individual freedom and respect for persons are pursued.

6. Universal Declaration of Human Rights 1948, Article 25 (1). Cited from James W. Nickel, *Making Sense of Human Rights: Philosophical Reflections on the Universal Declaration of Human Rights* (Berkeley, 1987), p. 185.

7. Ibid., Articles 23 (1) and (2), 26 (1) and 24 (pp. 185–6).

8. For the distinction between first-generation, second-generation, and third-generation human rights, see Philip Alston, "A third generation of solidarity rights: progressive development or obfuscation of international human rights law?," *Netherlands International Law Review*, 29 (1987), 307–65.

9. See Isaiah Berlin, "Two concepts of liberty," in his collection, *Four Essays on Liberty* (Oxford, 1969), esp. pp. 122–34. For a particularly virulent instance of this criticism, see Antony Flew, " 'Freedom Is Slavery': a slogan for our new philosopher kings," in A. Phillips Griffiths (ed.), *Of Liberty*, Royal Institute of Philosophy Lecture Series, 1983 (Cambridge, 1983).

10. It is difficult, though, to effect any rigid distinctions here. Amartya Sen persists in describing material self-sufficiency as "positive freedom," notwithstanding the fact that positive freedom, so conceived, has virtually nothing in common with the conceptions Berlin was attacking. See Amartya Sen, "Individual Freedom as Social Commitment," *New York Review of Books*, June 14, 1990, p. 49.

11. Berlin, op. cit., p. 124.

12. Isaiah Berlin, "Introduction" to *Four Essays on Liberty*, op. cit., pp. xlv–xlvi. (The whole passage on positive and negative liberty, pp. xxxvii–lxiii, is a wonderful amplification of "Two Concepts of Liberty.")

13. Ibid, p. liii.

14. John Rawls, *A Theory of Justice* (Cambridge, Mass., 1971), p. 204. Compare Rawls's view in "The basic liberties and their priority," in Sterling McMurrin (ed.), *Liberty, Equality, and Law: Selected Tanner Lecturers on Moral Philosophy* (Cambridge 1987), p. 41: "This distinction between liberty and the worth of liberty is, of course, merely a definition and settles no substantive question." Rawls adds in a footnote: "The paragraph which begins on p. 204 of [*A Theory of Justice*] can unfortunately be read so as to give the contrary impression."

15. Henry Shue, *Basic Rights: Subsistence, Affluence, and U.S. Foreign Policy* (Princeton, 1980), Ch. 1.
16. Cf. Mill, op. cit., Ch. 2, p. 39: "In respect to all persons but those whose pecuniary circumstances make them independent of the good will of other people, opinion, on this subject, is as efficacious as law; men might as well be imprisoned as excluded from the means of earning their bread." See also the discussion of economic security and the independence of the citizen in Chapter 12, below.
17. Shue, op. cit., pp. 24–5.
18. See Catherine MacKinnon, *Feminism Unmodified: Discourses on Life and Law* (Cambridge, Mass., 1987), pp. 93–6.
19. Shue, op. cit., p. 24.
20. David Hume, "Of the Original Contract," in *Essays: Moral, Political and Literary*, ed. E. F. Miller (Indianapolis, 1985), p. 475. (Cf. John Locke, *Two Treatises of Government*, edited by Peter Laslett [Cambridge, 1988], II, Sections 119–22.)
21. See also Ralf Dahrendorf, *The Modern Social Conflict: An Essay on the Politics of Liberty* (London, 1988), Ch. 7.
22. Cf. R. G. Mulgan, "The Theory of Human Rights," in K. J. Keith (ed.), *Essays on Human Rights* (Wellington, N.Z., 1968), p. 20: "The treatment required must also be crucial and fundamental to the welfare of the individual if it is to count as a human right. There is no point in calling every demand a human right because in this way the currency of our moral language becomes debased. Like the boy who cried 'wolf' we will have no words left to use in an emergency."
23. See, e.g., Maurice Cranston, "Human Rights – Real and Supposed," in D. D. Raphael (ed.), *Political Theory and the Rights of Man* (London, 1967).
24. In 1979 in India it was found that over 20,000 children aged five and upward worked at Sivakasi, the center of the match industry, starting every day at 3 A.M. and finishing at 7 P.M. (See L. J. MacFarlane, *The Theory and Practice of Human Rights* [London, 1985], p. 116.) I cannot imagine why anyone should think there are priorities in human rights that are more urgent than putting a stop to nightmarish abuses like this.
25. For the distinction between concept and conception, see Ronald Dworkin, *Taking Rights Seriously* (London, 1977), pp. 134–6. See also Ronald Dworkin, *Law's Empire* (Cambridge, Mass., 1986), pp. 71–2.

26. The distinction is most prominent in Immanuel Kant's *Groundwork of the Metaphysics of Morals*, trans. by H. J. Paton sub nom. *The Moral Law* (London, 1956), pp. 89–91.
27. This formulation better captures the force of Kant's fourth illustration of the categorical imperative: ibid., pp. 90–1.
28. D. N. MacCormick, "Rights in Legislation," in P. M. S. Hacker and J. Raz (eds.) *Law, Morality and Society: Essays in Honor of H. L. A. Hart* (Oxford, 1977), pp. 199–202.
29. See Dworkin, op. cit., p. 171; Joseph Raz, *The Morality of Freedom* (Oxford, 1986), pp. 183–6. See also Jeremy Waldron, *The Right to Private Property* (Oxford, 1988), pp. 68–73 and 79–87.
30. The argument that follows is due to Robert Goodin, "The State as Moral Agent," in A. Hamlin and P. Pettit, *The Good Polity: Normative Analysis of the State* (Oxford, 1989).
31. Robert Nozick, *Anarchy, State and Utopia* (Oxford, 1974), p. 238.
32. Ibid. p. 160.
33. Ibid., p. 206.
34. Ibid., p. 155.
35. Ibid., p. 160.
36. Ibid., p. 198. See also ibid., p. 219.
37. See the editor's "Introduction" in J. Paul (ed.), *Reading Nozick: Essays on "Anarchy, State and Utopia"* (Oxford, 1982).
38. Nozick, op. cit., p. 238.
39. See the discussion in Waldron, op. cit., p. 283, referring, for example, to John Locke's emphasis on the priority of need over individual property rights in *Two Treatises*, ed. P. Laslett (Cambridge, 1988), I, Section 42 and II, Section 25, and to John Rawls's insistence in *A Theory of Justice*, op. cit., pp. 64, 88, and 270 ff., that the determination of a basic structure by principles that respect everyone's interest in fair access to primary goods has priority over particular allocations and even over the decision as to whether there is to be private property in a whole range of resources.
40. Colonel Rainsborough in the Putney Debates (1647), in D. Wootton (ed.), *Divine Right and Democracy: An Anthology of Political Writing in Stuart England* (Harmondsworth, 1986), p. 286.
41. Locke, op. cit., I, Section 86.
42. Nozick, op. cit., p. 150.
43. Waldron, op. cit., pp. 278–80.

44. Once again, John Locke's explanation is the clearest. According to Locke, the starting point of a theory of property is the following:

    "God having made Man, and planted in him, as in all other Animals, a strong desire of Self-preservation, and furnished the World with things fit for Food and Rayment and other Necessaries of his Life, Subservient to his design, that Man should live and abide for some time upon the Face of the Earth, and not that so curious and wonderful a piece of Workmanship by its own Negligence, or want of Necessaries, should perish again, presently after a few moments continuance: God, I say, having made Man and the World thus, spoke to him, (that is) directed him by his Senses and Reason . . . to the use of those things, which were serviceable for his Subsistence, and given him as a means of his Preservation. (Locke, op. cit., I, Section 86)

45. For a survey, see L. J. Torne, *Property and Poverty* (Chapel Hill, 1992).
46. Locke, op. cit., I, Section 42.
47. Ibid., II, Sections 27 and 33.
48. Nozick, op. cit., p. 178.
49. See, e.g., Cranston, op. cit., pp. 50–1.
50. Ibid., p. 50.
51. See, e.g., Locke, op. cit., II, Sections 89 and 140; Nozick, op. cit., Part I.
52. See the excellent discussion in Shue, op. cit., pp. 35–64.
53. I have discussed this a little further in Waldron, op. cit., pp. 73–9.
54. See the discussion in Ch. 14, below.
55. Rawls, op. cit., pp. 126–30.
56. Ibid., pp. 11–17.
57. For alternative approaches in modern political philosophy that reflect similar concerns, see Bruce Ackerman, *Social Justice in the Liberal State* (New Haven, 1980); Ronald Dworkin, "What Is Equality? – II. Equality of Resources," *Philosophy and Public Affairs,* 11 (1981); Thomas Nagel, *Equality and Partiality* (Oxford, 1991), and Eric Rakowski, *Equal Justice* (Oxford, 1992).
58. See John Rawls, "The Basic Principles and their Priority," in S. McMurrin (ed.), *Liberty, Equality and Law: Selected Tanner Lectures on Moral Philosophy* (Cambridge, 1987).
59. Rawls, op. cit., p. 64. See also ibid., p. 88: "If it is asked in the abstract whether one distribution of a given stock of things to definite individuals with known desires and preferences is

better than another, then there is simply no answer to this question."

60. F. A. Hayek, in *Law, Legislation and Liberty*, Vol. II: *The Mirage of Social Justice* (London, 1976), p. xiii.

61. Ibid., p. 100, and the footnote to that passage on p. 183.

62. Ibid., p. 38, and the footnote on p. 166.

63. See Rawls, op. cit., pp. 54–60 and 235–43.

64. See F. A. Hayek, *The Road to Serfdom* (London, 1944) and *The Constitution of Liberty* (London, 1960).

65. Otherwise he would not take it for granted that a just basic structure will have a transfer branch which "guarantees a certain level of well-being and honors the claims of need." Rawls, op. cit., p. 276.

66. I have benefited greatly from discussions with Desmond King on all of this.

67. I agree with Henry Shue, op. cit., p. 16, when he writes that "a proclamation of a right is not the fulfillment of a right and may in fact be either a step toward or away from actually fulfilling the right."

68. See H. L. A. Hart, "Are There Any Natural Rights?" in Jeremy Waldron (ed.), *Theories of Rights* (Oxford, 1984), pp. 79–80.

69. See Bernard Williams, "A Critique of Utilitarianism," in J. J. C. Smart and Bernard Williams, *Utilitarianism: For and Against* (Cambridge, 1973), pp. 96–118. This is also the approach taken by Robert Nozick, op. cit., pp. 28 ff. Thomas Nagel, I think, gets it exactly right when he comments that Nozickian rights against, say, assault "cannot be explained simply by the fact that it is bad to be assaulted." The rights turn on the fact that it is bad *to be an assailant*, and this concern always carries priority over any concern over what it is like to be assaulted if the two concerns ever conflict. See T. Nagel, "Libertarianism without Foundations," in Jeffrey Paul (ed.), *Reading Nozick: Essays on "Anarchy, State, and Utopia"* (Oxford, 1982), p. 198.

CHAPTER 2   THEORETICAL FOUNDATIONS OF LIBERALISM

1. Ludwig Wittgenstein, *Philosophical Investigations*, trans. by G. E. M. Anscombe (Oxford, 1968), p. 32e.

2. See Larry Siedentop, "Two Liberal Traditions," in Alan Ryan (ed.), *The Idea of Freedom* (Oxford, 1979), p. 153.

3. Cf. Guido Calabresi and A. D. Melamed, "Property Rules, Liability Rules and Inalienability: One View of the Cathedral," *Harvard Law Review*, 85 (1972), p. 1089.

4. Though the difficulties of the liberal tradition are recognized, this is not an exercise in ideological pathology along the lines of R. P. Wolff, *The Poverty of Liberalism* (Boston, 1968) or T. A. Spragens, *The Irony of Liberal Reason* (Chicago, 1981).

5. Ronald Dworkin, "Liberalism," in his collection *A Matter of Principle* (Cambridge, Mass., 1985), pp. 188–91.

6. It cannot be stressed too strongly that a commitment to *equal freedom* is not a *compromise* between freedom and equality. What "equality" does in that formula is to pin down the form of our commitment to freedom; and what "freedom" does is to indicate what it is that we are concerned to equalize. The two concepts are of such different logical types that it is absurd to talk of striking a balance between them.

7. The argument alluded to here is one that has been made most persuasively in the socialist tradition: see, e.g., P.-J. Proudhon, *What Is Property?*, trans. by B. Tucker (New York, 1970); and G. A. Cohen, "Capitalism, Freedom, and the Proletariat," in Ryan, op. cit., pp. 10–17.

8. Dworkin, op. cit., pp. 192 ff.

9. See John Rawls, *A Theory of Justice* (Cambridge, Mass., 1971), p. 5; see also Ronald Dworkin, *Taking Rights Seriously* (London, 1978), pp. 134–6.

10. For these and similar epithets, see, e.g., Charles Taylor, "What's Wrong With Negative Liberty?" in Ryan, op. cit., p. 193; K. Minogue, "Freedom as a Skill," in A. Phillips Griffiths, *Of Liberty* (Cambridge, 1983), p. 200; Isaiah Berlin, *Four Essays on Liberty* (Oxford, 1969), pp. xliv and 131–72; and Anthony Flew, "Freedom Is Slavery," in Phillips Griffiths, op. cit.

11. Berlin, op. cit., pp. 131–4.

12. G. W. F. Hegel, *The Philosophy of Right*, trans. by T. M. Knox (Oxford, 1952), p. 279 (addition to paragraph 258) and p. 107 (paragraph 149). For the definition of "duty," see ibid., p. 106 (paragraph 148).

13. Thomas Nagel, "What is it like to be a Bat?" in his collection *Mortal Questions* (Cambridge, 1970).

14. This is an objection most commonly made against utilitarianism. For a useful discussion, see Rawls, op. cit., pp. 259–63.

15. Berlin, op. cit., pp. 124–6.

16. Though, of course, the limits of this will be controversial: should people be able to exercise their freedom by selling themselves into slavery? For an interesting discussion, see Robert Nozick, *Anarchy, State and Utopia* (Oxford, 1974), pp. 280–92.

17. It is sometimes argued that the Cartesian form of empiricism mentioned here had much more influence on English than on continental liberalism: see Siedentop, op. cit., p. 155.

18. The classic statement of the relation between Englightenment and liberal ideals is Immanuel Kant, "An Answer to the Question 'What Is Enlightenment?' " in H. Reiss (ed.), *Kant's Political Writings* (Cambridge, 1970), pp. 54–60.

19. John Locke, *Two Treatises of Government*, ed. P. Laslett (Cambridge, 1988), II, Section 95 (emphasis in the original).

20. Thomas Hobbes, *De Cive* (English Version), ed. H. Warrender (Oxford, 1983), p. 170 (Ch. 14, Section 2, annotation); and Thomas Hobbes, *Leviathan*, ed. C. B. Macpherson (Harmondsworth, 1968), Ch. 14, p. 191. I have often wondered whether this is an attempt at humor on Hobbes's part, at the expense of the Aristotlean logic chopping he despised so much.

21. Ibid., Ch. 21, p. 268.

22. For a useful discussion, see Richard Tuck, *Natural Rights Theories* (Cambridge, 1979), pp. 127 ff.

23. Michael Walzer, "The Obligation to Disobey," in his collection *Obligations: Essays on Disobedience, War and Citizenship* (Cambridge, Mass., 1970).

24. For the classic objection to contract theory along these lines, see David Hume, "Of the Original Contract," in his *Essays – Moral, Political and Literary* (Indianapolis, 1985), p. 474. For alternative versions, see F. Nietzsche, *The Genealogy of Morals* in *Basic Writings of Nietzsche*, trans. by W. Kaufman (New York, 1968), p. 522 (2, paragraph 17), and F. Engels, *The Origin of Private Property, the Family and the State*, in *Marx and Engels: Selected Works* (London, 1970), p. 576 (Ch. 9).

25. Locke, op. cit., II, Section 119.

26. Nozick, op. cit., p. 9; cf. Dworkin, op. cit., pp. 150–2.

27. Hobbes, op. cit., pp. 154–5 (Ch. 21).

28. Compare the discussion in Rawls, op. cit., pp. 363–91 with that in Dworkin, op. cit., pp. 192–3.

29. Jean-Jacques Rousseau, *The Social Contract*, in G. D. H. Cole's translation of *The Social Contract and Discourses* (London, 1968),

especially pp. 73–80 (III, Chs. 11–15). For a general discussion of contractualist voluntarism, see P. Riley, *Will and Political Legitimacy* (Cambridge, Mass., 1982).

30. Immanuel Kant, "On the Common Saying 'This may be True in Theory but it does not Apply in Practice'," in Reiss, op. cit., p. 77.
31. Ibid., p. 79.
32. Rawls, op. cit., p. 11.
33. Ibid., p. 13. Rawls also insists that the decision of the parties in the original position is not a so-called "radical choice," that is, a choice not based on reasons: see John Rawls, "Kantian Constructivism in Moral Theory," *Journal of Philosophy*, 77 (1980), p. 568. It is said to be closer to the idea of rational choice in welfare economics: see Rawls, *Theory of Justice*, op. cit., p. 119.
34. See the discussion in Michael Sandel, *Liberalism and the Limits of Justice* (Cambridge, 1983).
35. The passage is from James Tyrrell, *Patriarcha non Monarcha* (1681), and is quoted in Tuck, op. cit., p. 155. Locke uses similar arguments in places; see, e.g., Locke, op. cit., II, Section 138.
36. Locke, op. cit., II, Section 22–3, 135, and 149.
37. Rawls, op. cit., pp. 175–6.
38. Cf. H. L. A. Hart, *Essays in Jurisprudence and Philosophy* (Oxford, 1983), p. 200.
39. See, e.g., R. M. Hare, *Moral Thinking* (Oxford, 1982), and the debate in R. G. Frey (ed.), *Utility and Rights* (Oxford, 1984).
40. See Rawls, op. cit., p. 127.
41. J. S. Mill, *On Liberty* (Indianapolis, 1955), especially Chs. 2–3.
42. For the idea of "a conception of the good life," see Dworkin, "Liberalism," op. cit., p. 191.
43. In this paragraph, I have drawn heavily on Rawls's work and particularly on what he calls "the thin theory of human good": op. cit., pp. 90–5, 126–50, and 395–452.
44. This notion of "reasonableness" is discussed in Rawls, "Kantian Constructivism," op. cit., pp. 528 ff.
45. I do not think Rawls takes seriously enough the need to address the problem posed here: cf. his remarks in *Theory of Justice*, op. cit., pp. 215–6. The answer sketched here is necessary, I think, for a reply to objections set out in Sandel, op. cit., Ch. 4.

46. For the liberal claim to "neutrality," see Dworkin, op. cit., p. 191, and Bruce Ackerman, *Social Justice in the Liberal State* (New Haven, 1980), pp. 10–17.
47. Cf. Plato, *The Republic*, Bk. III (414b); Locke's remarks on the need to dispel mystification about politics are particularly apt here: Locke, op. cit., II, Sections 111–12.
48. Rawls, op. cit., pp. 55–6, 133, and 582. For an argument that publicity in this sense is a substantive moral principle and not a logical condition, see Samuel Scheffler, *The Rejection of Consequentialism* (Oxford, 1982), pp. 43–51.
49. Jeremy Bentham, *Deontology*, cited in Sheldon Wolin, *Politics and Vision* (London, 1961), p. 348. Cf. Michel Foucault's discussion of "panopticism" in *Discipline and Punish*, trans. by A. Sheridan (New York, 1979), Part III, Ch. 3.
50. Cf. Hannah Arendt, *The Human Condition* (Chicago, 1958), p. 71.
51. The classic expression of these apprehensions is Alexis de Tocqueville, *Democracy in America*, trans. by G. Lawrence (New York, 1969), Vol. II, and also Mill, op. cit., Ch. 3.
52. Karl Marx, *Capital*, Vol. III (Moscow, 1962), p. 800.
53. Steven Lukes, *Marxism and Morality* (Oxford, 1985), p. 9.
54. See Milton Friedman, *Capitalism and Freedom* (Chicago, 1982), Chs. 1–2; see also, from a quite different perspective, Dworkin, op. cit., pp. 194–5.
55. See Nozick, op. cit., Ch. 7, Pt. I.
56. Adam Smith, *An Inquiry into the Nature and Causes of the Wealth of Nations*, ed. R. Campbell and A. Skinner (Oxford, 1976), Vol I., p. 456 (Bk. IV, Ch. 2).
57. There is an excellent discussion in S. Moore, *Marx on the Choice between Socialism and Communism* (Cambridge, Mass., 1980).
58. Edmund Burke, *Reflections on the Revolution in France*, ed. C. C. O'Brien (Harmondsworth, 1968), p. 183. (See also Jeremy Waldron [ed.] *Nonsense Upon Stilts: Bentham, Burke and Marx on the Rights of Man* [London, 1988], p. 115.)

CHAPTER 3   A RIGHT TO DO WRONG

1. For the distinction between privileges and claim-rights, see Wesley Hohfeld, *Fundamental Legal Conceptions* (New Haven,

1923). See also Joel Feinberg, *Social Philosophy* (Englewood Cliffs, N.J., 1973), pp. 56–9, for a brief and aaccessible summary.

2. William Godwin, *Enquiry concerning Political Justice*, ed. K. Codell Carter (Oxford, 1971), p. 88.

3. John Mackie, "Can There Be a Right-based Moral Theory?" in Jeremy Waldron (ed.), *Theories of Rights* (Oxford, 1984), p. 169. A similar account is found in James Nickel, "Dworkin on the Nature and Consequences of Rights," *Georgia Law Review*, 11 (1977), p. 1117.: "And if P has a right to receive X then P does no wrong (morally, if it is a moral right, legally, if it is a legal right) in receiving X."

4. Ronald Dworkin, *Taking Rights Seriously* (London, 1978), p. 188: "Someone may have the right to do something that is the wrong thing for him to do."

5. Joseph Raz, *The Authority of Law: Essays on Law and Morality* (Oxford, 1979), p. 274: "To show that one has a right to perform the act is to show that even if it is wrong he is entitled to perform it."

6. The distinction was introduced in W. D. Ross, *The Right and the Good* (Oxford, 1930), Ch. 2, pp. 17–56.

7. See, e.g., Richard Brandt, *Ethical Theory* (Englewood Cliffs, N. J., 1959), pp. 437–9.

8. See Raz, op. cit., pp. 266–7.

9. A. I. Melden, *Rights and Persons* (Oxford, 1977), p. 1.

10. See Section II, above.

11. See R. M. Hare, *The Language of Morals* (Oxford, 1952), and esp. *Freedom and Reason* (Oxford, 1963), passim.

12. In this paragraph, I have drawn heavily on Hare's discussion of universality and generality in *Freedom and Reason*, op. cit., pp. 38–40.

13. This approach may be taken, e.g., by somebody committed to H. L. A. Hart's "choice theory" of rights: see H. L. A. Hart, "Are There Any Natural Rights?" in Waldron, op. cit., and also Hart, "Bentham on Legal Rights," in *Oxford Essays in Jurisprudence*, 2d series., ed. A. W. B. Simpson (Oxford, 1973), pp. 171–201. Despite superficial similarities, my emphasis on the role of *choice* in rights does not commit me to anything like Hart's "choice theory." One may say that a certain right is necessarily a right to make a certain choice, and that others have a duty to respect that choice, without saying (as Hart

does) that the respondent's duty is governed by the right-bearer's choice.

14. Dworkin, op. cit., pp. 269–72, presents this contrast nicely.
15. See, e.g., John Locke, *Two Treatises of Government*, ed. Peter Laslett (Cambridge, 1988), II, Section 11 (the "right" of self-preservation); see also Alan Ryan, "Locke and the Dictatorship of the Bourgeoisie," *Political Studies*, 13 (1965), pp. 223–4.
16. Godwin, op. cit., pp. 84–5: "There is not one of our avocations or amusements, that does not, by its effects, render us more or less fit to contribute our quota to the general utility. If then every one of our actions falls within the province of morals, it follows that we have no rights in relation to the selecting them."
17. See Section I, above.
18. See Dworkin, op. cit., p. 189, and footnote thereto.
19. Some such theory, linking "right" and "authority," seems to be espoused in G. E. M. Anscombe, "On the Authority of the State," *Ratio*, 20 (1978), pp. 1–28.
20. See J. L. Austin, *How to Do Things with Words*, ed. J. O. Urmson and Marian Sbisa (Oxford, 1975), pp. 101 ff., and Hare, *The Language of Morals*, op. cit., pp. 12–16.

CHAPTER 4 LOCKE, TOLERATION, AND THE RATIONALITY OF PERSECUTION

1. All page references in the text are to John Locke, *A Letter on Toleration*, ed. John Horton and Susan Mendus (London, 1991).
2. For the development of Locke's views on toleration, see Maurice Cranston, *John Locke: A Biography* (London, 1957), pp. 44 ff, 59–67, 111–13, 125–33, 314–21, and 331 ff. See also J. D. Mabbott, *John Locke* (London, 1973), pp. 171–5, and J. W. Gough, "The Development of Locke's Belief in Toleration," included in the Horton and Mendus edition of the *Letter*, op. cit., pp. 57–77.
3. It is of course controversial whether Locke's political arguments can be abstracted and deployed in this way. For the suggestion that there may be dangers here, see Quentin Skinner, "Meaning and Understanding in the History of Ideas,"

History and Theory, 8 (1969), and John Dunn, *The Political Thoughts of John Locke: An Historical Account of the "Two Treatises of Government"* (Cambridge, 1969), Chs. 1 and 19. For a less pessimistic view, see D. Boucher, "New Histories of Political Thought for Old," *Political Studies*, 31 (1983). There is an excellent discussion in James Tully (ed.) *Meaning and Context: Quentin Skinner and his Critics* (Princeton, 1988).

4. I use "persecute" in its dictionary sense of "to harass, afflict, hunt down, put to death, esp. for religious . . . opinions" (*Chambers Twentieth Century Dictionary*, ed. A. M. MacDonald [London, 1977], p. 994), as a general term to cover all acts at variance with toleration.

5. J. S. Mill, *On Liberty* (Indianapolis, 1955).

6. For modern theories of this kind, see especially John Rawls, *A Theory of Justice* (Cambridge, Mass., 1971), pp. 201–34 and 325–32; Ronald Dworkin, "Liberalism," in his collection *A Matter of Principle* (Cambridge, Mass., 1985); and Bruce Ackerman, *Social Justice in the Liberal State* (New Haven, 1980).

7. For the reception of the *Letter*, see Cranston, op. cit., pp. 331 ff. For the *Second, Third,* and *Fourth Letters concerning Toleration,* see *The Works of John Locke,* 11th ed. (London, 1812), Vol. VI, pp. 59–274.

8. For a contrary view, see Joseph Raz, *The Morality of Freedom* (Oxford, 1986), pp. 401 ff.

9. *Report of the Committee on Homosexual Offenses and Prostitution, 1957*, Cmnd. 247, para. 62.

10. Roger Scruton, *A Dictionary of Political Thought* (London, 1982), p. 464 (my emphasis).

11. Max Weber, "Politics as a Vocation" (1918), in H. Gerth and C. Wright Mills (eds.), *From Max Weber: Essays in Sociology* (London, 1970), p. 77; see also Max Weber, *Economy and Society,* eds. G. Roth and C. Wittich (Berkeley, 1978), Vol. I, p. 55.

12. Weber, "Politics as a Vocation," op. cit., p. 78; Weber, *Economy and Society,* op. cit., pp. 55–6.

13. John Locke, *Two Treatises of Government* (1689), ed. Peter Laslett (Cambridge, 1988), II, Section 3.

14. See also ibid., II, Section 86, and – for the organization of force – II, Section 137.

15. This incidentally undermines John Dunn's view that force and violence are presented in Locke's works as the ways of beasts

and the solvents of society and civilization (Dunn, op. cit., p. 165). A more accurate view is that Locke's account of force is ambiguous; rightful force is the essence of politics, but force without right is the epitome of bestiality.

16. For Scruton's acount, see note 10 above and the text thereto; see also Mabbott, op. cit., p. 176 (first premise of Mabbott's argument ii).

17. Locke defines it explicitly in these terms in the *Second Letter*, in *Works*, op. cit., VI, p. 62.

18. For some interesting questions about this assumption, see Robert Nozick, *Philosophical Explanations* (Cambridge, Mass., 1981), pp. 405–9.

19. Alan Gewirth, *Reason and Morality* (Chicago, 1978), especially pp. 22 ff.

20. See, for example, R. M. Unger, *Knowledge and Politics* (New York, 1976), p. 76: "From the start, liberal political thought has been in revolt against the concept of objective value." (Historically, of course, such a claim is utterly groundless.)

21. See the excellent argument by G. Harrison, "Relativism and Tolerance," in *Philosophy, Politics and Society*, 5th Series, ed. P. Laslett and J. Fishkin (Oxford, 1979), p. 273.

22. See John Locke, *An Essay concerning Human Understanding* (1690), ed. J. Yolton (London, 1961), Book IV, Chs. 3 (Section 21) and 10.

23. Raz, op. cit., pp. 395 ff.

24. Mill, op. cit., Ch. 2.

25. Ibid., pp. 43 and 49–50.

26. I am grateful to David Edwards and Tom Baldwin for impressing on me the need to treat this as a separate and important line of argument for toleration.

27. Gerald Dworkin, "Non-Neutral Principles," in Norman Daniels (ed.), *Reading Rawls: Critical Studies of "A Theory of Justice"* (Oxford, 1975), p. 124.

28. See Locke, *Third Letter*, in *Works*, VI, pp. 143 ff.

29. For Hobbes's views on toleration, see Thomas Hobbes, *Leviathan* (1651), ed. C. B. Macpherson (Harmondsworth, 1968), Chs. 18 and 31. See also Alan Ryan, "Hobbes, Toleration and the Inner Life," in D. Miller and L. Siedentop (eds.), *The Nature of Political Theory* (Oxford, 1983).

30. See R. Klibansky, Preface to the Klibansky and Gough edition of the *Letter* (Oxford, 1968), pp. ix ff.

31. P. Laslett, Introduction to his edition of Locke, *Two Treatises*, op. cit., Part III.
32. Locke, *Two Treatises*, op. cit., II, Section 209.
33. Ibid., II, Sections 210, 214, and 225.
34. Ibid., II, Sections 8–12, 86, and 126.
35. Ibid., II, Section 137.
36. Ibid., II, Sections 7–12.
37. For the doctrine that punishment should be waived when it does not serve these aims, see ibid., II, Section 159.
38. Ibid., II, Section 135.
39. W. von Leyden, *Hobbes and Locke: The Politics of Freedom and Obligation* (London, 1982), pp. 115 ff.
40. See Locke, op. cit., Section 8 (lines 21–3).
41. Ibid., II, Section 8 (lines 5 ff).
42. Ibid., Section 87 (lines 8–10).
43. Ibid., II, Section 184.
44. See note 17 above.
45. Raz, op. cit., pp. 110 ff.; see also C. L. Ten, *Mill on Liberty* (Oxford, 1980), p. 40.
46. See note 6 above; Dworkin, op. cit., p. 127; Ackerman, op. cit., p. 11.
47. Alan Montefiore, *Neutrality and Impartiality: The University and Political Commitment* (Cambridge, 1975), p. 5.
48. See, for example, Mill, op. cit., Ch. 2, pp. 53–4, 58, and 63–4.
49. For the distinction between concept and conceptions, see Rawls, op. cit., pp. 9–10, and Ronald Dworkin, *Taking Rights Seriously*, rev. ed. (London, 1978), pp. 134–6 and 226. This idea is indirectly linked to the views of Gallie on conceptual disagreement: see W. B. Gallie, "Essentially Contested Concepts," *Proceedings of the Aristotelian Society*, 56 (1955–56), p. 167. For discussion of this idea, see William Connolly, *The Terms of Political Discourse*, 2d ed. (Oxford, 1983), Chs. 1 and 5–6, and J. N. Gray, "Political Power, Social Theory and Essential Contestability," in Miller and Siedentop, op. cit.
50. Ackerman, op. cit., pp. 11–12.
51. Ibid., p. 359.
52. Locke, *Essay*, op. cit., Book IV, Ch. 13.
53. Ibid., Ch. 13, Sections 1–2.
54. Ibid., Ch. 13, Section 2.

55. I am grateful to Joseph Raz for suggesting this line of argument to me.

56. For an interesting discussion, see Daniel Dennett, "Mechanism and Responsibility," in Ted Honderich (ed.), *Essays on Freedom of Action* (London, 1973).

57. J. Proast, *The Argument of the Letter concerning Toleration Briefly Considered and Answered* (Oxford, 1690). See Mabbott, op. cit., pp. 180–2.

58. Proast is quoted in these terms by Locke in the *Second Letter,* in *Works,* op. cit., VI, p. 69.

59. Ibid., p. 74.

60. Mabbott, op. cit., p. 182.

CHAPTER 5   MILL AND THE VALUE OF
MORAL DISTRESS

1. See, e.g., Beverley Brown, "A Feminist Interest in Pornography—Some Modest Proposals," *m/f*, nos. 5–6 (1981); Andrea Dworkin, *Pornography: Men Possessing Women* (London, 1981); Susan Griffin, *Pornography and Silence* (London, 1981).

2. See Richard Wollheim, "John Stuart Mill and the Limits of State Action," *Social Research*, 7 (1973), pp. 1–30; also Ronald Dworkin, "Is There a Right to Pornography?," *Oxford Journal of Legal Studies*, 1 (1981), pp. 177–212.

3. Phenomenologically, an excellent starting point is the author's postscript in A. Dworkin, *Pornography,* op. cit., pp. 302–4.

4. J. S. Mill, *On Liberty* (Indianapolis, 1955), Ch. 1, p. 13.

5. See, e.g., Roger Scruton, *The Meaning of Conservatism* (Harmondsworth, 1980), pp. 76–9.

6. This appears to be the intention in R. P. Wolff, *The Poverty of Liberalism* (Boston, 1968), Ch. 1, and in Patrick Devlin, *The Enforcement of Morals* (Oxford, 1965), Ch. 6.

7. Cf. Ted Honderich, "*On Liberty* and morality-dependent harm," *Political Studies*, 30 (1982), pp. 507 and 510. I will discuss Honderich's article further in Section VI.

8. Mill, op. cit., Ch. 5, pp. 114–15. (See also C. L. Ten, *Mill on Liberty* [Oxford, 1980], p. 4.)

9. For a helpful review and discussion, see Ten, op. cit., Ch. 2.

10. See, e.g., J. C. Rees, "A re-reading of Mill on liberty," *Political Studies*, 7 (1960), pp. 113–29.

11. Wolff, op. cit., p. 24. See also Bernard Williams (ed.), *Ob-*

scenity and Film Censorship: An Abridgement of the Williams Report (Cambridge, 1981), p. 99, and Joel Feinberg, *Rights, Justice and the Bounds of Liberty: Essays in Social Philosophy* (Princeton, 1980), p. 71.

12. See the discussion in Section VI, below.

13. This heuristic is also adopted in Anthony Ellis, "Offense and the liberal conceptions of the law," *Philosophy and Public Affairs*, 13 (1984), p. 5, though Ellis pursues rather different lines of argument. A less satisfactory analytical strategy is pursued in Joel Feinberg, *Harm to Others: The Moral Limits of the Criminal Law* (New York, 1984), pp. 31 ff. and 65.

14. See, e.g., Mill, op. cit., Ch. 4; also J. S. Mill, *Utilitarianism* (London, 1962), Ch. 2, pp. 259 ff.

15. Mill, *On Liberty*, op. cit., Ch. 2, p. 34.

16. Ibid., Ch. 3, p. 88.

17. J. S. Mill, *Principles of Political Economy* (London, 1965), Book IV, Ch. 6 (Vol. II, pp. 752 ff.).

18. Mill, *On Liberty*, op. cit., Ch. 2, p. 58.

19. Ibid., Ch. 2, p. 64.

20. Ibid., Ch. 2, pp. 48–53.

21. Ibid., Ch. 2, p. 48.

22. See Section V, below.

23. Mill, *On Liberty*, op. cit., Ch. 2, pp. 49–50.

24. Ibid., Ch. 3, pp. 85–8.

25. Ibid., Ch. 2, p. 53.

26. Ibid., Ch. 2, p. 55.

27. David Gordon, "Honderich on morality-dependent harm," *Political Studies*, 32 (1984), p. 288.

28. Mill, *On Liberty*, op. cit., Ch. 2, p. 64. Mill's exasperation with this sort of objection is similar to his exasperation with the view (again typically English) that arguments for free discussions should not be "pushed to an extreme"; see ibid., Ch. 2, p. 26.

29. Ibid., Ch. 2, p. 65.

30. J. S. Mill, *Autobiography* (London, 1924), pp. 42–3. I am indebted for this reference to the discussion in Isaiah Berlin, *Four Essays on Liberty* (Oxford, 1969), p. 184 and note. See also Ellis, op. cit., pp. 9–10.

31. Mill, *Autobiography*, op. cit., p. 42.

32. Mill, *On Liberty*, op. cit., Ch. 2, p. 65.

33. Ibid., Ch. 2, pp. 65–6.

34. Ibid., Ch. 2, p. 66.
35. Ibid., Ch. 5, p. 119 (this passage is discussed at the end of the present section).
36. Ten, op. cit., pp. 40–1.
37. Mill, *On Liberty*, op. cit., Ch. 2, p. 63.
38. Ibid., Ch. 2, p. 40.
39. Idem.
40. See *Report of the Committee on Homosexual Offences and Prostitution* (London, 1957, Cmnd. 247), esp. para. 62.
41. Bruce Ackerman, *Social Justice in the Liberal State* (New Haven, 1980), pp. 179–80.
42. Mill, *On Liberty*, op. cit., Ch. 5, p. 119.
43. Cf. H. L. A. Hart, *Law, Liberty and Morality* (London, 1963), p. 45.
44. Cf. Williams, op. cit., p. 99.
45. See also Ellis, op. cit., pp. 15 ff.
46. On no account are Mill's views utterly consistent: see, e.g., Ted Honderich's concession, referred to in note 51, below.
47. Honderich, op. cit., p. 513.
48. Cf. the argument about external preferences in Dworkin, "A Right to Pornography?," op. cit., pp. 202 ff.
49. Honderich, op. cit., pp. 507 and 510.
50. See Mill, *On Liberty*, op. cit., Ch. 4, pp. 102–5.
51. This point appears to have been conceded in Honderich, op. cit., p. 511, where the author states that "if there were more along these lines," there might be a case for saying that Mill discounted morality-dependent harm as irrelevant.
52. Mill, *On Liberty*, op. cit., Ch. 1, p. 14.
53. Mill, *Utilitarianism*, op. cit., Ch. 2, p. 260.
54. Ibid., Ch. 2, pp. 260 ff.
55. Mill, *On Liberty*, op. cit., Ch. 2, p. 53.
56. Ibid., Ch. 2, p. 63.
57. This, I take it, is the force of the "corn dealer" example, ibid., Ch. 3, pp. 67–8.

CHAPTER 7   LEGISLATION AND MORAL NEUTRALITY

1. Ronald Dworkin, *A Matter of Principle* (Cambridge, Mass., 1985), pp. 191–204; Bruce Ackerman, *Social Justice in the Liberal State* (New Haven, 1980), pp. 10 ff.; Robert Nozick, *Anarchy, State and Utopia* (Oxford, 1974), p. 33.

2. Johnn Rawls, *A Theory of Justice* (Cambridge, Mass., 1971), pp. 205–16 and 325–32.

3. John Stuart Mill, *On Liberty* (Indianapolis, 1955); Immanuel Kant, *The Metaphysical Elements of Justice*, trans. by J. Ladd (Indianapolis, 1965); John Locke, *A Letter Concerning Toleration*, ed. J. Horton and S. Mendus (London, 1991).

4. Dworkin, op. cit., p. 191.

5. T. S. Eliot, *The Idea of a Christian Society* (London, 1939), pp. 9 and 35.

6. For a discussion, see Charles Taylor, "Neutrality in political science," in Peter Laslett and W. G. Runciman (eds.) *Philosophy, Politics and Society*, 3d series (Oxford, 1967), pp. 25–57.

7. See, for example, Joseph Raz, "Liberalism, autonomy and the politics of neutral concern," *Midwest Studies in Philosophy*, VII (1982), pp. 89–120.

8. For the distinction between *concept* and *conception*, see Ronald Dworkin, *Taking Rights Seriously* (London, 1977), pp. 134–6.

9. There is a good discussion in Julius Stone, *Legal Controls of International Conflict* (New York, 1954), pp. 408 ff.

10. Hugo Grotius: "It is the duty of those who keep out of a war to do nothing whereby he who supports a wicked cause may be rendered more powerful, or whereby the movements of him who wages a just war may be hampered." Quoted in Roderick Ogley (ed.), *The Theory and Practice of Neutrality in the Twentieth Century* (London, 1970), p. 34.

11. See Stone, op. cit., pp. 14–16 and 380–1, for a discussion of Vattel's influence.

12. Alan Montefiore, *Neutrality and Impartiality* (Cambridge, 1975), p. 5; Joseph Raz, *The Morality of Freedom* (Oxford, 1986), Ch. 5.

13. Mill, op. cit., Ch. 1, p. 13
    the sole *end* for which mankind are warranted . . . in interfering . . . is self-protection. That the only *purpose* for which power can rightfully be exercised over any member . . . is to prevent harm to others. His own good, either physical or moral, is not a sufficient *warrant*. He cannot rightfully be compelled . . . *because* it will be better for him to do so, *because* it will make him happier. . . . These are *good reasons for* remonstrating with him . . . but not for compelling him. (my emphasis)

    See also C. L. Ten, *Mill on Liberty* (Oxford, 1980) for an interpretation of Mill along these lines.

14. Locke, op. cit., pp. 36–7.

15. Nozick, op. cit., pp. 271–3.

16. See, e.g., the discussion of conservation in Dworkin, *A Matter of Principle*, op. cit., p. 202. But his discussion of the drawbacks of socialist economic decision-making, ibid., p. 195, seems to support a more intentionalist approach.
17. The argument for equality in Ackerman's work seems to rely on the consequentialist approach, whereas his overal orientation to neutral reasons presented in justificatory dialogue suggests a more intentionalist conception. See Ackerman, op. cit., pp. 11 and 53–9.
18. For an argument that moral skepticism implies nothing either way on the issue of neutrality, see Geoffrey Harrison, "Relativism and tolerance" in Peter Laslett and James Fishkin (eds.), *Philosophy, Politics and Society*, 5th series (Oxford, 1979), pp. 273–90. See also the text accompanying note 26, below.
19. Ackerman, op. cit., pp. 11–12 and 355–9.
20. Admittedly he is quite candid about this: Dworkin, op. cit., p. 203.
21. I have developed the same point in relation to the concept of *harm* in "Mill and the value of moral distress," Ch. 5 above.
22. There is a good discussion of this in relation to "treating people as equals" in Ronald Dworkin, *Law's Empire* (Cambridge, Mass., 1986), pp. 173–5.
23. For the issue of whether the requirement applies to voters and citizens acting in a political capacity, see Kent Greenawalt, *Religious Convictions and Political Choice* (New York, 1987).
24. Locke, op. cit., p. 18. "Confiscation of estate, imprisonment, torments, nothing of that nature can have any such efficacy as to make men change the inward judgement that they have framed of things." See also Jeremy Waldron, "Locke, Toleration and the Rationality of Persecution," Ch. 4, above. There is a similar sort of view in Kant, op. cit., pp. 19–30.
25. Neil McCormick, *Legal Right and Social Democracy: Essays in Legal and Social Philosophy* (Oxford, 1982), pp. 18–38.
26. Dworkin, *A Matter of Principle*, op. cit., p. 203. See also note 18 above.
27. Roberto Mangabeira Unger, *Knowledge and Politics* (New York, 1975), p. 76 and note. For Hobbes's moral skepticism and the consequences he drew from it, see Thomas Hobbes, *Leviathan*, ed. C. B. Macpherson (Harmondsworth, 1968), pp. 129 and 395 ff.

28. *Report of the Wolfenden Committee on Homosexual Offences and Prostitution*, 1957, Cmnd. 247, para. 62.
29. See P. F. Strawson, *Freedom and Resentment and Other Essays* (London, 1974), pp. 26–44; and R. M. Hare, *Freedom and Reason* (Oxford, 1963), pp. 137–85.
30. See Rawls, op. cit., pp. 90–5.
31. Lon Fuller, *The Morality of Law* (New Haven, 1964), pp. 33–94.
32. Dworkin, op. cit., p. 191.
33. Rawls, op. cit., pp. 395 ff.
34. See Raz, op. cit., p. 370.
35. See Harry Frankfurt, "Freedom of the will and the concept of a person," *Journal of Philosophy*, 68 (1971).
36. Locke, op. cit., pp. 46–7: "That church can have no right to be tolerated by the magistrate which is constituted upon such a bottom that all those who enter into it do thereby *ipso facto* deliver themselves up to the protection and service of another prince. . . . Lastly those are not at all to be tolerated who deny the being of a God."
37. Derek Parfit, *Reasons and Persons* (Oxford, 1984).
38. Thomas Nagel, "Rawls on justice," in Norman Daniels (ed.), *Reading Rawls: Critical Studies of "A Theory of Justice"* (Oxford, 1975), pp. 9–10.

CHAPTER 8   PARTICULAR VALUES AND CRITICAL MORALITY

1. *Bowers v. Hardwick* 478 U.S. 186 (1986).
2. Ibid., p. 194.
3. See ibid., pp. 204–5 (Blackmun, J., dissenting).
4. See, e.g., Charles Taylor, "Atomism," in A. Kontos (ed.), *Powers, Possessions and Freedom: Essays in Honour of C. B. MacPherson* (Toronto, 1979), pp. 48–50, and Michael Sandel, *Liberalism and the Limits of Justice* (Cambridge, 1982).
5. This line of communitarian argument is developed most fully in the work of Alasdair MacIntyre and Michael Walzer. See Alasdair MacIntyre, *After Virtue: A Study in Moral Theory* (London, 1981), and "Is Patriotism a Virtue?," The Lindley Lecture, University of Kansas (Mar. 26, 1984); Michael Walzer, *Spheres of Justice: A Defense of Pluralism and Equality* (Oxford, 1983). See also R. Bellah, R. Madsen, W. Sullivan, A. Swidler, and

S. Tipton, *Habits of the Heart: Individualism and Commitment in American Life* (Berkeley, 1985), pp. 142–63.

6. For different approaches along these lines, see Bernard Williams, "The Idea of Equality," in his collection *Problems of the Self*, 230 (Cambridge, 1973), pp. 232–9; J. Rawls, *A Theory of Justice* (Cambridge, Mass., 1971), pp. 90–5, 395–9. See also my own argument in "Theoretical Foundations of Liberalism," Ch. 2, above.

7. MacIntyre, *After Virtue*, op. cit., p. 220.

8. Sandel, op. cit., p. 62.

9. Ibid., p. 179.

10. Idem.

11. See Derek Parfit, *Reasons and Persons* (Oxford, 1984), p. 55; see also Amartya Sen, "Rights and Agency," in S. Scheffler (ed.), *Consequentialism and Its Critics* (Oxford, 1988), p. 187.

12. See Brian Medlin, "Ultimate Principles and Ethical Egoism," *Australasian Journal of Philosophy*, 35 (1957), pp. 111–18.

13. Cited in A. Smith, *The Ethnic Revival*, 166 (London, 1981). I am grateful to Glyn Morgan for this reference.

14. MacIntyre, "Is Patriotism a Virtue?," op. cit.

15. Ibid., p. 5.

16. Cf. Neil MacCormick, "Nation and Nationalism," in his collection *Legal Right and Social Democracy* (Oxford, 1982), pp. 253–4.

17. Robert Post, "The Social Foundations of Defamation Law: Reputation and the Constitution," *California Law Review*, 74 (1986), p. 736.

18. The *locus classicus* of this approach in recent legal philosophy is Patrick Devlin, *The Enforcement of Morals* (Oxford, 1965).

19. I have developed these points a little further in Jeremy Waldron (ed.), *Nonsense Upon Stilts: Bentham, Burke and Marx on the Rights of Man* (London, 1988), p. 169.

20. For the idea of an "Archimedean point," see Rawls, op. cit., pp. 260–3.

21. Walzer, op. cit., pp. 313–14.

22. Rawls, op. cit., p. 3.

23. John Rawls, "Kantian Constructivism in Moral Theory: The John Dewey Lectures," *Journal of Philosophy*, 77 (1980), p. 519.

24. See Simon Blackburn, "Reply: Rule Following and Moral Realism," in S. Holtzman and C. Leich (eds.), *Wittgenstein: To Follow a Rule* (London, 1981), p. 179: "To make an evaluative

remark is to commit yourself, not to describe yourself."

25. Ludwig Wittgenstein, *Tractatus Logico-Philosophicus* (London, 1961), p. 51 (prop. 4.1212, emphasis in original).

26. Michael Ignatieff, *The Needs of Strangers* (London, 1984), pp. 138–9.

27. This chapter was originally part of a symposium on community and moral values organized at the School of Law, University of California at Berkeley, in 1988.

28. For example, even within Georgia there was not a consensus regarding the immorality of homosexuality or the propriety of enforcing moral views about sodomy through the agency of the criminal law. See *Bowers v. Hardwick*, 478 U.S. 186 (1986), pp. 219–20 (Stevens, J., dissenting).

29. This point is well argued in Mark Tushnet, *Red, White, and Blue: A Critical Analysis of Constitutional Law* (New York, 1988), pp. 134–6.

30. Aristotle, *The Politics*, trans. by T. Sinclair (Harmondsworth, 1962), Bk. I, Ch. 2, p. 28 (1253a).

31. See Aristotle's discussion of the collective wisdom of the multitude; ibid., Bk. III, Ch. 11, p. 123, 1281b.

32. J. S. Mill, *On Liberty* (Indianapolis, 1955), Ch. 2, p. 58: "Truth, in the great practical concerns of life, is so much a question of reconciling and combining of opposites that very few have minds sufficiently capacious and impartial to make the adjustment with an approach to correctness, and it has to be made by the rough process of a struggle between combatants fighting under hostile banners." See also St. Thomas Aquinas, "On Princely Government," in A. D'Entreves (ed.), *Aquinas: Selected Political Writings* (Oxford, 1959), p. 3 (no one man can attain all necessary knowledge of well-being for himself, and so some division of labor is desirable).

33. This is the move that H. L. A. Hart accused Patrick Devlin of making in his argument for the enforcement of morals. See Devlin, op. cit., p. 9, and H. Hart, *Law, Liberty and Morality* (Oxford, 1963), p. 52.

34. Hart, op. cit., p. 20.

35. Sandel, op. cit., pp. 54–65.

36. Cf. Peter Laslett, "Introduction," in Peter Laslett (ed.), *Philosophy, Politics and Society* (Oxford, 1956), p. vii: "It is one of the assumptions of intellectual life in our country that there

should be amongst us men whom we think of as political philosophers."

37. Edmund Burke, *Reflections on the Revolution in France*, excerpted in Waldron, *Nonsense Upon Stilts*, op. cit., pp. 115–16.

38. See the account of the drafting of the "Declaration of the Rights of Man and the Citizen," in L. Gottschalk and M. Maddox, *Lafayette in the French Revolution* (Chicago, 1969), p. 8. See also Waldron, op. cit., pp. 22–5.

39. Karl Marx, "The Eighteenth Brumaire of Louis Bonaparte," in David McLellan (ed.), *Karl Marx: Selected Writings* (Oxford, 1977), p. 301.

40. See generally Hannah Arendt, *On Revolution* (Harmondsworth, 1963), Chs. 3–6.

41. See, e.g., Richard Rorty, *Philosophy and the Mirror of Nature* (Princeton, 1979).

CHAPTER 9 RIGHTS IN CONFLICT

1. Robert Nozick, *Anarchy, State and Utopia* (Oxford, 1974), pp. 28–9.

2. Ibid., p. 238.

3. Joseph Raz, *The Morality of Freedom* (Oxford, 1986), p. 166.

4. I shall say that two or more interests are "compossible" if it is practicable for them all to be promoted. More precisely, I shall call two or more duties "compossible" if it is possible for them all to be performed. (See Hillel Steiner, "The Structure of a Set of Compossible Rights," *Journal of Philosophy*, 74 [1977], pp. 767–75.)

5. See Thomas Nagel, "Libertarianism without Foundations," in Jeffrey Paul (ed.), *Reading Nozick: Essays on "Anarchy, State and Utopia"* (Oxford, 1982), p. 198, for the suggestion that a Nozickian concern for side constraints cannot be represented as a concern for the interests which the side constraints purport to protect. Nozick's approach in which each agent is more concerned with not being an attacker than with potential victims not being attacked (by anyone) seems more focused on issues related to agents' integrity than on issues related to victims' suffering.

6. Maurice Cranston, "Human Rights – Real and Supposed," in

D. D. Raphael (ed.), *Political Theory and the Rights of Man* (London, 1967), p. 50.

7. Of course, a claim of right must be universalizable. But universalizability demands only that the reasons for holding that there is a duty to serve the interest of one person should also apply to the same effect in the case of any other, if his interests and circumstances are relevantly similar. It does not require compossibility in the sense defined in note 4, above.

8. John Rawls, *A Theory of Justice* (Cambridge, Mass., 1971), p. 41.

9. Ronald Dworkin, *Taking Rights Seriously* (London, 1978), p. xi.

10. See Ronald Dworkin, *Law's Empire* (Cambridge, Mass., 1986), pp. 285–91, for a discussion of the role this sort of example should play in political philosophy.

11. See Cranston, op. cit., p. 51.

12. See also Henry Shue, *Basic Rights: Subsistence, Affluence, and U.S. Foreign Policy* (Princeton, 1980), pp. 35 ff.

13. The idea of "lexical priority" is explained in Rawls, op. cit., pp. 42–4.

14. Ibid., p. 43.

15. These questions are discussed also in James Griffin, "Towards a Substantive Theory of Rights," in R. G. Frey (ed.), *Utility and Rights* (Oxford, 1984), p. 137–60.

16. J. L. Mackie has suggested that for some rights conflicts, an equalizing rather than a maximizing approach might be appropriate. (See his article, "Rights, Utility and Universalization," in Frey, op. cit., p. 89.)

17. This approach is adopted by John Rawls in relation to the rights established by his principles of justice: rights of political liberty have lexical priority over rights of equal opportunity in the economic realm, and equal opportunity, in turn, has priority over the social and economic rights generated by the difference principle. (See Rawls, op. cit., pp. 243 and 298.)

18. Dworkin, *Taking Rights Seriously*, op. cit., pp. 231–8 and 257–8. The argument was attacked by H. L. A. Hart, "Between Utility and Rights," *Columbia Law Review*, 79 (1980), pp. 828–46, and defended by Dworkin in "Rights as Trumps," in Jeremy Waldron (ed.), *Theories of Rights* (Oxford, 1984), pp. 153–67.

19. The "internal relations" approach is captured in Dworkin's statement: "My aim is to develop a theory of rights that is

relative to the other elements in a political theory." (See Dworkin, "Rights as Trumps," op. cit., p. 165.)

20. John Stuart Mill, *On Liberty* (Indianapolis, 1956), Ch. 2.
21. I have expanded this argument in "Mill and the Value of Moral Distress," Ch. 5, above.

CHAPTER 10   WELFARE AND THE IMAGES OF CHARITY

1. There is a useful discussion of the complexity of Nietzsche's hostility to altruism in Walter Kaufman, *Nietzsche: Philosopher, Psychologist, Antichrist*, 4th ed. (Princeton, 1974), pp. 363–78.
2. Ayn Rand, *Atlas Shrugged* (New York, 1957), pp. 680 and 706.
3. Cf. the title of Rand's collection of essays – *The Virtue of Selfishness*. Her argument for egoism is criticized at length by Robert Nozick in his paper, "On the Randian Argument," in J. Paul (ed.), *Reading Nozick: Essays on "Anarchy, State and Utopia"* (Oxford, 1981), p. 206.
4. Murray Rothbard, *Power and Market: Government and the Economy* (Menlo Park, 1970), pp. 187 and 164.
5. Milton and Rose Friedman, *Free to Choose* (New York, 1980), p. 120.
6. Hannah Arendt, *On Revolution* (Harmondsworth, 1973), Ch. 2. The enormous difficulty of sorting out one's own motive, let alone that of anyone else, is emphasized by Kant in *Groundwork*: see Immanuel Kant, *The Moral Law*, ed. H. J. Paton (London, 1961), pp. 74–5 (Vol. IV, p. 407, of the Prussian Academy edition).
7. Kant, op. cit., pp. 90–1 (Vol. IV, p. 423).
8. Immanuel Kant, *The Metaphysical Elements of Justice*, trans. by J. Ladd (Indianapolis, 1965), pp. 18–34 (Vol. VI, pp. 218–30 of the Prussian Academy edition). For Kant's own account of welfare provision, see ibid., pp. 92–5 (Vol. IV, pp. 325–8).
9. This is particularly noticeable in Robert Nozick, *Anarchy, State and Utopia* (Oxford, 1974), pp. 32–3; John Rawls, *A Theory of Justice* (Oxford, 1971), pp. 251 ff; and Michael Sandel, *Liberalism and the Limits of Justice* (Cambridge, 1982), passim.
10. Nozick, op. cit., pp. 171–3.
11. See esp. ibid., pp. 265–8.
12. Ibid., p. 238.
13. Kant, *Metaphysical Elements of Justice*, op. cit., pp. 35–7 (Vol. VI, pp. 231–3).

14. Ted Honderich, *Violence for Equality* (Harmondsworth, 1980), Ch. 2.
15. For the best modern discussion, see Thomas Nagel, "The Limits of Objectivity," in S. McMurrin (ed.), *The Tanner Lectures on Human Values*, Vol. 1 (Cambridge, 1980), pp. 119–39.
16. Luke 10: 30–37.
17. In this, I follow the approach taken by John Rawls in "Kantian Constructivism and Moral Theory" (the John Dewey Lectures), *Journal of Philosophy*, 77 (1980), p. 546.
18. According to F. A. Hayek, *Law, Legislation and Liberty*, Vol. II: *The Mirage of Social Justice* (London, 1976), Ch. 9, this is the only basis on which any equality can be described as unjust.
19. Karl Marx, *Capital*, Vol. I (Harmondsworth, 1976), Chs. 27–9.
20. Cf. Isaiah Berlin, *Four Essays on Liberty* (Oxford, 1969), pp. 122–3.
21. Cf. Raymond Plant, *Equality, Markets and the State*, Fabian Tract 494 (London, 1984), p. 4.
22. For the common law rule, see *Southwark L.B.C.* v. *Williams* (1971) Ch. 734, at 744.
23. See note 13, above.
24. Kant, *Metaphysical Elements of Justice*, op. cit., pp. 51–64 (VI, 245–6).
25. For a similar principle in the foundations of liberal theory, see John Locke, *Two Treatises of Government*, ed. Peter Laslett (Cambridge, 1988), II, Section 42.
26. Cf. Thomas Hobbes, *Leviathan*, ed. C. B. Macpherson (Harmondsworth, 1968), Ch. 14; and also Locke, op. cit., II, Section 6: "Every one as he is bound to preserve himself, and not to quit his Station wilfully; so by the like reason *when his own Preservation comes not in competition*, ought he, as much as he can, to preserve the rest of Mankind" (my emphasis).
27. Cf. Rawls, "Kantian Constructivism," op. cit., p. 538.
28. Cf. Immanuel Kant, "Theory and Practice" in H. Reiss (ed.), *Kant's Political Writings* (Cambridge, 1970), p. 79: "For if the law is such that a whole people could not *possibly* agree to it . . . , it is unjust."
29. Hobbes, op. cit., pp. 192 and 268–70.
30. Locke, op. cit., II, Section 135. (See also Section 138.)
31. Rawls, *Theory of Justice*, op. cit., pp. 175–6.
32. Cf. ibid., pp. 240–3, and "Kantian Constructivism," op. cit., p. 538.

33. Cf. Rawls, "Kantian Constructivism," op. cit., p. 546.
34. Rawls is more optimistic about the possibility of extending contractarian ideas to cover relations between states: see *Theory of Justice*, op. cit., pp. 377 ff. (I am no longer as sure about the truth of the sentence in the text as I was when I wrote it in 1986, and I am obliged to Henry Shue for exacerbating these doubts.)

CHAPTER 11   JOHN RAWLS AND THE SOCIAL MINIMUM

1. See Albert Weale, *Political Theory and Social Policy* (Basingstoke, 1983), Ch. 2, for an excellent discussion.
2. See Raymond Plant, "Needs and Welfare," in Noel Timms (ed.), *Social Welfare: Why and How?* (London, 1980), and Michael Ignatieff, *The Needs of Strangers* (London, 1984), for recent accounts of the variability of need.
3. John Rawls, *A Theory of Justice* (Cambridge, Mass., 1971).
4. Ibid., pp. 124 and 316–17.
5. Ibid., pp. 75–8, 124, and 302.
6. See ibid., pp. 64 and 84–9. See also John Rawls, "The Basic Structure as Subject," *American Philosophical Quarterly*, 14 (1977), pp. 159–65, and the approving comments by F. A. Hayek in *The Mirage of Social Justice*, Vol. II of *Law, Legislation and Liberty* (London, 1976), p. 100. However, Robert Nozick, *Anarchy, State and Utopia* (Oxford, 1974), pp. 204–10 remains unconvinced that Rawls's conception is sufficiently procedural.
7. For example, Hayek, op. cit., and Milton Friedman, *Capitalism and Freedom* (Chicago, 1962).
8. Rawls, *A Theory of Justice*, op. cit., pp. 316–17.
9. Ibid., pp. 285–6.
10. See, e.g., R. M. Hare, "Rawls's Theory of Justice," in Norman Daniels (ed.), *Reading Rawls* (Oxford, 1975), pp. 103–6.
11. Rawls, op. cit., p. 155.
12. Ibid., p. 165.
13. Ibid., pp. 170–1.
14. For a useful discussion of realism, antirealism, and "quasi-realism" about probabilities, see Simon Blackburn, "Opinions and Chances," in *Prospects for Pragmatism: Essays in Memory of Frank Ramsey* (London, 1980).

15. Rawls, op. cit., pp. 150 and 157.
16. Ibid., p. 16.
17. E.g., Michael Sandel, *Liberalism and the Limits of Justice* (Cambridge, 1980), pp. 122 ff.
18. Rawls, op. cit., p. 176: I have reversed the order of two passages here.
19. Ibid., pp. 145 and 423.
20. For relative deprivation, see W. Runciman, *Relative Deprivation and Social Justice* (London, 1972). For this account of the French Revolution, see, e.g., Alexis De Tocqueville, *The Ancien Regime and the Revolution* (London, 1966).
21. Most clearly in the sympathetic discussion in Ronald Dworkin, *Taking Rights Seriously*, rev. ed. (London, 1978), pp. 150–83.
22. John Rawls, "Kantian Constructivism in Moral Theory (The John Dewey Lectures)," *Journal of Philosophy*, 77 (1980), p. 519.
23. G. E. M. Anscombe, *Intention* (Oxford, 1957).
24. Cf. Hannah Arendt, *On Revolution* (London, 1973), pp. 59–75.
25. Bruce Ackerman, *Social Justice in the Liberal State* (New Haven, 1980), pp. 19 ff.
26. John Locke, *Two Treatises of Government*, ed. Peter Laslett (Cambridge, 1988), II, Section 11 (p. 274).
27. Rawls, *A Theory of Justice*, op. cit., pp. 143–4 and 530 ff.
28. See, e.g., Claus Offe, *Contradictions of the Welfare State* (London, 1984), and J. Dearlove and P. Saunders, *Introduction to British Politics: Analyzing a Capitalist Democracy* (Cambridge, 1984), pp. 300 ff.
29. For an egalitarian critique see, e.g., Kai Nielsen, "Class and Justice," in J. Arthur and W. H. Shaw (eds.), *Justice and Economic Distribution* (Englewood Cliffs, NJ, 1978).
30. The classic statement of negative hypothetical contractarianism is by Immanuel Kant in H. Reiss (ed.), *Kant's Political Writings* (Cambridge, 1970), p. 79. See also the discussion in Ch. 2, above.
31. Nozick, op. cit., p. 238.
32. Rawls, *A Theory of Justice*, op. cit., pp. 170–1.

CHAPTER 12   SOCIAL CITIZENSHIP AND THE
DEFENSE OF WELFARE PROVISION

1. See, for example, Peter Taylor-Gooby, *Public Opinion, Ideology and State Welfare* (London, 1985). The 1986 British social atti-

tudes survey revealed growing support for the institutions of the welfare state: see Nick Bosanquet, "Interim Report: Public Spending and the Welfare State," in Roger Jowell, Sharon Witherspoon, and Lindsay Brook (eds.), *British Social Attitudes: The 1986 Report* (Aldershot, 1986). For an alternative view, and criticisms of these opinion polls, see Ralph Harris and Arthur Seldon, *Welfare Without the State: A Quarter-Century of Suppressed Choice* (London, 1987).

2. See John Dryzek and Robert E. Goodin, "Risk-Sharing and Social Justice: The Motivational Foundations of the Post-War Welfare State," *British Journal of Political Science*, 16 (1986), pp. 1–34; Desmond S. King, *The New Right: Politics, Markets and Citizenship* (London, 1987); and Kenneth O. Morgan, *Labour in Power 1945–1951* (Oxford, 1984).

3. See Richard Rose (ed.), *Public Employment in Western Nations* (Cambridge, 1985).

4. See David G. Davies, *United States' Taxes and Tax Policy* (Cambridge, 1986), regarding the United States.

5. See George Gilder, *Poverty and Wealth* (New York, 1981). For a similar but more effectively developed thesis, see Charles A. Murray, "The Two Wars Against Poverty: Economic Growth and the Great Society," *The Public Interest*, 69 (1982), pp. 3–16. Murray attributes the drop in husband-wife family units in the United States during the 1960s to the federal antipoverty programs associated with the Great Society: during the 1960s, he argues, "fundamental changes occurred in the philosophy, administration, and magnitude of social welfare programs for low-income families, and these changes altered – both directly and indirectly – the social risks and rewards, and the financial costs and benefits, of maintaining a husband-wife family" (ibid., p. 15).

6. Milton Friedman, *Capitalism and Freedom* (Chicago, 1962); F. A. Hayek, *The Road to Serfdom* (London, 1944); and F. A. Hayek, *The Constitution of Liberty* (London, 1960).

7. See, e.g., Robert Nozick, *Anarchy, State and Utopia* (Oxford, 1974), Chs. 7–8.

8. See Desmond S. King, "The State and the Social Structures of Welfare in Advanced Industrial Democracies," *Theory and Society*, 16 (1987), pp. 841–68; and Ray Robinson, "Restructuring the Welfare State: An Analysis of Public Expenditure, 1979/80–1984/85," *Journal of Social Policy*, 15 (1986), pp. 1–21.

9. Robert E. Goodin, *Reasons for Welfare* (Princeton, 1988); Raymond Plant, *Equality, Markets and the State* (London, 1984); and Raymond Plant, "Needs, Agency and Rights," in C. J. G. Sampford and D. J. Galligan (eds.), *Law, Rights, and the Welfare State* (London, 1986).

10. For the general argument, see Gosta Esping-Andersen, *Politics Against Markets* (Princeton, 1985) and "Power and Distributional Regimes," *Politics and Society*, 14 (1985), pp. 223–56; and, for Britain, King, *New Right*, op. cit., and recent publications of the Fabian Society, for example, Michael Mann, *Socialism Can Survive* (London, 1985).

11. T. H. Marshall, "Citizenship and Social Class," *Class, Citizenship and Social Development* (New York, 1964). This essay was first published in 1949.

12. Ibid., pp. 84, 92.

13. Ibid., p. 71.

14. Ibid., p. 72.

15. Idem.

16. As Marshall himself notes, "education . . . is a service of a unique kind" since

    > the education of children has a direct bearing on citizenship, and, when the State guarantees that all children shall be educated, it has the requirements and the nature of citizenship definitely in mind. It is trying to stimulate the growth of citizens in the making. The right to education is a genuine social right of citizenship, because the aim of education during childhood is to shape the future adult. . . . Education is a necessary prerequisite of civil freedom. (Ibid., pp. 81–2)

17. Ibid., p. 82.

18. Ibid., p. 72.

19. Ibid., p. 75.

20. Ibid., p. 80.

21. Ibid., p. 81.

22. As another scholar argues, "welfare statism is the twentieth century's response to the demands of citizens – however articulated – for material protection from contingencies that are beyond their pivately organized capacity to resist." Kathi V. Friedman, *Legitimation of Social Rights and the Western Welfare State: A Weberian Perspective* (Chapel Hill, 1981), p. 15.

23. See also King, op. cit., and Julia Parker, *Social Policy and Citizenship* (London, 1975).

24. With regard to the first set of issues, much of the debate has

occurred within stratification studies, where Marshall's essay was "one of the seminal works which resulted in the re-orientation of the whole discussion of the class structure in capitalist societies" according to David Lockwood, "For T. H. Marshall," *Sociology*, 8 (1974), pp. 363–7. Arguments about citizenship informed Ralf Dahrendorf's *Class and Class Conflict in Industrial Society* (Stanford, 1957), in which he considers the accuracy of Marshall's claims about the equalizing impact of social rights. The argument here is about empirical accuracy, not normative validity. Dahrendorf contends that Marshall's thesis neglects the social distribution of power: though greater equalization through citizenship rights has certainly occurred, it has not resolved the conflicts centered on class. But see Ralf Dahrendorf, *The Modern Social Conflict: An Essay on the Politics of Liberty* (London, 1988), Ch. 2, for a reassessment of Marshall's thesis. More recently, Giddens considers also the utility of Marshall's claims as a possible refutation of the centrality of class conflict. He argues that citizenship rights cannot be separated from the contradictory forms of modern capitalism, and more specifically, since the rights of citizenship do not extend to the workplace – where class conflict is most persistent according to Giddens – Marshall's thesis is an inadequate account of contemporary Western democracies: see Anthony Giddens, *A Contemporary Critique of Historical Materialism* (London, 1981), pp. 226–9. A more sympathetic treatment of Marshall's arguments is contributed by Turner, who argues that the pursuit and establishment of citizenship rights have altered the nature of capitalist society in fundamental and positive ways: Bryan S. Turner, *Citizenship and Capitalism* (London, 1986).

25. Such a proposal is advanced by Julia Parker when she observes that "the idea of citizenship implies that there should be no stigma attached to the use of public services, either because of popular attitudes condemning dependency or as a result of deterrent administrative procedures or poor standards of provision." Parker, op. cit., pp. 145–6.

26. Marshall, op. cit., pp. 102–3, my emphasis.

27. Ibid., p. 117.

28. Ibid., p. 84.

29. This is the view which Giddens appears to ascribe to Mar-

shall's analysis. See Anthony Giddens *Profiles and Critiques in Social Theory* (London, 1982).

30. The issue of full citizenship for women is another dimension in which developments can be expected. For an attack on the original version of the present chapter for ignoring this dimension, see Carole Pateman, *The Disorder of Women* (Cambridge, 1990), pp. 9 and 16.

31. Aristotle, *Politics*, trans. by T. A. Sinclair (Harmondsworth, 1962), Bk. III, Chs. 1 and 13.

32. Plato, *The Laws*, trans. by T. J. Sound (Harmondsworth, 1980), Bk. V, pp. 207–15.

33. Aristotle, *Politics*, Bk. II, Ch. 7.

34. Niccolo Machiavelli, *The Discourses*, ed. Bernard Crick (Harmondsworth, 1970), Bk. I, Ch. 55, pp. 243–8.

35. Jean-Jacques Rousseau, *Discourse on Political Economy*, trans. by and ed. G. D. H. Cole (London, 1966), p. 134.

36. See Steven Lukes, *Power: A Radical View* (London, 1974) and Herbert Marcuse, *One-Dimensional Man* (London, 1964).

37. Aristotle, *Politics*, Bk. III, Ch. 13.

38. Hannah Arendt, *On Revolution* (Harmondsworth, 1973), Ch. 2.

39. Arendt, op. cit., p. 114. See also her book, *The Human Condition* (Chicago, 1958), pp. 96 ff.

40. Aristotle, *Politics*, Bk. III, Ch. 5.

41. Plato, *The Republic*, Bk. VI, 495e.

42. As de Tocqueville puts it, once the workman becomes habituated to the concerns of, say, his particular place on the assembly line, "he no longer belongs to himself, but to the calling which he has chosen. . . . In proportion as the principle of the division of labour is more extensively applied, the workman becomes more weak, more narrow-minded, and more dependent." Alexis de Tocqueville, *Democracy in America*, eds. J. P. Mayer and Max Lerner (New York, 1970), Bk. II, Ch. 20. This seems to mean then that the workman lacks the necessary qualities for citizenship in the sense of an open and broad mind, an independent point of view, and sufficient experience of the world beyond his own hovel or workshop to allow him to address himself intelligently to the great and general issues of politics. See also J. S. Mill, *Considerations on Representative Government* (Buffalo, 1991), Ch. 3.

43. As John Stuart Mill puts it: "Those whose bread is already

secured, and who desire no favours from men in power, or from bodies of men, or from the public, have nothing to fear from the open avowal of opinions," *On Liberty* (Indianapolis, 1955), Ch. 2. p. 39.

44. "We receive, we hold, we transmit our government and our privileges, in the same manner as we enjoy and transmit our property," Burke claimed, as an inheritance from the past and a responsibility for the future. Edmund Burke, *Reflections on the Revolution in France*, ed. C. C. O'Brien (Harmondsworth, 1969), p. 120. He insisted therefore that "by the spirit of philosophic analogy," we should conclude that the skills which are developed in those who are used to handling landed property are the very skills which we should want the citizen to exercise. These are skills which are unavailable to the common masses, who "immersed in hopeless poverty, could regard all property . . . with no other eye than that of envy. Nothing lasting, and therefore in human life nothing useful, could be expected from such men." Ibid., p. 134.

45. G. W. F. Hegel, *The Philosophy of Right*, ed. T. M. Knox (Oxford, 1967), para. 4. See also the discussion in Jeremy Waldron, *The Right to Private Property* (Oxford, 1988), Ch. 10.

46. Jeremy Bentham, *The Theory of Legislation*, ed. C. K. Ogden (London, 1931), p. 113.

47. Ibid., p. 111.

48. See F. A. Hayek, *The Constitution of Liberty* (London, 1960), pp. 133 ff.

49. Max Weber, "Politics as a Vocation," in Hans Gerth and C. Wright Mills (eds.), *From Max Weber* (London, 1948), p. 77.

50. Michael Walzer, *Spheres of Justice* (Oxford, 1983), p. 68.

51. Ibid., p. 84.

52. Ibid., p. 68.

53. Ibid., p. 84.

54. Ibid., p. 66. See Goodin, op. cit., Ch. 4, for a general critique of "community" in arguments of this sort.

55. Walzer, op. cit., p. 67.

56. John Rawls, *A Theory of Justice* (Cambridge, Mass., 1971).

57. Ibid., pp. 275–84. Minimum provision in this context is discussed in "John Rawls and the Social Minimum," Ch. 11, above.

58. Anthony Flew, *The Politics of Procrustes: Contradictions of Enforced Equality* (London, 1981).

59. Nozick, op. cit.
60. F. A. Hayek, *Law, Legislation and Liberty*, Vol. II: *The Mirage of Social Justice* (London, 1976), p. 100.
61. Rawls, op. cit., pp. 138–9.
62. Ibid., p. 13, my emphasis.
63. Ibid., p. 13.
64. Ibid., pp. 176–8.
65. J. Rawls, "The Idea of an Overlapping Consensus," *Oxford Journal of Legal Studies*, 7 (1987), p. 4; see also Rawls, "Kantian Constructivism in Moral Theory," *Journal of Philosophy*, 77 (1980), pp. 515–72. For a critique of this relativism, see Jeremy Waldron, *Nonsense Upon Stilts: Bentham, Burke and Marx on the Rights of Man* (London, 1987), pp. 166–72.

CHAPTER 13   HOMELESSNESS AND THE ISSUE OF FREEDOM

1. See, e.g., R. Siebert, "Homeless People: Establishing Rights to Shelter," *Law and Inequality* (1986) p. 393, and P. Ades, "The Unconstitutionality of 'Antihomeless' Laws: Ordinances Prohibiting Sleeping in Outdoor Public Areas as a Violation of the Right to Travel," *California Law Review*, 77 (1989), p. 595.
2. The best discussion remains A. Honore, "Ownership," in A. G. Guest (ed.), *Oxford Essays in Jurisprudence* (Oxford, 1961), p. 107; see also Stephen Munzer, *A Theory of Property* (Cambridge, 1990), pp. 21–61, and Jeremy Waldron, *The Right to Private Property* (Oxford, 1988), pp. 15–36.
3. See Waldron, op. cit., pp. 40–2, and C. B. Macpherson, "The Meaning of Property," in C. B. Macpherson (ed.), *Property: Mainstream and Critical Positions* (Oxford, 1978), pp. 4–6.
4. In *Pruneyard Shopping Center* v. *Robins*, 447 U.S. 74 (1980), the United States Supreme Court held that the California courts may reasonably require the owners of a shopping mall to allow persons to exercise rights of free speech on their premises under the California Constitution, and that such a requirement does not constitute a "taking" for the purposes of the Fifth Amendment to the Constitution of the United States.
5. For a more complete discussion, see Waldron, op. cit., pp. 42–6.
6. But this ignores the fact that a large number of people with no home of their own are kept from having to wander the

streets only by virtue of the fact that friends and relatives are willing to let them share their homes, couches, and floors. If this generosity were less forthcoming, the number of "street people" would be much greater. Still, this generosity is contingent and precarious: those who offer it are often under great strain themselves. So the situation affords precious little security inasmuch as the friend or relative may have to move out at the first family crisis.

7. See, e.g., Murray Rothbard, *For a New Liberty* (Chicago, 1973), pp. 201–2:

> The ultimate libertarian program may be summed up in one phrase: the *abolition* of the public sector, the conversion of all operations and services performed by the government into activities performed voluntarily by the private enterprise economy.... Abolition of the public sector means, of course, that *all* pieces of land, all land areas, including streets and roads, would be owned privately, by individuals, corporations, cooperatives, or any other voluntary groupings of individuals and capital.... What we need to do is to reorient our thinking to consider a world in which all land areas are privately owned.

8. Herbert Spencer was so disconcerted by the possibility that he thought it a good reason to prohibit the private ownership of land altogether:

> For if *one* portion of the earth's surface may justly become the possession of an individual, and may be held by him for his sole use and benefit, as a thing to which he has an exclusive right, then *other* portions of the earth's surface may be so held; and eventually the *whole* of the earth's surface may be so held; and our planet may thus lapse altogether into private hands.... Supposing the entire habitable globe be so enclosed, it follows that if the landowners have a valid right to its surface, all who are not landowners, have no right at all to its surface. Hence, such can exist on the earth by sufferance only. They are all trespassers. Save by permission of the lords of the soil, they can have no room for the soles of their feet. Nay, should others think fit to deny them a resting-place, these landless men might equitably be expelled from the planet altogether.

This passage from Spencer's *Social Statics* (1851) is quoted in Andrew Reeve, *Property* (Oxford, 1986), p. 85.

9. For a useful discussion, see Isaiah Berlin, "Introduction," in *Four Essays on Liberty* (Oxford, 1969), pp. xiv–lv.

10. See also my discussion in "Welfare and the Images of Charity," Ch. 10, above.

11. For the contrast between "positive" and "negative" conceptions of freedom, see Isaiah Berlin, "Two Concepts of Liberty," in *Four Essays on Liberty*, op. cit., p. 118.

12. The *locus classicus* of negative liberty, defined in this way, is

Thomas Hobbes, *Leviathan*, ed. C. B. Macpherson (Harmondsworth, 1968), Ch. 21, pp. 261–74.

13. The claim that the poor are as free as the rest of us is sometimes associated with the view that they have the same *opportunity* as the rest of us to acquire property and become, if not rich, then at least well-off. This line of argument is discussed below in Section VI. For the moment, it does not affect the point that *being* poor amounts to being unfree, even if there are ways of extricating oneself from that predicament. An analogy may help here: a prisoner who has the opportunity to obtain parole and fails to take advantage of that opportunity, still remains unfree inasmuch as he remains imprisoned.

14. For a particularly clear statement, see G. A. Cohen, "Capitalism, Freedom and the Proletariat," in Alan Ryan (ed.), *The Idea of Freedom: Essays in Honour of Isaiah Berlin* (Oxford, 1979), pp. 11–14.

15. Reeve, op. cit., p. 107.

16. This distinction is found in Hobbes's discussion: he defines liberty as the absence of "externall impediments," and adds that "when the impediment of motion, is in the constitution of the thing it selfe, we use not to say, it wants the Liberty; but the Power to move, as when a stone lyeth still, or a man is fastned to his bed by sicknesse." Hobbes, op. cit., Ch. 21, p. 262. It is found also in Berlin's account: "If I say that I am unable to jump more than ten feet in the air, or cannot read because I am blind, or cannot understand the darker pages of Hegel, it would be eccentric to say that I am to that degree enslaved or coerced." Berlin, op. cit., p. 122.

17. Cf. Berlin, op. cit., p. 123:
    It is only because I believe that my inability to get a given thing is due to the fact that other human beings have made arrangements whereby I am, whereas others are not, prevented from having enough money with which to pay for it, that I think myself a victim of coercion or slavery. In other words, this use of the term depends on a particular social and economic theory about the causes of my poverty or weakness.

18. See Karl Marx, *Capital*, Vol. I, trans. by B. Fowkes (Harmondsworth, 1976), pp. 781–802.

19. For the idea of a "moralized" definition of freedom, see Cohen, op. cit., pp. 12–14.

20. Cf. Berlin, op. cit., p. 133:
    Once I take this view, I am in a position to ignore the actual wishes of men or societies, to bully, oppress, torture them in the name, and on

behalf, of their "real" selves, in the secure knowledge that whatever is the true goal of man (happiness, performance of duty, wisdom, a just society, self-fulfillment) must be identical with his freedom.

21. The whole burden of Isaiah Berlin's work has been that such tidy packaging is not to be expected.

22. It is not even to deny that they may enlarge the amount of freedom overall. Isaiah Berlin put the point precisely: "Every law seems to me to curtail *some* liberty, although it may be a means to increasing another. Whether it increases the total sum of attainable liberty will of course depend on the particular situation." Berlin, op. cit., p. xlix, note 1.

23. For the connection between generality, predictability, and the rule of law, see F. A. Hayek, *The Constitution of Liberty* (London, 1960), pp. 148–61.

24. See R. M. Hare, *Freedom and Reason* (Oxford, 1963).

25. For example, Albert Venn Dicey puts the following forward as the first principle of the rule of law: "no man is punishable or can be lawfully made to suffer in body or goods except for a distinct breach of law established in the ordinary legal manner before the ordinary courts of the land." A. V. Dicey, *Introduction to the Study of the Law of the Constitution*, 10th ed. (London, 1959), p. 188. Hobbes stated the same doctrine more succinctly: "As for other Lyberties, they depend on the silence of the Law. In cases where the Soveraign has prescribed no rule, there the Subject hath the liberty to do, or forbeare, according to his own discretion." Hobbes, op. cit., p. 271.

26. For a discussion of how a layperson applies the rules of property, see Bruce Ackerman, *Private Property and the Constitution* (New Haven, 1977), pp. 116–18.

27. Here are some examples. The City Code of Phoenix, Arizona, provides: "It shall be unlawful for any person to use a public street, highway, alley, lane, parkway, [or] sidewalk... for lying [or] sleeping... except in the case of a physical emergency or the administration of medical assistance." A St. Petersburg, Florida, ordinance similarly provides that: "No person shall sleep upon or in any street, park, wharf or other public place." I am indebted for these examples to Ades, op. cit., pp. 595–6, quoting Phoenix, Ariz., City Code sec. 23–48.01 (1981); St. Petersburg, Fla., Ordinance 25.57 (1973).

28. And New Yorkers have grown tired of confronting homeless people every day on the subway, at the train station and at the entrances to super-

markets and apartment buildings.

"People are tired of stepping over bodies," the advocacy director for the Coalition for the Homeless, Keith Summa, said.

Lynette Thompson, a Transit Authority official who oversees the outreach program for the homeless in the subway, said there had been a marked change this year in letters from riders.

"At the beginning of last year, the tenor of those letters was, 'Please do something to help the homeless,' " Ms. Thompson said. "But since August and September, they've been saying: 'Just get them out. I don't care. Just get them out any way you can.' It got worse and people got fed up." ...

For the homeless, the new restrictions mean it is more difficult than ever to find a place to rest. Charles Lark, 29 years old, who said he had spent the last three years sleeping on subway trains and platforms, left New York on the day the subway-enforcement program began: "This is a cold-hearted city," he said. "I'm going to Washington. I hope it'll be better there."

These are extracts from an article entitled "Doors Closing as Mood on the Homeless Sours," *New York Times*, Nov. 18, 1989, p. 1, col. 2; p. 32, cols. 1–2.

29. Anatole France, *Le Lys Rouge*, rev. ed. (Paris, 1923), pp. 117–18. ("The law in its majestic equality forbids the rich as well as the poor to sleep under the bridges.")

30. See Mike Davis, *City of Quartz: Excavating the Future in Los Angeles* (New York, 1990), pp. 232–6, for an excellent account of similar devices designed to render public spaces in downtown Los Angeles "off-limits" to the homeless. See also Davis's article, "Afterword – A Logic Like Hell's: Being Homeless in Los Angeles," which accompanied this chapter when it was first published in the *UCLA Law Review*, 39 (1991), p. 325.

31. See the extracts from the *New York Times*, note 28, above.

32. Bracing for the annual influx of homeless people fleeing the Northern cold, the police here [in Miami, Florida] have proposed an emergency ordinance that would allow them to arrest some street people as a way of keeping them on the move. ...

The new measure would replace a century-old law against sleeping in public that was abandoned after a similar statute in Clearwater, Fla., was struck down by Federal courts in January. The courts said the statute was too broad and would have applied even to a person sleeping in his car.

The new proposal seeks to get around the court's objection by being more specific. But it would also be more far-reaching than the original law, applying to such activities as cooking and the building of temporary shelters.

Terry Cunningham, a 23-year-old who lives on the steps of the Federal Courthouse, asked of the police, "Where do they expect me to sleep?"

City and county officials had no answer. "That's a good question,"

Sergeant Rivero of the Police Department said. "No one is willing to address the problem."

"Miami Police Want to Control Homeless by Arresting Them," *New York Times,* Nov. 4, 1988, pp. Al, Col. 1, and A16, col. 4.

33. Cf. F. Hayek, *Law, Legislation and Liberty: Volume II, The Mirage of Social Justice* (London, 1976), p. 64:

> It has of course to be admitted that the manner in which the benefits and burdens are apportioned by the market mechanism would in many instances have to be regarded as very unjust *if* it were the result of a deliberate allocation to particular people. But this is not the case. Those shares are the outcome of a process the effect of which on particular people was neither intended nor foreseen by anyone.

34. See Derek Parfit, *Reasons and Persons* (Oxford, 1984), pp. 67–86, and Don Regan, *Utilitarianism and Cooperation* (Oxford, 1980). The tenor of these works is that each person should pay attention, not only to the immediate consequences of his individual actions, but also to the consequences of a certain set of actions which includes actions by him and actions by others. As Parfit puts it:

> It is not enough to ask, "Will my act harm other people?" Even if the answer is No, my act may still be wrong, *because* of its effects on other people. I should ask, "Will my act be one of a set of acts that will *together* harm other people?" The answer may be Yes. And the harm to others may be great.

Ibid., p. 86 (emphasis in original)

35. See the extracts from the *New York Times,* note 28, above.
36. For a critique of the purely quantitative approach, see Charles Taylor, "What's Wrong with Negative Liberty?" in Ryan (ed.), op. cit., p. 183.
37. Cf. Ronald Dworkin, *Taking Rights Seriously* (London, 1978), pp. 270–2.
38. The failure of First Amendment challenges to restrictions on panhandling does not bode well for the survival of even those protections. See *Young* v. *New York City Transit Auth,* 903 F.2d 146 (2d Cir.), cert. denied, 111 S.Ct. 516 (1990). See generally, L. Hershkoff and J. Cohen, "Begging to Differ: The First Amendment and the Right to Beg," *Harvard Law Review,* 104 (1991), p. 896.
39. See note 4, above.
40. I hope it will not be regarded as an attempt at humor if I suggest that the Rawlsian doctrine of "the strains of commitment" is directly relevant here. J. Rawls, *A Theory of Justice*

(Cambridge, Mass., 1971), pp. 175–6. If the effect of a principle would be literally unbearable to some of those to whom it applies, it must be rejected by the parties in Rawls's contractarian thought experiment, known as the "original position": "They cannot enter into agreements that may have consequences they cannot accept. They will avoid those that they can adhere to only with great difficulty." As Rawls emphasizes, this is a matter of the bona fides of bargaining, not of any particular psychology of risk aversion.

41. See also the discussion in Waldron, op. cit., pp. 390–422.

42. This idea is sometimes expressed in terms of "social citizenship." See the discussion in "Citizenship, Social Citizenship, and the Defense of Welfare Provision," Ch. 12, above; see also Ralf Dahrendorf, *The Modern Social Conflict: An Essay on the Politics of Liberty* (London, 1988), pp. 29–47.

43. And this is to say nothing about the appalling deprivation of ordinary opportunity that will be experienced by those tens of thousands of *children* growing up homeless in America. To suggest that a child sleeping on the streets or in a dangerous, crowded shelter, with no place to store toys or books, and no sense of hope or security, has an opportunity equal to that of anyone in our society is a mockery.

CHAPTER 14 CAN COMMUNAL GOODS BE HUMAN RIGHTS?

1. The right to development is recognized in the African Charter of Human and Political Rights, 1985, and in a Declaration of the United Nations General Assembly of December, 1986. The right to a clean environment is also recognized in the African Charter. The right to peace is recognized in a 1984 Declaration of the General Assembly.

2. See, e.g., Philip Alston, "A Third Generation of Solidarity Rights: Progressive Development or Obfuscation of International Human Rights Law?," *Netherlands International Law Review*, 29 (1987), p. 307; also Ian Brownlie, "The Rights of Peoples in Modern International Law," *Bulletin of the Australian Society of Legal Philosophy*, 9 (1985), p. 104.

3. Karl Marx, "On the Jewish Question," in Jeremy Waldron (ed.), *Nonsense Upon Stilts: Bentham, Burke and Marx on the Rights of Man* (London, 1987), p. 147.

4. Ibid., p. 144.
5. Ibid., pp. 147 ff.
6. Karl Marx, "Critique of Hegel's *Philosophy of Right*," in David McLellan (ed.), *Karl Marx: Selected Writings* (Oxford, 1977), p. 33. I have been unable to track down the source of the Arendt reference.
7. R. M. Hare, *Freedom and Reason* (Oxford, 1963), Ch. 8–9.
8. For example, the theory considered but rejected by G. E. Moore in *Principia Ethica* (Cambridge, 1903), Ch. 6.
9. Neil MacCormick, "Rights in Legislation," in P. M. S. Hacker and J. Raz (eds.), *Law, Morality and Society* (Oxford, 1977), pp. 204–5.
10. Neil MacCormick, *Legal Right and Social Democracy* (Oxford, 1982), p. 143 (original emphasis).
11. Joseph Raz, *The Morality of Freedom* (Oxford, 1986), p. 198.
12. Ibid., p. 199.
13. Joseph Raz, "Right-based Moralities," in J. Waldron (ed.), *Theories of Rights* (Oxford, 1984), p. 183.
14. Denise Reaume, "Individuals, Groups and Rights to Public Goods" (unpublished paper presented to Centre for Criminology and the Social and Philosophical Study of Law, Edinburgh, 1985), pp. 5–6. I am indebted also to Reaume for some formulations in the previous paragraph.
15. Raz, *Morality of Freedom*, op. cit., p. 202.
16. Reaume, op. cit., pp. 6 ff.
17. The cases usually cited here include *Ricket* v. *Metropolitan Rly Co.* (1865) 5 B & S 156, and *Bundy Clarke and Co. Ltd.* v. *London and North East Rly Co.* [1931] 2 KB 334.
18. For recent discussions, see, e.g., J. Chambers, "Class Action Litigation – Presenting Divergent Interests of Class Members," *University of Dayton Law Review*, IV (1979); and S. C. Yeazell, "From Group Litigation to Class Actions," *UCLA Law Review*, 27 (1980).
19. H. L. A. Hart, "Are There Any Natural Rights," in Waldron, *Theories of Rights*, op. cit. For Hart's repudiation of this view, see H. L. A. Hart, *Essays in Jurisprudence and Philosophy* (Oxford, 1983), p. 17. See, generally, Jeremy Waldron, "Critical Notice of Hart's *Essays in Jurisprudence and Philosophy*," *Mind*, 94 (1985), pp. 291–3.
20. David Hume, *A Treatise of Human Nature*, ed. L. A. Selby-

Bigge (Oxford, 1888), Book I, Part 4, Section 6; see also Derek Parfit, *Reasons and Persons* (Oxford, 1983).

21. See Ronald Dworkin, *Taking Rights Seriously*, rev. ed. (London, 1978), p. 91, note.
22. See H. L. A. Hart, "Definition and Theory in Jurisprudence," in his *Essays in Jurisprudence and Philosophy*, op. cit., pp. 26 ff.
23. I am grateful to Steven Lukes for this point.
24. Dworkin, op. cit., p. 194.
25. Ibid., p. ix. See also Ronald Dworkin, "Rights as Trumps," in Waldron, *Theories of Rights*, op. cit.
26. Dworkin, *Taking Rights Seriously*, op. cit., p. 277.
27. This approach is rejected by Dworkin in "Rights as Trumps," op. cit., pp. 164–5.
28. Though Dworkin wants to leave open the *possibility* that there may be some rights which can be justified relative to all goals, and which may therefore be regarded as "natural" or "human" rights: see *Taking Rights Seriously*, op. cit., p. 365, and "Rights as Trumps," op. cit., p. 165.
29. See also my discussion of rights conflicts and internal relations in "Rights in Conflict," Ch. 9, above.
30. Hart, "Are There Any Natural Rights," op. cit.
31. Raz, *Morality of Freedom*, op. cit., pp. 200 ff.
32. See Peter Laslett, Introduction to *Philosophy, Politics and Society*, First Series (Oxford, 1956), p. vii: "It is one of the assumptions of intellectual life in our country that there should be amongst us men whom we think of as political philosophers."

CHAPTER 15   WHEN JUSTICE REPLACES AFFECTION: THE NEED FOR RIGHTS

1. Immanuel Kant, *The Philosophy of Law: An Exposition of the Fundamental Principles of Jurisprudence as the Science of Right*, trans. by W. Hastie (Edinburgh, 1887), p. 110.
2. Ibid., pp. 110–11.
3. Ibid., pp. 111–12.
4. Ibid., pp. 111.
5. G. W. F. Hegel, *Philosophy of Right*, trans. by T. M. Knox (Oxford, 1967), p. 58, para. 75.
6. Ibid., pp. 111–12, para. 162.
7. Ibid., pp. 113–14, para. 164; also p. 262, para. 161[A].

8. Ibid., p. 112, para. 163.

9. Idem.

10. See, e.g., Robert Young, "Dispensing with Moral Rights," *Political Theory*, 6 (1978), p. 68: "[O]ften not only is such an appeal to rights otiose, but it is morally jarring (rather than dignified) to insist on one's due. . . . This means of protecting what are conceived to be legitimate interests is, even if understandable, not morally desirable since it does nothing to mend the ruptured relations."

11. Hegel, op. cit., p. 235, para. 37[A].

12. See, e.g., Michael Sandel (ed.), *Liberalism and Its Critics* (Oxford, 1984); Michael Sandel, *Liberalism and the Limits of Justice* (Cambridge, 1982); Alasdair Macintyre, *After Virtue: A Study in Moral Theory* (London, 1981); Charles Taylor, "Atomism," in A. Kontos (ed.), *Powers, Possessions and Freedom: Essays in Honour of C. B. MacPherson* (Toronto, 1979); Roberto Unger, *Knowledge and Politics* (New York, 1976).

13. There is a good general discussion of the communitarian critique in Amy Gutmann, "Communitarian Critics of Liberalism," *Philosophy and Public Affairs*, 14 (1985), p. 308.

14. See Sandel, "Introduction," *Liberalism and its Critics*, op. cit., p. 5.

15. Macintyre, op. cit., pp. 204–5. See also Sandel, *Liberalism and the Limits of Justice*, op. cit., p. 179.

16. See Hannah Arendt, *On Revolution* (Harmondsworth, 1973); Bruce Smith, *Politics and Remembrance: Republican Themes in Machiavelli, Burke, and Tocqueville* (New York, 1985); and the symposium on "Civic Republicanism and its Critics," *Political Theory*, 14 (1986).

17. For the importance of new beginnings in human affairs, see Hannah Arendt, *The Human Condition* (Chicago, 1958), pp. 177–8.

18. J. S. Mill, *On Liberty* (Indianapolis, 1955), Ch. 3.

19. William Shakespeare, "Prologue, Romeo and Juliet," in S. Wells and G. Taylor (eds.), *The Complete Works of William Shakespeare* (Oxford, 1986), p. 379.

20. Ibid., p. 412. Act V, Scene 3 –PRINCE ESCALUS: "And I, for winking at your discords too / Have lost a brace of kinsmen. All are punished."

21. Ibid., pp. 402–3. Act III, Scene 5:

NURSE:. . . . Romeo
Is banished, and all the world to nothing
That he dares ne'er come back to challenge you.
Or, if he do, it needs must be by stealth.
. . . .

Beshrew my very heart,
I think you are happy in this second match,
For it excels your first; or if it did not,
Your first is dead, or 'twere as good as he were
As living hence and you no use of him.

22. Ibid., p. 412. Act V, Scene 3.

23. Ibid., p. 398. Act III, Scene 3.

24. Cf. Aristotle, *Politics*, Bk I, Ch. 2: "[M]an is by nature a political animal. And he who by nature and not by mere accident is without a state, is either a beast or a god."

25. See W. Hohfeld, *Fundamental Legal Conceptions as Applied in Judicial Reasoning* (New Haven, 1923); H. L. A. Hart, *The Concept of Law* (Oxford, 1961), note p. 27.

26. These reflections on *Romeo and Juliet* were first stimulated by Germaine Greer. See Greer, "Romeo and Juliet," in Roger Sales (ed.), *Shakespeare in Perspective*, Vol. 1 (London, 1982), pp. 22–3.

27. Michael Ignatieff, *The Needs of Strangers* (London, 1984), pp. 9–10.

28. Ibid., p. 17.

29. Marx, "Critique of the Gotha Programme," in David McLellan (ed.), *Karl Marx: Selected Writings* (Oxford, 1977), p. 569.

30. Ibid., pp. 568–9.

31. For a general discussion of the place of rights and justice in Marx's thought, see Allen Buchanan, *Marx and Justice: The Radical Critique of Liberalism* (Ithaca, 1982), and Marshall Cohen (ed.), *Marx, Justice, and History* (Princeton, 1980).

32. Sandel, op. cit., p. 33. Cf. John Rawls, *A Theory of Justice* (Oxford, 1971), p. 126, and David Hume, *A Treatise on Human Nature*, ed. L. Selby-Bigge (Oxford, 1888), p. 485.

33. Cf. Alec Nove, *The Economics of Feasible Socialism* (London, 1983), pp. 15–20. Marx's view was that the abolition of scarcity was a crucial prerequisite for socialism because without it and without what he called "a great increase in productive power . . . want is merely made general, and with destitution the struggle for necessities and all the old filthy business would

necessarily be reproduced." Marx, *The German Ideology,* in Marx, op. cit., p. 171.

34. For an explanation of how collective action problems may arise even among altruists, see Derek Parfit, *Reasons and Persons* (Oxford, 1984).

35. This raises an interesting question. When a theorist of justice evaluates the distribution of wealth in society, should he be concerned with what people are entitled to, or with what they actually get? The idea of rights as fallback guarantees suggests the former rather than the latter, because what people actually get may depend on an interplay of factors, including affective factors, which are independent of their rights. But still there are reasons to be cautious about concentrating too exclusively on formal entitlements. Such concentration can too easily lead us to look only at *legal* entitlements, ignoring the fact that certain nonlegal structures in society may determine not only what people actually get but also what they can rely on in *extremis*. There may also be a lot of interplay between people's sense of their formal entitlements and their sense of what they actually receive. Expectations are not fixed, and what may originally have been given out of affection may come in time to be regarded as a guarantee.

36. Karl Marx, *Capital,* Vol. I, ed. E. Mandel (Harmondsworth, 1976), p. 280.

37. See Emile Durkheim, *The Division of Labour in Society* (New York, 1933).

38. See Nove, op. cit., pp. 4–26.

39. In environments like this – black markets – there are no structures of rules, and hence no basis for security, expectations, and coordination in contractual dealings. That would be the fate of *all* dealings between strangers, if we were to insist on legitimating only those economic transactions that were clothed in the substantial affections of the community.

40. For a similar perspective on markets and affections, see Adam Smith, *An Inquiry into the Nature and Causes of the Wealth of Nations,* ed. E. Cannan (Chicago, 1976), p. 18: "In civilized society, [man] stands in need of the cooperation and assistance of great multitudes, while his whole life is scarce sufficient to gain the friendship of a few persons."

41. On group rights, see N. Glazer, "Individual Rights, Against Group Rights," in E. Kamenka and A. Tay (eds.), *Human*

Rights (London 1978). See also Ch. 14, above. For an excellent discussion of individualism in this context, see Joseph Raz, *The Morality of Freedom* (Oxford 1986), pp. 104–32.

42. Marx, "Grundrisse," in McLellan, op. cit., p. 346.
43. See Marshall Berman, *All That is Solid Melts Into the Air: The Experiment of Modernity* (London, 1982); Ignatieff, op. cit., note 27, at Ch. 5.
44. See Arendt, op. cit.
45. Sandel, op. cit., pp. 64–5.
46. Ibid., p. 62.
47. Ibid., p. 179.

CHAPTER 16   RIGHTS AND MAJORITIES:
ROUSSEAU REVISITED

1. I am not using "legitimacy" in the Weberian sense of something that as a matter of fact is widely approved of and accepted as valid: see Max Weber, *Economy and Society* (Berkeley, 1968), pp. 31–8.
2. My distinction between justification and legitimacy is similar to Ronald Dworkin's distinction between justice and fairness in *Law's Empire* (Cambridge, Mass., 1986), pp. 177–8.
3. This surely is part of the solution to the famous "paradox of democracy": Richard Wollheim, "A Paradox in the Theory of Democracy," in *Philosophy, Politics and Society*, ed. Peter Laslett and W.G. Runciman, 2d series (Oxford, 1969), pp. 153–67.
4. Ronald Dworkin, *Taking Rights Seriously* (London, 1977), p. ix; see also Ronald Dworkin, "Rights as Trumps," in Jeremy Waldron (ed.), *Theories of Rights* (Oxford, 1984), pp. 153–67.
5. Jeremy Bentham, *Introduction to the Principles of Morals and Legislation*, ed. J. Burns and H. L. A. Hart (London, 1982), Ch. 1, Sections 2–3.
6. See the discussion in David Lieberman, "Historiographical Review: From Bentham to Benthamism," *The Historical Journal*, 28 (1985), pp. 199–217.
7. The analogy is found in a Bentham manuscript in the University College collection in London; my source is Ross Harrison's excellent discussion in *Bentham* (London, 1983), p. 209.

Cf. Aristotle, *The Politics*, trans. by T. A. Sinclair (Harmonds-worth, 1962), Bk. 3, Ch. 11: "There are tasks of which the actual doer is not either the best or the only judge . . . it is the diner not the cook who pronounces upon the merits of the dinner" (p. 125).

8. See the discussion in Harrison, op. cit., pp. 215–23.

9. For a modern discussion, see Samuel Brittan, "The Economic Contradictions of Democracy," *British Journal of Political Science*, 5 (1975), pp. 135–61.

10. The classic discussion is Robert Dahl, *A Preface to Democratic Theory* (Chicago, 1956), p. 48.

11. Jean-Jacques Rousseau, *The Social Contract*, trans. by Maurice Cranston (Harmondsworth, 1968).

12. Ibid., Bk. 4, Ch. 2, p. 153.

13. Ibid., Bk. 2, Chs. 3–4, pp. 72–6.

14. Ibid., Bk. 2, Ch. 3, p. 72.

15. The point is taken up again in Section VII of this chapter. For differences between conceptions such as "general good," "common good," "social good," "public interest," and "the good of all," see Brian Barry, *Political Argument* (London, 1965), Chs. 11–15. See also John Rawls, *A Theory of Justice* (Oxford, 1971), pp. 61 ff.

16. Much of the impetus here comes from Bentham's critique of natural rights: see Jeremy Waldron (ed.), *Nonsense Upon Stilts: Bentham, Burke and Marx on the Rights of Man* (London, 1987), p. 36 ff.

17. Richard Rorty, "Solidarity or Objectivity?," in *Post-Analytic Philosophy*, ed. John Rajchman and Cornel West (New York, 1985), p. 14.

18. For the claim that acceptance of the slogan represents con-sensus on a certain concept, and that it tells us little about the detailed conception of particular rights, see Ronald Dwor-kin, *Taking Rights Seriously*, op. cit., pp. 134–6.

19. Alexis de Tocqueville, *Democracy in America* (New York, 1835–40), Pt. I, Ch., 15. See also Alexander Hamilton, James Mad-ison, and John Jay, *The Federalist Papers*, No. 10 (New York, 1961), pp. 77 ff; and John Stuart Mill, *On Liberty* (Indianapolis, 1955), Ch. 1, pp. 6 ff.

20. John Hart Ely, *Democracy and Distrust: A Theory of Judicial Re-view* (Cambridge, Mass., 1980).

21. See, e.g., Robert Dahl, "Procedural Democracy," in Peter Laslett and James Fishkin (eds.), *Philosophy, Politics and Society*, 5th series (Oxford, 1979), pp. 97–133.
22. See Hamilton, Madison, and Jay, op. cit., No. 47, pp. 300 ff.
23. Mill, op. cit., Ch. 1, pp. 13 and 18.
24. Ibid., Ch. 1, p. 18 (emphasis added).
25. Ibid., Ch. 3, p. 90 (emphasis added).
26. Hamilton, Madison, and Jay, op. cit., No. 48, p. 313.
27. For a modern contractarian argument along these lines, see Rawls, op. cit., pp. 221–34.
28. Of course, what people think about the general good will be colored by their own experiences and concerns. But it is surprising (from a cynical view) how often the expression even of one's own particular concerns (as a parent or as a member of a labor union or as a farmer) is already qualified to take account of what is thought to be its proper relation to other interests in society and the general good.
29. It is worth noting Ronald Dworkin's argument that the areas covered by rights are the areas where individual voting is most likely to be dominated by external rather than personal preferences – the areas where voting is least likely to conform to the pure Benthamite model. (Dworkin does not adduce any evidence for this, and it is not clear whether it is supposed to be an empirical claim or a normative claim about the proper function of rights.) Dworkin's theory diverges from mine, however, in his insistence that the dominance of external preferences in a decision process is a reason in favor of setting up institutional constraints of right. See *Taking Rights Seriously*, op. cit., pp. 231–8, 275–6, and 357–9. See also Dworkin's essay, "Rights as Trumps," op. cit., p. 153.
30. See Kristin Luker, *Abortion and the Politics of Motherhood* (Berkeley, 1984), esp. Chs. 7–8.
31. Rousseau, op. cit., Bk. 4, Ch. 2, p. 151.
32. Ibid., Bk. 4, Ch. 2, p. 152.
33. Ibid., Bk. 4, Ch. 2, p. 153.
34. Marquis de Condorcet, "Essay on the Application of Mathematics to the Theory of Decision-Making," in Keith Michael Baker (ed.), *Condorcet: Selected Writings* (Indianapolis, 1976), pp. 33–70.
35. Bernard Grofman and Scott Feld, "Rousseau's General Will: A Condorcetian Perspective," *American Political Science Review*,

82 (1988), pp. 567–76. For a response, see David Estlund and Jeremy Waldron, "Democratic Theory and the Public Interest: Condorcet and Rousseau Revisited," *American Political Science Review*, 83 (1989), p. 1309.

36. Condorcet, op. cit., p. 49.
37. See also the discussion of "the wisdom of the multitude" in Aristotle, op. cit., Bk. 3, Ch. 11.
38. See, e.g., Ronald Dworkin, *A Matter of Principle* (Cambridge, Mass., 1985), Ch. 2.
39. *Roe* v. *Wade* 410 U.S. 113, 93 S. Ct. 705 (1973).
40. We should also consider the implications of the fact that when the justices disagree among themselves on matters of principle, they think it perfectly proper to settle the matter by simple majority voting. It is not majoritarianism, as such, that is at issue here; it is simply a question of whose votes are counted in the final analysis.
41. See Ely, op. cit., esp. Chs. 4–6.
42. Dworkin, *A Matter of Principle*, op. cit., p. 70.
43. Ibid., p. 70.
44. Plato, *The Republic*, trans. by Desmond Lee (Harmondsworth, 1974), pp. 280–3 and 372–81 (Bk. 6, 487–89c; and Bk. 8, 555b–62a). See generally Paul Corcoran, "The Limits of Democratic Theory," in Graeme Duncan (ed.), *Democratic Theory and Practice* (Cambridge, 1983), pp. 13–24.
45. I have developed these reflections into a more general right-based attack on the idea of Bills of Rights and the institution of judicial review in "Constitutional Rights: A Right-Based Critique," forthcoming in *Oxford Journal of Legal Studies* (December, 1992).

Index

abortion, 8–9, 408, 410, 416
Ackerman, Bruce, 107, 129–30,
  265, 426, 431, 434, 436, 439, 450;
  on neutrality, 105, 143, 151–3,
  439, 441; on property 459
acts and omissions, 231
Ades, Paul, 456, 459
agent-relativity, 32–3, 173–6, 204–5
altruism, 384, 397, 467
Alston, Philip, 462
analysis, 119, 145–8, 153
anarchism, 43
animal sacrifice, 104
Anscombe, G.E.M., 264, 433, 450
Aquinas, Thomas, 196, 444
Archimedean Point, 189, 198, 376,
  443
Arendt, Hannah, 284, 342, 431,
  445, 447, 450, 465, 468; on compassion, 229, 447; on the social
  question, 287–8, 454
Aristotle, 79, 196, 201, 396, 444,
  466, 469; on citizenship, 283–4,
  289, 454; on the wisdom of the
  multitude, 196, 444, 471
art, 115
atheism, 101, 163
Augustine, 201
Austin, J.L., 86, 433
autonomy, 155–6, 228, 317, 334,
  367, 389

average utilitarianism, 252, 257–60;
  see also utilitarianism

Baldwin, Tom, 436
Barry, Brian, 469
Bellah, Robert, 442–3
Bentham, Jeremy, 59, 362, 385; on
  democracy, 394–400, 405, 407–
  16, 420–1, 468; panopticism, 58–
  9, 431; on pleasure, 132, 357; on
  security, 294, 455
Berlin, Isaiah, 321, 428, 438, 448,
  459; on positive and negative
  liberty, 5–7, 40, 318, 423,
  457–9
Berman, Marshall, 468
Bill of Rights, 136, 332–4, 403–9,
  418–19, 471
Blackburn, Simon, 443, 449
Bosanquet, Nick, 451
Boucher, David, 434
Bowers v. *Hardwick*, 168–9, 187,
  442, 444
Brandt, Richard, 432
Brittan, Samuel, 468
Brown, Beverley, 437
Brownlie, Ian, 462
Buchanan, Allen, 466
bureaucracy, 273
Burke, Edmund, 36, 61, 200–1,
  284, 290, 431, 445, 455

473

Index